Discovering the US on a Bicycle

Discovering the US on a Bicycle

AND 40 YEARS LATER

Edward Abair

DISCOVERING THE US ON A BICYCLE
AND 40 YEARS LATER

iUniverse books may be ordered through booksellers or by contacting:

iUniverse
1663 Liberty Drive
Bloomington, IN 47403
www.iuniverse.com
1-800-Authors (1-800-288-4677)

ISBN: 978-1-4917-7420-5 (sc)
ISBN: 978-1-4917-7421-2 (e)

Library of Congress Control Number: 2015913404

Print information available on the last page.

iUniverse rev. date: 10/27/2015

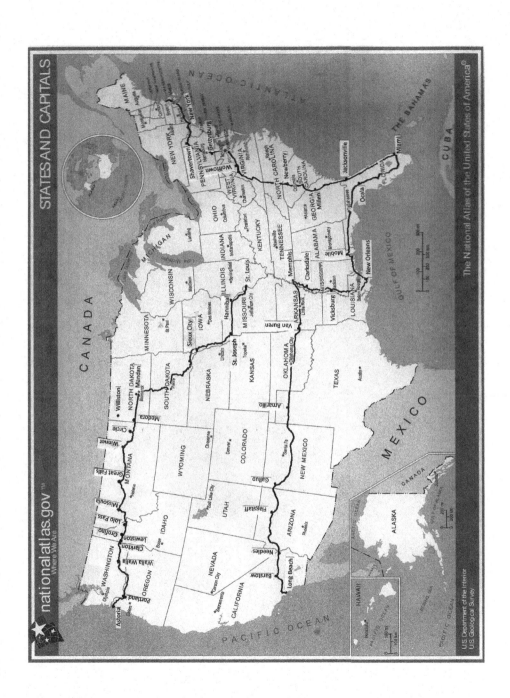

ACKNOWLEDGMENTS

This book is dedicated to the wonderful ladies on the trip who mothered me, taking me in, washing my clothes, generously providing free meals, giving me time to rest, and always with a cheerful demeanor. In quiet service, out of the limelight, they supported a stranger as if he were a son. This trip would have been miserable, and probably would have ceased with the misadventures that occurred. No, it would have been impossible. Thank you. Thank you. Thank you.

In particular, this book reverences two dear friends who were part of the love this book captured. Marie Costello died of cancer in September, 1973. Florence Bubla died of Lou Gehrig's Disease (ALS) in December 1973. A mother's love always reaches out beyond her own family. She cares when others heed not. She hopes when others despair. She cries when others feel no pain. And she loves when men see no "sense" to it. God Bless Mothers.

Thank you Paula Olinger of Reedley Bike Trax and her mechanic, Evaristo Mendoza, who were instrumental in bike repairs and refurbishing my old bike. Although the Italvega died before the 2012 trip, I benefitted from their repairs, advice, supplies, and safety tips which I had not considered.

My wife, Susan Kathleen Abair, was the instrument of survival. The Louis and Clark Trip would have been a failure without her. I misjudged that I could do the second trip alone. She was the planner, logistician, shopper, navigator, consoler, advisor, editor, laundress, financier, chauffeur, supply sergeant, cheerleader and indefatigable supporter the trip. I could not have done it without her.

INTRODUCTION

"You're crazy. You'll never make it out of California," said Mike, my coworker, at Kaiser Hospital in Bellflower, California. Others said the same. Some bet five dollars that I couldn't ride a bicycle across the United States. Wouldn't it be easier in a car? How are you going to deal with the desert? Where will you eat or sleep? What will you carry for protection? It isn't safe. Too many things could go wrong.

Why ride a bicycle across the United States? Since high school, I thought that every person should have an adventure in life. To experience things beyond the near horizon, to meet people, to share ideas and experiences, to see the country of my birth were my goals. Until the summer of 1972, I had considered my life humdrum, except for my Army stint in Viet Nam. My folks were poor, raising seven children. I couldn't afford a car. With my nose buried in high school and college texts, I was fortunate to have a bicycle for trips around Long Beach. California. I saw and heard sights and sounds that automobile passengers did not see, enjoying neighborhood activities and aromas. And, I liked swapping stories. Having become an English teacher, my life revolved around compositions, correcting grammar, and discussing literature, but it wasn't adventure. Sated with the asphalt, neon signs, and tract homes of the Los Angeles basin, I wanted adventure away from the city life I had lived all my life.

Drafted from teaching in 1969, I was one of the older men in boot camp. After serving as a medic in Viet Nam, I was discharged from the Army in February, 1971. Because of the Minorities Quota Law in California at the time (which aimed to raise the proportion of minority teachers to the level of the minority students within the school system) I was not hirable as a full time teacher, due to being a white male. Using Army medic skills, my employment was concurrent working as a substitute teacher and an orderly at Kaiser Hospital in Bellflower, California. I realized that if I didn't experience adventure by the age of 28, the dream would probably be relegated to the closet of unfulfilled wishes. And so began the adventure planning of an 28 year old unmarried, unemployed teacher with nothing to lose but the summer of 1972 on unknown roads.

My intention was to go quietly, observing life as it occurred, deliberately avoiding fanfare, sponsorship, and newspapers. I did not want "interference" while engaging the real United States and its people. Though it was a mistake, I did not take a camera. Instead, a diary accompanied me, which required pause to record daily events, the details of which I would have long ago forgotten if I had just taken photos. As a substitute teacher, I had little money in savings, so the trip was done without motels, daily restaurant meals, sponsorship, nor with subsidies from friends and family I would visit. My simple approach was to meet Americans by knocking on doors, asking to sleep on their lawns or front porches, and accepting their generosity as it occurred. Sightseeing would be spontaneous, meaning paying attention to the country, geography, geology, day to day experiences, and the people. Rest stops and sleeping accommodations were not pre-planned. As a practicing Catholic, Sunday mass would be required attendance unless there were an impediment. I would not lie, cheat or steal. Dialogue is as I remembered it, without embellishment and kept short. Events were written in a diary format, in the order of daily importance I perceived, with the desire to reveal stories and tidbits of American life. There was no theme, save the purposes of telling the story of America and Americans and contributing my philosophy of life. Not every day was a lesson in life. Sometimes it was just what happened.

Over the next 38 1/2 years, I taught various subjects and age levels including elementary grades 5-8, high school English, Social Studies, Spanish, Latin, Health, Driver Education, and served as a principal and school administrator. Other experiences included working on a ranch, cutting and selling oak firewood, cabinet making, handy man repairing, gardening, choir singing, and performing community service. In 1977, I married Susan Borgaro, Home Economics teacher and later Librarian. My daughter Rachel was born in 1982 and son David in 1983.

In 2012, forty years after the original trip, I took a second long distance bike trip and wrote a sequel, traveling the Lewis and Clark Trail from Astoria, Oregon, to St. Louis, Missouri, but this time married, using my wife and our car for support. Why? Because I had promised to finish the bike adventure when I retired, but this time, in the north.

My book is written in diary style. In the 2012 section of the book, I wrote a daily email to friends and family. In some cases a line may not have a verb or be in strict grammatical sentence form. It was enough to mention but not sufficient or necessary to make a complete thought. Sometimes I was just weary. On occasion I wrote present tense factual sentences mixed with past tense descriptions, because some situations are active and ongoing. I offer this report of my travels and perceptions, pains and pleasures, unadulterated. It was my adventure.

PART I

PART 1

GETTING ORGANIZED

Destination: Long Beach, CA to Miami, FL, to New York, NY, to Boston, MA

Dream: Cross the United States by bicycle. Discover the America not seen from a speeding car, or making front page news. Meet salt-of-the-earth Americans.

Equipment:

10 speed Italvega derrailleur	1 gallon canvas desert water bag
4 lb. sleeping bag	Orange tube tent (plastic)
Long brown pants	2 spare inner tubes (27")
Blue Bermuda shorts	Tire patches and cement
Green striped long-sleeve shirt	Metric bike wrenches
Red & white short-sleeve shirt	Salt tablets
Black leather loafer shoes	Suntan lotion
Transistor radio	Petroleum jelly
Razor and blades	Baby powder
Diary (6" x 8")	Tooth brush and paste
2 books (reading)	Aspirin
Orange fluorescent vest	Standard Auto tire pump
Red baseball cap	Bike generator light
Bike cable & lock	Bike rack (rear wheel)
Ink pen	A small bottle of Pacific Ocean water
$50.00 cash	$200.00 Traveler's Checks

Main route at start: Long Beach to El Monte, CA, to U.S. 66

Saturday, June 17, 1972   Long Beach to El Monte, CA   Day 1

First day of travel: Leaving my parents' home in Long Beach, California, at 7:15 p.m. with the sun slipping over the Palos Verdes Hills in the west, I gave the first check to the pack on the carry-all rack. My bike weighs 32 pounds, the pack 37. Only essentials are being taken. I haven't cared for publicity, so Mom took my official photograph. Tony, my brother, shook my hand, while sisters Therese and Monica shouted. Rita, Marylin, and Pete missed the send-off. Pop waved good-bye. For the next four months, a weekly phone call would be my only family contact. A single wave as I pushed off, the trip had started.

Simplicity must be the keynote of this trip. Though physically fit, I have no regimen. At 27 years of age, my body weight is 175 pounds. Conditioning was a matter of ten biking miles a day, for three months to school and back, plus thirty miles on weekends, and all the basketball I could play since Christmas. Distance and speed will increase as my body and circumstances permit.

Familiar neighborhoods in the sunny evening glided by: orderly communities with asphalt streets and cement curbs, spider web cables linked telephone poles to pastel stucco homes. A master street pattern interlocked the city blocks. Boulevards honked and grumbled with traffic. As if they were tempting moths, bright neon lights attracted hungry Southern Californians to fried chicken, taco, and hamburger havens.

Los Angeles suburbs pulsed in the twilight. Homeowners trimmed their lawns. Across a driveway, two mechanics flicked on a garage light to work on an engine. Kids bicycled noisily, girls running behind. Shouts drifted from a night baseball game under park lights. Mothers, sighing in relief, pulled out of shopping center parking lots. Slick customized cars gleamed under street lights, drivers revving engines, impressing girl friends. Saturday night in Los Angeles suburbs.

I stopped to make a tire pressure check at an El Monte gas station, 70 psi. Just right. Raul Grimes stared at me, not expecting my early show. Kate, his wife, and he had a camping date for tomorrow, and he had invited me to spend the night before jumping off. We raced each other to his apartment. While Kate's cooking warmed us, we three teachers talked up a storm. When the dust of conversation settled, we guessed at the future then hit the sack. The Grimes left at 4 a.m.   30 miles

THE FIRST DAY OF SUN

At 10:30 the apartment was silent. The Grimes have gotten lost in the so-called north woods. I cannot believe that the final demands of the school year have exhausted me so. Teaching has been a demanding profession. A light breakfast, quick pack up, and a scoot to church for the noon mass. The service was in Spanish. My blond gringo-hood contrasted with the deep brown skins in the white walled church. With a warm afternoon blessing, the congregation was dispersed. Filled cars deserted the parking lot. Maneuvering the cycle between cars, I zigzagged toward Highland Avenue's Sunday traffic, the San Gabriel Mountains, fifteen miles away, barely visible in the gray-purple haze, and gave a last smog salute.

Water loss was rapid in the 88° sultry sun. I hadn't yet filled the canvas water bag, suspended from the center bar of the brown bike frame, hoping to save on weight. (1 gallon = 5 1/2 pounds). Every half hour was a water stop. It would take several days for my body to acclimatize to desert heat. Until then, frequent service station breaks provided a cold slurp of water. Sun rays already stung my arms and legs, and salty sweat burned skin pores. While lunching in the shade of a gas station, a muscular twitching grabbed in my legs. Time for salt tablets.

The first uphill grade into Azusa warned my legs of cycling to come. At the bright sweaty red shirt and orange oblong rear bundle, residents gawked at the passing huffing and puffing cyclist. In the beginning, uphills required frequent rest stops. Later, as I gained stamina, I would ride for a solid hour, then take a 5 minute break for water and fruit.

In welcome contrast to city plastic, neon, and cement, small truck farms beyond Azusa colored the land in green felt. One ground squirrel flattened himself on a dirt mound, another dove into his hole in the grape orchards. A faint afternoon breeze stirred the heavy air to rasp my sunburned hands. Tanning lotion has not halted the wrath of the sun. My legs will need petroleum jelly because Bermuda shorts were not enough cover.

Although San Bernardino is at the desert's entrance, mountain water wells slake the thirst of emerald pastures. Drab wooden slat-board houses dating back to the 1920s and 30s dot the inroads. Throughout WWII, S.B. was an emergency postal airstrip during bad weather. Dispatches shuttled frequently by day, while night flights swooped up and over the mountains, guided by a chain system of beacon lights across the peaks. Since the war, S.B. had grown from 17,000 to 100,000. The CHP (California Highway Patrol) office, shades drawn, hung a sign: CLOSED. I had intended to ask road advice and tips for desert travel. Frustrated, I sat to rest my twitching legs, tilted over and fell asleep at the front door. An hour later, my stomach growled. A liquor store satisfied cravings for salt (Fritos), sugar (one quart of root beer), and protein (ice cream). Another half hour of achy sitting passed before I began knocking on front doors.

I explained, "I'm bicycling across the U.S. May I sleep on your porch or on the lawn?"

Though I promised to clean up and be gone by 8:00 a.m., six people refused. My intention was to let people know who I am and what was doing. It was for my safety and their peace of mind. Besides it was a good way to meet folks.

An elderly gentleman, Ben Nesser, crippled with arthritis, pointed to his back yard. I was rolling out the sleeping bag when he invited me inside the house to share his Father's Day cake and ice cream. We spent the late evening rocking on the porch, swapping tales, and slapping insects. Dew wet the ground. Fortunately the plastic tube tent was a good insulator. Freeway-hissing cars two blocks away, and barking dogs, snatched the soundness of my sleep.   60 miles

A PAIN IN THE....

Ben woke me for bacon & eggs and a chat. I sat and ate stiffly, then packed. A 9:30 check at the CHP office revealed the ancient Route 66 that paralleled most of the freeway up the Cajon Pass. The law required bicyclists to use alternate routes unless the freeway is the only route, or if there is no alternate within fifteen miles. According to the patrolman, I could ride untroubled up the valley until forced to join the freeway, ride three miles to the summit on the freeway, then exit to a side road at the 4,400 foot elevation mark.

Loaded with confidence and final provisions (canned food, fresh plums, a two quart canteen to back up the water bag), I crossed the railroad ties, circled over the bridge, down and around the freeway ramp, and glided onto a yellow dust road pointing to the blue north sky. While the sun bit at my exposed arms and legs, I reviewed the disappointing late start, resolving to leave no later than 6:30 each morning. This became one of many resolutions my body could not keep. It was not possible to foresee how cycling exhaustion would prevent me from rising early.

Elevation rose along the sand, weed, and trash lined asphalt. A brown creek wound its way along the left road edge, dotted by a few trees in washes. Occasionally a train or work gang inhabited the rocky perches near the tracks. At the highway junction, the tracks disappeared and the road lost its direction signs. A man in a scratched white pickup, who couldn't explain directions, resorted to offering a lift. Because no one else knew the way, I accepted a ride for a mile. At the on-ramp the driver suggested driving me over the pass-a twenty mile ride-but I refused. It wouldn't be a bike trip.

The climb was barely noticeable for the first half mile, until the curving incline steepened towards a 7 percent grade. Gears downshifted quickly to eighth, seventh, fourth and finally to the lowest gear. As the roadside gullies dropped off to tumble on the rocks below, I stood on the pedals to force them to turn. At the summit, a CHP patrolman stopped me, asked my business and gave warning to take the next exit.

Inside the Summit Cafe, air conditioning chills ran through my sweaty clothes as I ate a traveler's delight, a hamburger with everything. It was a pleasure to warm in the 94^0 outside heat. Next came the fun, a quiet downhill slope, not one hundred feet from the freeway, so gradual that there was no need to pedal, just enjoy the fourteen mile coasting into Victorville. Lush alfalfa farms lined creek banks, while in the distance the desert seared and parched the pitiful grass.

My two inner rump socket bones rubbed against the seat, causing irritation. In the beginning, the discomfort was slight. With each additional downward right thrust, the body weight shifted to the opposite left bone, rolling over the flesh, then, off-weighting on an upstroke, rolled free. This amounted to a pinching effect. To vary the motion, I tried sitting first on the right rump, then left rump, next, far back on the saddle, and finally up on the nose. It still pinched and pulled. All skin areas of the inner butt were tender, yet numb. There were moments when it felt like someone had hit me with a baseball bat in the anal crease.

Barstow's approach was a forbidding barren rock pile. Dry stucco and concrete homes scattered from the center of town. Why would 35,000 people choose this for a home? Asthma? Tuberculosis? Rheumatism? Arthritis? Goldmine fever? The CHP only offered advice for my driving safety: stick to the deserted 66 highway on the other side of the Marine base. It was never more than four miles from the highway proper, and it was safer.

In the golden sunset of the hills, I pedaled wearily and quietly up to a fenced house. A white husky charged from the porch for my hand. A teenage girl commanded, and the dog stopped. The girl brought me inside where the Merdis Merlini's (grandmother, mom, daughter, two sons) loaned a bathtub, washed my clothes and gave me an evening meal. We even went shopping for groceries. On their wide porch that night, heavy rumbling traffic buzzed loud enough to waken me often. Right now, my butt can't take much more strain.

[Today's lessons: Don't sleep near the highway. Limit travel to strain which the body will accept.] 80 miles

ORDEAL

Cranky stiffness and sunburned arms and legs. Gooey coatings of petroleum jelly and suntan lotion. Changed to protective long sleeves and pants. My head spun dizzily from lack of solid sleep. I sat like a weathered plank to a whopping breakfast. The Merlini's gave me a cheering sendoff at 7:30.

During warm-up pedaling, my leg muscles rubbed like grating splinters, knees tightly knotted. Five minutes later the joints limbered up. Neck and shoulders have cramped up, with the head drooped. Arms have become listless with repetitive leaning over the handlebars and lack of other use. Numbness has crept into the index and middle fingers of both hands. Exercise and slapping did not reawaken feeling. The dull sensation persisted through the night and grew in early morning. I feared that I would have deadened hands which could not grasp the brake handles for an emergency stop.

The road wandered out of sleepy-headed Barstow through a Marine camp. Soldiers moved in clipped rhythm--even the vehicles had a measured pace. A guard, in his shack, gave a quizzical look, eye-checked the ten speed for stolen military secrets, and waved me out the back gate into the desert. The old highway paralleled the freeway. According the Highway Patrol, help will always be in view. The morning became overcast as I wheeled past the houses of Daggett, a whistle stop. Houses sprouted scrub brush, sand, and cactus yards. A clattering diesel train honked unheeded through town. Then quiet. The last blossoming farm painted a green strip into the tanned desert. Brush lay dead and brown, grass too. With water this would be a fertile playground, otherwise, it is a gritty polka-dotted tumbleweed patch. The arid sand loomed, while the road bounced along dips in rising elevation.

Fortune smiled on me for a while. Low hanging clouds kept the morning comfortable in the 80s. Perhaps ten vehicles passed me on this fifty-one mile leg. The desert was not frightening as long as it stayed relatively cool, which meant only a few more hours. My thoughts roamed to the desolate hillsides deeper in the valley, where small specks could be recognized as modern factories, but whose purposes remained secret. A gentle downgrade allowed a half hour of coasting until late morning winds stirred up gusts which lashed across the bike, twisted, spun, and buffeted.

Sand specks danced, scratching my skin or jumped into my eyes forcing tears. Head-on winds cut speed by one-third. Tumbleweeds jogged along the road. Once, after pedaling up a steep hill, the fierce blasts forced me to pedal down the other side. To maintain strength, I halved rest stops to every 30 minutes, when I gobbled raisins and plums, and swigged from the water bag under the main bar of the bicycle.

Lunchtime in Ludlow, a three-gas-station-two-restaurant-four trailer town. I filled my water bag and canteen, opened two smashed baloney sandwiches, sniffed to see if the heat had turned the meat bad, and devoured them. There was no way to politely eat a smashed baloney sandwich. Western clouds farther back down the valley parted. I lolled on guardrail bumper posts, enjoying the diminishing wind and warming sun. Afternoon heat would overrun me. I had forgotten the tanning lotion at the Merlini's, fifty-one miles too late to return. [Lesson: Before leaving, check all belongings.]

The freeway merged with the old highway, jutting and swerving around sand and rock mounts, adding an extra ten desert miles. A shorter freeway was under construction, but without a water stop for fifty miles-a serious consideration when my water supply disappeared in forty miles. The body hasn't acclimated. While the pesky wind and baking sun played devilishly, I took the longer route, but stopped every half hour for water.

[Another lesson learned: Conserve water. Learn to live with thirst.]

The lesson came hard. Unstoppable sweat seeped out pores and soaked into clothing. Beads formed on my forehead, under the red hat bill, to dribble downwards, saltily stinging the eyes. Armpits, chest, back, groin and knees sported rings of wetness. Lungs became full and heavy with each gasp against the windpipe. After 30 minutes, saliva dried to glue consistency with the tongue stuck in the throat. I needed water, a small swig. Then larger. My mouth gulped fast. The throat choked at a potato sized swallow. Drinking water disappeared fast in the next thirty-seven boiling miles.

My body demanded to be fed constantly, and in larger quantities. Every hour I must stop for a nutrition break, at least an apple, orange, fruit tin, or half a package of cookies. [Lesson: Without sustenance, muscles twitched, shivered, and throbbed; soon they would refuse the order to pedal. The body demanded.] Thus, at every town or grocery/filling station, I'd need to stock up on a day's complete energy supply.

Amboy, eighty-eight miles from Barstow, boasted two restaurants and three gas stations. Dealers sold water. I bought a meatloaf dinner, $1.65, and then realized that, even with cheap meals, I couldn't afford restaurant fare. Carrying $37 in cash and $200 in Traveler's Checks to last until Miami, I must conserve money for the next 40-50 days.

Early morning enthusiasm faded. My fanny blanched with every pump while a tingling numbness crept down my legs. Strength ebbed with every pedal-pump. Thigh muscles just above the kneecap tightened, complained as they forced the stroke, straightened to a near cramp, then relaxed for 2/5 of a second before beginning the next cycle. From hip to knee, muscles grimaced as if bitten by ants. When slowing at a rest stop, I needed to be careful putting out my left leg as a kickstand, lest it buckle. But in a five minute rest period, muscles relaxed, sagged, cooled and tightened up. Upon remounting, knee bends were needed to loosen up. My legs had become wooden. I felt like Pinocchio on a ten speed.

My hands lost almost all sensation. Burning sun singed their backs, which have become deep red, the second layer of skin already peeling. Petroleum jelly lost its soothing coating. And circulation had been slowly cut off. Pins and needles jabbed hands from wrist to fingertips. To relieve them, I used every imaginable variation of hand and finger grips to ease the pressure of body weight pushing forward and down on the handles. At rest stops, I had trouble opening a small box of raisins, or tying my shoe laces. My hands acquired permanent handlebar curl grip, for it was difficult to close the fingers into a complete fist.

Gray asphalt cut the valley. Shushing traffic left a thin strip of road shoulder to pedal. Dark chocolate chip mountains passed slowly on the left; yellow-gold peaks on the right. Flash flood eroded sand and rock piles angled down steep canyons in three-mile long delta alluvial slants. Half-mile high sand dunes swallowed smaller peaks. The highway had its reliefs. Along the road edge, a thin thread of vegetation eked out life from traffic engine evaporation. In the distance a lonely black diesel engine pulled a hundred box car caravan of rectangles. Another diversion occurred at the periodic gulleys which run under the roadway. Short bridges, advertised by black and white striped guardrails, spanned these gouges. Their purpose was to allow floodwaters to drain under the road bed.

Yes, floods in the desert. Rain comes in sudden cloudbursts. Torrents may pour up to two inches of rain in an hour. Parched desert cannot soak up the sudden water, which rushes off the hills in a crest, sometimes five feet high. Wash bridges allow water to pass under the road without severe damage to the highway.

In evening shadows, I reached Essex, a Highway Department maintenance yard. Behind a fence, a thick green lawn looked inviting. However, a worker declined my request to sleep on state property, saying the dry river bed would be okay. He added that, if I saw lightning during the night, I should get up and get out fast! The mountains would be flash flooding. After 111 miles my body was too weak to beg or argue. My feet stumble-stepped through the sand, as aching hands pushed the bike into sand traps nearly tumbling everything into the riverbed. With camp set up on the hard, dry surface, I ate salami, Fritos, potato chips, an orange, and gulped water drawn from the state property well. A bat dived, then veered off into the scrub. Night stars stared unflinching from every direction. A full moon outlined mountain peaks. Distant trucks rumbled and train horns gave jarring blasts. I slept fitfully. Flashes of light ricocheted off the purple mountains. The glowing watch face said 12:30. A flash flood would be coming. Quickly I repacked and hurried out of the wash, my head cramped in a dreamy haze. Circling behind the maintenance yard, I dropped canned goods, rolled out the bag in the dirt, and slept too tired to care if the worker objected.   111 miles

BURNING DECISION

False call on the lightning-only slight rain. Instead, the night episode complicated breakfast with the hazy dizziness of sleep. Only a ghost could eat a morning meal of raisins, nectarines and salami. Head unclear. It was hard to sleep with the buzz of nearby traffic. Legs and shoulders were surprisingly comfortable, but the backs of both hands were covered with small yellow blisters. As the sun rose over the rim of the cloudless valley, its heat radiated through clothing, burning and tightening my skin. At 7:30 it was already 90^0 and dangerously late for a desert start.

A climb of two miles over a red sand mesa, exposed a series of orange sand mounds. Cars rocketed past, effortlessly rising the next mesa in three minutes. For me, it was a half hour's labor in fifth gear. A power relay station sign read: *No Facilities. No Water.* I was half way to the next water source with half my liquid gone and the sun heating up, twelve miles from Needles.

How odd that irritations and mishaps occur more frequently when a crisis mounts. My eyes were dry. Searing air burned my nostrils. The gear chain had several whistling squeaks-an abandoned oil can contained just enough lubrication drops. Next, the bike rack lost a nut and screw, allowing the bedroll to wobble sideways. Steering became unsafe. For a stop gap measure, on the road shoulder, I found a rusty nail, which, when bent, could hold the rack to the bike frame. Salty sweat beads burned my eyes. Tired with each mesa ascent, I had to rest at the summit, dizzy with six miles to go. For a few moments, I found refuge in the shade of a drainage ditch pipe. The longer I delayed, the greater my thirst danger. When the last swig of water disappeared, two nectarines were my last supply of liquid. I mounted the bike while shimmering waves of heat danced ahead on the highway. A mirage lake of water beckoned. And then, across the horizon, below the spinning wheels, a thin baby blue ribbon appeared, the Colorado River, sides embroidered with green plants. I pushed on harder because the dizziness was growing. I understood why grizzled cowboys and prospectors jumped into rivers and guzzled drink.

Needles. First stop in town was a service station drinking fountain. The owner grinned. He'd seen fools before. I sat cooling in his driveway, reading a map until I tilted over and fell asleep. He let me be. Some time later I woke to ride listlessly to a market. At 10:30 a.m., it was 110^0. Too hot to travel. Slow moving railroad workers leaned sluggishly on shovels in the rail yard. A lonely twosome walked on the green felt golf course. Heat waves danced the shrubs along the river, where I hoped to sleep off the heat. In the weed beds, a few children frolicked. A roaring speedboat towed a water skier. The tempting relief of river water was too cold for me at 50^0.

Frustrations continued to mount. Tickling bugs, choking dust and noise from the ski boat prevented rest. Oppressive heat lingered. Sunburned skin ached. My hands felt similar to a tooth with Novocain wearing off, their coordination and strength virtually gone. It had become difficult to hold a can opener, much less open with it. Couldn't button my shirt. Cold water neither refreshed nor cured. In a dilemma, with 500 miles of desert ahead, my body was in revolt. Stubbornness urged me to continue for at least three more days, until the ascent of the upper Arizona plateau. To reduce strain from pedaling extra weight, I began discarding anything unessential. Two books (no time to read), spare underwear, aspirin, radio batteries, automobile tire pump, spare inner tube and tire patches, and half of the plastic tube tent were given away or dropped. Weight loss: four pounds. I could have dumped the sleeping bag, but relented. I felt like quitting.

During the time spent at the river, I lost a screw to the temple piece of my eyeglasses. Though I could see well enough without glasses, I was fortunate to find a jeweler who located a replacement. Stocked and watered up, I weakly rolled off at 6 p.m. A store thermometer drowsed at 110^0 as I clumsily pedaled to the river crossing. The handlebar metal was like grabbing a hot potato. After two miles, I stopped to claim a lost towel from the dirt. Cut in half, and with five holes poked in the material, I fashioned makeshift gloves. Simple relief from the sun.

At the Arizona State Agricultural Checkpoint, a man screened poultry for the New Castle Disease chicken epidemic in California and Arizona. As we talked, I had an excuse to rest until the setting golden sun slanted over the western mountains. A gleaming silver girder bridge spanned the river. Immediately the road climbed in a three mile exercise to gain 1,500 feet in elevation. And the heat eased. Evening shadows lengthened during a brief cold dinner of ravioli-out-of-a-can-using-the-lid-for-a-spoon. Since the next town, Yucca, was twenty-five miles off, I intended night driving. For safety, I donned the fluorescent vest. Keeping to the extreme right shoulder of the road, and using reflectors and generator light, I glided along a gradual incline. In spite of my precautions, cars honked. They do not expect a bike here. Only headlights and traffic hiss broke the stillness of the desert.

Sometime after 10:00 p.m., I cycled wearily around the off ramp into neon smiles of motel faces. One manager, with only a glance, told me to move. Bad for business. He suggested an abandoned motel. It was a vacant line of squat adobe cottages, the only tenants being sage brush staring through battered windows. In one of the rooms, I spun the front wheel by hand to generate light. The stuffy interior contained a mattress, dirty, and losing its intestines. Pulled outside and flipped over, it seemed to offer a comfortable bed in warm winds. Lightning threatened in night clouds. Nearby hills were struck, but no rain. The radio broadcast news of a tornado in southern Arizona and a flood in Sacramento. Maybe I'm just lucky.   67 miles

A FRIEND

All night wind blew in smothering gusts. Because of the hot air, and glass, and dirt stuck in the mattress, comfortable sleep was impossible. Groggy morning pack-up. 6 a.m. Checked water. Left "sandy town." Easy road incline. I stayed silent, alone, until morning cars whooshed past. A sun baked weather beaten train snaked up through the sage brush and sand, crept along the highway, before it crossed the road to slink behind red rock sun mounds. Quiet. A wordless desert.

The left pedal began to click/slip forward. Each revolution lost power in the down stroke. As the slipping and noise increased, power loss grew to 25 percent. At a truck stop, amid hissing air brakes and diesels grunting up to fuel pumps, I tinkered unsuccessfully with the faulty retaining pin. Without proper tools, the bike would have to limp the next nine miles, forcing me to pedal like a man with a peg leg.

Nestled in a narrow brown rock gorge, an Arizona checkpoint inspected traffic. Two gray uniformed officers frowned their eyes at plants, fruit, animals, and then confiscated suspect items. The upper end of the gorge opened onto cliff-perched dwellings on either side of Kingman's railroad ties. Farther along were a chamber of commerce, other buildings, and a retired black hulking steam engine in a park.

At a bike shop in Kingman, a brown-haired teenager tried several tools to correct the faulty crank pin, without success. Since he wanted to examine the crank bearing, I excused myself to wash my sweaty foul smelling clothing. I stripped off everything except for blue shorts and a white tee shirt, then strolled about town while the clothes laundered. I wandered in and out of stores, looked at displays, and treated myself to a pastry breakfast. With jelly and sugar clinging to my lips, I whistled back to the laundry. The bike still wasn't ready, so I returned to the black train engine in the park. With an impish grin, I clambered aboard, listening to ancient ghostly train noises, whistles, and inspected phantom jiggling gauges. I played with the heavy throttle and boiler cranks, felt the mighty pistons and two-ton wheels. I even stood on the cowcatcher. Finally, tired, I napped in the shade of the high school. Back at the shop, the bike showed no improvement; it seemed worse. There were bigger shops in Flagstaff. But it was not appealing to pedal 165 miles when one-fourth of the power was wasted.

The town's afternoon shadows grew. Another cyclist paused at the bottom of a hill, his bike heavily laden with saddlebags, tool kits, clothes, bedroll, and water jugs. He looked back over his shoulder and I howdied. Dave Myer, who had left Southern California a day after me, was heading for Maine, hoping to return via Canada. By some miracle, he had survived a twelve hour ordeal on desert dirt roads, over sand hills without water on his bike, over weighted one hundred pounds. Yet he averaged a hundred miles a day. Together we rode.

A friend lends encouragement during an arduous test. We double-checked water and gear, exchanged tricks and tips, worked out hand signals, and set a demanding pace. As two knights of the road we charged a chocolate canyon split by rail line, the highway, and a few scraggly trees. The dragon wind spat its hot breath, raking our flesh with sand and pebbles. The unseen foe vanquished us until king sun hid his golden lamp behind the hills of royal lavender.

In the last hour of light we entered a serene meadow-village hemmed in by the yellow boulder cliffs of Valentine. We were tempted to increase mileage, but the wind and a steep climb threatened. We retreated back to a grassy driveway of a empty well-kept lawn. Hoping for permission to sleep on the lawn, we leaned bikes against a stone wall, wobbled up steps, and knocked. Two frisky dogs annoyed us, until the owner, an Indian, came around the yard. He refused permission, with reason. Scorpions, Gila monsters, and rattlers infested the Arizona rocks just behind on the hills. With the cool of the evening, they ventured down onto the lawn seeking water. It would be wiser to sleep high off the ground. He pointed to a cement loading dock behind his Bureau of Indian Affairs Office. In twilight blue-gray, Dave and I stripped to our shorts and washed with cold garden hose water. Without the sun's glare, the rocks chilled quickly. Evening slipped into silence, cracked twice by night train horns. In the evening shadows, jousting with the wind dragon ended.

Both of us were in pain from sun and wind burn. Dave wrapped bandages around the charley horses in both legs. My right leg throbbed from the extra work due to the pedal trouble. What was worse-I might have developed a butt blister. When I removed my underwear to wash in the morning, I did not put it back on. A blunder, for a single thickness of cloth did not protect from saddle friction. My rump had become frightfully tender.   65 miles

JAIL

Gray valley mist warmed to pale yellow. We hoped to reach Flagstaff (127 miles) before the weekend closed stores. The first few miles were awkward until we got the kinks out. Hills rolled and curved in sparse grassland. The left pedal worsened until 50 percent of its thrust was lost. Pedaling rhythm was impossible, the added strain telling in the right leg. At first, small pains stabbed the knee. Soon they shot downward along the shin to the ankle, until the whole leg swelled and grew numb. My hands continued numb. Handwriting resembled a worm with jagged bumps. Last, and not least, the butt chaffing has aggravated to two half-dollar-sized circles of "don't touch me" flesh. Pedaling increased every ache and pain. I hated sitting on the seat.

Peach Springs Indian Reservation Grocery opened at 9:00, giving us a breakfast of milk, canned pears, and cookies. Several barefoot kids in jeans and dirty dresses stared as we sat on the cool cement. Dogs strolled under a wooden hitching post to laze in the cool of the adobe.

Leaving town, my spirits sank. Wooden sign: *Flagstaff 112*. Both legs had tightened and ached. Dave was no better off with his charley horses. We forced ourselves to pedal, and somehow the kinks unraveled during the next hour, but by 11 o'clock, I wanted an excuse to stop.

Billboard advertisements for the Grand Canyon Caverns had blotted the hillsides with gray-white-red garish rectangles for over fifty miles. Dave, anxious for mileage, waved good-bye and rolled on. I paid $2.00 for walking the cool dusty labyrinth. A guide pointed out stone formations. Walking up and down, and crouching to enter portions of the cavern was a blessing in disguise, stretching sore muscles. One section of the vault housed five gallon water cans, portable commodes, stores of C-rations and medicines. It was all waiting for 2,000 people, pre-paid customers, who would streak for the caverns in the event of a nuclear war. Few, and probably none, of these individuals would arrive during such a catastrophe. Fifteen minutes warning would not be a great deal of time. They would be lucky to have that much alert in an atomic war. And then there would be the traffic jam with panic stricken folks abandoning vehicles any which way to rush to the bomb shelter. Worse, still, would be the insane chaos of 2,000 bodies living underground, in the dark, for two weeks. I'd rather be bicycling.

The tour provided rest and time to mull over a shrewd decision. If the stores were closed in Flagstaff on Saturday afternoon, a two day layover would be necessary. To be in striking distance, and capable of arriving in the morning for repairs, I'd have to push ninety-seven tough miles to Williams. And wouldn't you know it! All afternoon blustery winds sand-scratched face and limbs, and resisted every pedal forward. My eyes teared up as I concentrated, pressing down on the chrome pedals while hunkering to provide a smaller silhouette to the wind. On rubbery legs, I literally dropped into Ash Fork at 7:00 p.m. An unnerved grocery clerk in the window scowled as I untangled from the fallen bike, stood unsteadily, clinked his door entry bell, and lumbered down the aisles. I sat outside wolfing down spaghetti, cookies and milk, pausing before the final push.

The last bitter stretch ran fifteen miles, including a 2,000 foot climb up an extended twisting grade into darkening mountains. The wind fury died at the foothills. When dark held the sky, I donned the fluorescent vest to help motorists identify my presence. Trucks flicked high beams, honked and slid over the lane divider left. Oncoming vehicles' blinding high beams forced me off the road. Once the bike crested the summit, speed picked up and whizzed in black air. A bend in the asphalt ribbon and suddenly glamorous light flashed, like a circus! Carnival neons hawking to tired motorists.

At Williams, a fenced old wooden house had the appeal of a safe lawn camp. I knocked, hat in hand, and explained to the tremulous elderly lady what I was doing at her door at 9:30 at night.

"Why don't you go to the jail?" she quivered as her hand jutted up to lock the screen door.

Sheepishly, I loped down the steps, intent on asking a few houses down. No sooner had I reached the bike when a patrol car pulled alongside the curb.

"You the fella comin' to the jail?" a bull voice called out.

Grinning, trapped, I replied, "Yeah".

The officer let me park the bike in front of the headquarters window, took my belongings into custody, and let me creep-saunter to a burger joint on the corner. When I returned, he led me down a hall to a spare white room with green foam mattress bunk beds cemented into the wall, a sink and toilet, and locked the door. I ate a half cookie and fell asleep, the best sleep in seven days.   97 miles

A MEXICAN FAMILY

Jingling keys clanked. Thump went the door. Blinding light.

Hoarse voice, "It's six".

Eyes squinted in puffy sockets. Ears buzzed. Head spun. Flopped back on the bunk. Body refused to wake. Every muscle had cramps. Time passed. One hour.

A good natured sergeant jawed with me, helped collect gear, and gave advice and stories.

"Not many people want to stay extra in the jail," he said

My body hated waking up. A restaurant cooked homemade pancakes.

Yesterday desert, today forest. Yellow morning rays sliced through cool pine needles of the timbered hills. Crisp thin air made inhaling short, sharp exercise. To function at this altitude it was necessary to drop down a gear ratio. Excuses were easy to find for resting along running streams and forested pastures. At this rate, nine miles per hour was speeding.

Coconino National Forest surrounds Flagstaff. There is no escape. Firs, bending over homes, whisper into neighbors' yards. Houses, durable and modest, loll in the green shade. Nor are they jammed together and asphalted in the L.A. manner of uglification. Except for interstate traffic, it is a serene woodland panorama.

Contrary to the beauty, I was rolling into town with a head of self-righteous anger fortified by the aggravation pains in my leg and both rump cheeks. The anger had simmered for 165 awkward annoying pedal-slipping miles. My now boiling temper was ready to unleash a scalding complaint at the main repair center for the feeble job done by the teenager in Kingman. Rancor whirled through my mind. Huffing and puffing hot fumes, I slammed the bike against a shed door of the sporting goods store, marched up to the counter and demanded the mechanic. He calmly listened. As soon as the problem was stated, he smiled and began to fix the bike-no objections. He left me with a bellyful of argument and no one to holler at. Or talk to.

The victor of the local fifty mile ten speed race, Hugo Lopez, was checking gearing at the shop. After small talk, he offered lunch and friendship. We circled the pine grove park filled with set-ups for the July 4th Rodeo. Hugo pointed to a shingled pale green government housing project, and selected one long dwelling with a wooden porch. Low income families filled these cheap flats. Creaking steps announced us. Mrs. Lopez, a jolly plump woman in her forties, smiled a welcome, and spoke to her son in Spanish.

The home was bare, scantily furnished, with a small table and chairs, and a red velvet couch. The aging walls lacked paint. Worn holes in the linoleum showed the flooring. Three bedrooms were used and a fourth had become Senor Lopez' watch repair shop. Five small children played in the living room. Much later, a scampering parade revealed all eleven children! Senora Lopez begged me to sit while she served soup and frijoles. From that moment I was at a disadvantage. The family was indeed poor, yet made room for one more. Since moving from Monterey, Texas, the family had grown. The children spoke excellent English, though the parents did not. I conversed in stumbling Spanish, telling many stories. The kids poked and teased one another, but showed gentle behavior and discipline. Kids competed to give towels, clothing, or advice. Each gave without complaint from meager resources. They went fishing, shopped, joked, played baseball in the evening, and watched TV. Senora washed my clothes. It was too much. Their hospitality made me feel guilty, like stealing. Welcome everywhere, I was still anxious. I didn't know how to accept such generosity! Even at night the boys fought spiritedly over who would give up his bed to the gringo. To settle the dispute, I slept on the floor. Yes, they were "poor". Perhaps "the good life" spoils good lives.   37 miles

21

"YOU CARRYIN' A GUN?"

I dressed quietly at 6:30 and walked through pines to mass. Chilly. An Indian teen clad in old work clothes stood at the steps of the closed church. A station wagon loaded with a tourist family offered me a lift to another parish. The Indian boy began walking in same direction. Stop lights and railroad signals delayed us, so that the boy arrived at the second church just after we did. He entered quietly and stood in the rear, his presence an indictment against our bad manners. My personal sermon: selfishness and lack of concern hurt people.

When I returned, the Lopez children were in a last minute scurry to attend their Assembly of God service. The church, standing in a dried weed lot, was the only affordable building, a sadly weather beaten home, undergoing considerable repair, for thirty adults and children. A short Spanish prayer brought reverent silence. In a few moments, the youngsters departed to a separate room for questions and answers on sin, while adults received a formal lesson on responsibility. When the main body rejoined, there were songs and prayers accompanied by piano, electric guitar and drums, succeeded by two sermons. As we left, the minister thanked each person for attending. The children were already jostling for positions in the two Lopez's cars.

I had been complaining about butt soreness, so Hugo guided me to the hospital while Mama cooked. A reception desk nurse listened, smirked, and motioned to sit. After an uncomfortable hour, the counter sign's meaning registered: *Attention. All Patients are Notified of a $12.00 Emergency Room Fee in Addition to the Doctor's Fee.* Suddenly it was clear. The doctor would comment on the irritated skin, charge his fee, add $12.00, and recommend no more riding. We left the nurse open-mouthed. A drug store sold two inch gauze and adhesive tape. In the privacy of the bathroom I padded and taped the necessary locations as Mama called for lunch.

"Stay! Please!" the kids begged.

But I could impose no longer. A New Testament came forward as a gift. It became daily reading. Everyone signed his name on the inner cover. We held a waving contest until the pines hid the happy hands.

Businesses were taking their Sunday rest. Vending machines, however, spit out candy bar energy. Gas station stares and questions, then a hop, step, stretch, and hook a right leg over the seat. Surrounding forest listened to the whirling rhythm of the tires. A brown blur bounded between a yellow VW and the bike. I whistled as the coyote turned his head, belly laughed, and hustled down a culvert.

Geography changed quickly with the road's descent east. Trees thinned and shrunk in size. Dried grass and scrub clumps filled open spaces. A magic line on the hills indicated where the desert heat prohibited trees from growing any lower. Under powder blue sky, yellow desert spread to red mesas and deep purple ranges 80 miles distant. Hot, still air rasped deep in the nostrils, while unfiltered sun baked skin.

Winslow. 6 p.m. Mocha brown sandstone was the local Indian adobe building material. Isolated shacks, boarded windows. In a joint overrun by tourists, dinner was a burger and malt. Right knee stiff, but loosened when riding. Amid farms surrounding a small gas station, I took a 7:30 energy stop. A greasy mechanic and boy tilted back on chairs. Out front an icebox held a stack of fruit.

"Hi. Melons for sale?" I asked.

"Quarter. Ridin' far?" questioned the fellow leaning back on a wooden chair.

"L.A." I replied.

"You carryin' a gun?" he queried.

"No. Might scare some trigger finger holding me up. I'd rather hand over money and walk away," I countered.

"I'd get a two-by-four if I's you. You ain't got no hippie hair an' you dress good like you could get your hands on some money," he commented with an evaluating eye.

"You're just fooled by the red shirt and blue shorts," I chuckled.

He was right though, too middle class. I counted $20 in cash and $200 in travelers checks. How many others had sized me up as a mark? I still didn't want a weapon.

Holbrook. 8:30 p.m. Two different people refused to let me sleep on the lawn. A third, timidly peeking out the door, advised the court house. Not eager to sleep in jail again, I pedaled absently. A cycler drew abreast, decided I was a "friend" after a brief conversation, and showed the way to the park. A night softball game was just ending. Joe, a friend of his, rode up and invited us to his house. Joe's dad, Mr. Budenholzer opened the door, swept us in and gave royal treatment: dinner, TV, a shower, and a bed. I phoned long distance to tell Mom her eccentric son hadn't shriveled on the desert or become Gila monster stew.   97 miles

HIGHWAY BUNKO

Although breakfast began at 7:30, it ended at 10:00 sandwiched in between bacon and eggs, toast, cereal fruit, and hundreds of questions. Joe's friend, Richard, 16, asked to buddy with me as far as the Petrified Forest. He set the pace for twenty-five miles. Outlined distinctly in the yellow sage, stood the National Park's brown stone townhouse. Outside, government orderliness; inside clean counters, displays, and information booths. The park's specialty souvenir was a clock set in polished petrified wood. Exhibits were of excellent quality to emphasize the natural beauty of the locale. Outside were the stone concretion petrified logs. It only took thousands of years to substitute minerals for cellulose.

Roadside billboards were eyesores. Their bright red letters on yellow backing attracted sightseers like carny hawkers. Garish paint announced: *Indian Village Ahead. Official Moccasins, Tom-Toms, Jewelry, Kachina Dolls.* Such signs cluttered the view for 30 or more miles. The actual trading posts weren't what signs suggested-Indian trade centers. The "posts" were small square adobe affairs, sometimes a cement teepee, or perhaps a stucco western facade. Tourists apparently kept these frauds thriving. Once I leaned the bike against a fence, crawled under barbed wire, and visited an adobe post. A cash register sat at the door. Stuffed aisles, barely wide enough to walk down, permitted one to scan "real Indian made jewelry" and trinkets of turquoise. But it was not the quality an Indian would proudly display. On the tables, ferocious chiefs in feathered headdresses snarled from bottoms of ash trays; underneath the plaster was the stamp of Hong Kong manufacture. Shelves and walls were decorated with Indian maiden dolls, dressed in buckskin, made by Japanese Indians. Cardboard tom-toms drummed up war on black B.F. Goodrich rubber. No Indians were in the shop. The suspicious owner cocked an eye and sighted in on me browsing. He left his shirt open to advertize his hippo chest dripping sweat. A slouching girl in shorts guarded the till. I doubted that an Indian has been within a stone's throw of this place. The shoddiness of goods here was an insult to Indian culture. These posts sabotaged the landscape of Arizona.

State roads were well maintained, virtually free of refuse. The eastern state was drier and paler yellow. Route 66 crossed the state line into New Mexico in a long winding canyon. On both sides, the pigments of 500 foot bluffs varied in sediment strata lines from harsh reds to soft yellows. Dislodged boulders tottered at the edge of 300 foot drops, ready to bounce down to greet highway travelers. Once out of the canyons, the sightseer was impressed with the two block wide and seven miles of Gallup's gas stations, motels, restaurants, and liquor stores. The city lived off tourist trade.

Earlier I had removed my tee-shirt for an hour's tan. This proved disastrous in the thin clear air. I forgot the time, and by late afternoon developed a severe back sunburn. It hurt to stretch. When I asked a Gallup pharmacist to apply lotion, which I'd just bought, to my back, he gave a mortified blanch. So, I stood in the parking lot dribbling the ooze in places it shouldn't have gone.

At last, I rested in a restaurant, waiting for a hot supper. What a treat it would be since most of my meals were cold out of a can. Having ordered, I studied the figures in other booths. Three women, discussing distances, spoke as much with their hands as with their lips. One asked the miles to Las Vegas. Next, she inquired if I knew anything about tires. Would I check theirs? It seems a garage man in Grants had noticed cracks in their new Toyota tires. He pointed out that driving with such tread on the hot pavement might cause a blow out at any moment. When he quoted a stiff price for new tires, the ladies refused. Now, miles down the road, they were having second thoughts. Outside, on inspection, the tires showed only that they were dusty, with rain grooves as new as the spare tire. The odometer read 13,000. Another case of an unscrupulous salesman preying on naive female travelers. But it took fifteen minutes to convince the ladies of his deceit. By that time my supper had cooled to a tasteless sludge.

With a full moon rising, I pedaled a last seventeen miles for the night. Eerie light created phantoms. Witches' fingers beckoned from bushes whistling in the breeze. Banshee cattle moaned in the hollows. Like coffins leaning one upon another, stood the rigid black bluffs. Glaring traffic monsters blinded innocent souls with high beam piercing eyes, their fast fire breathing red tails receding at devilish speed.

Bone weary, legs resenting every stroke, I circled Fort Wingate into a full camper park, already snuggled down to sleep. A lone picnic table sat under a glaring light bulb. I placed the sleeping bag on top, rolled it open, and mechanically put my belongings on the seats. Applied sunburn lotion. Locked bike to table. Wrote in diary. More lotion. Tried to sleep. Twisted out light bulb. Cold desert night. 114 miles

TALES OF THE ROAD

The frying pan sun was cooking me on the picnic table. I crawled out of the sleeping bag, awakened by two boys armed with firecrackers. Aches and pains. Nothing new. Most of the other campers had left, so there was time for a leisurely fruit cocktail breakfast and diary writing. With another sunburn lotion application, I rode out the canyon neck. My first spurt of energy lasted a half hour until I reached a lonely Stuckey's Texaco and candy station. The Stuckey's concept seemed to work: a service station oasis in the barren hills, gas for an empty fuel tank, candy and coke for the kids, a powder room for the Mrs., and coffee for Dad.

Canyon colors varied from dusky reds and oranges to anemic yellows, the rims crowned with trees. Gulleys, cutting sideways through beige sand, revealed chocolate earth underneath. Barbed wire claimed this as ranch land. Rusting auto hulks in arroyos testified to long gone 300 horsepower cowboys. Although animals rarely appeared during the day, today a deer jumped out of a dwarf pine grove and circled back in. Jackrabbits scampered across the highway. There were other animals, for their mangled furry bodies lay beside the road, traffic victims. This applied to snakes as well. In the three states traveled so far, I expected to see at least one live wriggling snake. Even one sunning itself on a rock would be acceptable. However, the ten or twelve I've spotted all had tire treads for markings.

Trucks drove with controlled fury. A semi at sixty mph created a headwind that first buffeted any vehicle. As it passed, the backwash sucked inwards. I synchronized this and learned to slide in between rushes of wind to pick up speed. Needless to say, it was dangerous. Truckers were aware of the might of their metal behemoths. For traffic slower than themselves, they passed on the left after cautiously gauging distances and safety. Otherwise they blared their double horns well in advance of driving over their victim. The semis were equipped with air brakes capable of stopping their forty ton loads. If the load didn't shift and kill the driver forward, the only cost was tire tread. Road shoulders were littered with black snail shells of retread rubber sheared off in a panic stop. So far I hadn't seen an accident, though the damage of several has been towed past.

Most of the road to Albuquerque lay flat, straight and dry. During an apple break beneath a bridge, quadruple diesel engines whined past trailing a ninety-seven railcar earthquake. Nine Mile Hill, a series of three progressively higher bluffs up to a mesa became the evening challenge. Downshifted to the lowest gear, it was still a strenuous climb. With evening shadows, I coasted into the valley and city. Nearing town, I split from where Route 66 became freeway, rode leisurely, and began knocking on doors for lawn accommodations. After ten no's, an elderly gentleman gave permission. I bedded down, ate cold macaroni and beef, brushed teeth, and slept to the music of the cicadas.   119 miles

A HAIRY INCIDENT

Before I could pack and get off the lawn, Mrs. Laird invited me in for breakfast and bathroom use. A daily shave and combed hair makes me less gruesome to people. This morning, I reasoned that the pads taped to my rear end for cushioning would be foul. My fanny is hairy, making tape removal painful. I was too chicken to rip sensitive hair. Thus, the sticky ends dangled until I could find a medic to tear off the adhesive.

In a medical professional building, the desk nurse refused to pull the tapes, instead having me wait until the doctor arrived. After more than an hour, I pleaded for an orderly or nurse or even a janitor, anyone to pull the tape and get me an ABD pad (Abdominal pad) for sitting. Finally, inspired, she reconsidered, because she had a specialist in mind. She led down the corridor to Dr. Smart's office--the eye doctor. He ushered me to the treatment table, asked me to drop my pants and lean over. With two sharp yanks, he snapped off both Band-Aided pads, and about nine pounds of hair. There were no blisters or infections, an encouragement to ride. Unfortunately, eye doctors don't have soft abdominal medical pads, but flash! An idea! He stepped outside, rattled paper, and returned with a brown sack.

"This will fix you up," he said, handing me the sack.

The contents were two sanitary napkins, which he pinned to my shirt tail. How adaptable cross-country cycling can be!

After the hospital, market needs, and gear chain lubrication, the arduous climb of Tijeras Canyon began after 1:30. Worse than Nine Mile Hill, the narrow one lane passage of crumbling asphalt wound for sixteen miles, rising over ten thousand feet in altitude. The heavily trafficked undivided highway contained hidden curves which made passing impossible. Trucks had no room to pull onto the shoulder. Consequently, a line of cars snaked behind them. When approaching me, trucks gave a blast so they could get a couple extra inches of clearance. Twice they nearly forced me down deep ravines. Three hours of tortuous upward grind did not allow more than a brief glance across the ravines at flowing pastures, log cabins, and waving pines. Suddenly the road descended several hundred feet in a succession of steep rolling trenches, each 600 feet deep. My legs never dared to rest at the bottoms. Fearing the immediate demand of arduous climbing the next steep rise, I'd pedal fast up the next hill until gravity took its toll.

The Kotex pads, now sweat laden, lumped up, increasing irritation. When I could no longer stand the pain, I removed and threw them away. I'd rough it.

Behind, white clouds massed over the towering pass and changed to a sunset of puffy orange, lavender and golden cotton. The radio predicted thundershowers, blessed relief for arid land. There had been no services for fifty miles and the next stop would be thirty. So I debarked at Clines Corners, a gas station/restaurant complex. Next door, a new station under construction had building material scattered about. The pipe crew, having gone home, left giant dirt gopher mounds for me to camp among. Dinner was cold stew and sardines, followed by red licorice and water. Lightning flashed in the mountains causing radio static. Radio stations played from L.A., Oregon, Omaha, and El Paso.

As darkness invaded the sky, a tense low pitched buzz grew. The radio wasn't to blame, for the sound came from the pasture. Out of their underground burrows, fat brown beetles wriggled, took wing, and swarmed into the evening light. June bugs! Hundreds of thousands! They buzzed like a burping machine gun and splatted into the chain link fence. Every car and truck with its headlights on was greeted with a bug hail storm. Some vehicles, with headlights and windshields completely bug-smeared, stopped at the station to wash off the brown sludge ooze. Midnight frenzy.   50 miles

WET BACK

In the clinging morning heat, fifty cars had already gathered around the restaurant. Fathers gassed up while children squealed at the carpet of crushed June bugs on the pavement. Mothers shooed them inside for breakfast. I sat on a log stack catching up on two days of diary notes. Folks, spotting the bike, asked about the trip so frequently that the numerous tellings added three hours to get away, and one tar accident. The undersides of the logs had a gooey black coating which stained and ruined the long brown pants and long sleeve shirt, causing me to change to shorts and green windbreaker before heading into the hot morning.

The wind was a devil. Concealing treachery behind boulders, it lurked in depressions, then leapt out to tease and torment where there was no protection. During long sweaty inclines, not even a wisp of breeze cooled; on declines ferocious gusts forced <u>downhill pedaling</u>. Playful licks flicked pebbles at bare skin. Forward progress slowed to six mph. Religious progress stopped altogether as many sinful words came to mind.

An arc of cirrus clouds ahead were being swept by an east wind, while northwards black cloudbanks massed, threatening a storm. By mid afternoon, the weather had dropped low enough for gray mists to sprinkle on the horizon fringes and lightning danced from earth to sky on the hilltops three miles distant. Wind increased. Town was twelve miles; I would be trapped in the rain in the open. There was a slight hope in a Stuckey's sign: Free box of candy with ten gallons of gas. Four miles. As lightning zigzagged on the hills a mile off, the pedals churned to outrace each closer burst. It was dangerous being on a metal bike; there were neither houses nor trees for shelter. Thunder clouds tumbled towards me. Faster. Onward. A cement overpass loomed ahead, a temporary umbrella. I punished my weary legs to the bridge as a bolt struck 500 feet away. Out of breath, I squealed the brakes to stop under the bridge roof. Piercing winds whipped sand and grit into my face. I put on the tarred clothing for added warmth, and scrambled up the underside of the bridge seeking a nook for shelter. Finding none, I held out for a half hour, chilled to the bone.

Since only small raindrops were falling, and the lightning had passed, and Stuckey's was just three miles away, I was tempted to make a run for it. I pedaled perhaps a hundred feet when a gulley washer drenched me immediately. Large water marbles stung my ears and bare legs. Water streamed off the red hat visor, splashing my glasses and fogging them. Autos sloshed mud and road grit onto my clothes. Sodden socks slid down the ankles in wrinkles to help fill the bathtub shoes. I'd become a swimming pool on wheels.

Stuckey faces, staring out the picture windows, laughed at the spectacle. After switching to dried tarry clothes again, I came inside for warmth and coffee. Two motorcyclists wagging stringy hair had also been caught in the downpour. The owner, apprehensive of the crowd, announced closing time at 6:00, meaning we'd be hustling in another ten minutes. Back into wet clothes.

In the first laundromat of Santa Rosa, machines scrubbed tar and grime from clothing, while I washed caked mud off my legs. Soon I began knocking on doors hoping for a protective porch should the rain return, but townspeople were afraid of strangers. At the jail, the guard would not allow me to spend the night unless I had broken the law, and deserved it. The asking continued until well after 9:00. An elderly man finally let me use his open roofed porch. I bought groceries at a dingy market and stuffed my jowls with cold stew out of the can, and cookies. Wind swayed branches across a street lamp, as I put the day's frustrations to paper. Deep sleep.   56 miles

THE PEACOCK LADY

I lost two hours repairing a slipped brake cable. The owners did not venture out of the house. I shaved in a gas station restroom, then ate a breakfast of chocolate milk and bologna at a school bench. Tasted terrible.

The early morning basked in rain cleanliness; ranches breathed a dank hay odor; dripping water splashed into puddles lining the road edge; red dust had changed to orange mud as it mixed in the tumbling arroyo water. Above, on the green felt hills, cattle grazed in idle comfort, turning their heads to the unusual sight of a bicycle, then, lowering their heads, renewed chewing range grass. After forty miles the land reverted to dry dusty cliffs, canyons of parched weed, and red sand. No breeze stirred. The straight flat stretches allowed speed bursts up to 20mph--a long overdue pleasure. A few clouds appeared on the northern horizon, left, but the air remained arid and breathless. On the hourly five minute rest periods, I munched on peaches stored in the canvas water bag. Evaporation kept the fruit and water cool in 100^0 temperature.

For nearly three miles the bike steered awkwardly before I realized the trouble. The rear wheel swerved side to side as if it wanted to pass the front tire. Quick eye checks discovered no cause. Feeling innocently bold, I snickered, passing another Stuckey's outpost then coasted down a slope. Increasing speed revealed a slow tire leak-my first flat. It was a long walk back to Stuckey's. My tires had ridden over glass, rocks, nails, steel cables, scrap metal and other highway debris without damage, but this first flat was caused by an ordinary staple. The repair job was crude because of my stiff fingers, and the glue dried faster than the patch could be placed down. Several tries later, an air pressure test evidenced no leaks, yet after a half hour of riding pressure dropped from 70 psi to 64, and consequently another repair stop at a gas station.

On to Tucumcari, an elongated city lined with roadside services. Towering above, bare cement grain silo cylinders overlooked flat greenbelt. A co-op irrigation canal for 300 farmers paralleled the highway, and proudly advertised at the city entrance. Plowed fields surrounded the city. With stomach and tires refilled, I proceeded onto the narrow, dangerous, shoulderless two lane. At the road edge the bike was in tenuous control dodging construction, chuck holes, dips, and poor repair. I lost a race to a storm rushing from the north. Lightning flashed around me and the tire went flat again. A dilapidated shack far off the interstate offered shelter until I could reach town six miles east. At first I tried to pump up the tire pressure to reach town, but my numbed hands worked like boxing gloves, twice unable to untwist the screw down nozzle from the valve before the air pressure dropped. A gray drizzle fell. When the clouds moved on, I doubled back to an abandoned Enco gas station in a walk/run wobble-wheel trot. On the gravel entrance sat a pickup and an old Chevy under a leaky shingle roof. The pumps were old and rusty, the building's plaster chipped, and two plywood boards screwed together held the broken window together. A young man and elderly lady, the owner, were inside. They had been renovating for two days. Their air hose couplings were rusted beyond use. No repair possible. When he finished stocking a coke machine, the kid left in the dusty red pickup, the lady soon to follow.

Round-faced Lillian Murray, wearing a plain washed worn long hem print dress, pushed a graying lock of hair from her eyes. I accepted her promised ride to town only if she would fix up some of the leftovers of the day's business. A meal of chili, ham soup, ham, potato salad, cottage cheese and vegetables was tasty, plentiful and plain, like the woman. The four mismatched tables and chairs did not add adornment or complement her restaurant's tattered dusty walls and broken picture window. This had been Lillian's second day of business at the tumbledown Cedar Springs Station; it seemed a grandiose dream for a lady in her fifties, but her conversation displayed strong will power, moral fiber, and spunk that defied despair, even in a decayed building. For her whopping meal she asked only $1.50. She had to be forced to take $2.00.

Because of its quick-release tire feature, the bike was rapidly dismantled into her car. I swallowed my pride to accept a ride of eight miles into San Jon. Lillian kept a spirited talk about her diet, the President, hippies, her dislike to see anything die, war, her poverty ridden childhood on the farm, and her restaurant dreams. Just before the city limits, she offered her garage for a place to stay, provided that I: 1) didn't smoke, and 2) didn't mind peacocks. The first was easy; the second seemed no problem. We bounced along dusty dirt roads behind the high school to park in what appeared to be an auto wrecking yard. Old vehicles lay silently rusting in deep shadows. The red pickup was there with Guy, too. The yard was a hodge-podge of bric-a-brac, wood, machinery, tool sheds, chairs, old washing machines, boulders encircling a plain stucco house and porch, with a garage full of hay and feed. In back were fences separating cows and farm machinery, automobile skeletons and desert sage. Roaming over, around, under and through all this were three cats, a kitten, twelve dogs, two guinea hens, and five peacocks. Gunny sacks on the floor provided a mattress for the sleeping bag. A horse saddle became a pillow. Shortly, we picked up garbage scraps from a truckers' diner to feed the dogs who fought for morsels in the sand.

Lillian turned in; tomorrow would be busy at her restaurant. I sauntered across the school track field to a little league baseball game held under the lights. Moms and Dads screamed, hooted, and cheered while kids splashed in a muddy puddle around second base. The game broke up. Folks went home. I shuffled back to the farm house amid whelps of the dogs.

"Haaalp! Haaalp!" screeched out suddenly.

I ran toward the garage thinking someone was attacking Lillian. I searched about for the victim, but there was none. With the next scream, I realized for the first time the cry of a peacock. They were great watch birds because they sounded like damsels in distress. On the gunny sack bed, I listened all night to peacock calls.   82 miles

AM I CRAZY TO DO THIS RIDE?

Saturday, July 1   San Jon, NM to Amarillo, TX   Day 15

Muscle cramps in left chest. Toss and turn. Chickens cackled and peacocks wailed in the wind. Animal noises and bugs in hay. Restless.

"Ed! Ed!" Lillian called out. "I got to get feed from the garage".

While I dressed, she returned to the house, then bent under the jammed metal door for a scoop of meal. She was dressed in the same faded floral print dress and apron, and her hair tousle fell into her eyes all the time she was working. Amid the garage disorder Lillian displayed deft efficiency grabbing a tin of meal, a milk pail, dodging puppies under feet, gliding out to the corral, unlatching the gate, crossing the pen muck, positioning cows and spreading the dry meal. Then, she dropped a pad for her right knee, knelt, cleaned mud from the udder and began pulling teats with a squishy spray into the pail. A white bubbly froth filled the bucket. Puppies danced and scuffled next to her. Finished milking, we added a cube of hay to the trough. The milk was breakfast for "the family", a kitten in a broken down pickup, three cats in a shed, and the twelve dogs barking at three sloppy pans of milk. Feeding ended. Lillian left for the restaurant and station. I slept till 8:30.

After two hours wasted searching for the small puncture in the inner tube, I switched to a plain inner tube, not thorn resistant. Leaving Lillian's "family", I began chancing flats on the rugged exit from New Mexico. Eastward the road was narrow, in poor repair, and without shoulders. It was such a dangerous stretch that motorists were required to put on headlights during the day to make their vehicles more noticeable. Traffic was moderate; only a few cars and trucks beeped me off the pavement. On the shoulder I found a terrycloth towel, which I folded and put over the seat for cushioning. It seemed to cut down on butt ache.

The open road had moments of boredom. So did an assembly line or a secretary's typewriter. It was good to have Dave Meyer for a few days' companionship, sharing experiences. There was also safety in numbers. If trouble or injury occurred, there was someone to go for help. There might be conflict if one wanted to sightsee and the other didn't. It required cooperation to be compatible, to know when to agree or disagree. For my part, I simply liked doing things at my own pace without being a bother to others. Being alone gave time to think about things ordinarily taken for granted: home, family, school, teaching problems, personality and how to improve it. Perhaps some people were afraid to be alone with their thoughts. They needed distraction. Sometimes all I noticed was the weather.

Perhaps critics might say that I'm crazy to make this trip. I enjoy doing things out of the ordinary, not to be a nonconformist, but to experience things that others miss. At times I gain new insights into people's problems by suffering through a similar trouble. There is pleasure in taking things apart and reassembling them. Similarly, there is pleasure in doing something alone, being solely responsible for success or failure. I like pushing the limits of endurance, and conquering obstacles, whittling away at massive tasks, shaping out real form where there was once only a raw dream. I like being in control of myself.

Control is more than physical. There are intellectual and spiritual strengths, too. Learning about life and one's country from textbooks uses another person's experience to learn rapidly and more expertly in a shorter time. But theoretical knowledge is not a cure-all for problems. It must be put to work, applied to real life situations. Application is a process of purifying mastery. Self-control makes it easier to organize and function. The more situations one can handle smoothly and efficiently, the better self mastery. Our whole lives are spent learning control.

Spiritual strength is probably the most important ingredient of control, and the least developed. We all have notions of how people should be, how things should operate-standards, morals, laws. Ideas of perfection often don't match our particular situations, like persons who refused to let me sleep on their lawns. Emotions may stir to anger, resentment, fear. Kind, gentle words, and humor may be necessary to dissolve a tirade. Discouragement, too, weakens one's desire to retry, to go on, to succeed. Spiritual strength provides emotional control and thinking adjustment. It may require alternate solutions (knocking on other doors), or accepting that no solution exists for now. Learn to do without. For now sleep in the fields. Times will change and so will situations. The real strength of religion is learning how to live with others, the Ten Commandments and the Eight Beatitudes. The Good Lord provides. Have faith. Do what you can.

On the late morning horizon, heavy clouds were gathering as I entered Texas. The first fourteen miles east of the state line was desert ranch, flat, bare sand with scattered cactus and stubby grass. Smooth and fast pedaling. Ascending a series of hills to a plateau, the geography and weather changed dramatically. As far as the eye could see, level farmland extended in strips of tilled dark soil or sparkling golden hay or sprouting vegetables. Patterns of neat squared rows had a look of military discipline. Lonely outpost houses dotted the vista broken with lines of tree windbreaks. Prompted by the massing weather, fierce winds slowed speed and drained energy. Towns of Glenrio, Adrian, and Vega became grocery and rest stops; snacks, a nap, and hope that the wind-struggle would die. No such luck. Reluctantly I pedaled. And then luck changed. The wind ebbed, ceased, and reversed to a tailwind pushing me along. Dark clouds spread through the west canyon. A crooked finger of cloud stretched over the highway as jagged lightning strings crackled to the ground. With rain a certainty and no available shelter, it became a race against the overhead cloud and falling sheets behind.

On the right a lone set of farm buildings appeared. Pebbles crunched in the driveway under the tires while fat drops splattered. Two dogs barked angrily. When I knocked at the door of the wooden structure, a glimpse inside the picture window revealed a stocky tee-shirted man moving past two young boys to the bedroom. As he opened the door, a gust flew inwards, pushing the door wider. He stood at the entrance with his right hand held concealed behind his back, which made me think he was holding a pistol. Although suspicious after my explanation, he allowed that the old garage, though dirty and greasy, was water tight shelter, if I didn't mind. Heavy drops smacked my forearms as I pushed the bike through tall weeds and unlatched a rusted hasp bolt. Inside, light, angling through broken windows, fell upon the floor strewn with engine blocks, pails, and tires. The sleeping bag unrolled in a cleared corner. On the galvanized roof, rain splattered in a tick-tock staccato. I hadn't bathed in five days. Out came a bar of soap. Stripped to white undershorts, I stood under the rivulets off the roof lathering up and shivering in the foamy bubble chill. Then, as suddenly as the storm hit, the rain quit. Before I could rinse away the soap, water disappeared from the roof, leaving a goopy film. I dried off using the riding shorts and put on the dirty greasy long pants and shirt.

Above, the sky was still gray, but the horizon had slashes of blue heaven. Flat yellow fields were dotted with black silhouettes of barns, silos, and farmhouses with few trees. Cows lowed in golden pastures; wild sunflowers glistened with dark faces full of droplets. Cars sloshed watery rooster tails on the interstate. Solomon in all his glory was not so beautifully arrayed. The storm drifted to south counties amid pompous thunder and dazzling flashes.

Exiting the back door, the stocky farmer, accompanied by his wife and two boys, climbed into their pale green pickup, pulled up beside me and offered/commanded me to join them to the local spectacle, stock car races in Amarillo. I rode in the truck bed, wind whipping around for what seemed hours. The race track was closed due to mud, so we returned. The Collinses asked me in through the kitchen to watch roller derby and wrestling on TV, with tea and cheese snacks. A news flash reported thunder warnings and winds to one hundred mph in Hockle County, sixty miles south, an area that geographically attracted bad weather. The farmer said that rains were worthless unless they brought more than an inch and a half, in order to fill dried up wells and cisterns. Out the windows, a series of lightning flashes moved like electric caterpillars dancing on a griddle, their brilliance contrasting with the roadside fireworks being sold at roadside stands for the July fourth patrons and patriots. The garage was cool but comfortable.   70 miles

TEXAS BLUE LAWS

In the debris strewn garage, Sunday breakfast consisted of pears with juice dribbling onto my shirt. A glorious sunrise shone over grass clumps. Ditches sparkled dewy smiles as I rode by fresh, sweet, damp fields. I completed toilet and barber needs at yet another gas station. Two attendants gave peculiar winks when asked for directions to Catholic services. Information was accurate. On the other side of a weed filled road divider, energetic parishioners, walking from St. Hyacinth's to the parking lot chatted gaily.

"Hey, you just missed the 9 o'clock," called out Father Jim Comisky, in green vestments, standing at the front door, waving hello.

Without asking who I might be, he directed the way to the meeting hall for coffee and folks. I could probably get help to repair broken spokes and replace the leaky inner tube. Several people genially extended hands to bring me into their discussions, despite my dirty jeans and rough appearance. Frank Hollenbaugh, a jolly six-foot-four-inch football physique, took me under his wing, loaded bike and gear into his trunk, and invited both Father Jim and me to lunch after 10:30 mass. For church services, I secluded myself in a corner pew, ashamed of my dirty clothes, but thanking God for my fortune and these good people.

At lunch, Frank kept pushing plates my way, the first hot meal in a week. It was impossible to refuse the thick juicy steaks. Talk bounced happily among the four adults and two young girls, but I listened and ate three helpings.

Texas Blue Laws made it illegal to buy or sell on Sunday except for food and necessities. This was borne out as we searched for bike parts in the afternoon. Shopping centers, market, service stations and other businesses were as empty as their parking lots-a remarkable experience for a Los Angelino used to car dealers and discount stores open seven days a week. Counties have enacted Blue Laws in the Bible Belt. Baptists, in particular, demanded and got stringent laws closing businesses on Sundays. A parent may buy baby formula, but not a baby bottle; buy a hat but not clothing. Some stores circumvented the law by closing on Saturday, so they could open on Sunday. Work exceptions were police, hospital, restaurants, and gas stations. Needless to say, no bicycle shops were open, so I faced a layover day.

Amarillo homes spread out with fields interspersed, even in the center of town. We passed the city incinerator where all burning was done. Brick buildings sported extensive lawns and yards, but narrow clean streets. Law forbade any citizen from public burning of any kind. Pollution control was conducted using special filters to prevent even a noticeable smoke from escaping, giving the city clean air. In the far north of the city a smelter coughed chalky gray-brown soot day and night. The smoke was both an eye and lung sore, but because of the numerous jobs at stake and the cost of finding emission controls, the due date closure-of-facilities was several times set back. Smoke continued to belch.

Late in the day, Father Jim made the rounds to the rectory, a convent for coffee with seven nuns, and dinner with a family. Lively personalities talked of their city, work, love for fellow men and women. It rekindled a warmth in my own heart. Back at the rectory, Father Jim held his nose, gave me a blessing and sent me to shower first. The Hollenbaughs had given me fresh clothes to wear. I wrote for two hours about my kaleidoscope of blessings. No Miles

AMARILLO STORIES

Morning mass had no parishioners. I served as altar boy in brown and white plaid shorts. The service was quiet, simple, personal, the consecration of Christ's body and blood, and our lonely presence.

[Lesson: God must love us greatly, even when we forget Him.]

Father Jim was a slim graying, bespectacled man with the energy of two teenagers. His office reflected new breed ecumenism on bright wall posters whose sayings asserted: "Love is contagious", "No man is an Island", and "Repent and be Saved....If you've already repented, disregard this notice". His small parish contained 155 families within 680 square miles. Catholic population in Texas ran between 6 and 8 percent. As the only priest, Jim visited families, arranged conferences, counseling, and marriages. He spent the morning driving to various repair shops for bike parts. Most had closed for a four day holiday, so we ended touring the city again. But we did find an open bike shop.

There is a story attached to a mansion in Amarillo. Several months ago, the government dispossessed the owner who owned a farm tool company famous across the West. Over the years it ran afoul with taxes. Instead of the Federal Government closing him down, causing the loss of many jobs, it took over operations and <u>paid</u> the owner a dollar per implement made, until the taxes were satisfied. He was returned the business. An aging employee of thirty years at the company applied for retirement but was informed there would be no Social Security benefits, though he had dutifully paid from his wages. The owner had collected Social Security funds weekly, but never registered or paid them to the government. As federal retribution, the business was closed and the mansion taken away, yet, as of this writing, the old employee had no retirement funds, and there were no court proceedings against the owner.

Following an afternoon of chores, we spent a delightful evening meal with five priests and two nuns, each with stories of labors and neighbors. Later we retrieved the mended bike, and the Hollenbaugh family added first aid supplies to my clean laundry. We retired to the rectory after midnight coffee cake. My hunger is almost as huge as my inability to record the thousand events of the day. Like Vincent DeRose, drifter. He was sitting on the church steps this morning. Intending to be a gardener, he had a receipt for a bus to Las Vegas, New Mexico, but had lost the ticket.

He retraced his steps to end up on the edge of town. Father Jim drove him to the Salvation Army which gave him a discounted ticket. Vince was greeted cheerfully, but was afraid we would abandon him. He attempted to cover his fear with a patchwork of mumbled religious ideas from saints to the evils of alcohol. Father Jim paid the $10.80 fare. Vince bowed obsequiously, thanking us over and over again. Vincent is a permanent traveler in society. He has no home.   No miles

A FOURTH OF JULY UNLIKE ANY OTHER

Tuesday, July 4   Amarillo to McLean, TX   Day 18

July 4th began in a drizzle as the day's temperature peaked at 58^0, the coldest 4th in fifty years. Father Jim gave me a holiday nap until 10:00. Two ladies came to mass. Jim's breakfast of coffee, an orange, and toast were like hors d'oeuvres for my growling stomach. He left for an appointment as I prepared to leave. On the kitchen table on a scrap of shopping bag paper, I left a thank you note, and his keys.

The cotter pin on the left pedal stripped while I was tightening it, so rather than risk trouble on the open road, I returned to Mr. Rheas' bike shop. The spry 71 year old, who preferred a straw cowboy hat said he'd help at once. Rheas didn't advertise; his craftsmanship had built his business reputation, taking on work other shops turned away, especially wheel chairs. He was perhaps the only wheel chair repairer an owner could count on, otherwise they bought two or three chairs. As a widower and old ranch hand, Rheas was lively, happy and playful. He hated to say no. He fixed my bike.

Dismal clouds hung over Amarillo. By 3:30 the wind battle had resumed. Fortunately, I had bought gloves against the chill air. Amarillo Boulevard (U.S. 66) cut through the abandoned military airport, Texas Tech Institute, and an Army supply reservation before it opened onto green grain fields east. Although there were infrequent houses and barns, trees were rare. The next forty miles were monotonous, not because of the terrain, but numbing cold. It was difficult to concentrate on more than my feet and dull unfeeling hands, but my tail didn't hurt as much. On the road to Groom, dips in the land appeared, soon deepening from drains to washes, gullies, and then canyons. The asphalt ribbon weaved and dodged.

At nightfall, on the outskirts of McLean, trying a side road to ask a rancher's permission to sleep on his property, the bike slipped, skid, and tumbled into a mud lake. I must have looked suspicious with mud over the bike and on my clothes, so he sent me a half mile back and across the highway to a metal hay shed. In the dark it was difficult to find the door latch. The interior was black. Utilizing the bike generator light, I spun the friction generator wheel to get a dull light glimpse of hay blocks. Arranged in a bed, the hay was soft, warm, and comfortable. Dinner was a half tin of tamales, hard on a cold stomach. I settled for a comfortable sleep which lasted only ten minutes, because the hay was infested with tiny bugs which tickle-stepped over my face. Somehow I thought they would eventually stop bothering me, that is until they started biting. I moved outside the shed, lay down the plastic tarp, plunked down the bedroll and slept on the rocky ground. I'd had enough July 4th fireworks.   50 miles

HAPPY BIRTHDAY!

Two horses woke me with birthday kisses and snorts. We talked for a bit. When I rolled over for a snooze, they backed off, nibbled at grass, and stomped the turf. The palomino returned. It seemed they were looking to me for hay feed, but this might have invited reckless interference in the farmer's animal care. I tried to stay away, until it was obvious that the palomino had smelled an apple in my pocket. A gust of wind flapped the orange tarp spooking him off. On the shed latch, I left the rancher a thank you note, lifted the bike over the No Trespassing fence, climbed over myself, and began the morning ride. I felt strong and alert with the right leg pains diminished, but rode unenthused from sleep disrupted by night critters. Fifteen miles later, while eating an orange in a culvert, I fell asleep and woke stiffly. Dipping hills exacted strenuous cranking. At lunch I rationalized I should not push too hard on my birthday. A family drove up to the next picnic table, and invited me to a birthday baloney sandwich and coffee.

McLean, population 1,100, supplied a collection of rancher's shops and a free museum. A couple of older ladies roamed with me in the collection of antique tools and memorabilia, adding a stream of stories from the town's history. The drug store sold a special treat, a lime drink and soda. On the opposite side of the street a barbershop promised to shorten the five inch shag on my head.

In the barber's chair, I said, "I hear that they give good haircuts in Texas. You're the boss. Give me a good trim."

I never expected that a trim in Long Beach and Texas meant different things. When I left the shop, my red hat no longer fit. I wore white sidewalls!

My parting memory of McLean was a tour through the leather wares, harness, and saddlery of the bootsmith's shop. A homey western town.

Determined to cross the border before day's end, Shamrock became a brief water-hamburger-candy bar stop before I began the roller coaster dips of the eastern Texas panhandle. I was now seeing more trees, but a foul odor of crude oil escaped from drilling platforms and ponds hidden behind the foliage. Sticking above the tree tops were black refinery funnels. At Texola, where Texas and Oklahoma trade ownership of the interstate, I missed a road sign indicating the dead end ahead. Stubbornly, I continued over the bridge and into unpaved muck beyond. After several seconds, I realized my mistake of riding a portion of the Interstate construction. Backtracking meant mud. Taking a short cut seemed easier, which meant a walk/plow through thick roadside growth, trekking over railroad ties, and crawling up and down an embankment to attain the correct road.

The neon lights of Erick glittered from closed stores at 9:30. No place to stay. Farther on, a neatly trimmed lawn entrance to a farm offered possibilities but the farmer rejected the camp idea. Two miles down the road, a lighted billboard in the weeds tempted me to use its light to record notes. Weariness conquered my writing. The spot was unsafe. Across the road I approached the barbs of a wire fence, lifted the bike over, followed a path through sand and weed thicket to a mound of trees by a deserted feed corral and loading dock, and tripped over a low strand of barbed wire, scratching my legs. To avoid further trouble, the bike was left on the spot, while camp was laid out in the leaf mulch under the trees. Wind whispered through the night. A few mosquitoes hummed until the breeze increased. Trucks growled by like beasts with white night-eyes. Tossing turning sleep. Happy birthday!   116 miles

OKLAHOMA

Late morning sluggish waking. Noisy traffic. Wind. Camp in disarray. I had been sleeping on a tilt, and during nocturnal shifts, had slipped downhill amid stacked tin cans, tools and clothes. Peeking out of the sack, I viewed a stretching crop of desiccated weeds back to the wind break trees. I didn't put on shoes immediately, for they were occupied by a trail of ants en route to a Fig Newton party. Standing in white socks, I avoided the brown crawlies, since they hadn't disturbed me, and packed camp. After a polite chat with the six legged ants, we decided to split the remaining cookies for a "team" breakfast, to which I added canned pears.

Texas seemed as if it had been designed with military precision into geometrical patterns, exact rectangles, well groomed farms, manicured highway lawns, flower patches and infrequent trees. There were monuments, to be sure. Cement grain elevators 150 feet tall, visible from ten miles away, were connected by silvery rail lines across the Texas panhandle.

A drastic change occurred at the Oklahoma state line. An easy live-and-let-live attitude was expressed by tall swaths of weeds crowding around roadside fence posts out into pastureland. The landscape, broken by clumps of trees which farmers plowed around, left graceful curving furrows and intricate contour designs in the red-brown soil. Daisies, violets and mixed wild flowers infiltrated fields and decorated the hills. Deeper entry into the state brought denser green rollicking hills.

There were other contrasts. The stickiness of humidity had increased. Numerous streams wound beside and under the road bed. Wild animals became more numerous, as evidenced by shoulder graveyards of broken bodies: finches, sparrows, mockingbirds, opossum, skunks (There's no mistaking one!), turtles, snakes, badgers, armadillos, and other critters caught crossing the highway. For the farmer, there was one good type of carnage, grasshoppers. These pests, ranging from blacks and oranges to brilliant greens and yellows, hop-flew in droves as if chased by roundup cowboys. Speeding car windshields and grills were covered in grasshopper gore, much to the disgust of drivers. When hit, they cracked and oozed, their mangled carcasses littering the road shoulders. But farmers were delighted that tourist drivers avidly collected these insects. Oklahoma interstate roads skirted the small cities with by-pass semi-circles, the business centers being reached using exits. However, due to the constant up and down nature of the road, passengers needed sea sickness pills.

In Sayre, I bought a thirty pound birthday watermelon, the smallest available, to split with two gas station attendants. When the station got busy, I sat on the shaded lawn of the County Courthouse to admire the domed brick edifice. Fifteen pounds of watermelon was still too much for one man to eat. I tried donating the extra to a woman whose kids were playing in a nearby front yard. She declined, suggesting an old man down the road. Sitting on the porch of a shabby, paint peeling clapboard house, a yellow toothed fat man in coveralls was working on a refrigerator. He was slow of speech and mind. He took the melon. A pack of kids followed me, but the pied piper of watermelon was fresh out.

For the first time, I had actual trouble from motorists. In Elk City, a boy on a motor scooter, drove up behind, just out of the line of sight, revved his motor full throttle and shaved my left side, before cutting in front and jerk-squealing his brakes. Looking over his shoulder, he horse laughed. A second incident occurred on the open highway. While looking forward, a full beer can flashed past my head, splashing me with foam, before it bounced cart wheeling away. Disappearing up the hill was a van with California license plates.

Late afternoon meal at a truck stop. Wild cravings of milk, chocolate, and a family can of cold stew with an audience of three boys in baseball uniforms.

"How Far? Wow! Didja really? Howja do it?" tumbled the boys' questions.

With disappointment that I had covered just fifty miles, I was looking at a new rule to find evening shelter before dark. In the back of my mind came a voice saying that I should be whizzing along making crack time.

"What's the rush? See the country. You don't have to make a hundred miles a day," whispered a quiet internal voice. I never made the rule.

Because the sole of my right shoe was tearing away and the local store was high priced, I delayed buying until Oklahoma City. Uncertain how town would react to me, I headed to the city park. A white pickup made a U-turn, spun wheels and nudged me over to the curb. A roly-poly character stuck his head out and said he knew all about me. He'd seen on the news about the sixty bike riders from California. Where were the rest? He couldn't believe I was alone. Jim was a community relations man working as Clinton Park manager while studying business law. The only thing bigger than his body was his personality. After putting the bike in the truck, he went to close up the miniature golf range. A couple of poor kids sat watching others play. He gave them clubs and balls. Several local teenagers had projects he was vitally involved with. They talked earnestly. Later we drove little Willie home to "nigger town". This was the first time on the trip that I'd heard the term used. Finally, at the park house, his residence, we sat to sandwiches from his wife, then raided the concession stand for cold coke, candy and Fritos. In the swimming pool bath house, he gave me a fold down couch for a bed. While I showered, his wife washed my dirty laundry. We watched TV and talked until 2:00 a.m. Great sleep, but all too short.   50 miles

OKLAHOMA CITY HOSPITALITY

Friday, July 7   Clinton to Oklahoma City, OK   Day 21

Keys jangled in the pool house door at 6:30. A young man entered to clean the scattered towels and candy wrappers on the floor while I faked sleep. As other teen voices filled the echoing hall, it was useless to pretend. A giggling hoard of lifeguards readied the pool for opening time. Hurriedly, I slurped fruit cocktail and split without shaving. A National Guard Armory master sergeant gave me a cup of coffee before touching on re-enlistment advantages. I bowed out politely. I stopped at the Clinton High School offices to apply for a teaching position. The superintendent explained that state requirements were as stiff as New York or California, though salaries were lower. (Two years experience: Oklahoma $6,000; California $8,000. Housing and cost of living were cheaper, apartments being in the $50-$70 range compared to California's $110-$150.) Activity other than school was minimal. Life here was simple, carefree, unhurried by megalopolis ambition. Perhaps not rich, this community sold itself on small kindnesses, a cup of coffee, a sweet roll, gentle folks, and pleasant living.

Hazy sunshine baked the eighty-five sinuous miles to Oklahoma City with afternoon breeze. The route leveled onto a stretch of successive fields combed by wind. Ahead a heavy gray-brown smog cloud hung in the sky concealing Oklahoma City. Four hooting young men in a pickup honked and swerved toward me, forcing a ditch dive. There was no reason except Friday evening weekend joyride stupidity. The land rose toward the brown skyscrapers and city sprawl. I let out whoops and shouts to see a big city, knowing that soon I'd replace disintegrating shoes. The bike would get both a new cotter pin for the slipping pedal, and a new tire for the bald rear tread. Today I had conquered the elements. I considered spitting into the wind, but reconsidered it spitting back, and swallowed with a grin.

The free country feeling evaporated as the city loomed closer. Expressway congestion mounted. Oklahoma City held a reputation for years as the most spread out municipal territory until recently. And deservedly so: a patchwork of industry, farms, stockyards, homes, factories and feed pens broken by large fields of hay. Houses were packed tightly together more closely than those of Amarillo. On the south side of town, weather beaten homes were mostly constructed of wooden siding and shingles. Streets were narrow, barely permitting autos to pass, gutters choked with rocks and city debris. Sidewalks were virtually non-existent.

Weeds poked through fences and spurted up from cement cracks, except in the commercial areas which kept neat frontage. Large economy centers, competing for business, advertised with glowing plastic signs.

At a grocery store two young men, beer in hand, in a cluttered dirty Corvair, invited for a night's lodging. Their speed caused frantic pedaling for several blocks until they drove up on the lawn of a two story house. The driver hopped out, introducing six or seven teenagers. A few girls were introduced as wives. Inside other teens sat about a kitchen table playing poker, trying to impress each other with manly swearing and courage at cards. Three boys argued over a paper bag holding a bottle of wine. Other alcoholic refreshments were brought out. The host welcomed me to camp in the backyard with the chickens, where it would be quieter, since they were partying tonight. Aloud I told them it would be fine and then made excuse to cycle to the market for supplies, not eager to be arrested in the company of boozing teenagers. I didn't return.

An all night market charged such exorbitant prices I left with only a soda. I had neither eaten nor found a house as it was nearing 10:00. One man chased me off saying go to jail. A few blocks down, behind a chain-link fence, were a couple of ladies and three boys watching TV. At first, the lady said no.

"Please! Please!" chanted the boys from the rear of the house.

Relenting slightly, the woman told them to ask her husband next door. The frail man, when he saw my six foot size, hesitated, then allowed it to be all right to sleep in the outdoor clubhouse. The boys, Davey, Clifford, and Pat became a rustling whirlwind cleaning the floor of nails, moving boards, and furniture. The three were simple Huck Finns, their speech slow and drawled, but full of 13, 14, and 15 year old energy. Once set up, we strolled to McDonald's for dinner. Usual body aches and cramps commenced on the way home.

The boys were too excited to rest, or let me. We entered their home quarters, a white wooden shack in the rear. Out from a magic corner came malted milk balls and nuts. Momma, shy and plain, apologized for the house. It was all she could afford: two beds, fridge, table with worn red vinyl chairs, a small four-burner stove, and a closet. The whole house would fit into the average southern California living room. A cockroach jiggered on the wall and leapt to explore the stove unheeded. We exchanged stories of Oklahoma and Vietnam until Momma wanted the potato shavings from the family up front thrown out, because they had spoiled, and she couldn't cook them. Clifford obeyed religiously. By eleven my eyelids were sore. The playhouse had no walls, so a steady night breeze fluttered over the sleeping bag. I woke twice from the cold.   85 miles

BAPTIST MONKS

Though the boys left me alone until 10 o'clock, they had to be rounded up for goodbyes. I left the canteen in the clubhouse for a present. A time consuming day of chores began. Groceries in the super warehouse Economy Market meant walking aisles amidst towering cardboard container boxes stacked to the ceiling. No effort was wasted putting items in neat rows on shelves. Shoppers bought by the case, often exceeding four and five shopping carts full. I stood in line for a half hour waiting to pay for my puny armful of tins. Outside I wrapped everything in the sleeping bag, before proceeding next door to an optometrist. The screw in my glasses had fallen out again. A girl attempted an unsuccessful repair, stripping the threads, causing the glasses to tilt precariously on my nose. There was no charge, and no way to express displeasure, so I cooled my temper by eating a melon at a park pool. Next stop, a dependable bicycle shop. The rear tire had worn too quickly on hot chuckhole roads. The cotter pin in the left pedal crank had loosened again losing force each revolution. The expert mechanic at Wheel-o-Rama confidently ended the pedal troubles and gave me a compact tool kit. One of his assistants, overhearing us, asked if I'd met many girls, there being many to be found. I admitted that dating had been a problem.

"No time on the road. Besides, none of them want to pedal," I replied.

By mid afternoon, I had reached the final city destination, a shoe disposal warehouse, which specialized in selling out of style or smoke-damaged goods. I had no care for style or aroma, just solid leather bottoms that would deliver full compression force to the pedals. After careful inspection and trial, I selected a brown textured loafer, paid $5.00, then bid farewell to my old black shoes in a trash barrel. The new shoes were a bargain for they endured seventy days of harsh treatment.

The afternoon nearly spent, I stopped on the city's edge for a burger and quart of milk when an inspiration hit. Jewelers work with small tools, why not my crazy tilting glasses? Just before closing, a gentleman let me into his shop, bradded the screw, then balanced the glasses correctly on my face.

Today's travel would be fortunate to gain thirty miles to Shawnee. In light of local names (Arapaho, Anadarko, El Reno, Lookeba, Concho, Chicasha, Tecumseh, Watapatomie) I expected an Indian settlement. The town was a mile off the main highway, which meant retracing back to the highway, an added effort. A few quiet houses were ensconced in three foot high grass where a large billboard announced OBU (Oklahoma Baptist University). I turned into a Texaco station asking the attendant if it would be all right to sleep on the side of the road. He immediately picked up the phone and called the sheriff to find out if I was wanted. After an all clear, he laughed with a sneer.

"It's okay to sleep in the fields, providing you don't git et up by the chiggers," he chortled.

Not liking the tone of his voice, and not wanting to discover what a chigger was, I took a cut-off, Route 3, towards OBU and the college crowd. It might be safer.

The cut-off led up a narrow road, past two-storied mansions. Baptist land looked prosperous. More so on the north, where a long single lane, through a field, ended at a red brick four story college building. Its square battlements and central tower looked like a British fortress. I turned up the concrete path lined with graceful cedars. A green pickup with a hay load passed. The driver waved. An older man, clad in a white shirt and khakis, walked a large black dog.

"Anybody home, or did they all go home for the summer?" I asked.

"No," he replied, tapping his pipe. "The fathers have gone to do their work in the parishes for Sunday".

I knew Baptists referred to one another as sister and brother. That I could understand, but not "father". This was something new! He walked while I pedal-hopped.

"Would it be all right if I laid out a bedroll in a corner by the trees? I wouldn't disturb anybody, and I'll be gone by 8:00," I asked.

"Well, why don't we go over to Brother Marcus and see if we can fix you up with some Benedictine hospitality?" he rejoined.

I had never heard of Benedictine Baptists. I leaned the bike on a bench, and followed, gawking at the buildings, saints' statues, and holy inscriptions on the arches and roofing. Passing through a stained glass door, he gestured for me to sit, turned to leave, then looked back.

He inquired, "Have you ever been in a monastery before?"

Suddenly my eyes were opened. This was a Catholic learning center in Baptist country; I had presumed it to be OBU. I had not read the entrance sign. It was a merry joke on me repeating it to the religious brothers and priests about them being Benedictine Baptists.

Brother Marcus entered dressed in black pants and a blue shirt with its tails sticking out. He first led me to a guest room to freshen up, then returned to lead down the echoing halls to the monastic dining hall, a tall roofed echoing brick chamber. In the stainless steel kitchen, we found plates and utensils before picking the left-over pans of beef steaks, corn, fries, peas, and watermelon. Next, in a side room, Fr. Augustine, also casually attired in a white shirt, sat with us, but laid down his crutches, a reminder of a near fatal accident with a drunk driver who had not survived. Informal conversation continued with a night walk around the parking lot and into the trees before retiring to make up a bed. Marcus entreated me to stay over for a day's rest. Perhaps, I thought. For the first time in three days, I shaved, showered, and wrote in my diary barely a page when my eyes closed. 30 miles

BENEDICTINE HOSPITALITY

On summer Sundays the monks rose at 4:45 a.m., dressed in black robes, silently walked through the halls for devotions at 5:00. They woke me at 6:45. We walked to the dining room, selected a meal from a stainless steel cart, sat and ate in silence (discipline of the tongue). The men were young, healthy, and strong. Yesterday, the cutting and baling of 1,600 bales of hay was now betrayed in their sore postures, and pleasantly proud faces. After a tinkling bell, we were free to talk and leave the dining room. High mass convened in the great brick church at 8:00. Monks filed into ornate carved wooden stalls on both sides of the central altar. Twenty people, including nuns, sat in the main church pews. Three priests, in green vestments, entered to begin prayers at the foot of the altar. Fr. Augustine, though propped up by his crutches, assisted, but stood close by in one of the chapel stalls. Vibrant strong prayer responses echoed, as did singing, in the abbey. English has replaced Latin in the mass and in texts, while the altar faced the people. After concelebration, the black robed brothers stood to receive Communion, followed by the congregation. Mass ended. Brothers bowed in respect to the altar and filed silently out.

In cool morning sun we traded stories on the steps. There were peals of laughter over city boys' first experiences on Oklahoma farms. Some had been frightened by crickets and frogs; others couldn't relax without city noises. One brother earned loud guffaws when he told how he had gotten behind a nervous cow with diarrhea at branding time. Still chuckling, we entered chapel at 9:30 for Lauds, a fifteen minute prayer dedicating the day. Then free time. A lunch of cheese hot dogs, fruit, milk and juice graced lively chatter and playful teasing across the tables. We thanked God for His blessings and went out to a free afternoon. I wrote, read books in my room, and took a stroll. Vespers started at 5:30. Again a short prayer session. Brothers alternated readings and litany responses from side to side of the echoing sacristy. Should I consider being a monk? I had been in the seminary for three years until I was twenty. A happy smile spread on my face. My personality would have too much difficulty. I'm not monk material.

Supper was eaten in silence. Fr. Claude, the priest whom I had first met, took me for a long stroll about the grounds of St. Gregory Jr. College. Originally named St. Mary's, a fire had destroyed the buildings.

Administrators chose a site closer to the highway and Oklahoma City to attract college and high school students. As the new structures were nearly finished, during WWII, the Navy publicized the need for a new supply base, and all but solemnized the purchase of these grounds. Just as suddenly, the Navy let the plans collapse. Since Catholics comprised about 8 percent of Oklahoma population, and were mostly poor, it was deemed wiser to develop a junior college program, and open the school to women, students from out-of-state, and included those of other religious faiths. A federal grant for science aided in remodeling. High school was dropped. St. Gregory College boarded 300 students, 500 its total attendance, though capacity was 800. At $2,000 per year tuition and board, the school's goal was to serve Oklahoma Catholics, competing with state institutions.

Our stroll left the driveways and pebbled lanes crossing ball diamonds, open fields, and dormitories to join Brother Marcus and others in the big hall for a roundhouse discussion of American culture, animals in the locality, music, and Father Claude's special recipe for armadillo. Brother Marcus split a Coke later as we discussed our Vietnam experiences.

I called Mom in California by reversing charges. She seemed concerned for my safety, so we set up an emergency call signal. Any trouble that I couldn't discuss over the phone, I would use the code words Aunt Gertrude and somehow mention my location. I concluded the Sunday progress report, although Mom wasn't entirely convinced I wasn't being tarred, feathered, mugged and lynched. The part time monk slept well. No miles

RANCHING

Risen at 5 a.m., the monks had already finished prayers and mass before a knock woke me for breakfast. Another meal in silence. The brothers were off to the fields; I used three hours to write. Brother Marcus mailed some of my superfluous belongings home. He and Fr. Eugene bade farewell as I exited campus down the cedar lane. Shawnee was bustling, ambitious, green, lush, invigorating, and growing with a population of 40,000.

The soil changed to an orange-brown. After the Dust Bowl in the 1930's, Oklahoma had been stung with a recent drought lasting four or five years. Farmers sold off their cattle to save the ranches and farms. When a cholera outbreak was detected in swine in the west, whole areas were quarantined while government authorities inspected pigs, killed the diseased and burned their bodies, or delayed action for those under suspicion until safety could be determined. Farmers were reimbursed if swine were killed. Eastern Oklahoma increased thick woodland and brush. A picturesque center divider bisected the highway. Autos shot by in 95⁰ heat, oblivious of the pristine beauty. On the route to the Mississippi River, gentle breezes cooled.

Mobile homes studded small farm plots. This simplified dwelling-on-wheels made for inexpensive homesteads on isolated plots. Numbers of city folk bought lakeside property or ten acre sites, and staked claims with these aluminum homes. The 1920s exodus from farm to city was being reversed. The turmoil of city life has caused a hunger for nature on a patch of land with a chance to live country style.

Thirty miles of forest beyond Henryetta was the settlement of Lake Eufala, the largest man-made lake in the U.S. Sunrays ran through mint-fresh air of powder blue sky, tickled by pine needle arms stretched over syrup island mud banks. Clear lake water rippled deep and blue. A rock jetty poked a finger in a mile wide channel coursing miles east toward the great lake.

There were other man-made lakes and ponds in the area, but on a much smaller scale. If a rancher needed more rain collection, he notified the Department of Agriculture. Engineers studied the area for the best drainage sites, and calculated both the amount of water that will accumulate and the cost of construction. Services were free to all farmers and ranchers. However, if they decided to build, they must pay the major portion of earth banking; the government paid the rest and recorded these sites on official maps. The price was based on cubic yards of moved earth. In drought seasons, these ponds could store water for over two years. But there was a disadvantage. Water Moccasin snakes bred in them. Men and cattle must be wary.

For years men tried to farm eastern Oklahoma. They battled the grass that always grew with the crops. The struggle was long and fruitless. The farmers gave up, let the grass grow, sold their tractors or watched them rust, bought cattle and ranched. They found ranching was the answer. It made money and it was easier.

Cattle typically were raised until they weighed 600 pounds, whereupon they were sold to feed lots for fattening up to 1,500 pounds, fattening being necessary to bulk the meat. Flavor and tenderness not being present in unfattened meat-just toughness. Finally, beef was sold to slaughterhouses, sometimes thousands of miles distant. Trains used to haul cattle, but trucks had proven more economical and all but ended railroads in Oklahoma.

Before a cow is sold, a blood sample is taken. It is processed to determine if there are diseases such as anthrax or cow abortion disease. If detected, the whole herd is quarantined at the ranch for further inspection. Diseased cattle are killed as a preventative measure to protect herds in the county and adjoining areas.

A final animal note. Wolves patrol the land at night, sleeping in culverts or pond caves by day. Occasional howling parties send chills up one's spine. They frolic in new mown hay fields, for they like short grass. A lone wolf usually travels a regular path, or line, covering its territory in a few days. Generally, they do not harm cattle or men, but have raided chicken coops for unfried southern chicken. When wolves become too numerous, they are hunted by plane, locations marked, and riflemen roam the fields to thin packs.

As the day dimmed to evening purple, the road narrowed. Traffic volume increased, and several times cars did not see the bicycle until just behind it. With such danger on the road, I swung off the highway near Chickotah. A rancher and his wife sitting outside on the porch gave permission to sleep under his trees. Wolves occasionally serenaded through the night.   65 miles

ON TO ARKANSAS

Tuesday, July 11   Chickotah, OK to Van Buren, AR   Day 25

The rancher lived on the bypass of the soon to be completed expressway. Hundreds of trucks passed the house ruining sleep. At first light, amid singing birds, the wife emerged with coffee, toast, and sausage, her husband already at work. Heavily laden coal trucks thundered down the highway.

The region was laced with scars and gouges from open pit mining. In years past, mining companies cut through soil crust to harvest the earth's treasures. Top soil was covered over with waste rock creating mound hills. In time, a leafy ivy spread over the mounds, worthless as they were, giving a green cover. However, the mining companies never blended the terrain which had become impossible to plow. Rain collected in the mine pits that eventually became breeding ground for water moccasins. Subsequent laws required the land to be filled and groomed, but past sins were left to mar the countryside.

Rumbling trucks of iron ore, peanuts, beef, hides, and oil careened toward Muskogee to be loaded on barges for river shipment to processing plants on the Arkansas River, or later on the Mississippi. It used to be impossible to navigate the Arkansas due to shallow draft. Senator Kerr sponsored a bill for the Arkansas Dike System, the largest in the United States. A monumental series of locks and dams opened the river country to commerce and modern navigation as well as flood control. Deep water vessels passed upstream.

Rural Weber Falls was fronted by square dusty brick buildings, a cement plant, two service stations, and a post office. Postmaster Longden said that an Indian chief founded the community in the 1850s after whites had chased the Cherokees out on the Trail of Tears. Town ended at the green embankment sloping down to the half mile wide gravel beach of the Arkansas. The river meandered past willows, cedars, white oaks, elms, spruce, and maple trees under two tall concrete bridges then past the cement plant. The east bank was a favorite for swimming, fishing and boating. I succumbed immediately, divesting tools and clothing down to my shorts. Gingerly stepping over rocks, I waded into the warm water. A family splashed and frolicked with inner tubes a hundred feet from shore. A river shave was a scraping experience, followed by spaghetti, root beer, postcards, notes and a nap.

Of all the frustrations on this trip, writing has been the sorest. Condensing experiences into cohesive stories before the ideas disappeared from memory has been exacting work. The curiosity of tourist questions delayed opportunities to record promptly. Postcards promised to people who have so generously helped me also took time. It may only be five minutes per card, but ten cards have added up. Writing has always won out. The friends will last long after the trip.

Oklahoma hills rolled behind in the steamy afternoon. Drizzle swept over and continued until 7:00. I rode damp, mud spraying off tires onto my legs. As I crossed into Arkansas, a train slowed at the Dora post, greeting with a toot. Unfortunately, I passed up Ft. Smith, as it lay eight miles south, a mistake because of the history of Hanging Judge Parker and the Jesse James gang. In the evening, I exited the highway into Van Buren, a modern spacious beautiful community.

"When do you stop for the night?" asked a family at a burger stand.

"Oh, about now," I answered.

"Where?" the father asked.

"On somebody's lawn, if they let me".

The folks apologized for not being able to offer their house as they were visiting relatives in another town. They bought my dinner.

After rounding bends in the road I knocked on several houses for a night's refuge. Some people didn't answer the door, others had company, one man had sickness. It became too late to knock on doors, so I crossed an open field to a bright yellow light glaring out from a huge garage, rode up to the fire captain to ask if the Van Buren Fire Department would spare lawn for me. He looked at the shiny red engine.

"Okay, sure, but don't lay down in front of the door. We may have to come out in a hurry," he warned.

Camp was set under a tree in soft grass. I wrote under a street light. A gang of boys passed, teasing. The garage door closed, lights out.   80 miles

WHERE'S A RIVER FULL OF SNAKES?

Wednesday, July 12   Van Buren to Russelville, AR   Day 26

Van Buren displayed every decade of architectural and Wild West history from the 1870s on. It was western in flavor, farm in culture, and modern in activity. Besides a quaint main street of general merchandize, ladies' shops and bakeries, there were two railroad baggage damage shops. Leisurely pedestrians rested a spell in old church pews at store fronts. Coveralls were standard work wear, and pickups the vehicles of status. A collection of musty animal feed aromas and pesticides greeted the nostrils at the Farmers' Exchange. Shelves contained cages, tools and safety equipment along with saddle gear. There was no fancy department store pretense here. Sacks lay on pallets, feed dust coating the floor worn smooth. Along the wall were rows of seed bins with a choice of three types of radish or five types of watermelon, and corn varieties by the dozens. And the talk was about families and crops.

This brief encounter with Arkansas life inspired a backwoods excursion on Route 64 into the hills. Birds chirped among the thick trees. The winding thin lane gave peeks into squared-off grazing fields, brown Guernsey cows in one plot, Black Angus in another and Brahmas or Long Horns in a third. One extensive valley doubled as horse and cow ranch territory from tree line to tree line. A young man hauled tomatoes and melons in his truck bed. Then there were 500-1,000 foot long hen houses. Screen sidings permitted ventilation and sight of the different growth stages of downy yellow chicks to white feathered adults. Colonel Sanders must own this valley. Blue coveralled men in straw hats relaxed in chairs next to fruit stands packed with melons, peaches, peppers and vegetables. There were a few red barns like in school book pictures, but most barns were white with rusty galvanized roofs. Pedaling went smoothly with hills rarely taller than 200 feet, and lessening further to the east. With temperatures in the nineties, I regained the highway for its minimal breeze from traffic, and to complete today's eighty mile goal.

A swarm of mosquitoes dancing in the twilight attacked arms and legs. While glancing over the shoulder, a skeeter lodged in the left eye. The dead critter irritated the socket, but I dared not scratch the eye by rubbing. After a few minutes and lots of tears, the intruding insect corpse worked itself out. Eye pain eased while the stinging welts persisted for miles. At evening's end the Dardanelle Reservoir shimmered pale blue through the trees.

A sign announced Russelville at 9:30. I was annoyed at the prospect of a long bridge climb over this finger of the reservoir. About to curse my luck, I spied a picnic area on the right before climbing the bridge. Nestled in a small grove of trees were park benches and BBQ pits, with a hill forest behind. I curled right, approached the middle cement picnic table, locked the bike to a tree, and unrolled the sleeping bag on top of the table. A few late evening picnickers watched as I pulled off sweaty clothes and walked into the shallow water.

"Watch for the Rocks!" cautioned a fellow at the next table.

In waist deep water I wiggled toes in the mud, ducked under, splashed water, and rubbed soap over grimy skin. Back in camp I put a tin of spaghetti on the fire abandoned by the picnickers, dressed in the dark and ate dinner alone. The transistor radio blared news of the Democratic Convention which nominated McGovern.

At midnight I turned fitfully on the table top while a few mosquitoes sang about my ears. A large number of cars had been crossing the bridge spraying their high beams into my face. I dozed hoping, that after swing-shift, the traffic would ease. And then a car left the highway, crunching gravel with its blinding headlights illuminating my whole camp. It circled the parking lot, backed into position, in a dark recess, to stare at me. The motor cut off, as did the lights. It was 1 a.m. Mentally, I searched my possessions for weapons: a three inch Swiss Army Knife, a bike inner tube for a whip, two cans of ravioli and fruit cocktail for missiles, and a hunk of firewood for a bat. I didn't have my shoes on, but was prepared to run. My eyes kept vigilance on the auto outlined against the river. Lovers or thugs, I'd soon know.

A car door opened with dry squeaks, then shut. Again. A third time. But there was no crunching of gravel. Several times the high beams of passing cars revealed my position, but the mystery car was too far back to be lit up. For a half hour of mounting tension, I waited for the first move. It came simply. The engine started. When the car was past me, the lights flicked on. I sat up, grabbing for the tiny knife and my shoes. The car continued past, up the dirt road and into the woods. Silence.

Adrenalin does not turn off easily. With my ears blood-thumping, heart pounding, and arms shivering, I walked around shakily for a while, relaxed to eat fruit cocktail, then lay down again, with highway headlights still flashing over me. Because of the mosquitoes, I put on the long shirt and pants.

The dark car came back. Just as before, it parked with its lights shining on me. However, this time, when the light went out, I put on my shoes, rechecked possible weapons, and planned both attack and escape. I was ready to hurl the wood chunk into the windshield, damage the car for identification, and then run for the highway. Again the doors opened and slammed, opened, and slammed. But the car started, quickly drove past me, and joined the camper, which had originally been with the picnickers on the grounds. Both disappeared over the bridge. I lay down smiling. It was safe now. Probably a couple of guys on a drunk.

A bright beacon flashed, blinding my vision. When the light shifted, a sheriff's car came into view. The officers searched for several minutes, then, satisfied, drove off. I guessed they might have arrived in time to find my body. With all this hassle, I'd grown thirsty. Walking to my bike I sucked water out of my desert canvas bag.

Five vehicles, two of them pickups, stormed into the picnic area. I nearly choked on the water, as loud voices hooted and swore, slammed and banged doors. It looked like a set up. The first car, which had terrorized me and cased out the situation, now seemed to come back with chains for a beating. Five men noisily clanked metal in the pickups, then hustled over stones to the neighboring bench. They didn't bother me.

Curious, I called out, "Hey! What are you guys doing at 3 a.m.?"

"We don't mean to disturb you. We're just havin' a beer," answered a voice at the table.

"This is a heck of a time for a beer party," I chided.

"Naw! This is the best time. We just got off at the nuclear plant and we stopped here for a beer. This-here is a dry county!" said a worker.

"What's that?" I queried.

"You don't know? You can't drink alcohol here, that's the law. And the law's been lookin' for us. We keep the place clean though. Want a beer?"

"Well, I haven't had one since I left. Yeah!" I said thirstily.

By 4:30 they had filled me with carrot cake, cupcakes, and three cans of brew. Usually three is my limit. The men opened their repertoire of hunting, fishing and boating tales. One fellow asked where there was a river loaded with snakes. Seems his wife had overheard him talking about the fun of a drift trip downriver. He wanted a river, with overhanging limbs and so many snakes that she'd never ask to go on a trip again. Another storyteller, on a trip to Washatash, claimed to have killed a hundred snakes. I asked if these two were kidding.

They said, "No. Why the reservoir is full of snakes".

"Aw, come on," I objected. "I just took a bath in the lake".

A loud shout of surprise went up, amid cries of how crazy I was. The lake was reputed to have its banks loaded with water moccasins.

I listened until my groggy head bobbed. The sky, now overcast, began to sprinkle. I begged to leave, climbed on my table, dragged the orange plastic sheet over me to ward off rain and dozed.

"Get your gear and bike in the truck. You ain't gonna sleep in the rain," called out a driver.

He drove to a mobile home, and invited a buddy and me in. When he put a frying pan on the stove for breakfast, I slumped on the couch and slept.   80 miles

ALL YOU CAN EAT FOR $1.39

During the night, gusts rocked the single wide mobile home, but I didn't rouse until 8:30.

"Who's that man?" whispered a child's voice.

On sitting up, my head just wouldn't clear. Bill got up, fixed breakfast and lots of coffee. It was still raining when we finished. He handed me a can of 6-12 Insect Spray.

"You'll need it," he promised.

Bill Jenkins, a Cherokee Indian, was born in Oklahoma, but raised in Arkansas. After ten years in the Army, he retired to construction work to which his muscular build was well suited. He claimed that construction workers were a brotherhood. When a new man was getting settled with his family, fellow workers have offered $100 loans until the first check arrived. Bill was a prime example of this philosophy. Pass on a favor you've received.

I left in a muggy drizzle, sloshing the damp blacktop, rolling by sedate brick houses, brown, gray, white, and multi-colored. Passing St. Mary's Hospital, a whim turned me back. I entered the door, asking for the emergency room, desiring to check last night's stories.

"Have there been many cases of snakebite?" I asked.

"If you leave snakes alone they'll leave you alone. But since the first of the year, I think we may have treated one case of snakebite," replied the doc.

Snake stories!!!

Little Rock's hills swelled and fell under the bike's ten gear power-train. The cycle moved easily into the growing expressway whirlpool swirling torrents of cars and flushing them pell-mell into the bowels of the city. Too dangerous for me. The exit lane emptied into an enormous shopping center. I hadn't felt up to par lately, but was ready to make a fast dinner of soda and canned foods and leave town.

With the ten speed locked to a fence, I walked without relish toward the supermarket for yet another tasteless cold meal. A cafeteria sign: *$1.39 All You Can Eat* caught my eye. A hot meal is better than Coke and beans. I paid at the register and asked if seconds were allowed.

"Yes, all you can eat for $1.39," the young waitress replied.

"Lady, you don't know what you're saying. I'll eat you out of business!" I prompted.

"Go ahead and try," she challenged.

Any out-of-sorts feelings were dashed as my stomach crowded up to the eyeball sockets previewing the caloric bonanza. Then I started piling it on, making it impossible to see the bottom of the plate: turkey, wax beans, cottage cheese, salad, veggies, rolls, and vanilla cream pie with coffee. Getting permission to exit, I checked my bike, and returned. Second plate: a mountain of beef, macaroni, veggies, raisin-carrots, peach cobbler, coffee, pink lemonade. I returned from a second bike check.

"You must really be hungry!" the gal said.

Cucumbers, carrots, veggies, Jello, cobbler, tea, and coffee. But it wasn't until my fourth trip, for meat alone, that the girl's eyes bulged.

"We've seen thirds but never fourths, and this much!" she stood agape.

She begged my secret, and when told, refused to believe until she had seen the bicycle locked outside. I left with a rounded tummy, a slight top heaviness, and a very warm drowsy head.

With Memphis tomorrow's goal, I had to night-ride the ten miles to Lonoke. For safety's sake I secured the fluorescent orange vest, tied down the bedroll with bungee cords, and checked the reflectors. A sign on the expressway forbade bicycle entrance. I cut a path through the weeds and snuck onto Route 40 and out of town. As the final moments of twilight slipped into darkness, I started running into highway debris menaces: scattered lumber, rocks, chunks of truck tires, chuckholes, and hidden drainage trenches in the shoulder. A technique helped me. As headlights illuminated highway ahead of me, I watched the moving section of lit road, then mentally marked the location of hazards. When no traffic followed me, I'd slide out to the center of the cement surface for a smoother ride, always with a wary glance to the rear.

The night's entry to Lonoke was eerie. Street lights played on lonely asphalt down to a swampy tree lane. Frogs backfired, crickets rattle-whistled. A few empty-eye windows stared blindly into the night. Passing a fire-gutted building collapsed near the railroad tracks, a dog pack suddenly jumped forward, snapping at my heals. I talked quietly, slowly, and friendly to them, while pedaling, fearing a sudden move would cost me a leg for their dinner.

There were some nicely maintained homes, but it was too late to knock at 10:30. I set camp in the city park, under a brilliant white incandescent lamp. While spreading things in an inconspicuous corner of the ball field fence, mosquitoes were already dining. I sprayed the 6-12 insect bomb indiscriminately on hands face, neck, clothes, socks. Imagining myself safer from the pests, I wrote in the diary, under the bright incandescent park light, listening to the radio. Mosquitoes, discovering a visitor, came by the thousands to play. They danced and jiggled in the air, lit for a second until they sensed the spray, jumped off, then buzzed around my writing hand and up to my ears. I ignored them, for a moment. Soon the swelling numbers hummed in my ears, to interrupt pleasure listening. At last there were so many skeeters that it was hard to see the white paper I was writing on. Couldn't listen, couldn't write, couldn't think. I was even afraid to breathe hard for fear of sucking up a family or two.

Enough! Grabbing the radio, I scooted two blocks into town looking up and down deserted Main Street, spotting only the white police car. "Bowden" said the name tag on the young blond kid in a two-toned blue uniform. He talked earnestly to an older fellow lounging in an outdoor couch, his wife in the next chair. The lanky youngster, named Skip, drawled a welcome and said I smelled like 6-12. I started to explain the problem about camping in the park, but at this, all three roared in laughter. I mentioned about once sleeping in a jail. The older man asked if I was reporting myself for vagrancy. Getting a *no* answer, he asked Skip if he'd pick me up on a vagrancy charge. I countered that I had a destination, was not bothering people, and had funds. They snickered, saying that I sure must have learned about vagrancy laws. The deputy said he could put me in with one fellow, a little drunk, but he wouldn't hurt me, much. Then he kidded about putting me in with the homosexual, and, since I was writing a diary, this would add spicy notes on their Peyton Place. The older man propped his feet up on the counter wall.

"Let him sleep on the court floor and we'll set his trial in the morning," he said.

I asked what they were trying to do. Skip replied: "Well, we're making it easier for you to see the judge".

"Hey, what's going on here?" I questioned.

Pointing to the older man, Skip piped: "He's the judge!"

"Don't tell me this is a set up! You wouldn't be related to each other?"

"Oh, no. He's just my uncle". By then I was laughing with tears. They'd had a good joke and then gave me room on the court floor. It was hard, but mosquito free.   96 miles

IN MEMPHIS, BUT WHERE?

Shoes tattoo-tapped on the tile floor as clerks began morning organization. Since shift change, Skip was not around to be thanked. A charming secretary chatted briefly. When I became self-conscious of my delaying and getting tongue tied talking to the pretty gal, it was time to make tracks. Knowing today would be a 115 mile attempt, both bike and body grumbled. Right before the highway, a Minit Hamburger stand promised fast food. Simple, right? Enter. Make food selections. Pay. Sit. Wait. Wait. And Wait. Other customers grumbled at the long hold ups. A twenty minute delay for orange juice and a hot turnover, which was cold. *Aggravation.*

The road was level, smooth easy fifteen mph riding. Weather cloudy, warm, slight southwest breeze. Afternoon would be sweltering. Legs were strong and hardened. Fingers have regained some strength and feeling, and can now make a clumsy fist. This morning I feel herculean covering nineteen miles in an hour. Coffeecake break and orange juice, now my favorite drink. If conditions held, I could be in Memphis by 6 p.m. and on a date! For the next hour the bike whizzed swiftly down the heating highway. Cars no longer seemed to shoot by. Salty sweat trickled down my eyebrows, nose, and face. The shirt clung at the neck and armpits. Wind whipped through the hair on my legs. Speed.

Then the day's first flat tire. A man, stranded on the shoulder, was crouched in his car trunk trying to remove an awkwardly placed spare. It was soon evident there was more trouble. The threads on the retaining bracket were stripped, preventing removal of the spare, or the jack. It took muscle, a lot of twisting, and blisters. Eventually we changed the tire. He tried to pay me; I refused.

"Pass it on," I directed.

He begged. It was hot, so I let him buy me a Coke.

The second flat of the day was on the opposite side of the road, with a troublesome jack, but it did the job.

"What do I owe you?" he asked.

He preferred to pay. I refused. The afternoon was spent making up for the delays. A Memphis arrival before six was not in the cards, so no shopping or bank traveler check cashing. I took a brief water and snack break before returning to stuffy 95^0 air and cotton ball clouds.

West Memphis, Arkansas, population 26,000, 6 p.m. City trappings and sounds. Cars. Billboards. Stores. Railroad tracks, police sirens, sidewalks, traffic signs, stop and go lights, whistles, honks, lawn mowers. There was a noticeable change in society; more than half of the citizens were Black. And they sure waved friendly.

The city stopped a mile before the river, the last mile being a low beach of silt farms arranged in patchwork rows. Here, farming was risky business. During heavy rains or spring melt, this was the low extra mile of Mississippi River width. To cross one of the river bridges sixty feet above the farms, one must approach by a long preliminary access bridge constructed a mile earlier. In the main channel, heavy steel girders supported each of three enormous spans, two for autos, the middle for trains. On the north, a new bridge was unfolding. On the right, a forest stopped at the edge of the clay-brown water, a rusting barge tied to the riverbank. Two boys, who from the height of the bridge looked like insects, were fishing. The river moved its half mile girth downstream at eight mph, swirling eddies and whirlpools behind dock posts and bridge stanchions. Barge tugs churned a white froth foam as they pushed upstream at the edges of the current.

I stopped midway over the river. My watch read 7:00. For the traditional American celebration when meeting a body of water, I tossed a rock. It arched up, out and rapidly down, and marked its grave with a tiny momentary ripple. Nature and Man.

The bridge emptied onto the Memphis cliffs, fifty feet above the rivers' docks below. Historical landmarks were legion, but the tumult of Friday traffic gave no chance to inspect. A stream of cars funneled down Crump Street towards the business district. I channeled into Lamar Street and promptly got lost. From all appearances, I was in a Black section of town. And though I waved and smiled at the dark skinned people, I was displeased and frightened. Displeased because I couldn't find a White section, where I could perhaps meet a girl in a department store, and ask for a date. (I'd had a fantasy of dating a Southern Belle.) Frightened because I was in the Black district and began remembering stories of Negro reprisals against Whites at night. What a test of my Southern California liberalism. I asked several people where I was, and how to get out of this section.

I didn't want to sound prejudiced by saying, "I'd like to find some Whites".

Every Negro politely offered suggestions. I entered a department store, where I already felt ashamed, and left.

At an all White fire station, nine firemen on benches sat jawing. They laughed at my predicament.

"You wanna drink a little and go whoring?" One fireman boldly asked what kind of action I wanted.

"Well, I'd like to spend a quiet evening with a nice girl," I responded.

"We can tell you what street to go on, but they don't have any girls like that," he retorted.

The firemen gave directions but I got lost again. My wanderings passed a park and ended at a shopping center. I asked a grocery checker for a date and got turned down. I ordered dinner at a restaurant, and asked a waitress but struck out. She was already married. A grizzled old man, sitting in the next seat, introduced himself and began recounting his world travels. Our conversation led him to interrupt a young couple dining in a booth, and mentioned bicycling. The man, a fireman, claimed his father to be a cycling enthusiast and suggested talking to him at his beauty shop.

Silently, I thought, "Yeah. Yeah. Sure. Some story".

Persisting, he offered to take me to the YMCA for the night.

"This is a dangerous area," he warned.

In the morning I could locate on his father, Charles Finney, at Gould's Beauty Salon. I thanked him, politely, refused the ride, and hastened to get away. It sounded suspicious.

At 11:00 p.m., I was tired after 130 miles, fifteen wandering through the city. Leg muscles had stiffened, refusing to pedal unless with knotty pain. Needing a place to sleep, I urged my cramping legs towards the park I'd passed earlier. On the right came a darkened set of buildings, fenced off from the street, posted with a *Do Not Enter* sign above the driveway. I rode into the quiet dark. The two-story blackened buildings were lighted by a single yellow hall light, showing the midst of construction clutter. At first this appeared to be a hospital or convalescent home, but there were no nurses. A few white religious statues hinted maybe a Catholic school. Around back, looking for a safe spot among the shadows, I encountered a row of hedges, formed at an angle, that would be an ideal camp nest. Two cars were parked in a nearby carport, but there was no sign of life.

I locked the bike to a tree, laid out the bedroll in a corner of the hedge, and was instantly illuminated by a glaring security light. Spinning around, I found no one. High above the building, an automatic switch had lighted the grounds for safety of the owners. Breathing a sigh of relief, I relaxed on patio chairs outside a single story brick outbuilding, where I began writing. A banging door aroused suspicions. I stood up, grabbed the door and read: *Women*. Peering inside, the sinks and toilets were empty, save for a collection of tricycles gathered in a corner. The broken toilets bubbled water. I returned to the chair to write and watch big black cockroaches dance in the wall cracks and drunkenly stagger across the cement. The radio blared news of Memphis. At 1:15 I took soap and a tooth brush, marched into the restroom, stripped, turned on the faucet, washed in a slippery drench of cold water, rinsed, and put on my last clean shorts, which were really dirty. Late sleep. 130 miles

CHARLES FINNEY

Graybeard, the portly gardener, crunched up the gravel driveway at 6 a.m.

"Hey! What are you doin' here?" an elderly man called out.

"Mmmm, oooh, mmmm. I didn't mean to bother anybody, just sleep". He mumbled something else, but sleep ruled my ears. I laid down. Another crunch.

"Aw right, you, get up! Get outta there!" barked an authoritative voice.

I rolled to the right side, slid legs out of the bag, and opened heavy eyes to a light blue shirted police officer and partner, in dark pants, who stood out from the red brick wall of the toilet house, his hand on a riot stick.

"Let's see your identification," demanded the cop.

Dazed and awkwardly sore, I fumbled through my pocket, forgetting that I'd switched pants. When I remembered, and went through my other clothes. The officer shifted position with growing suspicion, fingering the nightstick. A pocket. The wallet. Stretch it out. Hand it.

Doing a double take the officer barked, "Who are you? What are you doing here? How'd you get here?"

I answered by pointing to the tree with the locked bike.

"On that? You're crazy!" he denied.

"Yup, that's right," I replied.

"Ya mean ya come all the way on that bike? Okay, get yer stuff together and go over to the park and sleep it off. No one'll bother ya. The caretaker here's a little nervous".

The two policemen watched the packing and placement of the bike. I grabbed the bike, but it wouldn't come off the tree. I'd forgotten to unlock, and now the key was in the bedroll. I had to unpack. The officers left, feeling there was no danger. The caretaker wandered back, apologized, but kept a wary eye until I was gone.

Overton Park. Forested lawn. Gardens, zoo, band shell, golf links. A shady copse made a bedroom. I slept atop the bag. Warm air. Cars motored by on the streets, occasionally waking me, but it was the pesky scampering squirrels, flies, and ants that finally woke me. Breakfast and a date with a Southern Belle. True, but not the way I expected. Combing the empty streets for a do-nut shop proved fruitless. A ten story hotel bore an ad: *Gould's Beauty Salon*. Memory flashed.

"What the heck, might as well check out yesterday's suggestion with the desk girl," I thought.

"Hi, I'm not here for a permanent. Do you have a Mr. Charles Finney here?"

"No," not to her knowledge. She asked other ladies under white aprons, their faces in mudpacks and heads lathered in shampoo. No luck. With my hand on the door, a woman, wiping mud from her lips, recommended trying the other salon three miles away.

In a giant shopping center stood the second, much larger, beauty shop. This time the girls replied: "Yes, Mr. Finney's here. Come with me."

At the rear of the shop, a slender, bushy silver-haired man wearing glasses, leaned over another gentleman whose hair he was trimming and balancing. I introduced myself, explaining how his son had urged me to see him. Charles Finney spoke softly, inserting a few questions about the adventure. When finished with the customer, he accompanied me outside to inspect the rig. Then, without asking me, he gave his phone and address with instructions, called his wife to announce a guest, and sent me off while he returned to work. Somewhat dumbfounded, I wandered the shopping center, cashed a check, bought underwear for what I'd worn out, feasted at the do-nut shop, and began the trek to the Finney house.

In the few minutes of cycling to the Finney home, my body was sweat drenched. A frizzy red-headed man, Richard, walked over the lawn. "You looking for my Dad? Come on in." He held open the door of a white wood-siding house. The temperature dropped twenty degrees in blessed air conditioning.

Blond Juanita Finney, cleaning house said: "Hi. Sit down and relax". Shortly she made sandwiches and heaped fruit and juice before Richard and me. Richard bought ice creams for both of us. He slipped out the back to mow the lawn, only allowing me to move the swing set. A phone call interrupted him, giving me the chance to repay, by working on the massive almond tree shaded back yard. Juanita called for my foul smelling clothing for the washing machine. The sleeping bag was aired on the clothes line. I was given a room and free roam of the house. It was unlike any previous experience.

And what was more, they knew a girl who might go out on a date! Juanita called friend Pat for several unsuccessful rings. With Charles home for dinner, he kept asking if I wanted more, pushing plate after plate before me. He spoke in his mild tone. As his wife left for Pat's house, he slyly called out, "Y'all come back now". Outside in his screened patio house we looked over bicycles, talked cross country touring and set possible plans for traveling downstream on a riverboat, another fantasy I had. Juanita returned with news. I had a date!

It was up to me to telephone first. We opened awkwardly, but the girl's frankness cut in sharply. "I don't know what kind of guy you are but I want you to know I'm a good girl and aim to stay that way," she frankly professed.

Clean clothes, a washed face, shave, and brushed teeth made a body feel sparkly. I waited in the living room with Richard. From a yellow Cougar convertible parked in the driveway, a slender brunette in white hip huggers, bare midriff and blue bolero got out. Richard introduced Juanita Frey, then disappeared. A brief, shy moment until we picked up the newspaper and selected "Junior Bonner" for a movie.

I was struck by Juanita's appearance, forthrightness, and background. Her father, a riverboat captain, spent thirty days working the river, then thirty days off. His desire was for a son, but Juanita came first. He virtually made her a son. They traveled the river, hunted, and fished together. She toiled on boat docks, rebuilt engines growing up, and understood men. She was charming, gentle, and sensitive, yet disarming because of plain, frank, concrete speech. Her current work in a chemistry lab got a lot of ribbing as the only girl. Once, when her long hair fell into chemicals, she had it cut short, complaining when men said they couldn't tell her from a boy.

After the film ended, we were more interested in conversation. In the humid night we stopped in a school yard. I asked her why the bolero top. I'd never been out with a girl that wore one. And why on a blind date? She said it was necessary for a morale boost. Many times people had misidentified her as a male. She wanted no mistaking. It was a twist, though, for her to be the driver on a date. She drove me home, and with a pleasant kiss, we said goodnight. I wished that time were not an enemy, that destinations and schedules were not the bosses of a traveler. I wished more time with her.   7 miles

BICYCLE CLUB PRESIDENT

Charles woke and accompanied me to mass. Next we attended an Interdenominational Angelical Church. By comparison, the ministers of both faiths were similar. They were jaded by years of religious repetition, using trite phrases and sayings. Their unenthusiastic sermons lacked interest, rambling on as the congregations found more interest in dancing flies.

What a tragedy in the pulpit! Clerics, unable to illuminate sermons with human examples and analogies, have lost the freshness of the message. Their sermons fall flat. "Believe in Christ", "Love God and neighbor", "Obey the commandments", yet where does Christ come in the selling of merchandise? or talking to the nasty kid next door? or counseling a pregnant teenager? Is taking corn from a farmer's field love of neighbor? Does Jesus expect us to do something about immoral neighbors, police, or elected officials? What? How does one love God, a thief, a hoodlum or loudmouth employee? How does a teenager act when his parents don't listen to his real needs? How do you forgive cheating, embezzlement, or murder? What does love look like in the flesh? Salvation sermons need more content on how to cope with the real world. Charles and I discussed more religion in the car than was experienced in church.

For the afternoon, we cycled to the park where Charles' bicycle club meets. He was club president, about to lead their thirty mile trip. At Memphis State University, we split off to tour the city. Charles was an up-to-date catalogue of cycling skill, equipment, and technique. Keeping in shape with an average of 150 miles per week, he had traveled to New Orleans, Nashville, St. Louis, Little Rock and other areas. Of course, he'd had bad experiences. One night, while riding the streets of Memphis, a car crossed the double line, bearing down on him. As he dodged, from an open window, a full beer bottle flew at him grazing his stomach. The car careened around the corner. Charles stood waiting. With lights out, the vehicle re-entered the street and parked. He changed to the left side of the street pedaling up hill. The car crept behind, crossed over and headed for him again. Pulling the bike onto the sidewalk, he unlatched the .38 revolver he carried, steadied the gun with both hands pointed at the windshield. The driver, seeing the weapon, veered sharply away, and weaved as Charles fired through the trunk. There was no more trouble.

A Memphis friend checked opportunities to ride or work on a barge downstream to New Orleans. Earliest word would be Wednesday, a delay that insured a second date with 'Nita. Back home, we witnessed a heated disagreement of neighbor Pat's sons over Bobby Fisher's temperamental complaints of TV camera noise during the World Chess Championships, then drifted to new topics, Judaism-race or religion? nationalism, ideals and religion in education, morality, premarital and common law sex. Having solved the world's problems by 2 a.m., we went to bed.   35 miles

TRUST

Monday was Charles' day off. He forced three men's breakfasts down my gullet. I wasn't hungry, well, not too hungry. We worked it off in the humid backyard removing varnish from a brass bed, under pecan trees, until it shone like gold. In the afternoon, we shopped for carpenter's tools for Richard's new construction job, window shopped quaint stores, leather goods, and a mattress factory for a new box spring for Charles' recently married daughter Charlene. Surprise!

Since his wife worked swing shift, Mr. Finney cooked the steaks and listened to the ooohs and aaahs of Charlene and Mike at their polished brass bed. Daddy earned a kiss. Talk on the swings, biking, jobs, a baseball game on the "tube", and a nagging conscience about not writing for five days. It was difficult to keep up.

I asked Charles why he trusted me so much in his house. He'd given no hint of suspicion. I was another son to him. It was hard to accept such generosity.

His reply: "My house is your house. If you want to abuse it, it's up to you. I've been disappointed a few times, but I prefer to trust people".

"This is the most trust anyone has shown on this trip," I complimented.

"I'm glad you feel that way".

I hadn't been able to see 'Nita for two days-car troubles. And barge trip news. No luck. Insurance regulations. Late night call to Mom assuring her for 45 minutes of my safety.   No miles

A DATE WITH 'NITA

Tuesday, July 18   Memphis, TN   Day 32

Noon wake up. Everyone at work. Restaurant lunch. Shopping for gift book and thank you card. Also a watermelon. Alone. It was eerie how much they trusted me, leaving money on the table, valuables at hand, yet not even a doubt of my honesty. Diary time. I already had a date with 'Nita, so when Richard came home late, I cooked his meal. By listening to his employer and using good sense, the boss already considered promoting the red head. Other employees quit, wasted time, or expected help where none was needed. After a week on the job, frizzy haired Richard was proving worth his $2.00 per hour. (Minimum wage was $1.65.)

A 7 p.m. dinner date decision. 'Nita asked the price range I wanted to stay in.

"As expensive as seventy-five cents allows," I quipped.

She drove into town while street eyes ogled the yellow convertible. The Luau Restaurant was decorated in a Polynesian decor of bamboo furniture and paneling. Palm fronds partitioned tables. A girl in a modest two-piece mini-suit waited. Using towels, she did not touch our dishes, when maneuvering plates or trays. The pampering was distracting me. 'Nita saved conversation by taking control of topics and teased me with her funny bone humor. We ate quickly so she could show me the river at sunset.

Down at the Memphis cliffs an ancient abandoned rail track sat suspended over the concrete levee wall. Painted on the wall in white stripes were high water marks. Once, the river crested fifty feet above normal. 'Nita pointed out eddies, shoals, sand bars, and Presidents' Island, an industrial park developed by the Army Corps of Engineers using built up river silt. We explored some of its immense manufacturing sites. Mark Twain's river description of an evening, in <u>Life on the Mississippi,</u> has not changed. Silver yellow waters swirling under bridges. Fertile banks graced by a black stretch of trees between river and dappled twilight sky. A sweet mossy odor wafted on cooled air currents. The first white lights blinked on for the night. Chain barges, 4-6 wide, and a quarter mile long coursed mid channel, pushed by pilot tugs, searched water ahead with a cyclops beacon light.

'Nita had a Bible school class to prepare for Wednesday, so we returned home. I hated to say good-bye, so kept the parting short. Getting out of the car, I turned, leaned solidly on the door,

"Thank you for being a lady".

"Thank you for being a gentleman".

10:30 Pat's house. Charles was in the midst of recounting adventures in the beauty parlor. A patron died and Charles was asked to do the funeral coiffure. After services, the family was remarking how well the lady had looked. A relative asked Charles how he had done the job. He said: "We dressed her up and tied her in a chair, so she wouldn't fall and get hurt. (This eased the relative somewhat.) Next we leaned her over the sink. We were gentle".

"Oh, thank you Charles," she responded.

"Oh, and I remembered how Miss................ never liked the heat, so I turned the dryer down to medium for her".

On another occasion, a woman of ponderous bulk sat in his chair for a shampoo and tint. Her girth undoubtedly had kept her single. During the rinse and coloring phase, some liquid inevitably fell down the double and triple chin line, dribbling toward her bosom. Charles took up a towel to mop the liquid before it stained her dress. He had no sooner touched the woman than she screamed that he was molesting her. After that event, whenever she came to his chair, he covered her with a towel and sloshed tint with sloppy abandon.

Midnight notes. Checked map of route to New Orleans. A ninety mile average a day would be needed to reach New Orleans by Sunday next. No miles

MISSISSIPPI IMPRESSIONS

Wednesday, July 19   Memphis, TN to Clarksdale, MS   Day 33

Charles left early. His wife kept finding grocery tidbits to squirrel into my bedroll corners. She wanted to drive me to the highway, but I turned her offer down. We did send souvenirs home at the post office, and bought post cards. Why was I so grouchy at a 10:30 leaving?

"You can't miss it," said the service station attendants when asked for directions.

I did miss the turn. On the outskirts of Memphis at 11:30, heading south on U.S. 61, I stopped for quart of milk and a phone call to say good-bye to 'Nita.

Heat and humidity made me a fortune teller, predicting that the remainder of the journey through the South would be well lubricated with sweat. I could also foretell that Mississippi roads would be dangerous. A line of trees hid the flat curving narrow road. Cars jammed up on the one-lane undivided highway and gambled on being able to pass. On three separate occasions, approaching cars veered out from behind autos, gunned the motor, and raced toward me. When they spotted the bicycle, they honked but bore down. I ditched it in the weeds and rocks, later picking grass out of my clothing. Travel time crawled. No enthusiasm. Whether Arkansas ague or Mississippi malaise, it was still lazy pedaling.

In low field rows, flush with bushy leaves, cotton was king, miles upon flat miles of cotton. Only tree lines and clumps broke the panorama. Black men jockeyed red tractors trailed by dust curls. In recesses of the fields, short squat brick houses sat. Amazingly, there were few Negro families in the weather beaten shacks, field workers by day, porch sitters by night. The houses looked nice though some were not plumbed well. They tilted on their foundations. Few billboards. At a weed-choked rail crossing a crudely drawn red and white sign warned: *Mississippi Law. Stop.*

The small brick houses had no roads up to them. If a car were present, it was old and dented. Black children and old folks waved from the porches. All houses were on cement blocks ten inches off the ground. Rains must pour heavily here. An then the revelation. Some brick shacks were <u>torn</u>! Black tarry lines wiggled up the walls, in reality, composition tar paper with a printed brick appearance! Where missing bricks should have been, weathered boards, gray from years of no paint. Deceptions by embarrassed prejudiced, slum lords and low paying farmers of servitude. A cheap facade to fool speeding travelers! Further south, the fake exteriors changed into creaky, leaning barren wood walls. Some shacks were abandoned, their doors and windows missing, stripped to cover up holes in other decrepit dwellings. Almost all had fallen chimneys. An occupied shanty always had clothing hanging from wash lines.

Occasionally, there were real brick houses, easily identified by straight walls, clean, long, low exteriors, washed windows with real glass, two-car garages, spacious lawns with shade trees, and toys or bikes. White folks lived in most.

Stubby yellow crop duster planes with pimple cockpits buzzed low over the fields spraying a white dust cloud down just over the cotton tips. The planes seemed to be afire, yet every time they nosed up, the smoke vanished. Modern technology vs. the insect menace.

Clarksdale. Evening. Mobile trailer. A friend of Charles promised to put me up. At the trailer door, dressed in a tee-shirt and fancy red silk pajamas, he greeted me, begging forgiveness for his appearance. He'd already eaten and bathed by 7:00, and was worried lest I met with an accident. He cooked a hamburger and offered little attentions which made me leery and uncomfortable regardless of weariness. The living room furniture, curtains, and carpet were a sensualist's dream, done in velvets and red felt. Daintiness and precision order for every article of the house. The same prissy neatness pervaded the bathroom. We talked for a while before I wrote post cards to ease my thoughts. I fell asleep fully dressed, with an ear on the closed door.   65 miles

MISSISSIPPI CHANGES

Thursday, July 20   Clarksdale to Hollandale, MS   Day 34

The owner tapped softly at the door at 7:00. Returning to the road regimen had made a grouch out of my body. I gulped coffee, shaved and showered, gathered belongings, and thanked my host. He bade good-bye, locked the front door, and went for his shower. Suspicions relieved, I smiled a hello to a Marine recruiter as I saddled the bike. In town, I mailed cards, wrote in the shade of the post office as patrons finished postal business.

Three girls approached, one holding a microphone as a second asked what I was doing. An unofficial interview. They left to contact the Clarksdale newspaper, begging me to stay put. Indeed, a few minutes later, a young woman in a green dress arrived, asked questions, and shot photos. Other cross-country riders had been in the news, and now was my turn. So far, I had deliberately avoided publicity and reporters, which probably explained why I froze up to the reporter's questions.

"Good things are done quietly," I commented.

She nodded with a promise to mail a copy of her article.

As I shopped a wholesale bread house, excited people gathered about. A woman asked for an autograph for her son. The owner added packages of cookies and candy bars to help out. Coffee and cakes ended the Clarksdale Restaurant excitement. Pleasant people, smiles, generosity. The back side of the city was crowded with rows of double room shanties, screened in, rotting, dirty on the outside. There were no Whites until fancier houses down the highway.

First impressions are lasting. Because of books and articles I've read, I have been expecting harsh, cruel Whites insulting Blacks, the term "nigger" commonly used, the refusal of service at shops, separate toilets, and perhaps a roughing up now and then. With my slow method of travel, no such treatment was discovered. Instead, Blacks and Whites in stores, working and shopping, talking or joking together. The majority of country population seemed to be Black, with Whites noticeably city dwellers. Both have been friendly and helpful. I have witnessed no ill feelings.

Warm morning sun brought expectations of fast riding, but shortly, narrow asphalt threatened travel. Two trucks barreled at me, one passing, leaving no room for a bike. Without a choice, I dumped into a ditch of rocks and weeds. Four more times this occurred. The hot sticky riding was breathless. Friction between the desert water bag and the angled bicycle frame bar frayed the canvas material causing a water leak at the rate of a quart per hour. There was no real danger of thirst, with many houses and businesses about. Mossy creeks cut across the land. They smelled like chicken coops. Rivers were mostly muddy brown, though a few ran clear all the way to the mighty Mississippi.

In Shaw, a group of teenage boys, working at the school, hailed me over, their shirts off, exposing dark bodies. We talked school and bicycles. At Joseph Calionici's Variety Store, he and his three daughters shared new insights. Mississippi has been the whipping post of segregation. It was true that segregation existed, but not to the exclusive focus of John Griffin's <u>Black Like Me</u>. There have been and were good Whites who knew and understood the Negro.

Since the freedom rides and marches of the early 1960s many fantastic changes had occurred. A cotton chopper before 1960 could earn $3.00 a day, and bought from his employer's company store at high prices. (Bread then sold for fifteen cents.) With the realization of voting and buying powers, earnings grew. Minimum wage was met-$1.60 per hour in most places or no work. A woman could make $30.00 a day chopping cotton. Farming and tractoring were no mean skills, so technical ability to handle expensive equipment or skilled proper use of chemicals became paid commodities. Cotton, previously selling at fifteen to twenty cents now brought thirty to thirty-five cents a pound. Conditions, too, changed. The fake brick facade wooden shacks used to be erected for $1,000 each and left without plumbing, or repairs. They have become empty remnants of the segregated past. The Federal Government financed real brick houses for Blacks.

Financial power was no longer in the exclusive hands of a few Whites. Negroes have learned how to earn and spend. Old habits and traditions curdled life of Southern society. The Negro was understood as having two personalities: the White's worker by day, and the bruised Black soul at night. A Black man's life was guided by wine, his women, and his music. Why? When frustrated and hopeless, what else? There was nothing to lose. Militancy became a keynote for Blacks. Strength in numbers. Rights or boycott. True, some extremists provoked trouble. A man raised on his parents' stories of unfair vile treatment will look for ways to repay cruelty for cruelty. Unfortunately, many years will pass before racial turmoil subsides.

Joe Calionici saw more than hope. In his last fifteen years, the changes had been startling with more coming. He was persecuted in the community for his Italian religious faith. So he lived in the cluster of Black homes.

Buying into a business, he traded with the Negro community guided by honest business policy. If folks had troubles he helped. His children went to the high school when it was first integrated. When the KKK (Klu Klux Klan) threatened him, burning crosses on his lawn, he quipped, "You can come and get me. Just remember, the biggest sheet is mine," meaning that the most important KKK leader would be the first person he would shoot.

His variety store sold glue for the water bag hole, and refreshing Icee drinks. My one hundred mile goal would be cut to seventy-five. Evening cycling was cooler and less demanding. Comfort blew in the breeze. Porch sitters watched traffic. Every house was equipped with a chair or rocker and an audience. Twenty miles produced only one billboard of corroded metal and faded paper: *Impeach Earl Warren*. Late evening passage through Leland. A decision to push on to Arcola took me down a darkening road. Cars honked before I caught their meaning. Reflectors, a light beam, and fluorescent vest were not sufficient to be seen. Just after 9:00, I camped under the pines of the Methodist Church in Arcola. On the opposite side, crickets chirped along the banks of the sluggish river. Mosquitoes bothered me constantly even with 6-12 spray on. Too hot to sleep in the bag. I put the plastic tarp over me which failed because it held heat and sweat moisture. An exposed arm or leg was instantly attacked. Believing the river the source of suffering, I packed drowsily and pedaled to the next town, Hollandale at 2:00 a.m. Fields were black with faint light from an occasional house. A rare truck or auto was surprised when its lights revealed my form. Almost asleep, I coasted down an embankment to a county hospital to set camp amid construction boards and fallen plaster. The mosquitoes found me immediately. Out of ideas, swollen and aching, I walked to the hospital entrance, and asked to sleep in the janitor's closet. Understandably nervous, the nurses called the deputy who let me sleep in the court house.   90 miles

VICKSBURG

At 6 a.m. the deputy said he was going to pick up the chief, and gave directions for a roadside park five miles away. Somewhat rested but suffering from a headache, I crept down the road, entered a gravel drive, parked behind bushes, and lay on the ground. The sun's heat woke me at 10:30, but my head never cleared all day. Writing was a struggle. My head pounded when I rode out at 1:30. Every bump activated a pain center. Mosquito punctures were not as swollen but still itched. Heat converted strength into languor. Most of the countryside went unnoticed.

I stopped in Rolling Fork to buy nectarines and apples. Outside the air conditioned market, a nose bleed dripped down my upper lip. A woman clerk ran out the door with Kleenex, and returned to make a phone call. Five minutes later, two reporters asked for an interview. News spread fast in small towns. (Ever talked to a reporter with tissues in your nose?)

Still heading south, at 7 p.m. it was a relief to glide through hills of dense woods and thickets overgrown with climbing vines and ivy. A husky chicken coop-like odor emanated from the swampy tributaries of the Mississippi. Courteous motorists passed slowly because there was no shoulder; one man blasted his horn with threats until the pack of cars behind forced him to drive on.

The street wove into a strand of dismal houses, lumber yards, shacks, and collapsed buildings. Rising smoke from a huge rubble pile gave the impression of the second siege of Vicksburg. Upon a green light's permission, the bike struggled up brick and stone pavement. Decaying 1880s store fronts stood silent. Small shops remained mute to the traffic trickle. Save for lingering voices and echoes, the city was empty. The hospitality house was closed. After a two cheeseburger dinner, a camp site search free of mosquitoes started. The bike's white generator light patrolled the dark streets of a riverbank, down dingy alleys to the train yard. Workmen in coveralls, pouring coffee from a pot, sent me back over the tracks to the old paddle wheeler Sprague.

Nine p.m. was an odd hour to visit the largest paddle wheeler ever built. Docked permanently against the river bank, the gray and white triple deck steamer shone under electric bulbs. Red bulbs lit the flat paddles. Insects by the hundreds danced about the lights. Shoe leather clacked on the steel deck. Inside the main fuel and cargo hold, now a museum, was a wooden floor. Sketches and panels depicted the history and tragedies of hundreds of riverboats during their heyday. Paddle wheelers once plied the Mississippi having stuffed cotton bales in every square inch of space from first deck to the pilot house. The craft lived in fire danger every moment. A spark from the wood burning engine room, a match idly dropped, or a smokestack cinder ignited many a fatal blaze.

In the old theater, a black-face dance troupe was performing. I skipped the show, clambering up to the bow winches, back down the other side to the engine room, now an oil burner. The conception, design and function of such enormous engines befuddled the mind on the complexity of the human intelligence. On the second deck, dinner was being served. The uppermost deck was the pilothouse filled with megaphones, klaxons, searchlights, guide bars, and a giant wooden pilot wheel with a *Do Not Touch* sign. Of course, I touched it! Leaving the boat was anti-climatic. The usual exit door was locked, requiring retracing the route. Mosquitoes hovered in anticipation of dining with me.

First camp was set up behind a market ice machine, but noise, dampness, roaches and foul air soon chased me away. The police gave directions for a camp. But dark streets played memory tricks, confused distances, and led along a memorial highway flanked by Civil War monuments and busts. In exhaustion, I hid in a corner of the high school parking area on dewy grass. 65 miles

SOCIAL CONFLICT

The sun dried the dew and sleeping roll readily. A Black caretaker greeted hello and brought a Coke. Between writing spells, I applied lotion to insect bites. I couldn't permit any more "free" meals, so I bought a mosquito net. The Hospitality House was open. Norma Daughtry repeated her monologue for a tour group prior to asking for hometowns. Hearing, "L.A.", she wanted a news interview, while I extracted information about the South.

A boycott was on in Vicksburg. Initially it began when rumor of a White man raping a Negro girl circulated. After some months of quieting, an incident arose in a grocery where a Black girl and her parents argued over money. The incident left a dead Black man and a beaten White man. The boycott flared anew. Blacks threatened and ordered other Blacks not to buy from White merchants, not even to work for them. Pocketbooks and pantries grew empty. On some days employees chanced coming to work, on other days they phoned in that it was too dangerous to risk leaving the house. Negro ladies carried guns to protect themselves against super-militants. Goods bought in a store were hidden in purses until they arrived home. The strike continued with White merchants trying to appease demands. Often they were met with new demands without warning. Some militants extorted money for programs and freedom activities but who could not account for the monies given them. Business and dishonesty trickled on.

The city itself was torn by those seeking to rebuild and modernize, and those who wanted to hang on to the old way of life. New homes and businesses have moved off the river, away from the center of town. Crumbling brick store fronts and deserted shanties still lined the highway in spite of a renewal program. Historical homes were beyond repair and Negroes lived in the rickety shacks, mainly because they paid no rent, accepting the fire trap danger. Change will come slowly.

Education was the answer, but it, too, must wait. Mississippi law required that the percentage of Black teachers correspond to a school's racial make-up. For this reason many White teachers were released regardless of seniority status or qualifications. Some left teaching altogether, others drifted to private schools supported by segregationists. Public education became essentially Black. Only to fulfill the law's requirement, some school administrators hired Negro teachers who were not well qualified. Most Black high school students were able to do simple math but could not handle two digit division problems. In the past, teachers were lax in pushing higher concepts. With patience and time there would be a rise of qualifications and standards. Life and the river moved on. Constant change.

I tried barges looking for a chance to ride down river. A tobacco chewing operator spit out a *No* reply. Insurance companies permitted only crew on ships. The end of day saw this Huck Finn dream die. Farmhouses sat in recessed coves and cattle roamed field thickets. Hours of dense forest lay south among the climbing ivy. The vines, called kudzu grew over anything, smothering trees, fences, or abandoned homes, giving the semblance of giant ghosts trapped under the dark green foliage. Undulating countryside, katydids and hissing autos were my companions.

Port Gibson, in the dark, was settling to sleep or a Saturday drunk. A sheriff sent me to a park eleven miles south with warnings to watch for drunks and snakes. Why did the law men always know of camp places far out of town? A car load of teenagers cruised by, stopped to offer a beer, then went to bother other kids at a drive-in movie. The park was on a wooded mound of thick soft mulch. Poking the ground with a rotten branch revealed no snakes. As I lay dozing in my mosquito tent, a couple of cars pulled into the parking loop aiming their headlights to illuminate a grassy swath. Two White drunks, cursing blue streaks, settled an argument, fighting it out, as others cheered the combatants. It was more of a wrestling match with dire oaths. They drove off. Except for a prowling raccoon it was peaceful. Hungry mosquitoes starved and cicadas laughed all night.   37 miles

CONFLICT: OLD VERSUS NEW

How blessed to wake to speckled green leaves against a blue sky, macaws squawking, jays and cardinals singing louder than cicadas. Pine cones, falling from their branches, clattered like pin balls on lower limbs to clunk into brown needles of the knoll. A whispering breeze wafted the air, unable to enter the mosquito canopy. No new welts on elbows, face, or back. Nature's glory is God's best church. Since there was no opportunity to adore Him in man's dwelling, prayers were said and scripture read under heaven's dome.

The famous Lorman Market, serving country folk since before the War of the States, raised its barnlike white-washed wooden frame out of the forest. Negroes of all ages gathered on benches and tree stumps alongside the road. Inside, were wooden shelves and cabinets stocked with bolts of cloth and trading goods, plus modern refrigerators and vending machines. The main attraction was the Civil War Museum. On display were firearms, flattened bullets, damaged cannon balls, soldier uniforms, boots, plows, leather harness, newspapers, store ledgers and catalogs, all remnants of lives long since gone. The replicas, tools, weapons, and monuments of steel and stone have received attention longer than the blood, sweat, and tears of those who made and used them.

The highway twisted through forest hills. Gouging earthmovers have flattened the land of the winding trail. Moss and vines grew down the vertical mud walls, hiding the soil. Humidity continued to rise. Fayette, a town run by Charles Evers, the Civil Rights activist, strictly enforced speed laws, especially against outsiders. On Sunday every store was closed. One man walked to the hospital to visit his wife. Beyond town, more hills. I stopped at a white-washed plywood beer joint. Three Blacks sat sweat drenched, sipping cokes. They revealed a hard fact; no matter how ambitious a man is, humidity is an unrelenting force sapping a man's energy. The weather has drained riding enthusiasm; I'd rather go catfishing. It was lonely. Often the only sign of life was a rusted rural mailbox.

Mississippi facts. It has the largest: 1) cotton plantation, 2) wood pulp factory, 3) catfish production, 4) telephone production, and 5) chicken farm. It raises cotton, cattle, sweet potatoes, corn, peanuts, and beans.

On the way to the state line, Natchez was supposed to be a grocery stop. With markets closed, I hit another burger joint. A Black boy on a bicycle rode beside me to the edge of town where I pointed to the gathering storm clouds. He dropped behind and waved. The sun still shone when the downpour occurred. Riding was out of the question with visibility less than a hundred feet. Puddles formed so fast and deep I could not navigate them. The asphalt was slick. My only choice was shelter under a tall pine in the yard of a new home. The drippings, clashing thunder, and soft pattering water created a symphony, but the increasing cloudburst forced me to seek cover in a garage. I intended to push on another thirty miles, when the right brake cable jammed again. Stuffy humidity required repairs at the edge of the open double door. Before repair was complete, Mr. Stearn invited me in.

The Stearns enjoyed a visitor. Their kids were away at camp, so man and wife lived in a quiet home. The doctor, after service in Korea, had been a long standing citizen of the community for the past fifteen years. He opened his practice as the first physician not having separate waiting rooms. It was unheard of to speak to a Negro as Mister or Mrs. Jones, and "improper" to greet with a handshake. These he did as a matter of custom. Now, a specialist in ophthalmology, his main complaint was alcoholics. They were difficult to sedate for operations, troublesome as patients (subject to D.T.s [delirium tremens] during hospital treatment unless given a dose of alcohol), and were unstable emotionally. About 70 percent of their operations resulted in poor healing or failure, due to alcoholic reaction.

Natchez was suffering the same agony as Vicksburg. Conservative elders opposed modernization, hoping to preserve the old genteel atmosphere-moss, old manses, and Civil War glories. In reality, decay was encroaching what nostalgic beauty remained. Several years ago, an oil company proposed a refinery site in Natchez, with an offer to assist in renewal. Council ladies rejected the offer, fearing change. Baton Rouge, given the same offer, accepted. In fifteen years its population swelled to 200,000 while Natchez declined to 25,000, keeping its historic atmosphere.

The orderly detail of a physician's mind was evident in the house: organization, neatness, precision, highly decorative furnishings, and formal comfort. The boys' room where I slept held similar precision-football hero posters mounted carefully on the walls in rectangular balance, multicolored team pennants in a perfect circle above the headboard. Parent example has deep roots. 45 miles

A MEAN COP

Dr. Stearns left early for the office, his wife coming to assist shortly. Because she appeared ill at ease being alone with me, I hurried the coffee and left. Cool shade in the hollows of piney hills and flats. Stagnant humidity. Perfect for a motorcycle run. Early lunch on a moist lichen covered stone table witnessed a young couple, towing a mobile trailer, pulling in, joined by the in-laws. The foursome camped out-of-doors in the aluminum trailer, but bickered over water and dishes.

A Ford dealership exhibited shiny blue tractors and accessories, yellow hay cutters, red plows, and silver bladed tillers. A small tractor, capable of ten acres of field preparation a day, ran about $3,000, the largest model, able to cultivate one hundred acres a day, cost $15,000. An office wall barometer indicated rain even though the sun shone brightly. In an hour, thunder roared through the sky for an hour's drenched riding.

Entering Louisiana. The drops grew fatter in welcome. A few more hills and I would be under the blackest of clouds. Peaking over the hill crest, I spotted a country store for shelter. Rain smacked down in stinging splashes. Glancing over the left shoulder, I turned to cross the wet asphalt. I never saw the car coming. A honk, screech of brakes, squealing, skidding tires. From the corner of my left eye appeared a white Datsun, water spraying up sideways, sliding straight at the bike. I was in the middle lane. Behind the windshield, the driver frantically spun the steering wheel. The tire tread caught briefly swerving the car left, skid again, passing less than a foot from the front bike wheel, caught traction again, shot off the road into a ditch on the left spitting gravel, bounced out of the ditch over the side access road, dodged a culvert, but bounced into a second ditch, and hopped the gravel in front of the store. The driver's head was lying on the steering wheel as I rode up immediately. He wagged his head. We apologized to each other in the torrent, both of us visibly shaking, as was his wife. In a few moments he drove on, slowly. I squished to the store, sat on a wooden bench trembling, knowing my legs were about to collapse. Undoubtedly, the orange vest had saved my life. Two hours were needed to calm down before I splashed my shoes and socks into the muddy road grit

Drizzle continued until St. Francisville when afternoon sun dried the streets. Crunchy moss, like a hair-scarf, dangled from trees. Tall wooden houses stood with flat eaves. Olive skinned men spoke a strange English, Cajun.

Ferry Landing at the muddy Mississippi. Trucks and cars waited in line on the dirt road for the next boat. Perspiring drivers swapped tall tales and swigs of water. Across the river, the ferry launch swung downstream, curved across, and gently docked. After red and white wooden rail guards rolled back, cars labored up the embankment. Then fresh cargo boarded. Gates closed and powerful engines churned foam. Passengers sat in their chairs, a few on deck.

The Louisiana south side of the Mississippi was flat. The land was reputed to be eleven feet below sea level, protected by a forty foot man-made levee. A two foot deep trench could reveal the water table. Rich alluvial soil produced sugar cane higher than a man's head like wild bamboo. Farmhouses were stubby affairs, with old boards and tin roofs like in "Old Miss".

Contrasts between the states. Old Mississippi had counties, towns with Indian names, drainage down to the big river and the largest number of churches in relation to population, mostly Protestant. Louisiana had French names adorning parishes (counties), cities and mailboxes, with lakes and rivers below sea level, and numerous statues honoring the Blessed Virgin Mary on front lawns.

The long way to Baton Rouge curved around idyllic False River. Flat bottomed boats lined the harbor while late afternoon fishermen were still chasing big ones. Small businesses advertised crayfish, shrimp, and bait. Wooden houses with sleepy docks occupied the riverside. The graceful road proceeded to sugar cane plantations and the I-10 expressway-the first road with shoulders in 400 miles. Fast and safe.

Squashed armadillo carcasses lay everywhere on the road edge. Hundreds. At night they were known to migrate over the highways grousing for bugs in grass and weeds. They snuffed out worms, leaving lawn divots for angered gardeners. Armadillos have emigrated from Texas in large numbers and have been found invading Kansas.

At dusk a galaxy of Baton Rouge lights radiated across the river. It was relatively easy to ascend the enormous steep green span. A state policeman, putting a flare at the top of the bridge, looked up in surprise. He jumped into his patrol car and followed me over, force-pinning the bike to exit at the next turnout. In a parking lot, he suspiciously checked identification, then issued a stern warning not to ride on the expressway as it was a federal violation. After 2,000 miles this was the first warning of federal law and road travel. There had been no sign prohibiting bikes on the bridge's approach. He further cautioned against: 1) staying in the Negro neighborhood ("They'll kill you".), 2) entering the downtown section, and 3) driving at night. He recommended going to the rescue mission for down-and-outers, or to a Catholic church-both would understand, since I was the vagrant type. I nodded my head and said whatever was necessary to appease him. When he left, I headed in the opposite direction he had given.

At the border entry to LSU, (Louisiana State University), I stopped for pizza and rest. The waitress directed me to Genesis House, a student self-help center. In the pressured world of higher education, there existed warm souls who cared for the lonely and problem-ridden. These students were the self help underground emergency backbones of educational life. In Genesis House, someone was on duty twenty-four hours a day to discuss anxieties, fear, drugs, studies, whatever. No one was refused help, though drug possession or drug talk was forbidden. As I entered, first aid classes were under way and someone was phoning in a problem. Ron Posey, a lean, bearded, Abe Lincoln type, ex-grunt from Vietnam, opened his small apartment to me. His possessions were few: three or four towels, perhaps twenty books, a few nick-knacks, and a loving plaque from his girlfriend, Kathy. It was a bachelor's pad with a cubby hole kitchen, bare walls, empty shelves, sparsely furnished, all for $80.00 per month. Ron somehow "got by". His finance problems evident, he asked what he could do for me. I tried to need nothing. I used a pay phone to call home.   85 miles

FRIENDS

Ron went to classes across the field outside the enormous football stadium. During a lazy morning, I washed clothes, adjusted brake cables and oiled the chain. In the mid afternoon, Ron was washing his car, getting it ready for sale. He couldn't afford the upkeep. Amid good-byes, he said he would help if needed, anywhere down the road.

Rain on the horizon would prevent arrival in New Orleans. It was spitting before supper and streaming down at a grocery store/bar near Dutch Town. From the market I bought milk and ravioli. A twenty something man, wearing a baseball cap protruding shaggy hair, out for a breath of air, ordered, in a friendly way, to come into the bar for a beer and watch the Baseball All-Star game on TV. I ate ravioli at the bar. Patrons, wearing baseball hats saying "Kank's", offered to buy drinks, too. Their softball team, having won district finals, was eager to go to state finals. When the TV game ended, Darrel Singletary led me to the house in back, where he cooked a rice and meat dish, and gave me his bed. The house was stuffy with humidity. When the mosquitoes got hungry, I went out to the garage and set up the net tent between two lawn chairs. I was comfortable until a small rat wandered in under the netting. We scared each other jumping around in the dark trying to get out of the tent.   20 miles

LOUISIANA TIDBITS, ED AND ADIE

Wednesday, July 26   Dutch Bar to New Orleans, LA   Day 40

Radio news announced a fourteen day season on alligators until a limit of 4,000 was taken. Hunting in the swamps, men would walk chest deep in mud, rifles overhead, stalking the beasts. Gators have been spotted up to sixteen feet long and weighing over a thousand pounds. Their thick plating has resisted all attacks, though a cotton mouth might win if it could bite the tongue inside the opened saw-toothed jaw. Men have shot at the head and had bullets ricochet. The tough skins have been sold for hand bag and boot leather, while the meat has been considered a delicacy. In winter, waterfowl are hunted and there is less danger from cotton mouths. Fishing goes year round. Louisiana's license plate proclaims: *Sportsman's Paradise.*

The swamp and lowland water table sportsmen revel in, was an engineer's nightmare. A proposed expressway through the western marshes proved an expensive failure. Pile drivers pounded steel pillars into the mush to hit solid rock for a stable raised bridge support. In one area of the swamp, pilings sunk hundreds of feet without hitting bottom. The sites were moved several times without success until the route was abandoned.

This was not the only headache for the state. A new constitution was in the process of being drawn up. The governor was elected on his campaign promise of cutting bureaucratic red tape. Laws as well as bonds, go through a maze of committees and officials for approval. Proposals that survived, must go before the people for election. It had come to this. Voting ballots were loaded with items seeking approval, sometimes more than one hundred separate proposals that a city commission could have handled. For example, the New Orleans Bridge. For more than ten years the city had dire need of a new span over the river. Traffic jams were two and three hours long on the present bridges. Each bond proposal had been defeated-not by the city residents, but by the other state citizens who felt they would be taxed to help New Orleans. So far the bridge had not been built, let alone designed.

The day's ride was uneventful on level ground, hot, humid, straight roads past bayous (swampy streams) and sugar cane. Turtles sunned on logs amid green scum. Rain threatened. The last ten miles into New Orleans was a jarring ride over cracked and bumpy potholes. Feverish traffic hustled by. Underpasses and factories wearing sooty coats stood stonily apathetic. Drizzle preceded a cloudburst that caught me on a ramp descending into a series of deep puddle-lakes ending before a hotel entrance. Astounded bystanders muffled giggles at the ridiculous bicycler's clinging red shirt and blue shorts. Around the side of the building, bikini-clad girls dived into the pool, laughing at the dressed onlookers sheltered under balconies. I used the lobby phone to locate a former college friend studying at Tulane Medical School. No answer, so at least the surprise visit was intact.

With the skies still crying in spurts, I cycled to the medical residence hotel. The manager gave permission to bring the bike in out of the rain and park in a lobby corner. Renovations were going on during the summer session. I went upstairs, to wait in the hall cluttered with beds, furniture, and carpet rolls. A door opened to a vacant room. Outside a tenth floor window spread the ugly roof tar tops above the maze of streets and tall buildings. Weak honks and sirens drifted up. On the horizon skyline, a ship's smokestack moved, its deck hidden. While I had been waiting three hours, Ed Shaheen was with a community help program for minority students considering medicine. Finally, to insure no one could miss me, I took up residence in a chair in front of the door.

Adie Shaheen exited the elevator and asked if I was waiting for someone. Without her glasses she couldn't identify me. Closer she came. I kept silent.

"Is it Jim?" she asked.

"No," I answered sparingly.

"No-is it.......Ed? Ed! Ed Abair???!!! Squeals and screams of girlish laughter filled the once drab hall. She opened the door. "Shhh! Ed's asleep!"

"Naw! I banged and no one answered," I replied.

Adie looked into the small bedroom, "Yes, he is!"

Indeed, the medical galoot was oblivious to the world. At the foot of the bed, I grabbed a big toe, and bellowed.

"Shaheen, this is a fine way to treat a guest. What are you doing when there's company to be taken care of? Get up Sweetie Pie!"

"Huh?" He mumbled, tossed, tried to dream. After ten minutes of more salty abuse and tweaking of toes, he roused to an inarticulate mass, grumbling, "Am I still dreaming or is that Abair?"

Somehow Ed had slipped into the apartment undetected, and then had the nerve to fall asleep.

Three years had separated us two Eds. Adie heard two replies when she called the name. In spite of having her prized chicken dinner praised, she refused my entreaty to come home and cook for me. She thinks she's happily married to Ed, almost-a-doctor, Shaheen.

In the late evening we wandered the French Quarter. Bourbon Street, as all other streets of the Quarter, was lined with French style two-story houses that touched shallow sidewalks and narrow lanes. Wrought iron balconies peered over the crowds wandering mid-street below. Shows under neon lights and windows all aglitter begged attention. Groups in every mode of dress from sloppy jeans and braless peasant blouses to tuxedos and evening gowns paraded together. Attentive ears caught strains of Dixieland and the delight of masterpiece jazz. Collectors marveled at antiques, jewelry, and art. Glitzy romance was everywhere.

Beyond the glitter existed a second French Quarter. Noisy streets and alleys were old, cracked, ridden with brazen roaches. Buildings were sooty and, from the exterior, appeared to be slums. Cheap souvenir merchants peddled trivia at steep markups; commercialism skyrocketed prices. Few people entered jazz bars, most stood outside, cheapskates unwilling to pay a cover charge or buy a drink. Vulgar girly shows blatantly traipsed nearly nude women on posters, and street barkers encouraged entrance to their houses. Two female impersonator shows competed for business, even luring dating couples or families. Great music and historic landmarks next to crass flesh peddlers.

Sights and sounds jangled saturated nerves. A quiet chat with friends along the river returned the joy of friendship. It was enough.   30 miles

TULANE MEDICAL SCHOOL

No one has yet discovered the antidote for early morning sleepyhead. Adie sacrificed heavy doses of coffee to my unawakened brain before she left for the ophthalmology lab. She'd been working in the medical center for three years. Ed and I soon followed, crossing a busy street to a tan brick nine story building. Charity Hospital connected to it. Inside the halls of Tulane Medical School, white jacketed doctors walked between departments and waited for elevators. Technicians carried equipment; lab assistants pushed carts. We checked into the gastroenterology department where Ed owned a cubby hole office of bottles, jars, chemicals, files, and analysis devices. He set out his work and gave directions on exploring.

Each floor was a medical labyrinth of separate, complex, highly specialized intelligence. One floor medicine, a second cardiology, a third, surgery, others neurology, pathology, anatomy and the list ran on, in beehive conference rooms and cubicles. Experiments were conducted in some rooms, classes in others. Lab workers prepared and checked specimens. Tubes, bottles, and stacked data sheets occupied shelves. Equipment was hospital clean. Paperwork helped employ secretaries typing and filing. The library was a storehouse of human health successes, failures, discoveries, and revolutions in medical knowledge.

On the third floor was a graphic summary of medical endeavor in the Souchon Anatomical Exhibits. Huge sealed glass jars housed anatomy examples: a leg's arteries and veins filled with red and blue dyes to expose blood routes; an arm lay open showing musculature, tissue, and bone structure; a cut away back bone revealed the delicate nervous system and the interlocking spine. Normal organs were compared against abnormal, whether by defect, disease, or injury. Parasite invasions were identified. Livers, lungs, abdomens depicted the intense study of dissection. In toto, the exhibit of this one man, Dr. Souchon (1846-1924), was a testament to the scientists who raised surgery from grave robbers to skilled physicians possessing the knowledge to heal.

Jim Lovelace, a parasitologist, joined us for supper at a Spanish restaurant. We entered a gilded alcove of red tile and brick leading to a main courtyard dining room ensconced below black wrought iron balconies. Roof tiles covered archways. Gay Spanish music stirred the atmosphere as our hungry crew lined up to sample dishes of tortillas, chile relleno, tamales, tacos, frijoles, and enchiladas. We could eat with abandon for the bill of fare was identical to a Spanish smorgasbord: $1.45 each. After two full plates, the Shaheens had saved a twenty dollar food bill. We teased the waitress who was surprised we spoke Spanish.

Jim returned home to study while Adie and we two Eds strolled the older section of New Orleans to admire leaded glass doors that twinkled light from within, pillared balconies, porch rails, tooled carpentry, grill work vignettes, inspected moss encrusted halls at Loyola and Tulane Universities, and caught the rickety-rackety electric trolley back to the neon city. In the hotel we contested each other at Perquacky spelling. Good company is life which money, booze, or luxury can't supply. Good fun is loving friends.   No miles

GARDEN OF LOOTING AND ART

Friday, July 28   New Orleans, LA   Day 42

Bad case of sleeping sickness. Returned to bed after breakfast. The grueling pace has caught up with me.

Friday after school was happy hour for the students. A party was in progress in the hotel's Zebra Room. Ed's group of minority Blacks sat drinking sodas or beer and eating chips. Friends milled around, joking and razzing Earl, the honored guest, it being his birthday, caught in his familiar eating pose. A polite, hilarious group, full of pep, enthusiasm, and talent. The Ron-ton Restaurant served gumbo soup, red fish and catfish with tasty delicate Creole seasoning. Humid night walking to the Quarter, with sticky finger ice cream eating in Jackson Park.

History surrounds the park. At the head stood the Catholic Cathedral, flanked by two stone government buildings. Originally used for governing, they have become apartments. Here, the Louisiana Purchase was signed. Both sides of the park were flanked by two story brick edifices with curlicue grill rails. The foot of the square, once the river, now was protected by a levee. On it stood mute boxcars waiting for loading from the massive brewery also at the foot of the park. Iron gates were locked at night to protect the garden and to prevent tramps and drunks from sleeping there. The locks also prevented souvenir looters from dismantling the statues. During the day artists painted and hung canvasses on the grills; at night guitarists serenaded with pop and romantic songs.

Home means air conditioning, a last talk of old times, and a book of Robert Frost poems in bed.   No miles

THE CARIBBEAN COAST

Saturday, July 29   New Orleans, LA to Biloxi, MS   Day 43

Good-byes. Bike down the elevator. Bed roll strapped tightly on the bike rack. Outside humidity stifling. Immediate sweat. Market and directions. Rough pavement bounced and banged the rubber tires hitting gouges and splits in concrete. Cars rushed by. Modern suburban homes watched stolidly under leafy trees until New Orleans fell behind and tall grasses stated marsh country. Clouds delivered a twenty minute drench. I huddled under a dripping tree. When it turned to drizzle, the tires sloshed on wet pavement. Grass gave way to reeds standing in excess of six feet. On marsh islands, spider leg pilings propped gaudy chartreuse, flamingo pink, and canary yellow wooden houses eight feet above the ground, their spacious yards under water during heavy rains. The islands resembled convoluted puzzle pieces interlocked by water. Frequently, rubbish was piled in the fore of the buildings and later burned. Trash dumps were any side road or vacant lot. Yellow and green Hefty bags cluttered in the weeds waiting the next flood. When the bags tore, foul contents spilled.

Marshes continued for thirty miles connected by thin landfills or short simple truss bridges. The ocean lay dark and muddy against the southern gray sky, while the north lake was dark and misty. Scudding cloud billows dumped rain ahead, behind, crooked witch's lightning fingers snapping thunder whips. Long sixteen foot boats dangling fish nets were anchored or tied to the bridges riding out the storm.

Then a last marsh stretch abutted a deep pine forest, as I entered the gulf neck of a great bay extending another twenty miles. Fishermen in bayous caught red and white fish and speckled trout. Occasionally sportsmen have become lost in the winding tall reed waterways. At best, they may have a tree for a landmark. Crouched in the driver seat of a police vehicle shielded from the traffic, a highway patrol officer monitored the speed trap indicator.

"Eleven miles an hour," he yelled out. Considering the damaged roadbed, it was speeding.

For the third time, the screw of my left glasses temple piece fell out, making them unusable. Blown sand and small insects lodged in and scratched my eyes from coastal gusts. Never had the protection of glasses been so well demonstrated.

101

The gulf was moody. Sun glistened as a storm gnashed its teeth offshore; squalls teased for hours during summer. Hurricanes have lashed boats, waterfront, homes, and companies destroying businesses and all forms of habitation. Clouds hung in the gulf, camouflaging their intent. Except for small breaking waves, the ocean was olive drab.

Buildings, deeply set back from the beach under shade trees, were divided from private wharves and docks by the highway. Without fences, people easily traversed white sand stretching 150 feet from curb to water's edge. Bathers parked in looping asphalt inlet bays every quarter mile. Pipeline jetties, every 500 feet, attempted to trap beach sand and prevent erosion. In reality, sand filled the east side of the jetty, and washed away on the west.

The street, banked towards the beach, was hampered by rounded curb, so grates permitted rain runoff to drop down and escape into emptying drain pipes. The grate had gaps 1 1/2inches wide and ten inches long. This was significant. Ten speed tires are 1 1/4 inches wide. A careless moment could lead to tragedy. If the front tire lodged into the crevice and twisted, the rider would be thrown into the traffic. For this reason I tried carefully dodging all grates seen. In the deepening twilight, autos had become more dangerous with the narrow lane, honking their horns to urge me closer to the curb. Then it happened. A shimmering puddle disguised a grate. I hit it full speed. Two thunks, a momentary loss of control. I corrected course, then stopped under a lighted driveway. The handle bars had twisted forward with the front fork bent, but still ride worthy. But the rear wheel held three broken spokes and a bend in the rim. The bike rode with an eccentric oval thump with each rotation. The tool kit trued the rim, but the thump would not disappear.

Six miles later, my energy gave out. I erected the mosquito tent camp in a vacant ten acre grass lot, where some trucks had also parked. A grocery sold milk. Lifesavers served as lozenges for my raspy throat. Writing under a telephone light, I listened to waves splash ashore and the progress of a beach party. A young Biloxi gas station operator offered his house in the west for shelter, which meant fifteen miles to be retraced tomorrow, too far. I turned him down.

Police were waiting when I returned to the camp in the grass. Neighbors had been spooked by a mysterious figure in the field. The officers accepted my explanation and allowed me to leave. Hustling back to the gas station, I asked if the offer still stood. It did. My bike had to be disassembled to fit into his small auto trunk. The attendant picked up his girl friend and another girl. They tried to make conversation while the sore throat worsened my watery eyes. I was annoyed at having to re-cycle fifteen miles. The two bedroom house was elegantly furnished. Another man was there. Then it dawned on me that both girls were living together with their boyfriends. I felt ill at ease. I showered, drank beer to ease the throat, and slept on a white shag carpet in the living room.   89 miles

INVISIBLE?

During the night the weather exploded. White brilliance flashed through the curtains. Thunder crashed at the front door. Furious rain pelted against the window finding weak seals to flood the floor. Twice I moved the bed from the growing puddles on the rug. It was fortunate that the police had run me off the field; I would have drowned. If I felt ill at ease, at least I was dry. In spite of the air conditioning, feverish perspiration set in. Spice jelly candies provided little relief for the raw throat. Anguished sleep ended at 11 a.m. No one was awake for a thank you, so I left a note.

A priest announced that I'd just missed local services, but Pascagoula had a.... I stopped listening because of intense throat pain. The fever was inconsiderate. Orange juice and pears for a cold remedy. I was nearly out of money, a mere $20.00 remaining. Averaging 120 miles per day for seven days, I might make Miami to wire home for more money. If not, I could try the BankAmericard. Would another state honor a California credit card? I didn't know.

Depressing travel. Headache and bouncing road. At 2 p.m., new rain. Two hours were spent under a market roof. Sardine lunch. Watched soaked shoppers run from their cars. The storm paused. Sloppy road. Long concrete bridge over Pascagoula River. Strong winds carried fish and marsh odors. Boats moored at bridge supports for tomorrow's sally to drop nets and harvest fish.

Pascagoula, homey and clean, was a growing city on the edge of swamp. Our Lady of Victory Church had mass at 5:30. I combed my hair using rain water, and urinated behind a building. Inside, a major mistake was discovered. My damp clothing together with air conditioning produced chills. Sermon: God turns all things, even evil, into good for man. Very little comfort for the fever and shivering-a poor attitude, yet the truth of the talk has certainly been proven in all my other mishaps and sudden fortunes.

For night driving, I donned the orange vest, ate a quick cold stew, and hurried to make Mobile, forty miles away. The sun set at 8:05. In the dark many, too many, vehicles honked, as if they couldn't see my generator light, florescent vest and red reflectors, although I was hugging the shoulder. The honks were insistent. Why were they beeping? Parking the bike on the road edge, I walked back a few hundred feet in the dark, turned around, and waited for a car's high beams to shine on the bike. No reflections, only dark. The bike could not be seen! I closed another 200 feet. Still no visible color. What was wrong with the reflectors? It wasn't until I was a hundred feet from the cycle that the florescent devices could be dimly seen! After more than 2,800 miles, the danger of my night driving was all too shocking!

At the very next off ramp, I exited toward streetlights. Swallowing a mouthful of service station water, I scouted an elementary school, selecting a recessed dry doorway, out of sight, tying mosquito protection to doors and bike. Frogs bellowed their songs. Sore throat.   70 miles

A CAR LOAN

Sick, I felt like the faces of cows in the meadows, dull.

Mobile's stark stone skyline poked into the air. Late Victorian era ironwork on three story balconies mixed with modern skyscrapers towering in the business district. The manager of a travel agency gave directions to an oculist, and added,

"Your legs should be in great shape".

"For a quarter, you can feel them," I offered.

"You're not the right shape," he retorted

An optometrist's assistant fixed the glasses in a minute. No charge. I felt foolish standing at the counter in a dirty red shirt and blue greasy pants. Street folks turned their heads at the odd sight as I walked to the park. A prolonged sneezing fit lasted for two minutes.

My next task was transit to the other side of the river. Bikes were forbidden in the Mobile tunnel entrance ahead, adding a ten mile extra circuit around the warehouses and rail yards. Rail yards were a scavenger's delight for finding cord, clothes, rags, wood, wire and other debris useful for replacement or extemporaneous repairs: a small chunk of wood supported the rack off the brake cable; a bungee cord held the pack more securely; a nylon rope secured my plastic water jug. The detour was a blessing!

Farther up, streams lead to the river which held listing and sunken ship hulks rusting at marine shops, disarray on all sides. A right turn onto U.S. 90 led past a small marsh, a factory, and then over a thin two lane girder bridge. The distance across was only 500 feet, yet if a construction flagmen hadn't been controlling traffic on the entrance, I could not have passed. There were no sidewalks and traffic was exceptionally heavy. The exit was unpleasant with sweet-foul air assailing the nostrils from garbage and mulch rot. East bank marsh lands were used as a landfill trash dump. Roaches gleefully skittered in the reeds. Factories and oil refineries occupied this section.

The route finally rejoined with the tunnel traffic along a narrow strip of islands, ten miles across, to the other side of the bay. Water lapped at one or both sides of the causeway. Fishermen, pulled off to sidings, and on islands, tried their luck. On the right, not twenty feet away, turtles and fish splashed among the seaweed. My shadow played over harbor scum washing the pilings. In the middle of the island throughway rested a giant gray steel structure, the battleship Alabama. Rising 200 feet out of the water, the mothballed warship's sixteen-inch guns pointed outward, searching for an imaginary enemy target. Its streamlined decks and armament identified it as deadly war machine. Children scampered up the ramp with their sightseeing parents. Permanently moored, old number 60, now retired, was an historic military museum. Picnickers visited this park dedicated to the Armed Forces.

After lunch, I traversed a split level bridge toward more island marsh and then solid land. The road forked at the stores of Spanish Fort. I bought provisions and drank chocolate milk with a gang of boys. A Shell gas station sold a Florida map. One state to go! I checked air pressure and rolled, but never made it down the hill. The bent spokes, carried for 2,000 miles, punctured the rear tire. It was difficult to patch because of an oddly shaped gash. With station attendants helping, it was fixed. But, filled with air, the inner tube had an air bubble sticking through the outer tire. It would explode with further riding. I was doomed! No bike shops this side of the river; I'd checked the phone book. A Western Auto Store was five miles away, but the tire couldn't last. The attendant, Mike Werneth, without hesitation, gave the keys to his new red Mustang. I hesitated.

"Go on. I'm insured," he stated.

For the first time in forty-five days I was behind a steering wheel. What a difference in speed! I arrived just before closing time and bought a new tire. Back at the station, it was a jiffy to replace the tire and adjust the wheel on the frame. After I'd gotten his address, we waved good-bye at 6:30. He'd get a postcard from Miami.

The last nine miles of the day wound through forests and pasture land. I would normally enjoy scenery, but the growing flu had me coughing, sneezing, dripping at the nose, stiffening up, and chilled, even in the 90° heat. Mileage sign: *Next Exit 18 Miles.*

No more riding. The off ramp led to a lonely all night gas station near Mossy Head. A man and his boy gave me the back of the building on a grassy slope. I wrote under florescent lights until the boy came out to shoot his air gun. Most of the time his dialect was unintelligible, so I nodded and smiled, hoping it would appease him. Small black insects, beetles, and gnats plagued my ears. I gave up, grabbed a bar of soap, clothes, and washed in the men's room. With a change of clothing I felt better, and could write. Under the insect netting, it was not so pleasant. Bugs somehow had entered the sleeping bag. Both nostrils were plugged, making breathing difficult. The full moon shone brightly in my face and heavy dew soaked the lawn and netting. And the last irritation, the slope's angle kept me sliding downwards toward the bike which supported the other side of the netting. The night passed slowly.   45 miles

THE LIMESTONE CAMP

Tuesday, August 1   Mossy Head to Ponce DeLeon to   Day 46
                       Caryville, FL

The dayshift man was annoyed at my presence.

"Hey, you! Hey! Come, get outta here. Yer bad fer business," yelled the day manager. He walked off with a scowl.

Everything was damp and took a long time to dry. To gain a few steadying moments, I shaved in the washroom, all the while my head throbbing from the flu hitting its peak, racking my body. The first neck of the trip lasted exactly one-and-one-half minutes, enough time to cross the overpass. My body wasn't ready, so I pulled into the competitor station for canned peaches. Feeling no better by 9:30, I pedaled in a mental fog.

Entering Florida seemed little different than Alabama. Neat orderly houses, farms, meadows, pine tree farms. Highway signs welcomed visitors, proclaimed speed limits, and warned litterbugs of $500 fines. As usual, brazen litterbugs had thrown refuse under the signs. A lady sponsor of the Florida Welcome House handed out tourist pamphlets and orange juice. Following her advice, I stayed on picturesque U.S. 90. Pilots from Pensacola Air Station, six miles away, tested Caribou helicopters and Army CH47 Chinooks. No detours, since I'm down to $12.00 and have 700 miles to go. I hoped the BankAmericard would be honored for a loan at a bank.

The afternoon was a blur. Occasionally I had spots before my eyes, and drove mechanically. Marshes, pine farms, low rolling hills, a railroad, and quiet 100^0 heat.

The day's last break was at De Funiak Springs at 7:00. The clock thermometer said 84^0, but I knew the temperature was above that. My reward for bravery above and beyond (or stupidity): a quart of soda and two ice creams. While I licked the ice cream cone on the Minit Store steps, a 300 pound lady looked at the bicycle, then me.

"You've got more guts than me," she remarked.

I smiled.

Once more I pushed into the dark, my goal, the town of Ponce de Leon. Cars could see me, but I felt guilty when they were surprised by the bike riding form. At the end of any cycling day, after sixty or more miles, it took ten minutes of rest to recover. Muscles full of lactic acid ached, joints were stiff, and tendons swelled. Slowly, by degrees, knees loosened by flexing. Numbed wrists, elbows, back, and shoulders, hunched by prolonged leaning forward, limbered up after rising from the crouched bike position. The sore fanny, no longer forced to support 175 pounds of side to side pedaling astride the hardnosed seat, said, "Aaaah," in relief.

A few store lights burned at the city wayside table, a sign warning against overnight camping. Seeing the town was asleep, I walked the bike behind the maintenance garage and set camp. Two couples in soft voices sat on the river bank. Frogs puppy-barked. I bathed in the men's room, indiscriminately sloshing water on body and floor. Refreshed, I wrote on a table until a long haired bearded fellow in leathers, rode up on a Harley motorcycle. He came to sleep on a picnic table. I laid down behind the garage.

I didn't get to sleep. Ponce de Leon was a limestone quarry for the I-10 expressway being built. Earth movers and giant front end loaders gouged white earth to feed hungry lime ore trucks which waddled away heavily laden. Day and night, gears ground and beepers warned of backing danger. Machines whined, diesels grunted. The noise a half mile away drowned out the river frogs.

Flight was inevitable. At 2:30 I gathered belongings in the cloak of night, dreading a ride with so many trucks on the road, especially after covering 126 miles. Strangely the muscles cooperated without complaint. A supercharged truck convoy growled by every other minute. I absentmindedly and sleepily had forgotten to put on the orange vest. Since only weak light came from the generator, I moved off the road as soon as I could hear trucks approach. At 3 a.m. I passed a long bridge with a park just below, but the truck noise was too great. Caryville. A couple street lights, a turn right, stop at railroad tracks, back into a church. Concealment behind a stack of bricks. Mosquitoes. Net up. 5 a.m. dozing. Roosters greeted the day.   126 + 7 miles

BANK SALVATION

Wednesday, August 2   Caryville to Tallahassee, FL   Day 47

Florida clouds neither cooled thermometers nor changed the barometric pressure. 9:30 was too uncomfortable for even pretend sleep. Caryville was a peaceful town, even with its sawmill. If anyone had seen me by the bricks, there were no repercussions, or maybe the church conferred peace.

Dwindled food supply: a handful of raisins, one plum, a nectarine, and a can of fruit cocktail. Food had never been a problem, but now with $8.00 left, a crisis was in the making. I needed money to finish the trip into Miami. I've counted on using the BankAmericard for a cash advance. In Chipley, a sizeable town, I asked a bank, three gas stations and a Sears store for credit card loan privileges, and was politely turned down. None honored the card at all. I was now worried. To help my financial thinking, I ordered a hamburger with everything.

Midway to Marianna, a roadside fruit market sold oranges for $1.25 (Vitamin C for cold) and a basketball watermelon. Lilly Guettlers, the sales clerk, invited me into the family home. They had sixteen kids, half of them married. Grandmother and younger girls watched a TV soap opera while I ate watermelon in the giant living room. Lilly played with her baby nephew. It was a close knit family. I bade good-bye, and placed oranges into the water bag, which now had a big frayed hole and no longer held water.

Mariana was perhaps twice the size of Chipley and more favorable for bank transactions. A service station and a Federal Savings & Loan refused, sending me to City Hall, which knew of no special fund or help, and referred to Citizens' National Bank. With great doubt I went. The banks here closed at 1 p.m. and it was already 2:50. The drive-up window clerk suggested the walkup window. I was astonished to find a teller.

"Yes, we can help you," she said.

I nearly fainted. A side door opened and a woman manager took charge, asking the necessary questions and identification. When she informed me that California allowed a minimum cash advance of $50.00, there was no delay in saying, "Acceptable".

Perhaps money made breathing easier, or quickened the appetite. I bought another hamburger. What else could you do with money, except spend it?

Fifty-six aggravating miles under a mental cloud, with a cold, hampered alertness. Low hills were just an inconvenience to progress. Rest periods were infested with tiny black gnats hopping on the sweaty red shirt, creeping on my face, and crawling into my ears. It was more pleasant to be on the saddle.

Further into Florida, near the Georgia border, Negroes were more in evidence than along the coast. Their living standards were nowhere close to the suburban homes of western Florida. Homes were again composition tar paper covering wooden shacks, some in worse condition than abandoned ones seen in Mississippi. Yet folks sat under rusting roofs, as the boards rotted, to watch sports cars whizz by. A market told a lot about a community. Gretna was all Blacks, good company, and peaceful.

After Quincy, evening riding glided along a divided two-lane. I pressed on to Tallahassee for two reasons, mileage and a laundromat. I haven't washed clothes for two weeks. Nothing dries in this humidity. Bacteria had created odors so foul that spare clothes had to be wrapped outside the bedroll. Route 27 was more hazardous than U.S. 90 having more vehicles, city drivers, drunks, pranksters, and unsuspecting motorists encountering a bicycle in the dark. Honks, swerves, curses, threats, and kicked up dust.

Universities have been safety zones. Students were lively, alert to the world, and eager to help. Florida State University was no exception. I purposely cycled in, knowing aid would be given. Dean, who never gave his last name, rolled alongside and offered his upstairs duplex. Students' bikes were chained to porches and doors of the 1920s gabled house. Junk cluttered the screen door entry and dusty hallway. A shabby dim front room, a bare kitchen, and a floppy bed. First a bath, then chicken stew. No more truckin' tonight! 100 miles

THE NAACP IN FLORIDA

Thursday, August 3   Tallahassee to High Springs, FL   Day 48

With Dean already in class, I left a thank you note. A bicycle shop sold three large red reflectors which I put on my hat, belt, and the bike rack for greater night visibility. Store owners backed away when conducting business with foul odors. Passersby gave annoyed stares. Smelling hot body steam, at the least, was unpleasant. Unfortunately, men rarely detect their own body odor. Clean laundry made a difference, whether worn, faded, threadbare, or torn.

A Black man and his son entered the laundry. The man, wearing a neat pin-striped dark suit, had mod sunglasses with metallic frames. He gave expert distance info and travel tips. I asked if he were a salesman.

"No. District Representative of the NAACP (National Association for the Advancement of Colored People)," replied the well dressed man. R.N. Gooden had been at the Association's recent convention in Detroit. There were conflicts between individuals or regions regarding priorities and tactics. Some individuals refused to come to order, because they weren't ready to. But that would be normal confusion when a delegation of individuals develop policy, compromises, and national strategy.

Florida ranked behind the states of Alabama, Mississippi, Georgia and Louisiana in integration. Alabama had more elected Blacks than the whole state of New York, and a county in which every election department had at least one Black. Similarly true in Mississippi, but Florida, according to the NAACP, had slid down the scale. On the surface, laws and public announcements proclaimed a liberal attitude and equal opportunities. In practice, segregation went on subtly. Only two Negroes were on the Florida State Patrol out of 1,500. All others were janitors. Minority councilmen and community programs were almost entirely White. The Urban Development Commissioner and his assistants were White. When complaints came from citizens, tokenism employed one or two individuals.

Housing was a simple matter. If one wished to know where the "nigger" section was, just head for the cemetery or the railroad tracks. The Negroes were on the other side. I found this to be consistently true in the towns visited.

Blacks, who got in school fights were suspended for the remainder of the year, while White students, after a reprimand, returned to class. In Jackson County, they objected to this injustice. While police watched on the school grounds, Whites beat the demonstrators with clubs furnished by the police. In the aftermath, Negroes were arrested for disturbing the peace. A demonstration march from Marianna to Tallahassee won little from the governor who claimed his hands were tied by the school system. Both the governor and the school system needed correction.

If the NAACP publicized facts, they were ignored. And one case was in point. In a different county, a Black man was arrested for speeding, but was taken to jail without permission to phone his lawyer. In the cell the sheriff beat and kicked him in the stomach. The prisoner subsequently died from his injuries. A complaint was registered, and the sheriff arrested. Bond was posted and he was released to continue his job. An indictment to bring him to trial was issued, but he argued for a change of venue because his White friends would let him off easy. It was granted. While the sheriff was being brought to trial for murder, he qualified and was allowed to run again for sheriff. The NAACP's part was to publicize and demand compliance with the laws, its main task being enforcement, for, although the courts have ruled for justice, the political administration must be coerced to act justly.

Travelers marveled at the lush beauty of Florida flora. A wayside park became an adventure out into the palms and ferns around a swamp.

At 9:00 p.m., the High Springs police recommended camping at a recreation park with a sand perimeter, fenced pool, boy scout hut, a stream, moss trees, and steel tables used in daylight by a farmer's market. Park lights revealed thriving roaches, and thus repulsed any thought of sleeping on the tables. Two girls clanked the bent pool's chain link fence and scurried away. Ripples rolled on the water surface belying their stolen swim. With the tent against the fence, I also stole a midnight dip. The head cold continued to interrupt sleep in the warm air.   54 miles

THE .22

Farmers arrived at the park at 7 a.m. to set up fruit and vegetable displays. Their kids played tag around the tables. With perhaps three hours of rest, I miserably consumed three cups of coffee with a ham and cheese sandwich. Still weak headed, I changed clothes. A half hour of riding, I found a second towel and doubled it to cushion my rear.

The sun beat down in breezeless force. Laconic grasshoppers didn't flinch, my warning shadow approaching, before tires squashed them. Even cars seemed slower in the humidity. Lots of reasons to stop: tire check; fill water jug; buy supplies; wipe forehead. My noon break excuse was to see the reptile farm (admission free). With a strawberry shake in hand, I gazed at wire cages holding monkeys, big cats, birds, and snakes in a private unkempt zoo. Since California, it has been true of most places advertizing animals-The Snakepit, Reptile Farm, Animal Land, Dogland, and others. Flapping pennants, flashing lights, and signs attracted the tourists. Gigantic signs in fresh red and yellow paint proclaimed a wonderland of animal sights, but the exhibits themselves were downtrodden and seedy, overgrown with bushes, trash littered, and decorated with green mold on walls and fences.

Turning south, Alternate 27 was bordered with ferns, oak and pines, and low palm fronds around marshes. Ponds dried to caked mud. The Suwannee River placidly crept under a short bridge, insect ripples visible. All other rivers flowed with red, gray, yellow, brown waters; the famous Suwannee was black. Fairy tale farms sat majestically behind long clean stable fences. Pastures were playgrounds for cattle and horses. A few Negro shacks stared out at the road. Sheds in peaceful cool sheltered groves, protected compressors and machinery.

Late sun blazed hypnotic rays on hay fields. My dizzy trance snapped just in time to avoid a black lump on the road. Backing up, I lifted a leather holster containing a .22 automatic. Releasing the safety and pointing at the ground. I squeezed the trigger. A resounding explosion startled cattle at the fence line. Checking to see if there were other shells, I fired a second round. This time the herd stampeded toward the barn. It was a tempting souvenir, but since I have not carried a weapon on this trip, in spite of advice, I chose to turn in the gun, rather than invite trouble.

At the sundrenched police station in Chiefland, I entered the office, sweating, pistol in hand.

"I've got something I don't want," I stated.

"What is it?" drawled the middle aged clerk.

"Probably a murder weapon, only I ain't confessing". It was a stupid attempt at humor.

He looked up at me, puzzled, laughed, then took down information, saying he'd check on the weapon. If nothing showed, the pistol would be turned over to the state armory. He used a sheet of paper to grip the hand gun and placed it on the desk. My fingerprints were all over the weapon. I thought about skipping the country.

To make Miami by Monday evening, I needed to average a hundred miles a day. Considering that the mornings took up to two hours to pack, check equipment, shave, and breakfast, I must ride an hour after dark. Road speed has been good at 12-14 mph with mild undulating hills. The four inch reflectors have been visible from 500 feet. Angry honking of surprised drivers ceased and, now quietly, they gave wide berth.

Modern Ocala had tripled its population in ten years to 40,000, its city life casting harsh neon and streetlight glare. Every intersection posed a cacophony of noises, dangers, posted laws, autos, and decisions. At 10:00 an elderly man gave me the front trees to sleep under. After dinner I sat in a lawn chair listening to the Atlanta Braves lose a double header. Under the netting I waited for the dew and drowsed, a neighbor's blaring party interrupting my slumber. A coughing fit refused to stop. Leaving my gear, I went in search of an all night market at 1:30. It took 40 minutes to buy cough medicine and Fritos. The medicine silenced the cough, the snack replaced excessive salt loss. Blissful sleep.   108 miles

A BAD DAY'S TRAVEL

The heat broke through the trees by 9:30. I sat in a lawn chair, groggy in the head, coughing fiercely. Exited from his house, Leonard Dukes greeted a neighbor and me. A police car circled the corner and stopped. The patrolman asked who I was.

"Did you have permission to be on the lawn?" asked the officer.

"Yes," replied Leonard. "It must be that nosey woman again".

"Yeah," the officer answered. "We get a call in this neighborhood every day or so about prowlers from a woman who refuses to identify herself. Sorry to have bothered you". He tipped his hat and returned to the car.

Leonard whisked me inside for breakfast. Besides assisting at a motel, he was an active 70 year old boating enthusiast, fisherman, and father of a 13 year old son. As I packed, the boy handed three packets of Kool-Aid to liven up drinking water. My noon leaving was too late to achieve one hundred miles for today. Resting under a tree, I wrote with an ice cream in hand. After 1:30 the bike rolled down the asphalt making slow progress and frequent stops. More spots before my eyes. Near 5 o'clock my head was spinning. A warning shivered through my body to get off the road. At a hillcrest stood a closed fruit market. I wheeled under its awning, sat on the hot cement, dizzy, lay back and slept for two hours.

Slow pedaling to Leesburg. Behind the school, I changed to cleaner sun-faded clothes, to attend evening mass at St. Paul's. Service ended with singing. While the congregation milled outside, I ducked back to the school, fearing my grimy presence would offend regular parishioners. With sweaty clothes back on, I repacked, eyeing rain clouds, made sure the reflectors were on, and bought travel food. The rear tire had a very slow leak. I hoped to ride until midnight to make up for the mere 30 miles I had made so far. In light traffic, under sprinkles and flickering lightning flashes, I pushed off into the shadows of orange groves.

Clermont's 200 foot tall Citrus Tower was the only witness of my arrival at 10:00 save for the puddles and lamp posts. A mobile trailer motel, in the completion stage, sat amid unpaved streets. Construction littered the area. One door was open. I decided not to sleep on the carpeted floor, as it would be considered trespassing. Instead, I connected the mosquito net from door to bike, and slept on the porch.   51 miles

CONFLICTS, FLATS, AND RAIN

Carpenters' hammering and wood sawing came from the Sunday construction crew rushing to complete the pre-fab motel and catch end-of-summer patrons. Bang, bang, bang, bang, buzz, whir invaded my makeshift Sunday revival tent. The radio was catching static on a single station airing a half hour religious commercial.

"Believe in Jesus. Give to our Southern Bible-centered church," the radio evangelist pleaded.

It was sad, listening to a minister retelling Bible stories through harrumphs and mispronunciations and bluster.

The construction foreman, accompanied by a bare-chested laborer, walked down the cement porch inspecting workmanship, frowned at my presence, and dodged my camp. Finished with morning rituals, I walked the bike over littered sand, past tourists at the souvenir shop of the Citrus Tower to a service station air pump. Fruit cocktail blessed the day's beginning. Kneecap bursitis felt like I'd knelt all night on a wooden floor. However, the flu seemed to be breaking up; coughing and sniffles lessened.

Sun cooked the orange grove soil. Free wild citrus melons at the grove's edge ripened like yellow striped rocks, but they were bitter. Walt Disney World lay less than fifteen miles east of Alternate 27. But I was dressed in shabby, dirty faded clothes. Besides, finances wouldn't permit. Disney imagination belongs to those who live other dreams. In the early afternoon, the slow tire leak became a rear flat in Haines City. My crushed tube of glue had leaked out and cemented socks together. A new repair kit came from the attendant who also asked for a postcard for his son's collection.

Florida road signs sported the motto: *Arrive Alive*. Other signs told of mechanical speed checks, or warned of $500 fines for littering. Wayside parks were announced periodically, though overnight camping was forbidden, a discouragement to low budget tourists. Travelers with money were welcome, but could not camp to enjoy the scenic beauty. This may encourage litter under shade tree pull-outs, where refuse was commonly thrown on the ground.

Far in the distance, autos swerved around a strange purple obstacle. Closer, the shape became an old woman in a sweater pushing a green wheelchair in the middle of the lane, heedless of danger or honking. Dumbly I passed her, and read the chair's title "Walker Hospital".

At the next service station I phoned a nurse.

"Ma'am, one of your patients is escaping. She's headed down the highway pushing a wheelchair," I informed her.

"Oh, dear, we'll check on it. She may be from the nursing home. Thank you".

The miles disappeared. Slow progress gave time to play games chasing cloud formations until they gathered to wash the orange leaves and spew on the small ponds and lakes. By evening in Sebring, it was pouring buckets. I've thought of a raincoat but discarded the idea. Rain has been warm, fresh, and cleansing. A coat would insulate, trapping sweat inside, making no difference. I dried in a truck stop over pie and a strawberry shake, then re-entered the rain, adjusted the reflectors and rode into the night.

Lightning flickered in the blackness. Then all the lights in town went out. My eyes searched desperately for pavement stripes. If there are hells for men other than fire, the terrors of darkness and the unknown rank high. A crashing overhead explosion rumbled and rattled the groves. Violent thunder ate away courage and infected the imagination. Wet pavement, sloshing mud, drizzle, laboring trucks were my highway demon companions.

As the night wore on, motels filled with cars. I was ready for rest when I reached Palmdale at 10:45. A downed power line had caused the blackout. Candles burned in distant windows. I lay down on the plastic tarp and bedroll late, too tired to care, a prisoner of the sandman.   122 miles

ALLIGATOR ALLEY AND ARRIVAL

Monday, August 7   Palmdale to Miami, FL   Day 52

Muscles refused to respond. Breakfast meant nothing. An hour's sit accomplished zero. There was only one recourse-bribery. A promise that with an excellent day of cycling, regardless of problems, I'd stop in Miami for a long rest, created instant enthusiasm passing the Miami marker: *121 Miles.*

Yes, the first hour's riding was shaky with leg spasms and twitches. Diagnosis: loss of blood sugar. Prescription: eat a whole bar of Hershey's Chocolate. In minutes, there was a surge of energy that never faltered the rest of the day. Each hour fruit, sandwiches, cookies, soda, and milk preserved the energy boost to slide by Lake Okeechobee, through the barren stretch towards Belle Glade.

Morning overcast did not reduce temperatures in the upper 90s. Desiccated brown swamp roots were encircled by rotting leaves on dark mud. The brief torrential rains were not enough to slake the ceaseless summer thirst of the land. Seared tall sugar cane discolored in the heat. Humidity permitted a thin green fuzz. The Everglade geography had no resemblance to the movie version of a dank marsh laden with hissing tongue-licking alligators lurking to gnaw arms and legs off unsuspecting nature lovers. The northern glades were covered with long saw grass blades 8-10 feet tall, thickly matted together, rooted in solid dry soil. If a man were to walk into these grasses, even for a few feet, he could easily become disoriented; there were no landmarks to obtain one's bearing. And the glades continued mile upon mile upon mile on the western side of Alternate 27. Water-pit sink holes every few hundred feet drained the land and preserved vegetation from the blistering summer evaporation. Along the eastern side ran a forty foot wide irrigation canal segregating pines, shrubs, low grass, intermittent rock quarries, and construction outfits. Farther south, sod farmers skimmed shaggy Bermuda grass, sectioned it, loaded squares on flatbed trucks, and shipped to the nearest client needing lawn.

Alligator Alley resembled the grassy bayous of Louisiana. Water meandered through treeless islands of brown reeds. A person, at water level in a flat-bottomed boat, had no distinguishable land masses, only reeds. For this reason, warning signs, posted on bridges and boat launch sites, demanded a red flag be mounted on a pole extending 10 feet above the boat for rescuers to sight; there was great danger of becoming lost in the monotonous grasses.

Men casting for bass on a causeway reeled in bouncing silvery fish on thin rods. At one muddy bank, an alligator chased a man's fish as he reeled in. The fellow turned his pole around and banged the gator on the snout. It reversed back across the water to hide in the reeds.

A storm raged violently far south. A tumult of clouds crossing my path dared me to ride farther. At a truck stop, I ate another of the countless burgers consumed on this trip, and changed into shorts in case of rain. At Andytown I tried calling relatives in Miami, but the phone was dead. Vending machines charged a quarter for a dime soda. In thirty-five miles, thirteen side roads led out of the swamp. Brown rabbits, used to traffic, scrambled into the bushes at the sound of a bicycle. A bar/fish-and-bait shop was the last rest break. The drunken owner and cohorts laughed at the bike and talked of other screwballs traveling the states.

Behind me the reflectors warded off cars and shone clear to California. Before me streetlights illuminated the path. Straight fast riding. Bumps meant nothing, nor did the rear wheel oval wobble. If necessary, I'd walk the last twenty miles. City lights grew in brightness. Stoplights winked a green go ahead. The outlying district fed to town to city. Hialeah glowed. Neons. A canal. A bridge underpass. Miami. I'd done it! Of course, one or two shouts were in order. It was 9 p.m. A quick thought of celebrating over a beer was scotched. Why do it? Drinking hadn't gotten me here.

Using a map, I roamed the strange streets. The numbering system made it simple to locate any address. The freight companies of 54th Street were closed down, but Negroes living in the vicinity gathered on porches and street corners. A few taunted, others warned Whitey to get into his own section. Most just ignored me. At a red light, a man and wife stared from and outdoor restaurant.

"Los Angeles," I yelled.

"Wow! You got a place to stay?" the boyfriend asked.

"Yeah, relatives".

Orange streetlights. Interstate. Side streets.

Finally, 67th Street. Pebble driveway. A girl, Chris, on the steps: "Hi, Edward!"

"Howdy, I'm the magic dwarf. Do you have any mail for me? No? Then I'll be on my way".

Aunt Irene came out and hugged me in my sweatiest. All the Bensons came to the front door, Karen, David, and Uncle Cliff in his shorts. Hugs and handshakes. But it was quiet. No fanfare. Just dwindling evening sounds.

Inside was a different story-a melee: questions, chicken popped in the oven, excitement. Suggestion of a bath, immediately acted upon. Hot water filled the tub with squeezes of dish soap for suds. I stripped off the rags and rewarded the faithful muscles with a soak. What a feeling to be really clean!

Back to the questions and chicken. A telephone call to Grandma. Another surprise, Mom was vacationing in Miami for a few days. Her fears and tensions about the trip disintegrated. My second call to California announced the safe arrival to the rest of my family. I had a bed on the living room floor, breeze, no covers, no mosquitoes, no interruptions, no noises, no trucks. Complete beautiful satisfying sleep.   121 miles

MIAMI

Miami Beach is a city of paradoxes. Beginning with its name, there is virtually no beach. Wave erosion has pulled tons of sand away from the coastline, now barely wider than a bikini. Skyscraper hotels are worried. Not only have they lost an attraction, the erosion hasn't ceased, and it threatens the hotels themselves. Cement dikes have been used to ward off the waves. Other hotels constructed jetties 200 feet out to catch migrating sands and "develop a beach". Sand accumulates on the southern side of the wall. At the same time the northern side is stripped clean. More sand disappears than is gained. Besides the hotel, the property owner on the north is enraged when his beach vanishes because of the jetty.

Hotel row, a series of 15-20 story buildings runs along a narrow coral reef on the ocean side of Biscayne Bay. Day or night the chain of high rise silhouettes can be seen. It is the mecca of the gods of sun and fun. Some have paraphrased it to "sin and din." Pleasure launches, sightseeing cruises, and fishing boats dot the inner harbor, a salt water lake. Fishing parties either troll or drift along the outside reefs for tarpon, sailfish, barracuda, red snapper, or sharks. Choppy waters prove men salty sailors or landlubbers in minutes; seasickness conquers men and women, boys and girls alike. First time fishermen are in for a bout. The trips sail for three hours, always within sight of shore, and then return for afternoon or evening groups.

Biscayne Bay varies in width from one mile. Both free and toll bridges cross the water to mainland Miami where weather rears contrary impressions. The reef beach receives constant cooling breezes up to three miles inland, whereas the interior swelters until winds arise. As long as breeze even trickles through the neighborhoods, it is cool. Summer is both sunshine and rainy season. Mornings are clear. Early afternoon squalls hit with random torrential downpours. In 10-30 minutes the sun shines again. Humidity stays in the 70s changing energy into lassitude.

Homes are CBS (concrete block stucco) construction, designed for strength, solidity, and coolness. Air conditioning is popular, but for those without it, the Florida room is used, a windowed space where louvers filter breezes. There are no residential curbs, excepting downtown and hotel row. Rain soaks into the ground rapidly. Where asphalt and curb meet, grass sprouts colorful strips in the streets and cars park off the green. In this semitropical locale, trees and bushes abound, peppered with roaches, nicknamed palmettos. No home is without one.

Canals lace communities near the bay and ducks swim peacefully. Residential areas are truly residential, for few neon signs clutter the night. Markets are generally confined to shopping centers, rather than sprawled on every street. Finding an address is simple. Instead of names, streets running east-west, avenues north-south, are numbered in four sections of the city: NE, NW, SE, SW. Example: 435 NW 56ᵗʰ Street. Any location is easily found. Rarely are roads named (e.g. Colorado Street); if so, they stick out readily.

For years, Miami had been the playland and second home for vacationing White businessmen. At one time there was a Negro town and Negro beach but now social and physical barriers have been eliminated at the beaches: rich or poor, black, white, Puerto Rican, or Cuban, the same sun and surf is enjoyed by all. Some people travel thousands of miles while others walk across the street. A number spend $100 a day at the hotels, a few tourists live in campers. Age, ability, background, language all wash away at the beach. The seashore is simply American.

In a clash of cultures, there has been hostility. Blacks preferred louder music and TV. Kids played more aggressively. Family fights spilled out windows and doors. English was spoken but used differently. Life styles varied greatly. Some Whites, out of fear or prejudice, put up For Sale signs and moved out. Sadly crime and prejudice followed the migration. Although Blacks have been attacked, victims were usually White. Windows have been broken and stores looted to the point that the windows have been bricked or cemented up. A few stores have a customer wait door so the proprietor can inspect before allowing entry. A gas station was robbed twelve times and the owner's wife killed. One particular corner business had been robbed with such frequency that it was labeled Crime Corner.

City officials and Black community representatives were trying to amend the status quo. Parks opened jazz festivals and concerts to lure young Blacks toward useful activities. A new effort had been undertaken where small businesses got a remodel or boost start. Counseling and complaint services were handled at a nearby office in the neighborhood. The model was Liberty City where the boulevard was renamed in honor of Martin Luther King. The results have been promising.

The southern tip of Florida is a loosely connected series of coral reefs called The Keys. Though some of the islands are large, most are thin, wooded grassy flats, dotted with houses on either side of the single highway linking all 165 miles of the Keys. Business executives and the more wealthy

123

citizens have built CBS homes on or near the water for vacation houses. Bays and inlets are perfect for lazy boating, fishing, or relaxation. Development companies, eager for profit, have bought up large tracts and are clearing away soil anchoring pines and sea grapes to build mobile parks. The selling of hideaways or senior citizen homes on the Keys creates a gross hazard for the future. These structures, built of flimsy plywood, supports, bracing, covered by thin aluminum sheets, and moldings to protect from the rain, are waiting disasters. The might of hurricane winds of one hundred mph would rip and tear all the mobile homes to rubble, if it didn't blow them out to sea. For ten years these parks have advanced down the keys. The next storm will be devastating.

I've taken several days to repair the lumpy rear wheel. The repair shop had a meager supply of materials. The repairman damaged the thorn proof tire while removing it, so the wheel was given an ordinary inner tube. Finally, the bike was cleaned and oiled. I bought new clothes, had my glasses fixed by an optometrist, discarded the desert water bag, gathered supplies, and most importantly, recovered from the flu.

There was a private ceremony. From out of a tucked away corner of the sleeping bag, I extracted the small vial of California ocean water. Walking across the beach, I opened the screw top and blessed the Atlantic Ocean with the Pacific Ocean water. Mission accomplished.

Relatives are the best people. Little attentions and courtesies, trips downtown, to the beach, sightseeing, cooking hearty meals. It was embarrassing to be a guest eating as much as a family of five, but I never refused a meal. In between regular meals, I found excuses for snacks, going to the bakers and shopping. Hunger consumed my thoughts for a whole week. I never considered how much the physical effort would tax my body. For one week we have been family. I'm strong again and reenergized. Tomorrow, I go north to New York.   No miles

UP THE FLORIDA COAST

Monday, August 14   Miami to Ft. Lucie, FL   Day 60

Quiet morning preparations. It was hard to say good-bye at breakfast. A written note was poor thanks for the Benson's hospitality. Besides, Cliff slipped me $10 for the road. At 9:00 the trip north began. A short stop at church to thank God for safety on the road, and to ask His continued blessings.

It was an easy decision to stay on the coast with the ocean breezes. A1A (Alternate) paralleled the beaches revealing mile after mile of cottages, motels and small cities. Often a bay separated the islands and mainland. Life was slow and patient. People lackadaisically strolled to market. Traffic was unhurried. Folks smiled and waved. Children played on spacious lawns. *No Parking* signs warded off bathers from private beaches in some areas; it was miles before the sun worshippers could find a public beach.

Some towns had snooty sounding names. Hallandale, Hollywood, Dania, Fort Lauderdale, Pompano Beach, Deerfield Park, Boca Raton, Boynton Beach. Names created images to attract a special type of immigrant, the sophisticated city escapee. Northerners have flocked to the balmy leisure life promised in the sunshine state, a cause-and-effect boom in condominiums. High rises fifteen stories were common. Advertisers touted the advantages of communal living for $20,000 and up, the curious end product being a whole new society settling in an "unspoiled beach" and "friendliness", and "security". Billboard glamour will fade. People will need to learn to live together.

Shirt off for a bit of tan. Because Palm Beach enticed, with the bike locked to a palm, I walked down wooden steps, removed shoes, wallet, and tools from pants pockets, and left everything in charge of an elderly woman. Soft white sand massaged itchy insteps. 80^0 water rippled in gentle waves. Tiny fish darted underfoot in clear water, tickling ankles and the unwary step. A dip in the waves was as good as a sauna bath, relaxing stiff muscles.

After Palm Beach, towns grew smaller. Tropical growth, thick along the white sand dunes, thinned out to a barren stretch by evening. A fish dinner at a small cafe brought a disappointing high price with poor quality and quantity. The owners were pleasant, though I felt irritated at their questions. Had the Miami layover altered my attitude?

Edward Abair

Late evening driving has become a habit since I bought the three large reflectors. The road bounced under the tires as the weak bike light sprayed twenty-five feet ahead. Neon lights and outspread houses welcomed in Fort St. Lucie as the body reached its limit. While talking at a service station, an insect landed on my left sideburn, which I swiped to brush off. A buzz later, stinging pain shot through my ring finger. The assailant disappeared but a red welt swelled the digit.

A man hesitated to loan his lawn, suggesting the water plant. It was unoccupied at night so if I left early no one would object. Furthermore, sleeping on the grass would be foolish because of fire ants. I cut across the wide lawn to the gray vat tower outline. Under dim street light reflections, buildings and tanks were neatly arranged. Two structures faced a side road, one a central office for the water utilities, the other housed water-plant controls. Behind these two were a thirty foot storage tank supported on cement blocks and two rinse tanks on steel legs. Sheltered between a corner of the control house and a ladder reaching up to the rinse tank, I made camp. A puddle underneath seemed no problem for the plastic drop sheet to cover. All food was placed high to avoid ants. Mosquito netting stretched from ladder to bike. Skeeters argued me into the tent with palmettos scampering on the net. Spare clothes rolled into a pillow cushioned the concrete. Technically, it was safe, though water leaked through the plastic wetting the sleeping roll. A crick in the neck made any sleeping position uncomfortable.   110 miles

ASSUMPTION AND RESUMPTION

Tuesday, August 15   Ft. Lucie to Titusville, FL   Day 61

The first workers clamored in at 6:30. Noisy cars, talk, clanging tools, footsteps. When they came upon me, two fellows stopped in their tracks, then laughed, saying it was lucky I hadn't drowned. The vat I slept under had an automatic blow valve. When the tank filled it spewed water everywhere. Fate had dictated that the vat shut down for the night. They told me to go on dozing, but the noise prevented it. I cleared out quickly, and none too soon. The blow valve spit just as I left.

I asked directions to church, because Catholics hold this day an obligation to attend mass in honor of the Assumption of Mary. With glistening morning dew, graceful boats on the canals, and first parishioners arriving, it was perfect timing for 8:00 a.m. mass. Inside air conditioning, outside 90⁰. People left for work. At a side door to the chapel I sat catching up on the diary, and fell asleep. The heat woke me at noon. Clouds gathered, and a heavy squall unleashed. I opened the side door for protection in church. It was cold but dry for writing and prayer. When the carpenter and his son arrived to finish cabinets, I was ending my notes and the rain ceased.

Already my schedule was in trouble for I had promised to meet cousins in Gainesville in three days. Total distance: 340 miles. With yesterday's mileage, I'd need to average 115 miles a day. It was 2:30 and not a mile covered. This meant no long rest periods, and night travel was a must. I had forgotten to get a telephone number just in case of a delay. Now the relatives would be worried if I did not arrive on time.

Farther north than Fort Pierce, rural communities are the rule. Flocks of billboards and road stands sold Indian River Fruit-tasty oranges and grapefruit.

"All the juice you can drink, 10c," said the come-on ads. Inside the policy was stated: "After a minimum purchase of $1.00".

Indian River coursed south, often wider than a mile, separated from the ocean by narrow reef islands; its salty water bred mosquitoes. Scenic grasslands and semi-tropic flora have anchored roots under water. Mainland rises were shallow, though increasing in frequency. Muscling against crosswinds used up the afternoon and early evening.

Titusville sat opposite the Kennedy Space Center. I regretted not having time for a tour because of single minded focus to arrive in Gainesville tomorrow. Weary legs, stiff elbows, sore hands and a neck ache denied comfortable biking positions. Entering Titusville around 10:20 p.m. was some relief, thinking I could make twenty miles extra by midnight. The flat tire took me by surprise. Ahead were two closed stations, no others in sight. Expensive motels on all sides glimmered under soft lights. I refused to accept the delay, trying to think of cuss words. The effort was too much, bewildered, angry, disappointed, and worried how to reach Gainesville on schedule.

On a spit of land, covered with dry grass, jutting out to the bay, white lighted missile gantries stood as skeletons across the water. A brisk wind arose. Plops and feverish splashing indicated night feeding fish. Mosquitoes did not heed the wind, necessitating a quick camp on the hard sand beach. A crusty plank across a solid bank held one side of the net. Straps were secured to the bike. Exhausted, I ate a cantaloupe, and fed a spoiled pack of meat to the fish before sorely settling into the net. The bites tonight were not from mosquitoes. Instead they were from sand fleas. I'd parked on top of a nest. All night they cavorted on the plastic. Little sleep.   99 miles

AGGRAVATIONS

Wednesday, August 16   Titusville to Gainesville, FL   Day 62

The Flea Olympics took place at dawn. Thousands of 1/16 inch insects bounced on the ground, hopped on the net, and did six-legged summersaults. A few frolicked on the tent netting, others simply dined. My hands were swollen itching clubs. Before leaving the protection of the net, I packed everything. Ridiculous! There was no room for a clumsy six footer to maneuver under a 2 1/2 foot ceiling.

Compressed air for the repaired tire leak, a bathroom and sink for shaving, plus peace for breakfast. Today's drive of 142 miles began at 8:30. Expected saddle time: thirteen hours.

The road moved inland where ground palms covered open spaces between pine forest groves. Many flat areas lay under water. Dead snakes, rattlers, coral, and water moccasins lay on the road edge, crumpled victims trying to cross the highway. Black vultures swooped down from tree tops to feast on armadillo carcass cuisine.

From the start, I misdiagnosed a queasy feeling to be low blood sugar, and filled my stomach with a quart of soda. I did the same at Edgewater, adding candy bars and coffee cake. The woozy head remained dizzy, so I slept on a weather beaten bench while passersby gawked. Eleven o'clock showed small improvement after a bowel movement. Heat in the nineties relieved the dizziness. Toby's Fruit Stand offered citrus for 50c, one grapefruit and five oranges. I ate two oranges quickly. No gastric change. In Daytona Beach, I tried another bottle of 7-up to settle my stomach. The hot sun turned it to sweat. I pushed on. It wasn't until I ate the grapefruit that my system came under control. Almost instantly I felt the change. Sixty miles of misery.

Bunnell turned inland, west on State 100, through successive groves of sixty foot pines. With a tailwind, the bike hit express speed. The chain whirred around the sprocket, gears whirled and the wheels spun in fresh rhythm. Western sun faced the oncoming bike, offering a chest sun tan-a rare occurrence; the back normally received most of the sun's rays. Because traffic was light, I attempted removing the red shirt without first stopping. Steering the handlebars with the left hand, I grasped the left side of the jersey awkwardly pulling it toward the shoulder. Then I switched hands and pulled up the right side. It proved easy-too easy. And stupid. The contents of the shirt pocket, my glasses included, spilled out onto the pavement shooting by. Items bounced, hopped and skipped. A lens popped free, tinked, and rolled. I jammed the brakes, dropped the bike and ran back. A car was coming. I snatched up the gold frames and the undamaged lens, guessing the Good Lord was still blessing me when acting stupid.

Speed into Palatka was better than seventeen mph-the best in several weeks. A luxurious dinner, rest and conversation lasted for an hour, the reward of the first one hundred miles. The last forty-two miles raced by rolling hills amid peaceful lakes and ponds, where homes lolled and lazed. Clouds gave delicate blues to the deepening shadows. By Hawthorne, at dusk, there were but sixteen miles of night travel.

Gainesville was a loosely cropped town. Houses spread into the dark without neon clutter. Streets were arranged in numerical order as in Miami, but I still got confused. At 9:30 I knocked at a green stucco house. Dennis Benson answered, his wife came sharing his amazement. They had waited for a cousin dine out. That first required a shower and change of clothes. Dinner was merely an excuse to laugh at our idiosyncrasies. I made up for lost sleep.   142 miles

UNIVERSITY OF FLORIDA SCENES

Thursday-Sunday, August 17-20   Gainesville, FL   Days 63-66

Gainesville, home of the University of Florida Gators was sequestered in a forest. After parking a mile from the classrooms, then catching a bus to the interior department clusters, 23,000 students venerated its halls of learning. The University had acquired land and a few odd properties-a plane for the football team and a two-man sub for the psychology department. The inner workings and expenditures of a university are amazing. Several specialty journals cost $100, the library spending $20,000 a year in periodicals alone.

Exploring the campus, I gained access to a special research building where study of the activity of individual brain cells in chinchillas was being conducted. In the lab, the animal was first anesthetized to prevent any interference from muscular twitching. Two earphones were inserted, one in each ear. These helped steady the head on the table. Next the head was shaved and the skin carefully cut down to expose the cranium. Then, using a microscope, three holes were drilled in a triangular pattern, delicately avoiding rupture of the durum protecting the brain. Finally, a stainless steel electrode, drawn to a thousandth of an inch in diameter, was inserted into the top layer of red and white durum. When preparations were completed, the experimenter closed the sound proof door to the chamber and began monitoring the brain's response to varied sound waves, noises, intensity, and pitch. Using an oscilloscope, he estimated the cellular field responses and recorded data on a computer and tape. When the electrode came into contact with a single cell, the experiment ran through a wide range of activities until the cell died in three to four hours. Then began a search for a new single cell. The chinchilla remained marginally awake but paralyzed throughout, until it was given a lethal overdose of a drug. A chinchilla's brain has a structure and stimuli pattern similar to that of humans. The scientist's purpose was to gain more accurate knowledge of how the brain correctly receives, interprets, analyzes, concludes and responds to stimuli.

The mystery of brain reaction can be seen in this example. A match burns the fingers of the left hand. Nerves fire electronic impulses to pain centers in the hand. The severity of the pain is immediately chain-relayed up the arm to the central nervous system which interprets the problem, notifies the brain and waits for the right half of the brain (which controls function on the opposite side body) to order the response back to the hand: *Remove from Fire.* All the activities take place in a split second. If scientists can crack the response pattern and understand the mechanisms, they will have a better picture from which to treat brain damaged victims. So experiments continued into the engineering design in God's orderly universe.

In the afternoon, I sought out another cousin, Rick who was the University photographer. We spent time developing pictures, comparing automatic processes, wide angle lenses and photos. He answered my flow of questions as to what makes a good photograph. How is a picture composed? balanced? lighted? In the darkroom, he taught me how to develop and add tone. For years it had been easy to glance at a photo and shrug, "So what?" Rick demonstrated knowledge of black and white shots and explained that color is much more difficult to control because it required critical developing procedure.

At night, we hauled cameras with friend Bob, roaming the campus with lighting experiments, variances in poses, flashes, trick shots, and gimmicks, such as standing headless or bodiless behind walls, or like contorted football referees, or two-headed goblins, or in jumping poses. We even tested delayed action shots on a busy street corner. In the dark room, we viewed our artistic endeavors. Some were complete failures, others good. Most were mediocre-a predicament that photographers accept. Much of their work does not pan out as expected, so they shoot several pictures to get one good one. In this sense, photo art is wasteful and consumptive.

Near midnight we went for beer at a topless bar. The atmosphere was subdued, lit by ultraviolets. The walls were painted black. Raucous shouts came from some of the men seated at tables. No one stood. A burly doorman insured that there would be nothing out of hand. Customers were almost entirely male. At one time there were five women with their husbands or boyfriends. The whole room was filled with blue choking smoke, which soon caused eyes to water and burn. Girls danced in relays. When it was her turn, a girl would remove her bikini top and dance on stage, or, for a dollar extra, on the patron's table. The dances were supposed to be seductive bump and grind, but the distant, bored look on the girls' faces belied their disinterest. One dancer's gaiety made her seem the life of the party, until she spoke, revealing her ignorance and shallow thinking. How could a woman make topless dancing her life work? What does it say about her talents and limitations? Would Women's Lib sanction this career? I get one credit: for having gone to a topless for the first time, my eyes didn't pop out of their sockets. It's weird to envision cellular composition, nerve impulses, skeletal structure and biological systems dancing on a platform.

Gainesville, as a college town, took advantage of the youth job market. Bosses begrudged giving the $1.65 minimum wage, but knew that they could avoid higher salaries because of the large number of students looking for work. That attitude had spread to department stores and city businesses which depended upon and exploited students. The University, the main business of the city, employed over 6,000 adults for school functions. If the school and its 23,000 students suddenly were to leave the city, it would become an instant ghost town.

Mary, Dennis's wife, taught Law at the school, studied for her bar exam, and worked for the District Federal Court-a busy woman's life. Her involvement in the court has indicted kidnappers, hijackers, white slavers, extortionists and killers. On occasion, cases settled out of court saved judicial expenses, though some people would prefer to see the full penalty of the law applied. The accused, not getting the maximum penalty, must accept 10-30 years. And the problems of justice go on.   No miles

MOVING ON

Dennis and Mary were both gone early, leaving me to writing. Journal keeping is nearly impossible when one relaxes. Then, when the harness of putting thoughts to paper resumes, half a day disappears under an ink pen.

Today, a half day of travel began at 4:30 with a jaunt to town for a map of Georgia and directions to Highway 301. Dismal, brooding clouds built on the horizon. In an hour they cried on the pine forests. Cars spewed mist high over the narrow pavement during heavy downpour. On the left, a shed lean-to housed calves penned in narrow stalls. A large woman watched from a corner of the shed, then beckoned two old hands to come out into the rain with the tractor. They were clearing low ground palms. The three talked of their baby calf farm, and their new problem of an alligator which had just commandeered the drinking hole to lay its eggs. After the rain passed, the highway dried under winds stirred by speeding vehicles. Clean forests are a remarkable sight along the roadbed.

Night. Baldwin on the edge of Jacksonville. Weekly phone call to reassure parents and learn home news. As I hung up, a police car circled the closed gas station and I signaled. The officer recommended not sleeping in town, nor asking for a lawn to sleep on. His advice was a park a mile further up. I bought a quart of 7-up from a package store, talked with the girl for a half hour, and rolled on. Quiet. Breezy.

The wayside park had eight tables to choose from, under trees. In the dusk, by the stream, a man, his wife and son fished for minnows by flashlight. More annoyed by mosquitoes than stories about snakes and streams, I set camp on the ground, heavy truck traffic bouncing over the bridge. Navy jets streaked overhead on night scrambles from the Jackson Airbase, crickets and frogs joked on the riverbank, and trains rumbled past. At least I think I slept.   52miles

GEORGIA ENTRY

Tuesday, August 22   Baldwin, FL to Jesup, GA   Day 68

From the riverbank, two young boys splashed the water with their fishing poles. Two chubby girls, also with poles, stood under branches leaning into the water. Together they giggled, snickered, and snuck furtive glances. I spent a morning lazing in the netting, watching clouds drift above the tree leaves, listening to quiet sounds of the stream, walking along the water's edge looking for pollywogs and minnows, writing on cool shaded benches with the radio playing softly. Early afternoon clogged with clouds. The kids left, and picnickers arrived for family lunches and frolicking at the stream. I pedaled to a garage/market to buy sardines and peanut butter crackers. My body dictated what it felt like eating and then washed it all down with soda. The stream kids returned to the store and made fun, but their father's presence tamed them.

[Lesson: I have a new attitude. Enjoy each state. Do not worry about mileage. Why be anxious if I make less than fifty miles a day? I want to visit the country.]

Swift and smooth narrow Highway 301 grew easier as it joined a wider double lane stretch at Callahan. Pine forests along the sides grew tall and dense. Occasional patches were bare from loggers' chain saws. Some sections already sprouted grass, others had two foot replants. Logging trucks chugged under their loads. One sort of load was a log pile of forty footers extending their stripped trunks out behind the flatbed, waving a red flag. The second type of load was a stack of eight foot lengths widthwise against the cab, and ten feet tall to the end of the bed, the wood being secured with chains. The logging trucks rode throughout the day.

Crossing into Georgia over St. Mary's River had little change in terrain. Hills, slightly more frequent and steep were hardly a cycling problem at 60-70 feet high. Ground palms had disappeared, while pines were as thick as Florida's. More noticeable was the landscape free of billboard clutter. Smaller towns were limited to essentials of grocery, gas and dry goods. Buildings were smaller, simpler in design, and their wooden sides had a less rigid appearance. Lawns were not scrupulously kept, but were neat. Blacks and Whites mixed together. Judging from rural freedom, crudely made posters, and the absence of neon lights and city headaches, sophistication was unknown and unwanted here.

Forests were no place to hide during rain. Skinny trees were branchless and leafless from base to fifty feet above. Gusty winds announced just prior to rainfall, but there was no shelter. If one estimated a light rain, and misjudged the torrent, there was no pity. Trying to dodge raindrops behind a pine tree was like standing under a sieve sifting champagne; it tickled as it wet. You know you're soaked when socks crawl down the ankles to swim in your water-tank shoes. It was quite an experience to wash clothes while still in them. The last thing to do was wring them out.

I stopped at a restaurant to squeeze clothes dry a second time, and moan over my shortsightedness. I had neglected to wrap the sleeping bag properly in the plastic tarp. Both rolled ends were soggy. Fortunately, the other patrons ignored my wrinkled duds after I ordered a traveler's delight burger. There was a problem knowing where I was. Many small communities, i.e. a bar, barn, grocery, or three houses perched together, were not listed on the map. At times it was not evident whether a city was near. Some side roads attached to the main artery, but were not shown on the map.

[Lesson: Because night travel difficulties had increased, and rural folk would be more leery, (meaning shotguns at a late night door knock) I must find a place before dark.]

Fifteen miles from Jesup, a tall pointed black roof jutted out of the skyline. I turned into the driveway of a barn converted into a market. A man watched silently as I asked to sleep on the lawn. Without saying a word, he rose, climbed the wooden steps, and got the owner.

"Yes," responded a jovial Jim Davis giving a sharp look.

After encouraging me inside, a fullisade of opinions, questions, and conversation began. Except for a coke and a few breaths, there was no chance to stop talking. In the next three hours, he and Jeff Manning touched every subject that crossed their minds: bikes, war, Vietnam, schools, poverty, death, ulcers, food, accidents, poison, books, TV, Democrats, movies. Jim sat on an old red Coca-Cola cooler. Jeff mooched pastries and soda. During the gab, roaches ran up and down the tables, scampered on the floor, and investigated the trash. At 11:30, I camped under a lone pine next to a hog pen. Mosquitoes landed in a crease in the net ceiling, and I applauded their acrobatics. They got caught between claps. Hog aromas drifted over occasionally. Trucks growled by. My sleeping bag was wet.   75 miles

UP IN THE AIR

Ants were feasting on the spent ravioli can of last night's dinner. I began to wonder about my diet. The appetite was healthy. I ate plenty of fruit, veggies, pastry, sweets, soda, and milk often, at least every hour. But worry existed over the weird taste combinations, for instance, today's lunch. Guayaba fruit bar (sweet), canned pears, cokes, and a can of chili. The chili lost its taste after a few forkfuls. A look at an old bony hound dog gave me an excuse. I poured the can contents on a cardboard. He ate with relish, licking paper and the ground. The peppers, however, must have been hot, since he went for a drink shortly afterwards. So, what's happened to *my* stomach?

Rejoining Highway 301 on the other side of Jesup, a struggle commenced. Heavier traffic buzzed past. Drivers, fearful of a bike on the road, slowed behind until they could cut around wide, and sped past. But such action was not necessary, even though there were no shoulders. The lanes were wide enough, and I wasn't daring to ride out into an accident in the traffic lane.

After the sweet-sour choking odors from the ITT Chemical Cellulose plant outside Jesup, traffic was building. Steady nerves held the bike true to course on the extreme edge of pavement. Cars shot by, a pickup honked angrily, trucks lumbered heedlessly. Paralleling Highway 301 on the right, across a median strip, lay the old abandoned highway whose asphalt was split and badly cracked. All its bridges were removed or washed away. For safety's sake, since it contained no vehicles, I chose to ride its length, cutting through the grass dividing strip and pumping for maximum speed. There were chuck holes to dodge. Then I discovered the reasoning of the abandonment. A deep trench cut across the entire width of the road. With less than fifty feet for stopping, I grabbed both brakes, squeezing as hard as possible. Squealing rubber pads slipped against the aluminum rims. The front wheel dropped suddenly into the ditch gap, banging into the asphalt abutment on the other side. The rear tire lifted straight up, suspended in the air, balancing on the front wheel. For a split second, the bike stood on its nose, threatening to flop over. The gold rim glasses fell off and smacked the ground. My arms completely supported my weight. I did not dare move either foot for the bike would topple to the opposite side. Then, like a reprieve, the rear tire fell back to earth, bounced and stayed upright.

Shaken, I laughed, picked up my glasses, and sprawl-rested on the bike. More trenches loomed on this old side road. Enough of the dangerous "safe" road. I cut left to fight vehicles for ownership of the highway.

In Claxton, I phoned a Statesboro army buddy not seen since he left boot camp for Germany. (Pay phones were different in the Southeast. The caller placed a dime in the slot *after* reaching his party.) Mrs. C.L. Daughtry, mother, answered. She called her son while I cycled to Statesboro. All traffic lessened, except for logging trucks. In the dusk, yellow and red truck lights outlined semis crawling up grades. And a new cargo was identified by the aroma of tobacco. Honks frequently insisted that I drive off the pavement lip. As I rounded the curve into the street lighting of Statesboro, the danger of vehicle volume ended. Phone directions to the farm were denied.

Mrs. Daughtry said, "Patience. Wait to be picked up".

While slurping a celebratory strawberry shake in front of a swanky restaurant, a scratched blue pickup braked to a stop in the parking lot. The stocky driver behind the wheel, C.L., was no longer the skinny farm boy in the San Antonio, Texas, army barracks, though as calm and gentle as ever. Bicycle in the load bed, we jounced down moonlit dirt roads, weed patches, gardens, and farms with searching headlights. I could never have found the farm.

We paid respects to C.L.'s mother and sister before riding to Herndon, population 28. Our route wound under arching trees, over wooden plank bridges, back roads, past darkened solitary houses hidden in the fields. Not another vehicle was seen for thirty miles. C.L. dropped left down an embankment to a mobile trailer, honked, and parked under the trees. Sandy woke up to cook steaks for the two of us, then went back to bed. C.L. and I laced together three years of life threads. Way after midnight he hit the sack. I confiscated the couch.   71 miles

GEORGIA SCHOOLS

Sandy and 2 1/2 year old Brian made kitchen noises until C.L. twisted my toe for breakfast. We ate with gusto and dressed for school in sport shirts, Sandy in jeans. Sandy taught kindergarten; C.L. was an industrial arts instructor. Morning roads were shrouded in fog-mist, cool, ghostly, mysterious. It crept over hedges and swirled around cars. We dropped Brian off at the babysitter's and clocked in 8 a.m., as required at Millen Elementary School. Georgia schools had a 180 day year. Teachers began the last full week of August; students came the next week.

Millen included grades 1 through 8. Junior high grades 7 and 8 were deliberately added to elementary for financial reasons. Rural schools were as costly as in the city, but funds were harder to come by. The school was arranged in a series of one story red brick buildings. In the rear, two mobile trailers under Title I federal grants (subsidies to schools) served primary and kindergarten for socially and economically deprived children (S. & E. D.). Basically, it allowed a fixed sum per student, up to a maximum of 20 per class. In order to obtain such funds, the school must have initiated a course outline together with certification of students who take the course, on the basis of a qualifying test.

School administrators throughout the nation have rethought this process in hopes of acquiring more money. By making course outlines vague, the money could be channeled into areas on the periphery of original intent, such as typewriters or painting the classrooms. Also teachers who have classes composed entirely of S. & E. D. children would thus have their salaries paid by the Federal Government and the county could shift that local salary money elsewhere.

But problems arose. Limitations on some of the grants prevented money from being spent on some school essentials; it was to be spent only on a qualifying class program. This excluded remodeling the school or repairing plumbing. Teachers were disgruntled by this system, because they were tied with money they couldn't use for things they needed. Furthermore, the system encouraged principals to develop classes composed entirely of S. & E. D. students. A good teacher faced an enormous teaching burden. Because they were not S. & E. D., advanced students were precluded from woodwork or drafting They were steered to other studies. School financing gained money but sacrificed the student's electives.

About 17 percent of Millen students were Black. When the courts ordered integration, in 1968, segregationists revolted, pulled their children out of public schools in the South, and started private ones. In certain instances, White public school superintendants sold unused school houses for nominal fees. In one case a county high school was sold for $1.00. The courts banished this practice. Financing for the private schools came from big money operators and people with political and social pull. A road was paved out to a private school in the same area where Negroes waited ten years without success for pavement.

Segregation was struggling to survive, but at a costly price, not money. A number of White children were being educated away from the community they lived in. How could they learn to get along with Blacks or anyone else who thought and lived differently? Unfortunately, the students became victims of their parents' fears and frustrations. Few teenagers could refuse their parents' demand to attend segregated schools. Eventually, they must and will mix in college, hence, the farce of the private segregated school. If adults denied the existence of segregation, all one needed to do was read the sports page of the local newspaper to see the pictures of the high school football team. The photos were black and white, the teams were not.

Negro students also suffered from the White pull-outs. It was more difficult to advance socially and culturally without crosscurrents and peer learning. When a child saw another doing math, writing, sewing, drawing, or cutting wood on a jigsaw, she/he learned by imitation. Parallel interests allowed people to see how others think, work, and relax. Without peer-to-peer cross learning, separatists crippled Southern progress. Certainly, learning standards would be temporarily lowered as both groups adjusted and bolstered each other's education. Though it may take years, youngsters will survive and learn to get along.

Sixth grade teacher, Mrs. Howard, was appalled at the lack of education her students had been provided by supposedly good White teachers. Some children could not read or spell words of more than five letters. She used first grade reading charts that had pictures to remind students which picture matches the word: plane, ball, cup, hat, etc. Few children could write, and were easily frustrated putting words, much less ideas, on paper. She asked pointed questions: "Where have they been all this time? What were the teachers teaching for five years? How was this allowed to pass?" A guess would hold that prejudiced educators expected Negro children to always be farm laborers, chopping cotton, hauling tobacco and doing menial tasks. Therefore, why educate them? Another answer might be that teachers never realized the cultural blight children might grow up with. If his parents couldn't read, whom did the child ask for help with homework? How could he grow to love books when there was no dictionary at home to look up unknown words. Over the years teachers expected children to absorb the material quickly, when, really, the livelihood of a crude shanty is crushing. How did a kid study homework without electricity? How much educational makeup and review was necessary to develop a powerful vocabulary? What would it take to teach writing and self expression after 5 years of wasted incompetent teaching? Was it any wonder that absenteeism ranked high among Negro students?

C.L. dedicated himself to developing pride and enthusiasm in his classes. He started the year with a quickie project, usually woodshop. Students operated a saw, used hammers and nails to manufacture a puzzle. Having surprised themselves, they realized they <u>could</u> accomplish something. During the remainder of the year he helped them do projects that showed the scope of business: Product need, capital (stocks), tools, designing, machinery, refining, salesmanship and profit.

His methods succeeded beyond expectations, one year, when the classes designed their own fancy, miniature wooden racing cars powered by CO_2 cartridges. Students spent the day in racing competitions in the gym as children from other classes cheered. Regardless of winners, all the boys were noticeably wearing proud smiles. So remarkable was the event that the newspaper produced a photographed article on the races. C.L. brought clippings to the former principal, who glanced at the Negro girl and White boy in the photo, and complained, "What are people going to think?" C.L. took the clipping and found no reason to speak to the principal for the remainder of the year.

The afternoon thermometer rose above 95^0; humidity topped 86 percent. At 2:30, we entered the library for a faculty meeting. Five male teachers, outnumbered eight to one, were responsible for importing fans to cool the room. The meeting began, progressed, and ended with the usual first week of school confusion. Schedules indicated class arrangements and size. A few teachers were angered, others griped according to custom. C.L., given six S. & E. D. classes, was dismayed. Sandy met us and cried over C.L.'s schedule.

We sat in hot car seats, rode silently to the market, and picked up Brian who was crying because he thought Mommy had gotten lost. We cooled off with ice cream cones. We cooled better with the air conditioner.

"Want to go fishing?" he asked.

"Sure," I smiled.

"Well, let's load up the truck".

An aluminum flat-bottom draft, two brown cane poles, a tackle box, and we were ready. At the country store, a bait clerk reached into a deep wooden box for a scoop of crickets and shoveled them into a cricket cage. Back down the road, over the bridge, a dirt path overgrown with thicket scratching at the truck. A river clearing showed a ramp down to the green-brown water. Sliding the craft down from the pickup bed, we pushed off the muddy bank, drifted, momentarily rocked, started the five horsepower motor and chugged downstream. The sandy riverbanks were impossible to see for they were covered with bushes, pines, cypress, and oak. Except for the river, there were no open spaces. Dead tree trunks lay in the water. Sometimes branches hid just under the surface lying in wait to snag a boat. We glided around these traps looking for quiet deep pools where big fish hid, testing their hunger. Occasionally we'd tie up at a log mid river or try still water lily ponds where insects frolicked on the surface. The stream slowed, cool and refreshing. Overhead clouds gathered, hid the sun, and drizzled. We paddled into a cove of overhanging limbs and continued to fish. The rain splattered circles in silver splashes; drips from the trees wiggled tickles down our shirts. Suddenly the poles' lines pulled straight down, tangling under logs. We braved the drops to come around the sunken logs, and placed new line and hooks into the sink hole. Nibbles. Yanks. Bass began slapping the floorboards. We both caught one pounders. C.L. had skill to pull his line taut with his left hand, aim, release, and have it land exactly where he wanted. However, he managed a paltry three fish to my eight. At dusk we motored back up-stream. It became dark before we had gone far, and had to cautiously study ripples by the moon's light to detect snags. Trees were silhouetted black against a deep blue purple sky. The evening spoke peacefully with chirps, croaks, and rustling leaves.

Home. A loving meal. A woman asking about her husband's adventure. A soft chair propped before a TV. A shared day.   No miles

GEORGIA FISHIN' AND EATIN'

Friday, August 25   Millen, GA   Day 71

A new day's fishing. A deep swift flow at the bridge met shallows slowing water to a twisting meander around bends, stumps, old cutoffs, sandbars, and islands. Brilliant daylight played on hundreds of speckled shades of green in the river brush. Drifting with the river, we cast into hollows of the growth, over stumps, behind rocks, and under branches. The rising river, gathering mud and leaves, skittered the fish. Even our lucky spot, the deep sink hole, was poor fishing. Two sunburned fishermen quit at 4:00, with three fish, others were so small they had to be thrown back.

Out for family dinner, we drove ten miles on open highway, lush with ripening corn, soy beans, and peaches, to a pond resort restaurant. We turned up a lane of pines to a row of dark red cabins. Kids were splashing mightily in the swimming pool. In the whitewashed lodge, we waited our turn for the knotty pine paneled room. A black waiter served shrimp. Brian said grace. After supper, we strolled the winding path around the evening lake. Large trout swam lazily in the pond, like shadows under the reflecting yellow surface. A waterwheel dumped its spinning tubfuls on rocks below. Shadows painted the land in dark blue tints. A fish hatchery park had the same beauty as the farms. Sweet artesian water welled from a blue sand lagoon. In the dark, we drove home on dirt roads, C.L. looking for snakes, because we hadn't spotted any live ones all day. Kicked up sand pelted the rear fenders; tires ground on hard tractor ruts. Trees protected us from moonlight peeking out of clouds. Weeds stood as dark brooms at the culverts. Headlights sped over orange sand. A rare amber house light stood in a field. We found dead ends and sleepy old shacks, but no snakes.   No miles

GEORGIA CROPS

Saturday, August 26   Millen, GA   Day 72

Georgia farms were arranged in squat crowded geometrical designs. Over short distances, terrain changed from corn squares to triangular tobacco and rectangular bean fields. Peach groves sat in chunks, while forests filled irregular designs. Statesboro area farms were among the state's richest soils. Acres sold for $500 and up. Since taxes were rising, as was the skill required of modern farming and machinery, so was the demand for higher salaries. In order to make $5,000 to $6,000 in a year, a farmer needed at least 200 acres. He must calculate against his limitations. Citrus crops and watermelons were not profitable; Florida's early growing season captured the market before Georgia had a chance, and the Carolinas caught the tail end of the season. Soil was not fitted to some crops, so farmers spread out risk. Peaches were popular, soybeans sold to the ever-increasing plastics industry, and wheat could be grown after the soybean harvest, which permitted doubling crops on the land.

Another crop was tobacco. The harvesting method was to pick the bottommost leaves as they ripened every 5-6 days. Leaves were tied in bundles and laid over a long pole placed in a curing shed. The farmer carefully maintained the temperature to dry out the leaves. During the night he rose to air the poles from the shed, and replaced them before the dew affected the tobacco. The final step was bringing the product to market under the auctioneer's staccato-tongue salesmanship. No matter what the tobacco sold for, the farmer's efforts went up in smoke. Oddly enough, in spite of the Surgeon General's danger warning on cigarettes, the tobacco industry was apparently unaffected. If anything, it was as big as ever.

Corn was left to dry on the stalks, then gathered as hog feed. At market, prize choice hog weight was 180-220 twenty pounds for 28c-29c per pound. #2 choice was 160-180 pounds (leaner but acceptable) for 24c-27c per pound. #3 heavyweights were 220-250 pounds for 20c-23c per pound. It was evident that farmers lost money on fat hogs.

Planning for future logging, lumber companies bought up many farms, fenced off the forests and tacked up no trespassing, no hunting, no camping, no fishing signs. Soon after, fires began breaking out in the forest. Whole areas were devastated. Company officials decided to forget the signs and open access routes through the woodlands to the rivers. They had been cutting the river access to men who lived nearby. Magically, the fires ceased.

C.L. and I sneaked out of housework while Sandy went shopping. Cane poles and tackle box in hand, we walked the thickets into the cypress swamp. A high leaf canopy kept us in gloom. Mud underfoot was slippery. During spring, high waters rose 4-6 feet higher than where we stood. Consequently, mud covered the low tree bark. At the edge of the swamp, we discovered a pond of trapped fish. With sunrays breaking through the leaves, we jumped over logs to launch our hooked crickets. The fish weren't biting. We explored into the deep dark trunk forest, slipping on the gushy mud, tripping on stumps, and plunging in gooey puddles. The growth was too thick to penetrate, so we backtracked to the pond. I lost my enthusiasm early, and sat to watch as my friend crossed the log bridge to toss his line. He slipped on slimy round wood, double shuffled, waved his arms, turned backwards, put a right foot on another log, waved frantically, stepped and fell backwards, creating a huge wave in the pond. Only his nose and glasses stuck above water. When he climbed out, C.L.'s first reaction was to bait his hook.

We waited until at last a jackfish fell for the hook. I promised not to tell Sandy about the bath. When we entered the house, she screamed.

"Get offa my clean rug with those shoes! C.L., you been swimming?" she scolded.

Shame-faced we ate. And argued football over a preseason game.   No miles

LEAVE MILLEN, ENTER AUGUSTA

Sunday, August 27   Millen, GA to North Augusta, SC   Day 73

Since there are just twenty Catholics in the area, there was one Sunday mass, which we missed. The schedule had been changed. C.L. used the trip as a final tour through Millen. Dark red brick homes sat on one acre plots, shaded by lofty trees. Tall grass divided property lines rather than fences. Streets curved around hillsides. Main Street's orange concrete buildings faced the railroad tracks along six city blocks. A farm equipment business displayed plows, scrapers, bailers, and other equipment unfenced and unguarded by the tracks. People of this community were not thieves. Across the tracks were the police station, a grain elevator and Negro homes. Most houses were of wood, gabled roofs, white exterior paint, usually weathered to dry patches or to bare brown lumber. Even with a yellow light bulb glaring, the interiors were gloomy, with furniture old, torn, faded. Two bedrooms never satisfied space for four, five, or six children. The neighborhood bordered on rundown.

Government funds started financing Blacks so that they may buy modern brick houses. These structures stood solidly and cleanly apart. Some families had already moved in. One of the cleaning ladies at the school said she went without breakfast and wore the same dress to church every Sunday just so she could buy her house. She was so proud. Everyone listened to her revel about the sinks, closets, bathroom, and kitchen at least five times. Progress had seeped into the community.

Tuna fish lunch, mushroom soup on bread, a departure meal. C.L. tape recorded the story of the bike trip to play to his students in class, as an example of dreams come true. Willie and James hung around at the door. They would be C.L.'s students. He inspected their non-turning front wheel, and promised to fix the bike after school tomorrow, when he could buy bearings. We piled into the truck, Willie in the cab, James with me watching the ten speed in the back. Wind rushed past our faces as the corn ears listened to our whoops and hollers. C.L. gassed up in Waynesboro-he'd been driving three days on empty-and took me to the city limits. We shook hands, the boys waved goodbye. I pedaled off to the beep-beeping trucks.

Hills teetered up and down, curved and rolled into Augusta. The city three lane highways were jammed with quick lane-change artists and red light traps. Augusta was situated in the bowl of a smoky valley watered by the Savannah River. Just off the bridge, three sunken wrecks lay on their sides. In the brief passage through the city, I learned two anecdotes. When the rains came to fill storm drains, residents called the police to save them from snakes crawling to higher ground. Augusta had the second highest murder rate in the nation.

An overpass led to South Carolina's North Augusta, a quiet pleasant town. Homes spread under leafy trees. Ben and Pam Johnson leant the front porch of their rented house, and let me watch television while a cloudburst broke outside. A mechanical architect and an artist by hobby, Ben was expertly skilled in both. An avid do-it-yourselfer, in three months, the husband and wife team remodeled the house interior, bricking the kitchen. After investing more than $800, the owner told them to move. They were buying a home and moving in five days. Bunked on the porch, trucks rumbled by. The 6-12 Insect Spray didn't prevent a couple of mosquito bites, one on the cheekbone, the other on the rump.   52 miles

A SAD HOUSE AND JAIL

Monday, August 28   North Augusta to Newberry, SC   Day 74

Pam gave coffee and juice for breakfast. I stocked groceries at the supermarket and sat on a lawn writing and drowsing. At 3 p.m., the road lifted up and out of town. As before, South Carolina roads were narrow and tree lined. Forest signs: *Prevent Wild Fires. Use Your Ashtray. Littering Highways Punishable by up to $100 Fine.* Slopes became 150 foot climbs. Countryside changed like the speed of a camera's click. Corn rows basked in the sun. A windfall of trees hid a bean field. Timber surrounded a groomed farm, followed by a bend, cutting through rolling pastures looking like golf links. Yellow hay lay stacked under a rusting tin roof. Fallow acres lay among fields of weeds. Cattle munched contentedly as semis shifted twenty-five yards away. A steep hill overlooked a placid meadow and another series of hills yet to be climbed.

A Johnston grocery clerk didn't believe someone could drink a quart of orange juice. She also refused to believe a cross country bicycle trip. The folks were kind, happy and gentle, even the undertaker, who worked in the store.

A deserted shanty off to the right appeared in a grove. During a peach-and-raisin break, I waded through a bed of weeds surrounding a porch. No snakes. Braver now, I mounted creaking boards to spy through the broken windows. It was too dim, so I pushed against the door. Dusty, moldering clothes lay strewn over the entire floor, worn shoes scattered on top. Walls exposed scrawny skeleton construction ribs. Some walls had a yellow fiberboard coating, as did the partially covered ceiling. A blackened chimney in the center of the house sat over a double-sided fireplace for the two front rooms. No kitchen sink or table. No pump for running water. No toilet. A gutted stove, the size of a five gallon paint can sat alone in a dingy corner. In the rear, a long bedroom had just exterior wallboards showing, making winter a severely cold experience here. A three foot drop to the back yard had no steps. Behind the shack, the forest grew dense.

Late evening shadows. The town of Chappels did not appear on the map. Two husky young Negroes said it was far off on a side road. Breaking my resolution, I rode in the dark. The generator light stopped working. I relied on reflectors. A Boys Farm watchman assured that the road, diverging into the dark, connected back to Highway 121 and Newberry.

At night, Newberry, South Carolina, looked like Main Street, Disneyland. Turn-of-the-century buildings in heavy gay reds, blues, and greens stood lit by bright street lights. Over the old opera house chimed a tower bell. A neatly kept park marked the center of town. The movie house ticket taker allowed the use of a wall phone for a long distance call home. I had just talked to my Dad, and was assuring Mom of my safety, when she asked what all the shooting was about. John Wayne was getting killed in "The Cowboys".

A young man showed the way to the police station behind the opera house, and pointed out barrel-chested Sergeant Campbell. The policeman offered an empty cell, a mattress, and a shower. The day's heat vanished under water spray, and two days' whiskers parted company. Following a dinner of two tins of fish steaks and pineapple, patrolmen grilled me with bike touring questions until 2 a.m., when I plunked on the jail bed. The cell occupied the center of the police station, where green steel bars let in whirring fan air, and the door stayed open. Once, during the night, a drunk, who thought he was in the next town, was admitted. He said he'd rot before paying a $15 bail.   64 miles

SMALL TOWN LIVING

Chief peeked in on me several times to make sure I hadn't died. He did order his men not to wake me, since a good bunk couldn't be guaranteed up the road. The banging screen door to the office finally became an alarm clock. I straightened to gather belongings from the storeroom, and strapped the bundle to the bike rack. When I came into the office to say goodbye, the chief was on the phone to the newspaper. I couldn't very well duck out with the chief of police standing there, so I consented for the third news paper interview and photo of the trip. The Newberry Observer paper came out twice weekly, and the reporter claimed that they rarely had anything exciting happen. This interview was a real treat.

I rolled back uptown to the doughnut shop across from the movie theater. One old store with a wizened gray woman sold day-old coffeecake. She ordered me next door to the magazine shop for milk. The second shop keeper talked excitedly, presented two homemade doughnuts and cans of catfish stew and chili.

"Look. See!" she told everybody, to my embarrassment.

Coasting down Main Street, past the jail, and around the corner, I left old white-washed wooden homes surrounded by geraniums and roses and yellow weeds. Towering above the city was a five story textile mill, one of three in the area. Northern industries were moving south. Plagues of labor union wage demands had blighted management profits. Businesses looked to the South for cheap labor, large areas open for development, and low tax incentives or tax-free five year plans. Companies built in small towns and even complete wilderness areas. Small cities benefitted as did Blacks, who learned skills, earned higher wages, and grew in experience and self-esteem.

Religious signs nailed along forest roads: "Do You Believe in Jesus? Then Follow Him." "Do You Believe That Jesus is Your Lord and Master? Then Obey and Serve Him.?" No denomination claimed the numerous poster works cluttering the woods.

For amusement, and curiosity, I began counting hills. In a thirteen mile section, twenty-six major climbs and drops occurred. Excepting bridges, straight-aways were uncommon. Broad River dropped as a chasm, between heavy brush and a hundred foot side bank growth. The river was almost spanned in some areas by arching limbs. Water ripples spilled over rocks and scurried around logs. Then the river hid.

A circular by-pass system, developed for the city of Chester, skirted noisy commercial vehicles around the city limits, leaving citizens unharried. Dusk descended at a hillcrest rescue station. Inside, county voting polls had closed, so counters tabulated the results. The police okayed camping on the park tennis courts. Bright lights played on the basketball courts where two groups of Whites and Blacks played at opposite ends. The Negroes played a faster and more aggressive game.

On a warped bench, I sat listening to the radio vote returns. For weeks the air waves had vibrated to the impassioned local political squabbles. A sheriff fought for his twenty-four year job on account of experience; the contender protested that experience, unused, was worthless, as seen in the county's unsolved crime rate. Councilmen, representatives, and other vote seekers all expressed a plethora of concern for the voter-lower taxes, more recreation, openness, justice, equality.

Earlier in the year, in Georgia, a candidate, running for County Sheriff, bought TV air time for his campaign. His platform held that he wanted his White friends to vote for him.

"To protect White women from niggers," he said. "You can't have justice and niggers, too". The TV station was appalled, rejected his views, and apologized to viewers, then complained, asking CBS (Columbia Broadcasting System) to prevent future incidents of tasteless politics. CBS refused, stating that citizens were educated sufficiently to discern for themselves. The candidate lost his bid for election, but 2,000 people thought enough of his appeal to vote for him.

Local politicians denied that they have bought votes, but rumors and gossip say that their tactics are virtually the same. Party backers paid drivers $25.00 to pick up voters from the rural areas, almost insuring votes. It was inexpensive in a small community of 6,000 where the winning margin might be only 200 votes. The most common inexpensive vote buy was a booze party within a week of election.

The boys stopped playing basketball, shut off the lights, and drove away. After camp was set on the tennis court, the White boys returned, flipped on the lights again, and sat down to drink and sling the bull. They offered a beer which I accepted. Shortly, when a car turned up the parkway, they heaved their cans into the bushes-underage kids. It was a false alarm and swearing broke out. They hopped back in the car for another beer sale. I sat reading Robert Frost feeling woozy, then crawled under the net with the lights still glaring. A fresh round of beer, loud talking, more bragging, and a stolen sex book from the store rack returned with the boys. One lad read while the others interrupted and horsed around. Conversation drifted to the local girls and who would and who wouldn't. Two girls were especially popular. They had more votes than all the politicians. Katydids cackled to each other in the trees.   43 Miles

Pauses In Newberry

An unemployed California high school teacher is using his time to see the United States — the hard way.

Ed Abair of Long Beach, Calif., paused last week in Newberry during a bicycle journey which up to that point had taken him more than 4,400 miles via leg power.

He spent a restful night at the Newberry jail, as a volunteer guest of the Police Dept. Staying there was his own idea.

Abair, a Vietnam veteran in his middle 20s, is both unemployed and single. He left Long Beach on June 17 with a free mind, a 10-speed touring bike and not much money.

Zig-zagging his way across the country, he has visited Memphis, New Orleans and Gainesville, Fla., among other places.

From Newberry last week, he headed for Charlotte, another way-station on a route which will take him to the Shenandoah Valley, Washington and New York.

Being without steady work in his West Coast hometown where teachers outnumber classrooms, he could take time to pedal all the way home if he wished. But he guesses he'll take a train after he sees New York.

His money is beginning to run out. He thought he had his budget figured closely before he left Long Beach, but didn't reckon on the amount of food he'd require to provide the calories for long-distance bike riding.

"It's amazing how much I eat," said the trim and well-muscled young teacher. "I find I have to stop for a meal five or six times a day. Food is costing me a lot more than I thought it would.

"Some days, I eat something every hour or so."

Except for two short rides made necessary by mechanical problems, he has pedaled all the way. In some cities, he has paused for a day or two to visit Vietnam buddies.

(Continued on Page 4)

HITTING THE ROAD: Ed Abair, cyclist from Long Beach, Calif., says a symbolic goodbye to a Newberry parking meter as he leaves town to continue his all-summer-long pedaling. Abair spent a night last week as a volunteer guest of Newberry police, pausing after covering 4,400 miles of a roundabout journey which won't be complete until he has toured Washington and New York. —Observer Photo.

Ed Abair photo taken by the Newberry Observer,
Newberry, South Carolina, August 28-29, 1972.

INTELLECTUALS

Wednesday, August 30,   Chester, SC to Charlotte, NC   Day 76

Lazy morning. Sun bath. A shave kept my face friendly for the locals. A speedy afternoon to Rock Hill. Kids on the 3 o'clock busses waved and shouted. Truck traffic was the heaviest yet seen. Often it was necessary to dodge into the weeds for refuge from heavy duty radial tires. At the North Carolina state border, the Interstate blended into Highway 29. Faster travel, but driving problems swelled. Factories, warehouses, parking lots jammed full of semis explained the traffic volume. Charlotte was a major trucking route, the second largest in the U.S. Two thousand vehicles left every morning. City roads were so narrow that diesel tires actually scraped against curbs to stay in the lane. Five o'clock rush hour tied up the drivers in debris muddled streets. Stop lights winked and ignored sweltering drivers caught by the red eye. The bike was forced up and down sidewalks, curbs, dirt paths, stone walks, and lawns, past ramshackle houses to the inner city, making good time-a possible eighty mile day-when a metal hunk sliced through the rear tire wall, punctured the tube, and left me staring at a green light at 5:30.

Although superstick tire patches covered the tube perfectly, the slashed tire wall bulged as if it were chewing gum, blowing a black bubble. I needed a new tire but had to ride over bumps and asphalt gouges. Easy does it. Neither the shopping center nor department stores carried the correct size tire. Phone calls reached closed bike shops. Overnight delay. To be close to a shop I pedaled forty blocks, then looked for a charitable homeowner. A brick home did not answer a knock. Next door, two bicycles on kickstands were on the lawn. At my knock, a young woman opened, called her red headed husband and let him decide. The backyard was okay. He introduced himself, Mike Mosley, who taught music, and his friend Chuck, a German instructor. Both taught at the University of North Carolina. Sharon invited me to eat while the two men asked me to join them at table discussing languages.

Our technical conversation concerned the rigid sentence pattern of English, subject-verb-object (S-V-O), and looked at variations permitted in German, Spanish and Latin. A question arose as to how grammar patterns and sound might influence the thought perceptions or psychology of various nations. Did the guttural sounds of German make them more brusque as people? Did language develop or retard intellectual growth?

Academic questions to be sure, but worthy of linguistic and psychological study.

We sat in the living room while Sharon, listening, painted the doorway white and finished the brown trim on the mantle and baseboards. At the university, Mike was involved with a BCA program, Bachelor of Creative Arts, unique in this country. The concept allowed a student to develop a program of study, along personal interests, mixing classes as she/he saw necessary, under the guidance of a resource counselor, the controlling principle being that students must show effort and progress in developmental lines. He might pair modern art with a seminar in dance. If next week, a ceramics course or classical guitar session provoked his interest, he would not only be allowed, but encouraged to switch classes, so that his creativity would not be stifled by complete-the-entire-course instruction. Though not as orderly as the traditional, it did avoid lockstep education. Students would not be required to assimilate the achievement of all the recognized masters. In this manner, an appreciation of modern efforts in classical music, art and architecture were hoped for. At the time there was difficulty accepting recent achievements in the arts. Academics hung tightly to the accepted masters.

How to avoid superficial art? "Let me do my own thing" offered no criterion of quality. What allowed Picasso to paint a blue guitarist and be acceptable? Yet why would his angular shapes and gaudy colors be rejected in another picture? Difficulty arose when all art was expected to have an easily understandable form. Must art or music make sense? Must it have universal appeal? We had no answers, but agreed to Sharon's definition of superficial: "Not going beyond the present moment". Petty conversation falls flat for this same reason.

Four hours had flown by. At 1:30, Mike told me to bring my things inside. A shower, a little Robert Frost, and sleep in the spare bedroom.   46 miles

THE LOST HUSBAND

Thursday, August 31   Charlotte to Lexington, NC   Day 77

Sharon's pancakes coated the stomach like a milkshake. Kirstin, her two year old, smiled playing with the syrup. Mike left for school while I circled the block for a new gum wall tire. By noon I rolled through a city park laced with maples and gravel paths. Children integrated on the ball fields, climbed swings and played in the sand. A picnic lunch of catfish stew and pineapple. Juice slipped down my chin to splash on the table. Bees with yellow faces and black body stripes came to lap the juice puddle. Kids stopped by inquiring about the bike. Two flirting girls came to tease and ask personal questions. They whispered secrets of nasty things boy and girls were doing back in the trees.

"She wants to kiss you," said one girl of her friend as they left.

Oh, the puppy love rewards of cross country riding!

Outside Charlotte, traffic on Route 29 rushed, turned, and twisted forty miles. Twice I stopped when both arms and legs felt odd. I tried sweets but it wasn't sugar depletion. A third time I felt dizzy and weak in the stomach, yet ginger ale had no relief from nausea. Dinner equaled an apple. Twenty-five miles to Lexington side-by-side with snarling semis bullying their way. Northern winds blew steadily slowing progress.

A white pickup was parked on the shoulder, with the driver watching patiently through the rear view mirror. I wheeled forward to a truck stop a half mile ahead, where a distressed woman turned onto the exit ramp.

"Need help, ma'am?" I inquired.

"Well, yes," she replied. "My husband and I are traveling together. I think that's him back down the road. I thought he saw me pass, but now I'm worried if he's back there. I'm worried if he's sick and I don't want to walk out on the road. Could you check for me? His name is Mr. Willis".

I had to wait several minutes for a hole in the traffic so that I could cut across the center divider and roll back south. Indeed, the man had not seen his wife pass, and was worried for her safety. Assured that his wife was safe, he drove up to the rest area, shared a few words, and continued driving. I waved to the woman as I passed a second time.

At dark the Lexington turnoff led down a neon lit access road. *Fish, All You Can Eat.* I stopped, combed my hair and entered. I lost my appetite after 15 minutes of non service. My body said ice cream, a quart of orange juice and fruit cocktail. I still didn't feel well. A man, whose house was up for auction, provided his lawn. No real disturbances, but irritations kept me awake till 4 a.m.   60 miles

TAKING STOCK

Friday, September 1   Lexington, NC to Danville, VA   Day 78

Status quo #1: Belongings. Everything displayed rough treatment; clothing torn, patched, faded; white athletic socks, muddy gray, saggy; sleeping bag lumpy and torn. Hat, having lost elasticity, fell off with the slightest gust. I was tired of chasing it. Mosquito net and plastic drop cloth have holes. Radio, dented, bent aerial. Bike: scratched with rust spots, but rides smoothly in spite of bent fork. The generator light enjoyed a new bulb.

Status quo #2: Health. No severe physical problems noted, aches and pains to be endured. Neck still strained. While riding it was difficult to glance up at approaching traffic. Arms have regained their strength, but no steering position was comfortable. Elbows stiffened at day's end. Rough calluses have built up on the hands with fingers clumsy for delicate work and little strength for turning a can opener or twisting sealed bottles. Torso and back excellent, no pains. Groin has suffered a burning itch for last two weeks from prickly heat. Legs powerful and hard with thighs and knees sore after each daily ride; a few minutes and they tightened into knots. Bursitis. Must be exercised before riding. Thighs have swelled so much they were too fat for the walking shorts. They filled the brown jeans skin tight. Overall there has been no weight gain or loss-still 175 pounds. Appetite: Constantly hungry. Diagnosis: Tapeworm. Prescription: More bike riding. Attitude: Good enthusiasm, unless a big truck sneaks up behind.

Route 29 out of Lexington was deceptively dangerous on two lanes, no paved shoulder. The pavement dropped 4-6 inches at the edge. Hills rose and fell sharply. Side exits were traps for the unfamiliar motorist. Cars entering the highway must stop first, perpendicular to the road. For twenty-five miles there were no graduated speed acceleration/deceleration lanes to blend with traffic; it was floor it, and pray. Greensboro had small shoulders, but short, sharp, turn exits were significant hazards. It was more of a race to leave the city before rush hour and Labor Day Holiday traffic. When Route 29 split from Interstate 85, under a bridge, country atmosphere returned. Houses wore simple designs, wooden sideboards, and stucco. Weathered old barns tilted their walls; rusted machinery hunkered, disused in the fields; spangled groves displayed the season's first yellow leaf changes.

Reidsville was the tobacco market of North Carolina. In the center of town, a red cigarette emblem announced the Pall Mall Company. Railroad tracks nuzzled a long series of sheds and processing plants gathering the crop for the American Tobacco Company. The aroma was unmistakably strong, deep, warm.

Sunset passion overlooked the western mountains. Soft flamingo feathers touched pastel violet clouds on a blue veil, slipping to purple hills. Welcome to Virginia! High beams outlined my shadow against reflecting signs. In bustling Danville, the search for a quiet house was impossible. As my energy gauge signaled empty, I turned the handlebars toward the floodlights of a football field. Two teams met for a scrimmage. I pedaled up the heights of George Washington High, rounded the front offices and made tracks over the grassy knolls to the field. A nook of brick outcropping and recessed walls afforded shelter from night winds. Low on the hill, football squads practiced under the lights, while I watched, eating chop suey and melon. 91 miles

TEMPTING OFFER

Saturday, September 2   Danville to Amherst, VA   Day 79

The school lawn rounded down to the highway fence. Brown ascents toward Danville sat in bright morning splendor. Silver light poles stood as sentries over gray concrete bridges shuttling traffic. It was a good day for riding. Route 29 zigzagged along the city to a shopping center on a crest. The usual marketing stop received the usual stares, so for a peaceful meal I pedaled to a deserted paint peeled and faded hamburger stand. Shattered glass lay scattered over the asphalt, trash containers sat inside the windows, and counters were empty of prices and customers. A sun table, out front, asked for company to sit on its broken seat. Breakfast: pears and milk. The sun's caress glinted off a white VW in a parking stall. It was new, clean, yet strangely, its rear tires folded inward and wires dangled. Munching on a chocolate chip cookie, I lifted the hood. No motor. What does a man do when he discovers a stolen vehicle without its motor? Finish his milk and cookies. Two grease monkeys, mechanics, at a hill station let me report the theft. My fingerprints were all over the hood. Would I be convicted if I stayed in town?

Civilization's trappings lined the Virginia countryside. Restaurants, purveyors of antiques, mechanics, repair businesses, motels blocked the serene beauty of the knolls. Farms were divided from the highway by lines of fence posts. Wild flowers clustered at field edges and timber borders. And everywhere were hills. Virginia possessed no level land. A sailor would be at home with its wavy landscape.

On a particularly long climb, in late afternoon, a car with two fellows stopped ahead and waited for me. With clinging sweaty clothes, I drew abreast and passed.

The driver shouted: "Where you goin'?"

"New York, eventually," I replied.

"Well, we're jus' headin' to Charlottesville, about ninety miles up. We'll give you a lift," he said.

"That's mighty tempting, but I've refused all rides. I've gotta do this by bike".

They drove up the hill handily, as I began to wonder if perhaps I'd made a mistake. The steep hill said yes.

Lynchburg. Late Saturday afternoon peace amid white stone and clapboard homes; easy chairs and evening gossip on porches. Churches to the left and right-Baptist, Methodist, Assembly of God Lutheran, Jehovah Witness. I hoped for a Catholic evening mass so that Sunday would be non-stop travel, but no church was to be found. I detected a weakness of our upbringing in organized religion. Have we properly worshipped God only if we attend our particular denomination? If we love God did it make any difference if we used another church one Sunday? Wasn't God in all churches?

The civic center and business district towered above San Francisco-like cross streets in cement canyons. Town dropped to the rail yard, buttressed by a restraining wall channeling traffic over a bridge, spanning the river as well, then disappeared up a forested embankment.

Evening shadows returned the magic of yesterday. Mountain humps twenty miles west painted the horizon, true to their name, Blue Ridge. Later, the foothills sang the glory of America: purple mountain majesty.

Amherst's sign greeted: *Bicycles Prohibited*. Last minute Saturday shoppers prepared for the Blue Laws against Sunday business. Two bars invited early drinking. An elderly couple pointed to the Methodist parsonage with its light on. No answer to knocking. At a third house, a woman said staying in the neighborhood was unwise, local trouble and all. Methodical house-to-house search of six more doors. A woman renter allowed the front bush which would block the streetlights. After my weekly call home, the phone book gave no listings for a Catholic church.

Under the orange tarp, I was protected from the heavy dew, while poking my head out of the sleeping bag to count stars, imagining shapes, and reflecting on distances and the vastness of space. It seemed I lay on a raft being spun through the air, too far away to latch onto a star and too small to feel important in the ocean of space. Human accomplishment is but a dust mote in creation's eye. 79 miles

STARVATION AND SHENANDOAH

Sunday, September 3   Amherst, VA to Shenandoah   Day 80
                                 National Park

Virginians rose early for church, banged around the kitchen, walked outside in robes and slippers to collect the Sunday paper, and rinsed off their cars. Children squawked. Chill night air hung, making 9 a.m. travel uncomfortable. A metal curve-guard looked restful for a stop, but unsafe. Sitting on a curbstone with cows on a hill overlooking pastures, I read Scripture and meditated. A cattle truck drove by with protesting steers. My private prayers were in the center of God's creation and outdoors.

Food supplies were low, but every stop at a grocery was closed. Today looked like a day of fasting and hunger. Valley scenery changed to a mighty timber army marching down the mountains to placid farms. Houses occupied patchwork fields. I became so hungry I could have eaten the scenery. Perched on a rock, I ate the last can of sweet peas. It took but minutes for the air to warm, and 30 minutes developed a heat wave, or so it seemed. And the rises became tougher climbs.

I called out, "Hey, look at those young gentlemen, all spruced up. Wonder where they're going?"

"Church!" replied a group of boys waiting for service to begin.

A wooden fruit stand across the center strip held baskets piled with corn, green apples, melons, and peaches. A blond boy filled baskets while a man lay on a picnic bench, sick from a Saturday drunk. Jerry sold a large sack of peaches, ten for 60c, and handed out a soda. He and Uncle Doug indentified tree names, oak, poplar, wild cherry, hickory, chestnut, peach, apple.

Route 6/159 to Shenandoah National Park meandered over a clanking steel girder bridge. A run of clear creek water dribbled and gurgled over smooth round stones. Cornfields saluted at attention, guiding to tree lines, tidy pastures, and a valley begging for a Sunday Drive. An hour of tortuous climbs and curves took the next three miles. The road shoulder was brittle and cracked, full of chuckholes. I strapped the shirt to the bike rack and enjoyed a tanning session.

At the summit of the pass, an entrance divider guided past the marker on the right: *Elev. 1900 Ft.* Cars lined up at the ranger station, to pay an entrance fee of $2.00 per vehicle, 50c per bus passenger. The ranger who poked his head out of the brown shack, handing change to the vehicle ahead, turned and asked, "Are you sixteen?"

"On occasion".

"That'll be 50c." He held out a park map, waved and said, "Enjoy your ride through".

Shenandoah National Park nestled atop a one hundred mile mountain chain in quiet forest majesty. Two lane Skyline Drive wound along the crests, up and down, around clefts, passed through sloping glades and wildflower dens. Breaks in the timber lines telescoped out to mountain palisades towering above rich, fertile checkerboard farms in the valleys below. Insect chirps, bird whistles, hidden grunts, and undergrowth patter told of a life unknown to the motorist. Steep ascents rose elevation up to 3,500 feet, then swiftly coasted down to 2,400, only to begin another climb.

As the sun eased toward the horizon, chill air rustled through the trees. Late afternoon storm clouds scudded up the peaks, making no pretence of their purpose. Rumbling clouds and tossing winds forewarned. Rain was not far off, but the nearest shelter was fifteen miles. First delightful mists increased to sprinkles and graduated to soaking rain. Trapped on a slope, I sought shelter in a grassy strand under two poplars. A sharp plummet lay left off the road edge, a steep rock pile commanded the other side. Black clouds overhead pounded forest leaves, rocks, grass, pavement, deer, bird nests. Nothing was exempt. I stood under a thick limb hoping that the storm would quickly pass, playing dodge ball with the drops until they became too numerous. Cold splashes caught me by surprise. In five minutes I was thoroughly soaked; in fifteen I began thumbing cars for a hitch. No luck. The outer sleeping bag was wet and couldn't be allowed any further dampening, for all my dry clothes and tonight's sleep depended on its dryness. Swiftly, I unhooked the rubber bungee cords, spilling canned goods on the ground. Taking the orange plastic tarp off the bag, I opened to its full eight foot by four foot size, and placed one end down flat. On top, I plunked the sleeping bag, sat on its rolled lumps, and pulled the remainder of the plastic over my back and head, holding the cover over my hair, and pinned it under my chin like a granny scarf. Only my face and shoes protruded from the mass that looked like a giant lumpy pumpkin. When a car sloshed by, a thumbed hand stuck out to hitch a ride. No offers came.

Evening rain eased enough to ride. Repacked, bike and gear strained uphill. Chill was in the air, while warm pavement created fog that slithered into the trees and lurked on mountain lookouts. The valley vanished in the mists. With slow going, perhaps six mph, it was a race against time to reach the Loft Mountain Campsites before dark. My knotty sore knees pumped. Wind cut through the green long sleeve shirt, slowly drying with body heat. At dusk, the camp entrance. Vehicles, some with lights on, occupied spacious tent sites interspersed amid age old trees. Barbecue pits were near at hand. Two deer occupied the pavement. Vehicles and campers approached the animals while cameras flashed. Children in a station wagon teased a doe with a stalk of celery before tossing it on the ground, next to the National Park sign: *Please Do Not Feed the Animals*. Daddy thought it was cute.

I eased past the spectators, advanced to the corner, and turned up the last incline which was the most severe climb of the day. At the summit was a campers' store where I stiffly walked the bike to lay it against the wall. Inside was warmth. The waft of delicious aromas assaulted my stomach growls. My grocery list included bread, jelly, honey, corn chips, candy, cookies, milk, licorice, sandwich meat. Overbought, there was no way to carry all the food, so it was left in the store, while I munched candy bars looking for a tent site. Then I ran back to the store just as it closed, and clumsily hiked back to camp with a wet disintegrating paper sack.

Dinner comprised six jelly sandwiches, corn chips, four candy bars and two peaches. I opened the sleeping bag and laid it out to dry in the wind. The clothes were dry. Because of the chill air, I donned all three shirts, windbreaker, and two pairs of long pants. From the next table Susan called to her husband that they were out of milk. I offered mine. In return, they invited me to eat with them. In the dark, we cast eerie shadows from the light of a Coleman lantern. It took an hour to build a fire to cook steaks, and minutes to eat on the cold wooden benches. Of course, I cleaned up the leftovers and the extra piece of steak. Afterwards we placed our food in bear proof lockers. A stroll to the restrooms at 10 p.m. and a late evening sit-about-the-fire. All bodily needs met.

The sleeping bag had dried in the wind. I got in, placed a clothing pillow roll on an exposed tree root, and maneuvered among sharp rocks until I was comfortable. Wind was blocked by a tree and a dirt ledge. I slept peacefully, except for a light rain at 3 a.m., when I slid under a picnic table and covered up with the plastic again. A bear came into the neighboring campsite looking for a late snack. He wasn't vicious, just hungry. One of six college guys slept in the open having left peanut butter and jelly jars next to his sleeping bag. The black bear stood on his chest to reach. The ensuing scream woke the tent people, and scared off the lumbering animal. 54 miles

LABOR DAY

Daybreak was full of chill and clouds. I moodily exited from the warm sleeping bag cocoon and gobbled three jelly sandwiches. Susan and Elit invited to a second breakfast. It took an hour to cook bacon and eggs in the cold. We broke camp, Susan and Elit compressing their tent to fit in their VW trunk and drove home to Arlington. Two-tenths of a mile to the camper's store supplied public washing machines where I laundered clothes while I scrubbed off body germs in a steamy 50c shower. Since there was nothing to do until clothing dried, I ate the last of the jelly and bread, six more sandwiches.

Light summer wear was not sufficiently warm on the mountain peaks. Pedaling was a chore. Up slope gear changing has been getting sloppy, slipping into an unwanted higher gear without notice. Tightening the shift levers hadn't worked. Wear was affecting the bike. Twice my red baseball cap blew off racing downhill, causing me to stop to retrieve it. Turning it backwards prevented the visor from catching a puff of wind. Fourteen miles of idyllic forest mist and dew, clouded dark and bright snatches of quilt farms below, ran to Swift Run Gap and an exit. The bike left behind the park for easier travel.

Route 330 slashed across the park with overland travel from Kentucky. Turning east down the Virginia slope, the descending road shot like a runaway rollercoaster bending and whipping its passengers in hair-raising perilous turns. The shoulder was spongy soft. Impatient cars, anxious to speed home from the holiday, honked. Once, I rolled onto the shoulder and instantly realized the mistake. Brakes cannot rapidly slow a bicycle careening down a mountainside. A steep angle pulled the bike faster, even as the rubber pads grabbed the wheel. When I hit the gravel shoulder, the bike lost control, pitching and tossing left and right, sometimes bogging front while back wheel spun. It slipped on the stones instead of gripping. The car just behind me jammed the gas pedal and zoomed ahead; succeeding cars could not see the dilemma I was in. Each time I tried to regain control by muscling the ten speed onto the road, they honked. Once I brushed a stone wall with the right handle bar and pedal, cutting up the handlebar tape grip, narrowly missing my head on an abutment. I squeezed the brakes again and again, until they burned on the wheel. It took nearly half a mile to stop the bike. When I looked around there were no cars. A speed sign read: *Speed Limit 45.*

Lower levels of the route slackened the pace as warm afternoon beams raked the fields. Country pride poured a lavish green smile. White diamonds of interlocking fences touched on knolls. Wedges of houses and barns separated cows from combed hay. A steepled church pointed heavenward and blessed the ground encircling it. In small Standardville the rustic charm was preserved, although a closed psychedelic shop hinted invasion by city slickers.

An offshoot road, 230, continued the pastoral fantasy. Several modern homes had discovered this peaceful scene, but the farms rolled on. The Roaring 20s Antique Car Museum passed on the left with scant notice, as did the Wolftown Mill Museum. Then, on reflection, never having seen a mill, I retraced the path to black gravel fronting a solid wooden step of the three story clapboard structure.

"Helloooooh," I called out. "Anybody home?"

Next door a gray haired woman opened the white house trailer and stepped out. With twinkling eyes and smooth face, she introduced herself as Mary Turner, and began her tour of the wooden recesses, thumping footsteps on the floorboards. Flour millers were acutely intelligent about their buildings which had to be solid and sturdy, built from forest lumber materials at hand, and square blacksmith's nails. Their choice of woods were oak, hickory and chestnut. Most woods contained acids or chemicals that would change corn or wheat flavor, so millers selected lumber that remained neutral. The upper floor stored grain and shunted it down wooden tubes to be ground between two circular grindstones. Expert chiseling on the stone faces was required to allow the grain to crush properly. All machinery operated by a system of gears, belts and winches from a waterwheel.

Wolftown Mill had been built before the turn of the 20th century, with sawmill lumber. However, there were many sheds and homes in the area that were built before the age of sawmills. Mary had her tools on display together with relics of pioneer days. Her private collection of wooden tubs, adzes, cogs, household tools, wooden toys, dresses and lithographs took one's imagination back into the dark forest where survival depended on an axe, an adz, a knife, courage and ingenuity.

A local Negro minister arrived with his soft spoken wife. Robert Jones stood tall, a mighty man of stony hand. His size matched the enormity of his ideas. Kindness glinted from his eyes, and gentleness wrapped itself in his words. He worked the land where he preached, and his religious talks

165

were flavored with words from nature, animals, trees, and the seasons. Before becoming a minister, he remembered his lumberjacking, the sizes and strengths of timber, smells of fresh sawdust, log rolling and pinning. He identified several types of lumber in the mill. When younger, his father owned a mule. The boys felt it their duty to drag logs across the snow to open roads for poorer folk. Other memories included using wild cherry trees as a medicinal aid, and chewing a dogwood branch and shaping it for a tooth brush. There were hand games and handmade toys. Cooking was a scrumptious art that filled empty bellies and warmed hearths with sweet aromas on cold winter nights. Farmers had superstitions. Plant by light of the moon, the corn will come up; plant by dark of the moon, the corn will stay down. Put in fence posts by light of the moon, they'll come out; put in posts by dark of the moon, they'll stay till they rot. (Some of the chestnut fence posts in the area were ninety years old and still sound.)

Hours of fascinating stories. At dusk, the Rev. Jones and wife drove home. Mary invited me to stay; the mill would make a comfortable hotel. She entered the trailer to cook supper. I went to play in the field and run along the rocky stream, clacking smooth boulders underfoot, skipping stones over the rippling stream by the pasture. In purple twilight Mary sang out her dinner chime, her menu fresh from the garden: corn, tomatoes, potatoes, pickles, and watermelon for desert.

Mary had driven across the U.S. six times by herself and as recently as six years ago. Physically spry and mentally alert, she conversed on politics, religion, history, philosophy and the sports page. Her personal interest in pioneer life began thirty-seven years ago, as well as her historical collection. She owned other museums but had to give them up due to conflicting problems. When not collecting, she used the winter's confinement to write about what she had learned. Spring became her publishing season. She claimed to be on the verge of retiring, but one might question why a 50 year old would quit. Mary confessed she was 71.

We watched an ABC Sports Special, then said good night. The mill was lit by a small table lamp casting a yellowed glow on the tubs, pick axes, shovels, barrels, walls, and wooden floors. I wrote a few moments, then went outside to enjoy cricket songs and watch stars outline the horizon. Off flicked the light. In the dark I snuggled into the cozy sleeping bag. A hoot owl cooed in a roof eave. The cats pounced one another in playful thumps and bumps. The cooling boards of the mill creaked and echoed an evening song.   35 miles

THE STAUBS

Soft muted rain ticked the window panes. Mary knocked on the loading dock door, entered, and fed her cats. When she left, I climbed out of the sleeping bag, packed, and wrote at one of the desks till Mrs. Turner called to eat a heaping breakfast. Mothers never stop mothering, and they love a man who eats. Filled to capacity, I returned to the mill to finish my journal.

Mary dressed for shopping in her blue Mustang. Ready to leave, I tried to give her two extra dollars for the meals. She refused, and we spent several minutes trying to outmaneuver each other about whether or not she'd keep the money. As a last resort, Mary stuck the two bills in the rear wheel gears. We talked pleasantly for a while, then she ran to the trailer. I put the dollar bills inside on the floor, and closed the door.

I said, "I'm not going to keep it".

Mary conceded, "All right, give it to my favorite charity".

"What is it?"

"The Society for Helping Hungry Bike Riders". We parted the best of friends.

Pastoral farms under afternoon cloud. At Highway 29, the rural flavor ceased. Metropolitan life sped past on steeper hills. Small factories puffed smoke and banged and hummed. Though city life has not truly crept out ninety miles from Washington, D.C., these were the first ambassadors. Roads were plain and simple for two hours. Lunch in a cornfield, with the bike on its kickstand, I extracted a plastic bag of tomatoes, cucumbers and cookies Mrs. Turner had given me and climbed a bank of fresh cut grass. I bit into a red sphere. Tomato juice dripped into my hand, making the applesauce cookies even stickier. Passing drivers made quizzical faces.

Two precocious twelve year old girls wandered downhill to the fence line. Casey and Bonnie first thought I was a road worker. They asked why I was still working after five. Their eyes bulged as I told them I was a teacher riding cross country. A barrage of questions popped, and a lot of school chat. Mom drove up in a station wagon-it was time to go. I tramped down the grass to the bike. The girls raced back to the fence, and mother followed. She asked if I was the teacher in the news.

"No. I've avoided publicity," I answered.

"We...Would you like to come to our house for the night? My son would love to meet you".

I pedaled back to the turnoff where Patsy Staub waited in the station wagon. Disassembling the bike, we fit it in the back, and began an animated conversation as we drove through Culpepper, through rustic Boston, Virginia, into the back hills. Pat stopped in the dirt driveway of the "new" home-a white washed wood clapboard house, two stories, built 130 years earlier! Which meant that all the wood on the house had been cut and squared and flat surfaced completely by hand using tools like those in the Mill Museum. A pre-Civil War house. And there were two floors of craftsmanship to explore!

The house rested on a sloping eleven acre parcel of grape orchard, vegetable patch, and grazing land. The grass, rich and tall, was being cut by a neighbor on a tractor. The Staubs were enduring two weeks of moving pains, painting, patching, and cleaning what had not been finished. Consequently, they lived out of boxes and crowded rooms no one could yet enjoy. The first week they got along without water; the second week without hot water. They have, with loving care, remodeled, plumbed, heated the house, and in their "free time" gone to a cattle auction and horse show.

Each bedroom had a fireplace, one in the dining room and one in the living room, for a total of six. Mantles were wooden, faux painted by a 19th century artist to look like marble. The paint was chipping, the craft being a lost art, so restoration was impossible. Doors of inlaid panel were smoothly finished by a craftsman before the age of electric tools. Stair landings, wall panels, and floors were also smooth and solidly constructed. The floor was trued with an adz. Limestone walls were both painted and papered. One wall was being remodeled to add another toilet. The only modern conveniences the house had on moving day were electricity, two sinks, and a toilet.

Ten year old Lin hopped off the school bus, walked up the lane, and heard his mother's introduction. The last hours of sunlight faded as two "boy" scouts swapped stories and planned trips of discovery and conquest. After supper, the kids argued over who would take a bath, vying to be the last one.

To leave the monotony of the partying set, the family moved to the country, desiring to be at ease, experience the seasons, and raise animals. Casey was a first rank equestrian; the horses had room to prance. Pride, their gentle Doberman, could frolic. The kids knew secret hiding places and explored forest deeps. And the winter season was fast approaching.

Another reason for the move was nature education, away from the distractions and luxuries of the city. Lin and Casey thought it novel to show visitors their outhouse. Once they invited a local boy from one of the poorer homes to dinner. He was well mannered, but couldn't stand sugar in his iced tea. His folks had never been rich enough to buy sugar. He also never had inside plumbing. But segregationist pride reared its head when the Staub girls announced the school they would attend.

The neighbor boy said, "I wouldn't go to that nigger school for a million dollars". Though the poorest of Whites, he considered himself better than any Black.

The girls were dumbfounded.

Nature was also a teacher. One observation was the naturalness of mating animals, no longer keeping sex a lurid topic. When the kids asked questions, they received an answer appropriate to their age. Questions were never put off, and with this attitude, the fears or embarrassment about sex were avoided.

Jim Staub, a stocky blond headed IBM program manager, came home from work about one o'clock. As a West Point graduate, performing as a tactician and teacher at military schools, he exuded military discipline. After the 5th or 6th year, it was customary to update one's education. Most military men, who have attended liberal universities, and returned to the conservative traditions of the military mold, faced intellectual and moral frustration. At social gatherings, a lieutenant was looked down upon if he disagreed with his captain. A lieutenant colonel was expected to never display better knowledge of a situation than a full bird colonel. There were countless stories of higher ranking officers who revenged upstart fellow officers. But this was also true in the hallowed education halls of the Academy. If a colonel was responsible for missing equipment, and a captain mentioned to whom it was last issued, reprisals had the captain pulling extra duty and receiving numerous difficult assignments-the object being to cause him to fail, and blot his record. Thus, protocol demanded one to ease through social encounters, never broaching controversy, and leaving, instead, bland conversation. The result reduced ability of the soldiers to question. It was defended as needed discipline and respect of a senior officer. Senior officers clearly don't know everything. But thinking and knowledge under fire was not to be challenged by the lesser ranked soldiers. Any command given was subject to bias that the senior officer had superior knowledge. This may apply to the battlefield and tactics, but it did not apply to conversations outside military expertise. Was an officer superior because he dominated an argument by virtue of his insignia or rank? Rather, the officer was no better than his ability to think on his own two feet before a critical audience. Unfortunately, Jim and I had both experienced officers who didn't know what they were talking about, and yet expected no one to contradict their statements. Seven years ago, Jim left the Army. He taught private school and roughed it until IBM selected him. He was a troubleshooter and director of computer operations. His country home beckoned him to build and repair, craft woodwork, plant, raise animals and pasturage. At 4 a.m. we stopped, the night almost gone. After a shower I hopped into the chilly bed vacated by Lin. He slept on the cot while Pride, the Doberman, slept on his feet.   28 miles

VIRGINIANS

Jim was up, readying for work, to tie loose ends together. The kids had waken at six, dressed, ridden the yellow bus to school, before house noises woke me. Pat was moving dishes and washing clothes.

Casey excelled at school, music and horse riding. Perhaps, because he is younger, Lin felt the need to fight for attention, so sometimes he was disruptive in class. In counseling, the cause emerged-competition, and the safety outlet became sports with his natural agility and quickness. He loved chess. Though he teases Casey, the two have a tight friendship, as when riding his ten speed. On the first morning after moving in, both had vanished. Casey was sitting on the bike crossbars while Lin pedaled.

Pat and Jim were competitive adults and thorough researchers. Pat read the background and all of an author's writings in order to understand and appreciate the works. This characteristic was infused in her gardening, dog breeding, and house purchase. Jim, in like manner, studied photography books and magazines prior to selecting camera equipment, expecting to know strengths and weakness of a product before buying. The house was an example of detailed choices.

Other city dwellers exited the city for rural atmosphere, space, relaxation, helpful neighbors, Civil War history, and gardening beauty. Real estate agents promoted residential developments and tract houses. The result, outside Washington, D.C., was metropolitan sprawl. Rural counties were banding together to fight off the menace. They wanted legislation limiting future sales of real estate to a minimum of twenty-five acres to preserve a green belt to the mountains. Construction outfits were racing the lawmakers; five tract homes had gone up near the Staubs.

Neighborliness was a key word in the country. Folks knew and looked after each other. It took 5-8 years to be accepted as other than city folk. The 70 year old woman mayor knew everyone by name and spoke personally with shoppers, or tool buyers. She had the reputation of carrying city hall in her purse, knew all the goings on in town, organized public functions, listened to problems, and had been seen cleaning the street. Out of a population of 250, she never had more than ten votes against her.

The tractor man returned in the afternoon with clanking machinery to scoop and bale hay. Without a word, he chugged into the field and harvested the hay field. When the machine bogged down, he stopped, slid under the trailer to jimmy the baling mechanism, hopped back in the seat, and chugged merrily on.

Now it was time for the Doberman to showoff canine obedience. Hand and word signals directed all movements. The dog went through its paces with grace and speed. Then play period. Both girls wrestled and tugged at the halter strap in the sauna sun. Contrary to common opinion, Pride was not a dangerous animal. However, she was treated specially by Lin, her owner, and deservedly so. Two years earlier the parents, sitting before the fireplace, heard late night barking. Ordinarily, they would have passed it off, except for Pride's constancy. When they reached Lin's door, they smelled a faint odor of smoke not coming from the fireplace. Upon opening the door, they were choked by smoke. An electric Christmas decoration had fallen from the window and lodged in the bed covers. The built up heat smoldered in the mattress. Pride, the dog, had saved Lin's life; since then she has been spoiled. The kids came home noisily to look at photographs while I analyzed character from their faces. Later we threw a football around, and the children tried to get out of their chores.

June and Stuart, neighbors, invited us for dinner. Country cooking held a unique delicious aroma in late summer. After the blessing, the meal ended much too quickly. Seventy year old June displayed her flair for oil and grease paintings. And Stuart's woodcraft wizardry was displayed in his garage converted into a guest room rivaling any modern apartment. The kids, pretending to be sleepy, hinted that they had visited long enough. Playing along I carried Lin fireman-style down the dark lane. Stars were spattered dots from a painter's flicked brush. Night walked in cold silence, its icy fingers turned flesh into goose pimples. The only defense would be a warm bed. And, if you are a boy, a dog sleeping on your feet.   No miles

ON TO SILVER SPRING

The school bus had left. Jim had come home late due to holiday traffic build up. The kitchen creaked underfoot while Pat commandeered the phone, wearing out the ear piece. Jim roused by noon, ready for work, offering to drive me to Washington, D.C. I could not accept. Pat drove the station wagon back to the highway, showing a safer smooth Road 15/29. Removing the ten speed from the back, I reassembled the wheels. Black pre-school children sat agape before their modern suburban house. All exchanged goodbyes; Pat honked.

Washington goal? Sixty-six miles. Counterculture folks, rejecting social status and high incomes, moved in droves to the rural districts, reveling in a simpler life style. One chemistry doctorate grad, a girl, worked in the city, but came home to a log cabin, cooked on a wood burning stove and sewed by candle light. She wore blue jean quilt dresses. Her pony-tailed husband, a carpenter, still worked in the city, but developed business in the backwoods.

Several Protestant denominations have *Welcome Visitors* signs. From scattered folklore, and religious rumor, stories could be pieced together. Some churches manifested Free Baptist and Free Methodist names. Years ago congregations had to pay for their pew seats. Indigent farmers could not afford a seat, so ministers established branch churches where the seating was free. A few Virginians believed Catholics have devil horns-the reason why nuns wore head coverings (habits) and priests black hats (birettas). A particular sect believed that rosaries were a bead prayer used to call the devil to capture Christian Scientists.

While the highway snaked around, dipped under a stone rail trestle, and crossed trickling water runs, the level bed of train rails divided the hills. At Brandy Station, I bought stamps. The postmaster, detecting a westerner's accent, said the Civil War was still being fought in the area, and this time the Rebs aimed to win.

He asked, "You see that oak tree yonder?"

"Yes," I replied innocently.

"Well, better get over there when we start the shootin', Yankee".

We chuckled. He was a Civil War preservationist who enjoyed refighting ancient battles at historical society meetings. A souvenir folder told the story of the Battle of Brandy Station, the last of the great cavalry battles.

Mid afternoon milk break. A couple of old men sat in a worn wooden church pew at the country store. The stately elder one told how hurricane Agnes flooded the area and floated the bench down river to lodge in a tree. He chucked his great-grandson under the chin and played games with artificial flowers. For a 91 year old, his knowledge was encyclopedic as was his awareness of the U.S. Olympic team.

Miles of congested residential avenues were cropping up alongside the road. Civil War battle plaques commemorated fierce engagements behind these thickets, across this fence line, and over that hill. Cemeteries haunted the sleeping farms and ghostly battlefields.

Dusk at Arlington's rush hour offered city road repairs, billboards, pilings, barricades, traffic jams, barrel markers, and road-closed signs. The rumors passed around by the city dwellers when asked for directions:

"Don't stay in D.C. at night. It isn't safe".

According to the map, it was an easy ride through D.C. I would pay respects to friends of my uncle Cliff Benson (Miami), and find a place for the night. The D.C. hills prolonged the riding an hour into the night, but traffic drove with speeding abandon. Horns blared. Glaring orange incandescent lights illuminated far beyond the intersections. Many Negro faces on the doorsteps. Children played games or chased one another.

The simple directions given to find Silver Springs were forgotten by 8:30. Lost, I steered to the Wheaton Library to obtain the residential address. Finding the driveway, I climbed the porch and knocked. A heavyset bespectacled gentleman with graying temples answered.

"Hello, sir. Are you Captain Costello?" I inquired.

"No," he answered.

"Do I have the Costello residence?"

"Yes," he returned.

"Do you know the Cliff and Irene Benson family in Miami?"

For a moment he was mesmerized in thought, then sparked, "Why, yes. Where did you come from? When did you see them last?"

Introductions broken, we entered the house. He was not a captain, but a chief warrant officer in the Coast Guard Reserves, the basis of his friendship with Cliff. John Costello had many years of Coast Guard experience. He had worked for the CCC (Civilian Conservation Corps) during the Depression, when he worked under military authority at night, and under the jurisdiction of the Department of Forestry by day. Later he applied as a government messenger while he studied business and economics. At last he received a position with the Internal Revenue Service (IRS), where he prepared a prospectus to advise the responsibilities and tax benefits for business. He had worked in and for the Government for over thirty-nine years. Marie Costello greeted and begged me to stay, then descended to the cellar to prepare a bed. Without asking, she made sandwiches. Twelve year old Johnny shyly listened. The family went to bed, and I clomped on the wooden stairs to the basement.   75 miles

A TOUR OF WASHINGTON D.C.

John puttered about the kitchen at 6 a.m. His chipper voice, contrasted by my morning grouch, woke the kids for school. Mary Alice graced the table for a quick teenage breakfast, and left with Dad. With a head full of coffee, I planned a tour of the Capitol. Marie made me leave belongings at the house to be picked up at night, wouldn't take no for an answer, and whirled about preparing a king sized breakfast. I dressed in brown slacks and red shirt for the Capitol.

The White House had many visitors, but no permanent owner. Guards permitted bike parking at a side entrance where strollers and carriages could remain undisturbed. A rich golden oak entranceway received guests. Velvet chain guardrails restricted passage of the crowds passing through the hall and rooms. Walls were adorned with presidential and first lady portraits. Stationed guards with earphones appraised tourists entering each room, and doubled as information guides. At first no one talked, until a guide spoke; then a cascade of questions spilled. The furnishings were in the finest provincial taste and regal splendor. More presidential portraits, in the red, green, and white rooms. This was a house of dignity.

Facing the White House was the most important branch of government, the Treasury. A whirlwind electronic tour in a darkened labyrinth exhibit left the tourists out of breath, asking, "What did we just see?" It certainly wasn't money. A guard suggested seeing money being printed at the Bureau of Printing and Engraving.

I was sidetracked to the Federal Bureau of Investigation headquarters, where I locked the bike to a tree and headed for an open door.

A policeman asked, "Where you going sir?"

"Tour the FBI," I said.

"Around the block sir".

I had bumbled into the wrong door. The guards checked identifications of every person entering. No I.D. no entry. All packages and women's purses were inspected. The reason was a rash of bomb threats and an explosion on the Capitol steps. On the other side of the building a line formed to wait fifteen minutes for a tour. At peak season, guests may spend two hours in the sun before gaining admittance through the iron gate to the courtyard. A courteous agent escorted us. Crime detection by scientific analysis and electronic gadgetry were the marvel of 20th century criminology. The Hall of Crooks showcased famous scoundrels trapped and convicted by their shoe heel marks, torn stamps, paint chips, and body hair. Firearms technology, in the armory, was highlighted by pistol and Tommy gun demonstrations. A gray haired agent leveled a .38 and squeezed off the entire magazine. He flicked a light and proved every bullet had hit the target head. The distance? Seventy-five feet. Although a small child screamed during the loud burst of the Thompson's machine gun blast, the adults chuckled. When the target was returned, all shots had hit the vital zone.

Requirements were stiff to become an agent. The caliber of its agents gave the FBI its outstanding reputation. Two women have gone through training, one an ex-Army officer, the other an ex-nun. They must perform the same as men; there are no eased standards. Though the organization was moving to new buildings, and changes have occurred in administration, the same integrity was expected by its forty-eight year director, J. Edgar Hoover.

Resting on a lightbox, in the shade of the Justice Building, a pretty lass dressed in white Capri's and red blouse approached me, aahloooing (helloing). It was a Corsican girl who had given me directions earlier. She had to be coaxed to sit next to me, even though she was obviously tired. She had accepted a summer governess job advertised by Americans. Besides watching the children, Paola Denis helped the woman practice French. On days off, the girl toured various U.S. Cities. We made a date to see the Smithsonian tomorrow. She had been reluctant to discuss home and family, and I was startled when she asked if I believed in God.

"Eet ees a problem, no?"

We were going to have a long discussion when we met again.

Library of Congress. [Lesson: Skipping lunch is a major mistake when touring D.C.] A back metal entrance led through a new maze of corridors, side passages, secretaries' and administrators' offices.

A lobby guide took the elevator to the gallery floor to explain library workings. We looked down on readers at the desks, listening to the talk on preservation of rare manuscripts, historic documents, efficient gathering, and control of research materials. Pneumatic tubes sucked notes to far away nooks and crannies. Underground conveyor belts brought requested materials from across the street. Books were then placed on the study table reserved for use. There was no limit to the number of book requests, though no one may check out a book. Anyone over 17 years of age may use the library.

The conception and decoration of the library is an artistic astonishment. Fifty American artists collaborated in the architecture of a hall that represented all aspects of learning. Their limitations were the twofold themes of education and the fields of knowledge. The collected genius of these artisans produced a monument unequalled in the halls of library institutions. Frescoes depicted the world history of culture; statues reverenced the fathers of science and industry; mosaics hallowed the fathers of American culture. Stained glasses, prism craftsmanship, ceiling, colonnades, and marble stairwells portrayed growth from gangling youth to a mature man, blessing the perfections of knowledge, science, art, philosophy, and crafts. The National Library blended many diverse skills into one glorious edifice. The experience was stupefying.

West of the House of Congress, the Lincoln Memorial overlooked a two mile lawn, called The Mall. I climbed the steps of the western white colossus to talk with the President, who sat in white marble silence, seventeen feet tall, between the wall ciphers. His words, etched in the white walls, spoke from a soul conflicted by the nation's dissension, words of peace more than the heartbreak of war torn society.

Shadows crossed the Potomac as the sun's last yellow-pink rays slipped below the horizon. Passing the Kennedy Center, I stopped along the riverbank, where boys were fishing, drew out my wallet and removed a half dollar given by a California girl friend. Cocking the arm, snapping, and releasing, the coin glided up, arched, and fell into the river about a football field away. Not even half across. George Washington's record feat of throwing a silver dollar across the river was still intact. Friday evening, traffic radiated outward from the Capitol hub from which wheel spoke-streets exited. Its diagonals cut through the square neighborhood boundaries. Residences, designed in two and three story Revolutionary and Philadelphian brick architecture, held triangular cornices, with roofs sharply angled to shed winter snows. Small ten foot lawns fronted the porches on tree lined streets.

D.C. neighborhoods were 90 percent Negro. Many Blacks emigrated to the District hoping it to be the Promised Land of Government Miracles (new leases on life or handouts). Some hoped for handouts. Others used it for as educational or social stepping stones out of poverty. Residences varied from well kept blocks to outright ghettos. Large sections were becoming rundown. Papers littered streets and front lawns and no one cared. Blacks sat on porches; children played summer evening games; young men held down the block at the corner; drivers double-parked to talk and impede traffic. Broken windows sat unrepaired. Some store fronts were forts hung with heavy iron grating screens to ward off burglary. Rattling cars and suped-up engines cruised dirty streets. Corroded green bronze Civil War monuments, were surrounded by grass stubble leaning over park curbs. Vacant lots gathered trash and broken glass. Litter gathered faster than sanitation crews swept. Desolation slithered back to haunt Negro ambition. Discouragement loitered at back doors and fear walked the streets in surly contempt. Phantom despair twisted perspective. Hatred bared its teeth and violence growled at night.

Whites did not travel D.C. at night. It was unsafe. Drunks molested passersby; beatings, stabbings and murders were common. Cars had been attacked with drivers in them.

Supermarkets were rare in the ghetto. Some Blacks asked for credit. Too often they lost Friday salaries to the alcohol ghosts before paying their bills. Supermarkets did not function on a credit system. Thus small corner Ma & Pa stores catered to Black shopping needs, and extended credit. They also charged higher food prices as a result. During the riots in 1968, after Martin Luther King, Jr. was assassinated, the neighborhoods erupted, smashing and looting White stores. Corner markets were prime targets. Burned out, gutted, and destroyed shoe stores, clothiers and groceries disappeared. Almost none reopened. Nothing was really solved, leaving the poor and innocent and aged to travel farther to buy their goods. Despair knocked again.

My northwards zigzag journey was unmolested, but night shadows crept a fear in me. I watched street play and the social gatherings on front steps. There must be some mistake or exaggeration. This was the Capitol of the United States! These people lived here. They can't leave at night. True. Where would they go?

Silver Spring city limits. Silent road home. Synagogue dispersing. On the sidewalks, Jewish men, wearing Yarmulkes, walked proudly with an arm on a son's shoulder; mothers strolled with daughters. Where else but America can freedom mean so much and have so many contrasts?

Johnny erected his miniature golf course in the driveway. He and Mary Ellen, from next door, had designed the course from boards, taped cups and broomsticks. They were charging a nickel per game, and once I'd arrived they did land office business. John and Marie had gone out, leaving meatballs, noodles, and stew. Perfection for an empty tummy. Later, Johnny, Mary Ellen, and I disassembled bikes for tire repairs. We visited Mary Ellen's clan who listened with rapt attention to my adventures. When 18 year old Pat's boyfriend left, I kidded that she was two-timing by staying to talk with me, "Mr. Charm." I brushed my pants' lap and motioned for her to sit. She blushed and we belly laughed. Mr. Murphy offered a ride into the Capitol in the morning.   30 miles in D.C.

PAOLA

You can guess who woke late. Pete Murphy phoned, and I had to tell him to leave. I dressed and made ready to meet Paola at the YWCA (Young Women's Christian Association). Marie knew I would be late, and saw to it that I phoned the girl. Then Marie refused to let me out of the house without breakfast. Some mother!

Saturday traffic was as busy as the weekdays. Stop lights seemed to work extra fast to catch all movement. Detours and short cuts led to blind alleys or cul-de-sac streets. There were no time savers. I rushed to the YMCA at 11:00, but Paola wasn't in; her key was missing. A check of the drawing room and the nearby lunch counters proved futile. Then the raven haired beauty came from the street, in flowing tresses, clothed in a blue floral sleeveless top, and white Capri's. Being a gentleman, I gave her a ride on the metal bike rack. She gingerly sat on the folded windbreaker cushion, swinging her legs out free of the spinning spokes, hair blowing perpendicularly in the wind. Her laughter grew in small giggles and hiccups. Geared down, the bike rolled slowly to accommodate balancing our weight. A Black man rollicked at our cavorting mode of travel. Eyes at intersections followed our path toward the museum buildings.

The Smithsonian Institute is the largest collection of memorabilia in the world. Six buildings contained exhibits ranging from a stuffed elephant, and Lindberg's Spirit of St. Louis plane to a full scale steam engine. It was impossible to see all the exhibits in a full week. Beginning with the Museum of Science and History, in three hours we had covered only half of two floors. And, what was on display was only 2 percent of the collection, the rest was stored underground.

Paola's exhaustion showed. Her breakfast had been coffee and juice. The basement cafeteria was packed by excited visitors in animated conversations. Before we had adjusted ourselves in a booth, Paola raised the topic of God. Hamburgers and religion are hard to mix well in a noisy lunch hall. Paola explained. Europeans are idealistically and artistically oriented. They begin conversations with broad universal topics, law, justice, religion, birth control, politics. They are well versed in abstract discussion. The difficulty for Americans lies in their materialist upbringings. Time is money; money is dear; the home and furnishings are costly; families are expensive. Thus Americans begin conversations with what is closest-the family, home, and money. Europeans do not discuss their home life until a familiarity has developed over several weeks. The best way to know a person is to learn his/her philosophy.

We adjourned to the shade of a park tree, to discuss the existence of God. I brought up proofs for the existence of God, based on causality, perfection of the world/universe, motion, and conscience. Paola was unaffected.

"It is easy to explain the world if you have a God".

My insight was that a person ensconced in religion might be lead to a mistaken assumption that, if given proof of the Divine, automatically others should/would instantly accept it. However, acceptance required more than words. It took grace and faith.

Paola was tired. Her hosts the previous evening had kept her up until 4 a.m. Passing a construction site, she rode silently on the bike rack. At the Y she aimed for the elevator. I caught her hand, said good bye, and kissed it. She was embarrassed and annoyed. European customs do not permit such familiarity.

Late afternoon shopping for the Costellos, a gift book and poems. I rode back home up the ghetto streets. Just before the iron fence of Walter Reed Hospital, on Georgia Street, two small black Civil War cannons sat poised in opposite directions. A National Cemetery. Since the steps were blocked by a locked gate, I hoisted the bike over the wall, and walked about the white grave markers arranged in two concentric circles. Number 13 marker: John Kennedy, N.Y. At the walkway were two black iron plaques. The first remarked how the War Department had discovered disgraceful behavior of visitors to the National Cemetery; vending in the park limits, picnics, running over graves, racing, defacing monuments. By order of the Commanding General, vending was prohibited, and defacing was considered a misdemeanor, punishable by a fine of not less than $25, no more than $100. The second plaque established regulations of the park. All vehicles and movements through the park would be conducted at the pace of a walk. Picnics and vending were disallowed. And parks were to be closed to the public from sunset to sunrise. Signed by the Adjutant General. The first plaque was dated 1867, the second, 1875.

At the Costellos, we finished bicycle repairs in the evening. A bunch of new youngsters gathered asking about their bikes. Johnny learned to repair tire flats. Another boy succeeded in taking wheels apart. Dinner call saved us. Marie and John had gone out for dinner again; Mary Alice had cooking honors. The kids came into the kitchen where joke telling was the evening's entertainment. Mom and Dad returned to join the merriment until our sides ached from the laughter. They each got a kiss as the kids went to bed. 25 miles in D.C.

MY COSTELLO FAMILY

Sunday, September 10   Silver Spring, MD   Day 87

Sunday mass with the Costellos and an afternoon drive in the woods. Marie entreated me to stay the remainder of the weekend, and use the time to write. The warm afternoon made me too drowsy to resist. The neighborhood descended upon us when we arrived home. It was difficult to separate kids, bikes, jokes, and the basketball. Kids got the attention.

John and I played with the barbeque fire after setting the table. In privacy, he asked if I was aware that Marie was very sick. I replied no, that my uncle had only mentioned that she wasn't feeling well.

"Marie's had five serious operations in the last two years," reported John.

We were interrupted by the clamor of plates and last minute preparations. Table dining was a family affair with succulent aromas of meat, sweet corn, hot potatoes, and creamy buttered peas. As guest of honor, I closed my eyes and said grace. Perhaps that was a misinterpreted courtesy, for when I opened my eyes the plates were empty, the food had vanished. Johnny and Carolyn teased Marie about being a human pharmacy since she takes seventeen pills daily. The food was re-placed on the table but it disappeared rapidly with the diners. Dishes were promptly cleared, and the kids were anxious to finish school assignments.

Mary Alice brought out the tape machine to record my guitar singing, and a few new jokes. The Murphys came over with a group of college boys. One told the latest political tomfoolery. A Persian diplomat, thinking he understood American ways with women, pinched an elderly waitress in a restaurant. She jumped, yelled unladylike oaths, and bashed him sideways with a tray. Thereafter the diplomat walked to the opposite side of the dining hall to avoid her, and clued his countrymen about American women.

"You don't pinch them-especially that one," cautioned the diplomat.

A long evening of stories, political arguments and disagreement on every topic. I was truly sad to leave. These have been three wonderful days.   No miles

HEARTBREAK

Monday, September 11   Silver Spring to Baltimore, MD   Day 88

Everyone was gone to school and work. Marie washed clothes in the pantry. She fixed a special departure breakfast and added packed sandwiches for lunch. Eve Murphy came over with daughter Pat to take a remembrance photo. When Mrs. Costello had gone upstairs, Eve pulled me into the pantry. "Did you know Marie is very ill?" questioned Eve.

"Yes, her husband said she was sick, but not how sick," I answered.

"She's dying of cancer".

Outside the bicycle was packed and, dressed in my road togs, it was leave time. Eve and Marie snapped photos, Pat, too.

Marie, with her deep-set eyes and a smile on her face, complimented: "Thanks for coming, Ed. The kids enjoyed you. You were a real treat. Why don't you come back and see us".

The road out of Silver Spring was saddest part of my journey.

Intermittent clouds graced misty Route 29 to Baltimore. Eight days behind on my diary. I wrote in uncomfortable places then moved on. Flies on a garbage heap drove me away from one spot. A long slope rose on the Baltimore beltway. I had no concentration at a fruit stand, bowling alley, shopping center or grassy field behind a nest of trees. When it became too cold outside, writing ended until inside the Normandy Bowling Alley at a warm empty table. Amid crashing balls and raucous shouts, three days' notes were finished. However, air conditioning was colder than outside, forcing me to drink hot tea. At 1 a.m. I stumbled into a copse of trees and slept on top of tree root lumps.   49 miles

NO PROGRESS BOWLING ALLEY

Tuesday, September 12   Baltimore, MD   Day 89

Drizzle. Breakfast, pears and ten doughnuts. I locked the bike against a pole at the bowling alley. Rain poured. I used the morning and afternoon women's league bowling cacophony to finish another two days' writing. The noise finally jumbled my thinking. I had to escape the din. Mounting the saddle, an unusual bike sensation occurred. The rear tire squished. My seventh flat! Two hours were consumed trying to find an infinitesimally small puncture. Another problem surfaced when attempting to adjust an erratic wheel revolution. Since spokes did not sit on the rim correctly, the bounce stayed.

Too late to ride. I re-entered the bowling alley to retrieve my razor from Bill Edwards at the desk, the owner who discovered it in the restroom. He and manager Mike Fiori invited me to stay. Dinner made me feel at home until the evening bowling balls crashed and rumbled like thunder. I lost all concentration, suffered a bout of diarrhea and a pounding headache. My body demanded to leave. I scooted back to last night's camp but, although this time I selected a flat dirt bed, couldn't sleep. Under a Fotomat night light, I read Robert Frost. A pimply faced boy with an irritating stutter asked for directions to a town. He'd traveled all day without getting a ride, consequently he had walked 28 miles so far, to attend a funeral tomorrow. My maps were no help. I could only give tips on hitching. He disappeared into the night.   100 yards

FANTASYLAND OR CEMETERY?

Wednesday, September 13   Baltimore, MD to   Day 90
                              Gettysburg, PA

My feelings matched the overcast. At the bank, a Traveler's Check changed into money. I wrote for perhaps a half hour, then left for Baltimore in an sour frame of mind, my body listless. I couldn't remember a station attendant's directions. On increasingly steep hills I remembered my goal of visiting Gettysburg National Cemetery.

Just after the Pennsylvania border, I saw my first live snake wriggling its black and yellow stripes on the road, more like a fish out of water. Asphalt was poor friction for a walking snake. Considering that five cars were coming from both ends of the road, he needed to grow legs fast or become permanent tarmac.

Maryland and Pennsylvania farms wove contours of circular brown dirt around hills. Furrows, interlaced with cuts of yellow straw, looked like scarecrows buried side by side with green corn stalk hair. Corn ears stood at attention, dangling golden mops. In the rear, triple-decker red barns, trimmed in white with windows at each level, stood above Guernsey cows bellowing for the evening hay feed and milking. Tractors parked at house edges. Lonely fence posts guarded the farm from sunset.

It couldn't have happened to a nicer guy. Flat number eight was a blowout so loud, a man running a power mower thought it was a gunshot. Eight miles from Gettysburg I began walking at 6:30. The heavy laden bike was unwieldy to push and balance with a mushy rear tire. During the second mile I began thumbing. Three construction men in a pickup passed, circled, and stopped. They loaded the bike on top of their cement encrusted sawhorses and tools, shoved a beer in my hand, and sang wildly as the rushing wind whipped through our hair.

A Gettysburg billboard entrance greeting read: *Shenandoah Park With Homes.* Fertile crop rows glimmered in late summer splendor. Houses reserved the charm of the 1800s. Further in, a garish sign. A florescent green elf on a black background smiled: Enjoy Fantasyland-Gettysburg. Then we passed the somber National Cemetery.

Town was closed up for the night. So were bicycle tire dealers. The first light sparkled out of leaded windows and glass doors. The construction workers suggested asking for a room at the college. I wobble-walked across railroad tracks. Amid a cluster of smoke bricked edifices, two men from

Phi Kappa Psi regretted not having room. Instead they gave directions to the Frosh dorms. But halfway across campus, Blaze came huffing back; they'd forgotten a vacant room. The frat opened their house and hearts to a temporary brother. Greg greeted acquaintance and found the upstairs room. Tony, a collector and re-enactor of American wars, fussed like a playful puppy, supplying towels and shower needs. Others came to help or talk. Names flashed. Bill, Stick, Doc, Pa, Ace, Steve, and before long, the brothers were my brothers.

Just before sack time, a commotion on the lawn outside drew attention. At another fraternity, one fellow had gotten deliriously drunk. While taking a shower, he took umbrage at a frat brother. Thereupon, in the dripping nude, he chased the fellow out the dorm, over the landscape, and across campus to the street. Unable to pursue further, though he'd started, he returned staggering to his house for a pair of trunks and resumed the chase. Isn't college fun?   51 miles

GETTYSBURG

The brothers tried three times to feed me, then gave up. When I woke, all efforts went to pushing the cycle to a sporting goods store for a tire and tube. The eighth flat ceased ownership of the rear wheel at 11:45.

The frat house ate lunch at 12:30 in the basement. Its number of diners varied from 10-20, plus guests. The room sat up to forty with two side couches, a ping pong table, pool table, and pinball machine. Prexy Lee High, alias Stick, rang the fraternity to attention with a bell, then called a name. Said brother prayed the blessing, usually a brief, "God bless this food. Amen". Everyone sat, the meal devoured or criticized depending on cooking or students' moods. All helped clear the table by bringing dishes into the kitchen where the day's waiters washed and dried. Then it was class, study, or goof-off time. The latter was most popular.

As the nation's most famous Civil War graveyard, Gettysburg was sedate amidst farmland. However, downtown was a jumble of plastic neon and trade. Tranquil roads drifted through the city to the vast National Cemetery. A large modern white Park Service Building commanded a low green hill. Inside the cyclorama recreated the immense struggle.

A battle explanation before the actual tour set the war drama. Impact? Vietnam has been touted as a massive loss of American soldiers, more than 58,000 lives in ten years. The Battle of Gettysburg lasted three days. It counted 50,000 men (Union and Confederate) as killed, wounded and missing. The tour building rested behind the focus of the Confederate charge. Pickett's 15,000 men marched/ran a mile's distance down one shallow hill and up another rise into the face of cannon fire. They reached the defenses but were beaten back. In that one charge, 6,000 men died. A hundred plus years later, marble, cement and bronze statues stood as silent Honor Sentries. Union cannonball piles waited next to silent artillery pieces aimed across the corn field at the Reb line of defense. Engraved metal markers recorded states, regiments, names and dates, and the hastily scribbled diary entries of the fierce encounters. Mammoth inscribed stones and lifeless monuments endured. The rocky Union Line road embraced automobiles gliding by, passengers occasionally exiting to read names or diary accounts. They tired before long, and remained in the cars more frequently. Dreary clouds gathered overhead; rain was certain.

Culp's Hill. Combat onslaught had butchered nearly all surrounding forest growth. 1863 photographs showed bared rocks, hillsides, and foreground. After 100 years, once again thick woods enveloped the rocky perches. Sharpshooter lookout points spied down boulders to the peach orchard and wheat field, where another 6,000 bodies lay crumpled after a flanking attack the second day of Devil's Den. The trail sloped down to cross the central hollows, No Man's Land, now a tilled battlefield, as gray and white raindrops drummed marching tattoos on a wooden fence, tree leaves, corn field, a red barn. An asphalt highway divided the Yanks and the Rebs.

A mile away, on the battlefield's other side, the Confederate monument line was marked by plaques describing artillery engagements and tragic losses. The hill was not more than forty feet above the hollow of the field. More cannon and shot soundlessly pointed back at the Union line. In a park juncture, a tape recording related Pickett's Charge. A few huddled visitors braved the dripping trees. The multitude of statues became a blur, the mind saturated with regiment facts, dates, faceless names and loss statistics. Hence, the back leg of the thirty-nine mile park route received half-hearted tourist glances. At 6 p.m. the park closed to the public.

Upon return to the college entrance, young men and women, leaving the dining halls, scattered conversation with bursts of laughter. Football fanatics sprinted to a lawn for a pickup game. Phi Kappa brothers finished a stew, and talk focused on 1) the local "fence" for stolen goods, 2) a girl who wanted marriage for money rather than love, and 3) the weekend.

A brother guided a tour of the school grounds. We accepted an invitation to play basketball. I hadn't exercised muscles other than cycling, and welcomed the opportunity, a costly error. Without tennis shoes, I played with bare feet on the gym floor. Quick starts, stops, jumps, twists and slapping feet irritated the skin on the balls of both feet. A blood blister on the left big toe broke, calling an end to the game and jeopardized the end of the trip. We stuffed in the car, like a six pack, back to the house. Blisters meant soreness, limping, hobbling on stairs, and possible infection. I slept in the disheveled room with painful tootsies.   39 miles

CLOSE CALL

Friday's morning classes had done their damage to student ignorance. I was shaven and well lunched as the brothers shook hands goodbye and wished luck. It has become harder to leave friends and acquaintances. They have become dear. I find myself not wanting to finish this odyssey.

A leisurely pace reaped a scenic harvest. Disciplined farms, green and brown plowed stretches boxed both sides of the asphalt strip. Golden straw lined shoulder of Route 15 on tempered hills and sunny fields. Mop head cornstalks swiping the breeze. Mottled cows grazed in belly high hay.

The highway into Harrisburg clogged with weekenders. Campers blocked the view ahead; cars followed behind loping trailers and semis. Impatience grew in bumper-to-bumper progress. A ten speed was the best speedy transportation during rush hour, and fun to watch 300 horsepower vehicles in a mile long traffic tie-up eat bicycle dust! However, an impatient sports car pulled out sharply before me, without signaling, suddenly veering right, onto a side road. Caught mid daydream, I grabbed at the handbrakes in fumbling desperation, squeezing with all the strength an awkward finger grip could give. Momentum pushed me perilously forward while the driver continued his turn, never looking in my direction. The front brakes screeched. I twisted the wheel right, to prevent being snagged by the bumper. Avoiding collision, meant going out of control into a ditch, over a dirt hole, and skidding on loose rock until the bike flopped over leaving me with a palpitating heart and a few bruises. The damage survey: twisted handlebars, easily rotated back into position. A stopped motorist who witnessed the scene, wagged his head woefully, and wiped his brow in exaggerated relief. Caution weighed for a few moments. Then, putting on calloused nerves to counter near accidents, I soon jounced merrily past the fuming stalled traffic.

The Susquehanna River spread a flat blue half mile wide ribbon down the valley of thousand foot mountains. On the other side, a gold and green dome marked the state capitol, Harrisburg. The square faces of public buildings stood shoulder to shoulder. Three bridges linked the opposing riverbanks. On the near shoreline railroad yard, hundreds of sooty orange and red boxcars, black tankers, and rusty flatbeds congregated. Thirty rows of paired silver rails sidelined boxcars or switched through incoming trains.

During the June, 1972, hurricane floods, this switchyard, normally fifteen feet above the river, was under water.

Northward bent the stream bisecting wooded peaks. While a safety wall jutted out into the highway towards the meandering river's edge, fishermen scrambled on rocks fly casting into the shallow weeds mid-river. Boaters drifted carefully among boulder clumps. Below the safety wall, diesel engines whined and thundered. With chattering teeth I donned the thin windbreaker, and, with no means of heating, ate a two pound can of stew, grease and all. Upriver travel was quiet. On the opposite bank, insect sized cars moved on the toy highway below.

The last of the chilly blue twilight seeped out of the sky as I entered elongated Liverpool. Shivering with demented hunger, I bought lavishly from a warm market, then crossed over the river. Biting chill and road noise drove me back to town to sit in the porch shelter of the Good Samaritan Convalescent Home. Trembling fingers opened a can of spaghetti and poured honey on bread. I layered clothes on top of clothes in an effort to warm up. Walking the street helped, but there were notes to record, and no camp. I asked the nurses of the home for permission to write in a warm corner. They acceded. Lonely patients wanted to talk to the fresh face and share life stories. In two hours, when the nurses had to ask me to leave at the 11 p.m. shift change, I'd scrawled two paragraphs.

With cold nipping outside, a night patrol sheriff pointed to a camp ground up the road. I rolled out into the dark, expecting the red reflectors on my back would rebound auto high beams. $3.00 for an outdoor campsite? Forget it. There would be a free spot further down the river road. A mile. Two miles. Tiredness, cold, and a sore butt begged me to pull over at an opening in the dark. Black matted trees lined a dirt path on the right into a deserted work yard of moonless shadows, junk tractors, and trucks. The yard dipped to the river. Under starlight, I flattened a sand bed into the river bank. Dew formed quickly on the bike and sleeping bag. I pulled the ground tarp over for protection. Clear sky, bright stars, light breeze. Fish splashed me to sleep.   67 miles

HURRICANE EFFECTS IN A RIVER VALLEY

Saturday, September 16   Liverpool, PA to Shavertown, PA   Day 93

Skip, Plink! Skip, Plop! Clack! Crack! Two boys, in red and orange shirts, walking the riverbed, bounced stones. I poked a nose out of the covering bedroll. Sun splashed on willow trees. A tiny canoe drifted under pine boughs uplifted in prayer above the mountain. Exit the gypsy moth from his cocoon. Trees bent to touch a mirrored water-reflection of the woodland. In such surroundings one can sit cross legged all morning. Soft dark sand gave way underfoot. The property was an abandoned rock/sand quarry. Flood water had ruined the conveyor belts; sun warped wooden troughs; rust ate the machinery. An industrial graveyard.

Two Amish women sold breads and sweet rolls to Saturday crowds mingling on quaint streets. Mother wore a long plain black gown draped modestly from neck to ankle, her daughter dressed similarly in purple, both in matching white bonnets covering their rolled hair. The husband rode a black surrey, whip-flicking his steed for true horsepower. He chased the road out of town, making deliveries. Farms sprouted on river islands. River cuts spawned fishing holes.

Autumn Harvest Festival banners greeted visitors to Bloomsburg. The shady lane approach was blocked to traffic downtown. Sirens wailed. Fire trucks paraded with children as riders, the winners of a contest, clowns, a high school band high-stepping in style, antique cars, comical floats, an old time pump wagon, a water fight between firemen-with the crowds getting sprayed, teenagers standoffishly interested, unsure how to accept the hi-jinks as adult or childish? Onlookers wormed through sidewalk throngs enjoying the gaiety.

Ride, ride, ride. My rendezvous, Shavertown, Pennsylvania, was unlisted on the map, tucked back in the mountains. Uphill pumping needed. Before I started the climb, I checked for directions at a grimy service station littered with old tires, car parts, and trash. The owners had been caught in the Susquehanna River flood of Hurricane Agnes, three months earlier. Rain saturated the ground for seven days. Then the storm focused its might on the half-mile wide valley for three more days. A flood was inevitable. Police ordered everyone to evacuate river towns, supervised emergency packing and food storage, and began rescue efforts. The service station was twenty feet above the river level. Two partners who had just bought the station, having seen floods before, packed food three feet above the floor for safety, secured tools and hoisted their new soda refrigerator up to the garage ceiling thinking it would be safe. Then they protected any loose property. No one expected the river to rise forty feet, but the garage was covered completely, even the upstairs. Just across the street, a two story white house on higher ground, showed the muddy water line above the upper windows. Power and gas lines were shut off. Telephones went dead. There was no communication except by boat. Sewers backed up and raw sewage floated. People moved uphill, or tried to stick it out in second floor houses. It took waters twenty-four hours to crest and three days to subside.

River chaos remained. The great dig-out began. With martial law declared, the city was off limits from dusk to dawn. Looters were apprehended, but confusion reigned. All flooded areas had a three to twelve inch coat of gooey thick mud: roads, sidewalks, store aisles, counters, roofs, cars. Vehicles attempting to enter the cities skidded and bogged down. Many took flats. Nails, under the mud, punctured tires mercilessly. Busses hauled workers, merchants and civilians to ease traffic swell. One bridge to Wilkes-Barre was destroyed. Teenagers pitched in round-the-clock alongside adults to aid with the massive clean-up/throw out. All wood products warped, buckled or cracked. Rugs were soggy rags. Steel rusted. Furnishings, in disarray, in every building, moldered. File cabinets held smeared records and receipts that were unreadable and worthless. Small businesses were hardest hit. Many could not re-open. Those that could, threw everything out. Army trucks, day and night, hauled away the rubbish piles stacked in the streets ten feet high on every storefront and on every avenue. Whatever was salvaged was washed, scrubbed, washed and scrubbed over and over. It still looked mud-caked. In this green lush valley, it seemed incredible-like a stupendous hoax, the hoodwinking of a practical joker. Yet, evidence was everywhere: new wood, carpet rolls, do-it-yourself home repairs, makeshift braces, and mud water lines.

A playful brook skipped down rock paths as I rode up the canyon winding along the mountain spine. Saturday car washing and polishing was conducted on turnouts. A few dry leaves crunched under tires traveling into forest recesses. Twice I took wrong lanes; the correct path loped up a grade into a quiet glen of ranches. Yellow sun dots broke through green maple branches, a scenic eyeful worth slow climbing on downshifted gears.

Shavertown was the birth place of a famous American, at least to me, Jack Eck, Jr., his two story white clapboard home nestled in the arms of poplars. At my knock, a silver haired man opened the screen door.

"Hi! Is this the Eck residence? Do you have a son who spent a lot of time patching up guys overseas?"

Mr. Eck, Sr., somewhat baffled, called back over his shoulder. "Jack, Jack. There's someone here to see you".

A barrel-chested bespectacled man, strode roly-poly to the door, dropped his jaw, smiled and exclaimed, "Uncle Ed! I didn't know if you'd make it. All the way from California! By bike! It's good to see you. Mom, this is a friend of mine from Vietnam, one of the medics".

Mrs. Eck, in a red dress came outside, took a brief look. "Have you had anything to eat? We're just about to eat. Bring your things around back". She disappeared into the kitchen. Ah, the motherliness of women!

Jack accompanied me upstairs to the spare room vacated by his sister. Mrs. Eck had to pry our reminiscing selves apart to get dinner served. I had worked as a medical assistant for Jack in a Vietnam dispensary for fourteen months. His goodness to the medics won lasting respect and friendship. Jack chauffeured a tour of the five finger lakes. Friendship is a love saga.   89 miles

THE DOCTOR AND THE MEDIC

Sunday, September 17   Shavertown, PA   Day 94

The Eck home was a showcase of tasteful brocade furniture and finely woven materials. A grand piano commanded the living room. Porcelain figurines adorned table tops. Delicate china pieces served as wall and shelf decorations. An embroidered cloth covered the dining table. Warm artistic detail provided family comfort and enjoyment.

Jack stole me from the house after church to finally pay off the airplane trip promised last February. His sports car roamed golden flocked Pennsylvania mountains like hunkered sleeping dinosaurs with forest feather coats. The first nips of autumn chills were already changing tree leaves to spots of red, gold, orange. In two more weeks the hills would be afire with color. We slipped onto the field of the local airport, and waited for Jack's reserved rental plane to return. He could practice flying while giving a bird's eye commentary of the geography. We waited two hours. The overdue plane and rising air turbulence discouraged us from further flighty ideas.

Jack contented himself no matter what he did, no matter where he did it. In the Army, at our overseas medical station in Phu Bai, he was the only consistently even-tempered man I met. He refused to stoop to petty bickering, yet he arbitrated many arguments. Efficiently and skillfully he performed every task, both large and small, even the most unpleasant, like recovering charred bodies from a helicopter crash (no one else helped), or mouth-to-mouth resuscitation of an overdosed soldier. Caring for his medics was a continual effort, insuring first rate treatment, thoroughly done jobs and fair distribution of tasks. We nine medics and doctor cared for three thousand G.I.s directly under us. When word leaked out how competent and efficient our medical care and flight physicals were, we soon had men from other battalions sneaking over for service and treatment. We took medical histories, sewed and bandaged all cuts, sassed a few ornery men, prescribed for ills, tested blood and urine, trapped and killed rats, inspected kitchens, sprayed against cockroaches, flew medical helicopter missions, performed village health checks, handled minor gunshot wounds (usually self-inflicted) before sending to the hospital, and in general mothered soldiers who, not seeing enough action, created accidents, beat each other senseless, fell on sharp metal, broke bones, took heroin. This last casualty area, Jack developed into a special commander's report, under orders, when he had four days left in Vietnam. He wrote a drug abuse paper analyzing and criticizing the Army attitudes and treatment of drug users, and asked me to proofread. The scathing report was instrumental in revolutionizing the military's punishment approach to addicts. His last year of Army practice, in the States, was frustrated by regulations, military rank, snobbishness, and pettiness. On discharge day, he grinned at the re-up (recruitment) officer: F.T.A. That did not mean Fun, Travel and Adventure.

Jack applied soon thereafter to specialize in orthopedics, but then discovered just-got-out-of-the-military-blues. His heart was not in it, so he changed his mind, and began practice in Vail, Colorado, where he could be a ski freak while setting the broken bones of less fortunate fanatics. General medical practice was pure enjoyment.

I often wondered how tacit Jack could be so skilled at medicine when he claimed, "It's no more difficult than any other job. You just know where the reference books are".

There were exploits he had never mentioned, for he was not the bragging type: a track star, outdoor enthusiast, and sportsman. As an Eagle Scout with a chest full of merit badges, he built and operated his own ham radio, had been a camp counselor, canoeist, tennis player, water and snow skier, photographer, and an accomplished musician. At twelve, he learned to pick out pieces on the piano. In church one Sunday, the organist became ill. Mrs. Eck asked Jack to finish the service which he did. For fun he picked up the guitar and banjo. And one of his big thrills was piloting a Cessna aircraft. (In Vietnam, he added helicopters.) How could Jack be so modest?

During an afternoon cruise to the finger lakes, a friend, Walt, invited us to play tennis with his wife Judy, who two years earlier had been in a near fatal car accident. Recovery was slow, but the mangled left elbow never regained use; it hung limp at her side. Judy refused to let it limit her spirited activities. Jack and I teamed against the couple, who beat us soundly. Down at the boathouse, Jack secured a white safety vest and dove into the water. Grabbing the tow rope, he waited as the line tightened. The engine revved pulling him up on water skis. Tilting from side to side, he slashed through the water raising a white rooster tail. Judy got in next. She rose out of the water holding the tow line with one hand, and stood on a single ski, repeating the weaving maneuvers for 15 minutes. Then it was my turn. Ha, ha! I'd never water skied, but took the dare, plunging into the icy lake. As the towrope stretched taut heavy drag pressed against my chest, rushing water swirled around bent knees, as my body lifted over the water! Amazed, I gasped, swallowed water running up my chest, and

195

fell splat backwards. On the second attempt, I fell releasing the tow bar awkwardly, bruising the inner thighs. The third try was a charm. I stood. Waterskiing was like roller skating on glass, smooth, fast. We cruised into a lake finger, turned, and shot back to the main lake. Growing bolder, I began cutting out of the V-wash behind the motorboat and weaving like a pro. Man, oh man! It was so easy. I giggled. That's when I lost my balance, caught a ski tip in a wave, and drank half the lake. Walt finished the skiing with an exhibition of back twists, one arm pulls, buoy dodges, and a neck-in-the-tow-line trick.

Judy winced, "That's how he plans to divorce me".

Back home, Jack prepared for swing shift in the Philadelphia hospital where he assisted for the summer. We made plans to meet again. At night, chess games with a family friend.   No miles

FLOOD AFTERMATH AND CLAIMS

Monday, September 18   Shavertown, PA to Portland, PA   Day 95

Mrs. Eck packed lunch and wagged her head as I strapped her goodies to my sleeping bag. She wondered if I'd be safe. Mr. Eck, already at his bank in Wilkes-Barre, had invited a visit.

If stories about flood devastation seemed incredulous, a visit into Wilkes-Barre, three months after Hurricane Agnes, verified the catastrophe. A cement bridge to the city lay crumbled; the one usable bridge was entirely discolored and caked with mud. The best description of downtown, grime. Regardless of many buildings having been scrubbed inside and out, water and mud lines showed across first floor walls and windowsills. Above clean, below soot, scum, and mud. Nailed boards sealed businesses closed, nearly every other store on Main Street, more on side streets. Back alleys and streets were boarded up, windows soaped. Mud crusted many sidewalks. Street police directed the whirlwind of traffic, trying to organize vehicle movements, where disabled signal lights failed.

Until normal transportation could resume, free city busses were jammed with standing adults and teenagers. Students were on half day schedules. At noon the second shift of classes traded attendance. All day the city was crowded with students waiting on sidewalks for an empty bus.

Mr. Eck, in the bank foyer, pointed out the vast disorder, both outside and inside. Four to five feet of water had entered the building. Furniture was nearly a total loss. The niceties of banks were missing, counters, desks, tables, extra chairs, decorations. Brown mildew and scum stuck to the walls. Partitions, desks and wall panels were cracked, buckled or splitting. Loosened masonry had gaps between sections. Filing cabinets were virtually empty; paperwork obliterated, smeared, and mildewed had to be thrown out. Stainless steel safe-deposit boxes rusted; they had already been cleaned and polished three times. Everything in the bank had been scrubbed at least three times and still looked dingy. By comparison, the bank was perhaps the cleanest business in town. During the critical peak of aftershock, the bank gave its help. Every employee was given $500.00 outright. Desperate families received more. Loans and assistance were given, as speedily as possible, at low interest rates.

A worried father called Mr. Eck multiple times about his home. It had been washed off its foundation. Army engineers ordered it demolished. The man had lived in the house one year, and still owed $20,000.

"Mr. Eck, what will I do?" he pleaded anxiously.

As a banker he could do nothing until the government took a crucial step to replace lost homes. Regretfully he had to accept the man's $100 due payment for a house that did not exist. Other buildings washed off foundations, settled intact, but had to be demolished because of where they landed-against other homes or in intersections.

Declared a national disaster area, federal aid was pumped into the locale-low cost loans on little or no security. Many plighted families were sheltered in other homes temporarily. The Ecks put up two families and found clothing for them. A certain Mr. X accepted help but would not assist in house duties; he did not clean his portion of the charitable home. When a truck was dispensing free federal brooms, he stood in line several times collecting brooms to give away to friends. His own was never used. When the waters receded, he delayed leaving because his house was messy, and expected National Guard troops to be assigned to clean it for him. Two elderly ladies next door, asked his assistance to mop their flooded basement. He was "too busy". Having received damage claim paperwork, he listed an old dish set, which he threw out, as corroded, and further, declared rug rot. He didn't own carpeting. The government accepted his word. Bankers noticed a 20 percent increase in carpeting claims over their listings prior to the flood. Houses, in general, were worth another $5,000 after the hurricane, according to beefed up declarations. The government honored the word of claimants.

Afternoon. Shifting gears down to seven, six, smoothed motion. Southward into the Bear Creek and Pocono forests. Brooding cloud cover lay over pines, poplars, oaks, and maples as the route continued to New York. Bone racking hills bent, rambled, and twisted. A light drizzle wet pavement from Lake Pocono to rock strewn Swiftwater. A market clerk advised to avoid the river camp. There were lots of cottonmouths. I deliberately ate supper on a boulder just to observe snake action. No luck.

Paralleling Route 611, the road descended into Stroudsburg towards the Delaware River. Rain. Rain. Rain. The last two miles to Portland were gully washers. On a woman's front porch, a reprieve-change-of-clothing allowed walking dry to a delicatessen for pickled sandwiches and milk. A renewed downpour forced hustling under overhangs, trees and roofs. Radio static crackled with lightning flashes. After the rain passed, I wrote, excited. Tomorrow would be the last riding day!   70 miles

NEW YORK ARRIVAL

Tuesday, September 18   Portland, PA to New York, NY   Day 96

Delaware woodland truck farms. Tomatoes, melons, cucumbers, squash, pumpkins. Route 46 angled through the mountains. Decay ate at the road, potholes, cracks, frost splits, and overuse crumble. Crews were trying to repair the damage as traffic drove by. It was exceedingly dangerous cycling road, and worse with each mile to New York.

Delaware hunting had become a cruel sport. Game laws prohibited rifle use under the guise of giving deer a chance to escape. Hunters used shotguns. Unless the deer was killed outright, the animal limped out of range of a weapon. Hunters rarely chased wounded creatures, feeling plenty more were available. A young man had seen numerous deer with gangrenous wounds hobbling through windbreaks, hiding their blood-scabbed crippled bodies in thickets.

Drizzle. Asphalt grit blackened my lower body. Intersection horns blared from an auto army creeping through Hackettstown, Budd Lake, Dover, Caldwell, Clifton, Passaic. No traffic breaks. Surly drivers honked, cussed, swerved, jammed brakes, and squeezed the bicycle to ram curbs, lunge into potholes, run over highway litter. Sixty miles in six hours. Almost over.

Lincoln Tunnel Toll prohibited bicycles. At 3 p.m. I detoured north to JFK Boulevard. Blue clad policemen with octagon hats and Manhattan accents, dropping Rs and dragging out As and Os, barked directions.

"Okay bud, ya goes downa pahk, tuhn tah yas right and goes ovah da watah," directed one cop.

George Washington Bridge bundled eight lanes and a wide footpath over the Hudson river. Lovers walked, kids chased, hopped and skipped, graffiti scrawls identified street names and gangs. Fabled Manhattan skyline rose like a giant gray prison. Stark, tall rigid apartment cages of human life jutted up like guarded towers overlooking the river. Citizens seemed imprisoned on the island with bridges, ferries, and tunnels their escapes.

Five and six story apartments lined the Hudson River banks. Taller ones appeared nearer the heart of the city with exterior fire escapes, cement, and asphalt lawns. Street and telephone poles poked skyward posted with official signs: *Tow Away Zone. Curb Your Dog. No Parking.* A roller-skate hockey game played on a side street. Mothers strolled baby carriages or sat on stoops. Walkers uncurbed their leashed dogs. Cars parked in fecal aftermath. Police towed away a car and some aftermath. A street sweeper would clean the remainder next week, if there wasn't a strike. Trash piled on every corner. Wind delivered dirty newspaper across streets.

Central Park. An island of green in a cement city. Curving paths encircled the park center. Horse carriages, benches, ball fields, lakes, kiddie rides, club houses, swings, joggers, football teams, loners, lovers. The stories of Central Park muggers were not apparent; I didn't run over any black-jacketed knife-wielding thugs, or their victims.

59th Street Bridge posted *No Bikes*, but had a pedestrian walk. I asked two cops what the story was. They didn't know.

"Go ahead an' see if yas get away wid it," they said.

Okay. I sauntered stiff legged over the old steel beam walkway up to a locked barrier gate. The only remedy was to walk out into stop-and-go traffic and spiral down into Queens borough. New Yorkers were equally helpful with misinformation and wrong directions. No city maps. At 7 p.m. a familiar residential street.

On 56 Drive, a tranquil, green two story shingle house sat. Knock.

Uncle Johnny Paige chuckled: "Oh, ho, ho, it's Edward. Well, well, so you made the trip. Come in. Florence! It's Edward".

The Bubla house was still. One by one, relatives coming home throughout the evening greeted: Fred Bubla, who never sat; Cecile, who always had something to talk about and liked to be teased; Larry, catcher on a Detroit Tigers baseball farm team; Barbara, his bouncy, chipper girlfriend; Johnny, head payroll manager for United Airlines; Florence, Fred's wife, a former school aide and postal worker, who suffered from Lou Gehrig's Disease (muscle atrophy), was the heart of the family. I was with family. The trip was over, or so I thought.   74 miles

NEW YORK, BOSTON, HOME AND A LESSON IN HUMILITY

September 19-28   New York to Boston MA, to New   Days 97-106
                   York to Long Beach, CA

N.Y. City sights. Greenwich Village, rattling subways, crowds, pop art, fish markets, skyscraper canyons, stores galore packed with customers and cornucopias of merchandize. Parks, panhandlers, poets and preachers. High brow, hijinx, hoot and holler. Cabbies and flabbies. Streetwalkers and street cleaners. Hot dogs and hot tempers. Theaters and TV broadcasters. Jews, Italians, Blacks, Puerto Ricans, Polacks, Germans, Greeks, Cubans, French, and all nationalities mixing together on the streets going home to private social ghettoes. It was all here. It was a place to visit, investigate, absorb.

I stayed seven days, technically finished, but I wanted to add Boston, another 250 miles, glimpse a bit more of the famed changing autumn leaves. It took three days of numbing, freezing travel on Old Boston Post Road: Connecticut lowlands, harbors, Mystic's whaling museum, ancient historic graveyards with markers from the 1600s, Rhode Island's insurance canyons and polluted rivers, and the turning leaves. It was getting too cold. I didn't enjoy the riding, or the scenery, because sweat chilled me to the bone at each stop. A new yellow heavy ski parka was too warm. My knees were super tender with bursitis. I spent no time touring Boston, but took an Amtrak train back to New York.

A promised teaching job was waiting back in Long Beach for a long term substitute, not my real wish, but it was the opportunity to work with students, and fight off winter hunger.

I bade farewell to the Bublas, and Uncle John. For a plane ticket, $168 was a lot of money. It would have lasted easily to Denver on a bike, but not in winter. The ten speed, now affectionately referred to as my wife, was dismantled, stuffed into a cardboard box and flown as baggage in a 747 jet hold. Out the cabin window, I watched New York shrink into ant sized dirt mounds, and for five hours at 35,000 feet, sadly watched the land passing below: Appalachian Mountains, rivers, forests, Ohio, the Great Plains and Bad Lands, Rocky Mountains, desert mesas, gorges of Utah, Arizona desert, and the Colorado River disappeared without any investigation. And I missed meeting all sorts of good folks.

At the L.A. plane terminal, eager passengers pushed and shoved out of the exits. I took my time, collected the bike box, re-assembled the wheels, adjusted the handlebars, and made ready to bike home. For a few moments I sat outside on a taxi bench. Albert, a security guard, speaking with an Hungarian accent, approached.

"Yoo beeen riding, no?" he questioned.

"Yep," I bragged, "about five thousand eight hundred miles".

"I did too, vhen I vass young. Nine t'ousan six hundred miles acrosst der U.S. in nineteen turty-six. I had only vun speed. I didn't know der Eenglish so goot. I got der address book, too, as souvenir".

He pulled out a worn tattered leather diary from his back pocket and showed the cities he had visited and hundreds of signatures of people who attested to his travels throughout the West.

Adventures may be sources of pride, accomplishment achieved. But when it goes to the head, fattening one's ego, a taste of humble pie needs to be served. My dream wasn't shattered, but it was tempered. Others have done this and more.   5,800 miles

Thus, be thankful for all the adventure and those who helped. Relish the goodness of Americans. Take time. Truly enjoy America. Be still. You have been loved.

My next bicycle adventure will occur after I retire at age 65. I expect to take the northern route across the upper U.S., the Lewis and Clark Trail.

As a parting thought, I invite cyclers to dream, whether a city ride, a state journey or a continental trek. There is beauty, fun, adventure. Americans are good people, well worth meeting. It is possible to "make it", if one begins with the first step, the first pedal push, the first block. The rest comes naturally. Take it one day at a time, one bite, one pedal stroke, one battle. It cannot be done all at once. Choose moments. Good planning and common sense will guide over the rough spots. Maybe take a friend or two along. Adventure is in the challenge of a bicycle tour.

PART II

PART II

40 YEARS LATER

Okay, I lied. I promised to do a second trip across the U.S. when I turned sixty-five. I'm now 67, advancing to 68 this summer. When I retired from teaching, at age sixty-three, it seemed that the promise would be kept a little bit earlier. However, my wife made it plain that she was not available to go bicycle gallivanting across the country due to the book orders, grants, cataloging, coordinating with library aides, and the thousand and one details of being a district librarian serving eight school libraries. Each year she hinted that maybe when she retired, then it would be possible. This year, being older and more crotchety, I told her I'm going, with or without her.

Susan was not ecstatic about a bicycle trip, saying that she never expected me to go, that it was just idle man talk, because I wasn't riding my ten speed or getting preparations underway. It was probably a passing fancy. Well, there might have been truth to that. I hadn't ridden for three years and my bike sat idle in an open shed collecting dust and moisture and rust. This winter after some honest self-talk, I realized that to make such an arduous trek, time was running out for my body. It had to be this year.

For my wife, there was a complication. Her father, Ernie, died before Christmas in 2009. That was stress enough. Since Ernie had died, we went monthly to the Borgaro home in Santa Barbara, CA, providing relief to her sister Laurie, until her mom moved to a convalescent hospital. Sally died midsummer 2011, six weeks after Susan retired. It fell to Susan to be the executor of her parents' estate. We assumed estate care for the house, went through belongings and pared down the accumulated possessions of 60 years, and gardened the acre-and-a-third of hillside orchard, front and back yards. Susan found that, even though there was an excellent trust set up, administering it was a significant task. In addition, two of her sisters were on chemo. More stress. She really didn't want me to go.

In part, she said she would go along with me, if I'd just wait one more year. She wanted to be at hand for her sisters and conclude the estate business. She asked me to spend a year getting in condition; didn't like me going off alone; worried that the worst would happen to me; feared that I would be abandoning her for ninety days; agonized that it would not be good for our marriage.

I explained that I couldn't put the bike trip off any longer. Though I have done many strenuous handy-man tasks, heavy duty gardening, remodeling, carpentry, and construction, my body was giving signs that it did not have the energy or drive it once had. Next year might be too late. The trip had been put off for too long. When we married, it was never kept a secret that, when sixty-five, I wanted to do the second half of the trip which I had taken by bicycle from Long Beach, CA to Miami, FL to Boston, MA (5,800 miles). It was never held as a requirement that my wife had to accompany me for moral or physical support. I was willing to go alone without any negative feelings or regrets. There was no lack of love. We were simply two spouses with a conflict. I intended to go.

As far as health was concerned, I rated myself as a seven on a scale of one to ten. At 6 feet tall, I weighed 240 pounds, 65 more than the 1972 trip. Both shoulders had rotator cuff surgery, and functioned without pain. I bench pressed a hundred pounds, walked two miles a day, and did the daily dozen army stretches. Some muscles and joints were stiff partly due to age and maybe arthritis-mostly my lower back. Four months ago, my doctor said I had diabetes, so there were medications and diet restrictions to which I am adhering. Because I have neither smoked nor been a drinker, there are no other complications of health known. Tomorrow I go to the doctor to ask if I'm healthy enough to take on part two of the adventure.

PREPARATION WEEK TWO

Today Dr. Shannon gave me approval, saying that I was disciplined and stubborn enough to do the bike trip. He has enjoined me to continue monitoring my blood sugar daily. I am usually in the 120-140 range after fasting through the night. Medications will also be maintained. He questioned me about meals, conditioning, length of daily riding goals, and cautioned not to push hard if the hills were too challenging. He admired the ambition but as a precaution, he wanted lab tests to make certain there were no surprises. At present my medicines were Metformin, one-a-day, Glyburide, two-a-day, and other pills for losing weight. I spent the rest of the morning getting lab tests.

Susan was furious: "How dare he tell you, you could go on the trip! He doesn't know if you're healthy enough. You haven't practiced. You need a year of training. What about your heart? Is it healthy enough?" Susan and I disagree as to whether she demanded Doctor Shannon that he schedule an appointment with a heart specialist. We both have definite strong feelings about how the doctor was urged to set up a heart test. But I agree with myself that I have the only true memory. The bottom line was that I had to see a cardiologist.

For training, I started with a mile a day, adding one extra mile each day thereafter, now up to six. Knees at first recognized the unaccustomed stress of pressing down on the pedals. Breathing has not seemed laborious or strained. It will take a while for hands and arms to adjust to leaning over the handlebars. Because of the extra 65 pounds, sitting on the seat will be a pain, at least until I find the right padding. Putting all one's weight on the two bottom bones of the pelvis is self-imposed torture. Every pedal stroke rubs one side or the other. This is what saddle sore means. At the moment, folded bath towels are the preferred experiment.

Late in the day, the cardiologist's office called to schedule an EKG. I'm not fearful of my age, but I do not expect any serious circumstances, since I last had the test done about five years ago, with no problems. Ten weeks to go.

CONDITIONING WEEKS THREE THROUGH SEVEN

By slowly increasing the mileage each day, no significant aches or pains surfaced. Sure, at the end of the day, I can feel the lactic acid build up in muscles, but a massage usually takes care of the tiredness. Two benefits have come along with the conditioning. A sore knee had swelled up three years ago. An orthopedic doctor said to keep a watch on it, but gave no medication or directions for exercise or care. It has since ceased being tender and annoying. I can now genuflect in church without stiffness or moaning pain. Secondly, my energy and endurance have increased (duh?). However, there is a drawback. I want to sleep 12 hours a day.

On April 27, I did 32 miles in three riding segments of about an hour each. Normally I rode between 8-12 miles then took a 15-30 minute break, ate fruit or a meal, drank juice or water, and made adjustments to the bike or equipment. I'd like to say that the training has been consistent, but it hasn't. The San Joaquin Valley has had unusual spring weather. Maybe I'm too wimpy in my old age to bear the elements. There have been heavier winds than normal, 20-25 mph range, rain squalls and thunder showers that I want no part of. I see no benefits from a metal bicycle conducting electricity through a person into the ground. The heavy late season storms are not the type worth training for. I still do the military daily dozen stretch exercises with some modifications three days a week, and lift moderate weights the other three days. Being consistent is a struggle. And yes, I do suffer from acute laziness, as opposed to ugly laziness.

Reconditioning my Italvega bike was another thing all together. First, the "heavy duty light weight bike" was built 40 years ago, no longer made and neither were replacement parts. By modern standards its plain aluminum frame was a beast at 31.2 pounds. Due to carelessness, the bike had been relegated to an open air shed where for over three years it suffered moisture damage-amazing how much rust accumulated from dew. Many hours were spent with a toothbrush, a rag, and oil, rubbing (polishing?) metal surfaces not coated with brown spray paint. With elbow grease added in, the rust reduced but lay hidden in a few spots. However, mechanical aspects of the bike needed professional help from the Reedley Bike Trax Shop. New tires and tubes. New brakes. The drive chain was replaced, as was the needle nosed leather seat of 40 years ago. After three different attempts to acquire a seat that reduced the pressure on the butt, I finally purchased a wide Avenir gel seat. Then it was a problem to find the correct angle seat position to prevent sliding forward and developing hand, arm and rump cramps. The solution appeared to be new handle bars which raised up the hand position four inches thus relieving the stressed body parts. A complete tune up, new pedals, and handle bar tape rounded out the reconditioning. The repair cost more than the original bike at $172.

In addition, the safety was also updated: new reflectors, front and back; small head and tail lights using AA batteries, and a clip-on mirror attached to my glasses to see rearward. I already had a riding helmet, but I expect bright colored shirts would ensure easy visibility. I have considered a lime yellow highway vest, but have not yet made up my mind. During the conditioning rides, the old bugaboo of a sore butt resurfaced. The gel seat and raising of the handle bar helped, but it wasn't until I bought a pair of padded riding shorts that the sitting soreness receded to a mere ache.

Dr. Telles, a cardiologist, required visual confirmation of all medicines taken, and comfortable shoes and clothes for a stress test. The good news? The doctor was an avid bike rider himself. The bad news? My wife was surprised that the family doctor had declared my health satisfactory to allow for this foolhardy trip. So now she hoped the cardiologist would declare me too enfeebled to proceed. Other bad news? The appointment was delayed forty minutes. Could that add stress? The nurse lead me into the room and requested me to remove my shirt. After waiting another ten minutes the sonogram proceeded smoothly with no oh-ohs or humms.

The doctor entered, looked at the monitor and said: "Good. Let's go on".

I was moved to the inclined stress walking machine, without switching shoes from stiff hiking boots to soft broken-in tennis shoes. All things considered, it was just a walk, right? *On an eighteen degree slope.* Hold on to a bar directly in front (to prevent falling), which impeded a normal arm swing. I walked for three minutes, increased the speed for another three, then sped up for two more. Of course, a body was going to huff and puff. What I did not expect was that my right arm would cramp up getting pins and needles from not being able to swing naturally. When the machine stopped the doctor took a second blood pressure check, then the nurse provided a second sonogram test with me lying down once more. The doctor left the room.

The nurse ordered: "Put your shirt on. Follow me," and edged into the labyrinthine hallway. Now should that create stress? Apparently not.

In the office, the doctor said, "There's nothing to be concerned about. There is no blockage. The heart looks normal. You can go on your trip. However, there are a few things to consider. Get your conditioning to 40 miles a day before you leave. Practice on hill climbing before you go. Buy a pair of padded riding shorts. I know you're poo-pooing them, but they really do help. Lose some weight. It will help with sitting on the seat. Cut the carbohydrates and you'll lose the weight. And since you are not a junk food eater, cut the amount you eat".

I promised to follow instructions, and thanked my fellow biking enthusiast. Stress? What stress? (At the supermarket later in the day, it was astounding how much of what's on the shelves is carbs.)

The real stress was in the car. I asked Susan if she wanted the good news or the bad news.

First the good news: "There is no problem with my heart. The bad news: The doctor says I can proceed with the trip". Susan drove silently, dejectedly to the shopping center, where I bought a pair of padded bike pants. We ate a late lunch and drove home in silence. I was healthy enough to bicycle. She drove in a blue funk. Now that's stress!

PREPARATION WEEK EIGHT

If Susan were going with me then she wanted to plan our accommodations. The internet provided lots of RVs for sale along with trailers and motel stops. So far the motel option called for about $10,000, adding gas for the car and meals. Ten to fifteen year old RVs tended to be in the $10,000-$25,000 range offering about ten miles per gallon of gas or less, compared to our Subaru's 24 mpg. The upside would be that, after the trip, we could vacation else wise, or resell the vehicle. Unfortunately, the Subaru could only haul up to 2,500 pounds which limited any trailer to a very small size-like a teardrop variety. We've looked over several vehicles, but since Susan will be doing the driving, the emphasis must be on her comfort and driving safety, and to this point nothing has been satisfactory.

Each day I've increased the distance cycled and by the end of April I hit 41 miles. Although the padded bike shorts have helped the sitting soreness, they have not proven to be the miracle cure-all for butt pain. The longer the distance, my hands numbed. Because of the other activities and requirements, training was broken up into basically three or four periods of riding about 12 miles at a session, taking a break, sometimes hours, and then doing another riding stint. It meant riding at night around a four mile square in our town of Dinuba, so I carried a small but powerful headlight, reflectors, a red taillight, and wore a fluorescent yellow vest. I began developing driving and traffic strategies. Most vehicles were courteous, giving a wide berth.

BOISE: MAY 2-9

We had planned to visit our daughter, Rachel, toward the end of the school year. She worked in the Boise YMCA as a Health and Fitness director. The "Y" was populated by a veritable flurry of exercising indoor and and outdoor devotees from high schoolers, college kids, young professionals, families, single moms, and loads of vibrant retirees. Facilities were heavily scheduled, brimming with coming and going enthusiasts. Rachel oversaw several coordinators, and taught classes herself, one of these being cycling.

Together we went to Idaho Mountain Touring to rent a bicycle for ongoing training during the visit. I admit that I'm basically cheap, hating to spend a buck, especially on myself. Well, there were several styles of bikes to choose from, but the only appropriate one was a touring racer bike worth $1,200, renting at $25 per day. After balking at the price of $175 for a week, Susan said that she would rent it if I wouldn't, and Rachel induced me to realize what a modern bike might offer that my forty year old Italvega didn't. In addition, we purchased another padded bike short, and a guide book Biking the Lewis and Clark Trail.

The book revealed many tips and insights of the L. & C. trip, although its travel course was the direction of the original Discovery party, east to west, while my intent was to reverse the direction. However, the big news to my stubborn thinking was that the book listed the total distance of 3,254 miles from St. Louis to the West. The itinerary listed the daily distance as typically between 70 and 90 miles, with the entire tour completed in 40 days, thus demonstrating what several people had been asking me to do: shorten the trip; cut out the distance from Dinuba, CA to Astoria, OR, (900+ miles) which would make the trip over four thousand miles. My estimation was a daily distance of forty to fifty miles expecting to finish in sixty days. It was sobering that, when planning to ascend the Sierra Nevada Mountains, it would be unlikely that I maintain forty miles daily. I must eat my pride and make compromises. Susan was thoroughly pleased when I relented and agreed to drive to Astoria at the mouth of the Columbia River to begin the tour.

As a comparison, the rented bike had eighteen speeds, two front sprockets with nine at the rear, ram horn handlebars, a needle nose seat, light weight (22 pounds), water bottle holders and handlebar gear shifters. This last was a revelation. With a flick of the finger inward, the bike chain dropped to a lower gear quickly, smoothly, and efficiently. A push with the thumb reversed the gears back to a higher speed demanding more forceful stronger pedaling. It was pure pleasure to shift gears up and down. My old bike struggled to shift ten speeds (two sprockets front, five rear) from higher to lower gears, and the rider must reach down below the center bar to manipulate a cable lever, which is an awkward and off-balance maneuver especially when turning a corner, or encountering hills. And the gears took time to synchronize the shift. The old bike carried a rear rack to hold traveling needs, a kick stand, no water holders, a wide seat, straight handle bars raised four inches, and weighed 31.2 pounds.

Needless to say, the rental outperformed my Italvega in every way. It was a delight to ride, fast, efficient and could smoothly shift down to take steep hills outside the Boise area. Although it was a vacation visit, I put in at least 12 miles a day, with two 20-24milers. Now the bad news (stubborn me) was that I wanted to do the trip with my Old Faithful. I have seen the future, but I wanted the past, bike and man 40 years later.

For the duration, we stayed at the home of Kevin and Mary Shaner, parents of our daughter-in-law, Sammy. The accommodations were in the five star category. Information about the roads, impassable mountain ranges, steep ascents, and 5,000 foot passes of just Idaho alone reinforced the seriousness of the trek. Bullheadedness wouldn't get one up a mountain. I might have to admit that some climbs might be more than my 67 year old body could deliver, unless I'd be willing to walk if need be. Facing facts was a requirement here. And there may be some heavy Northwest weather to encounter. Kevin voiced the Lolo Pass would probably be my toughest challenge.

PREPARATION WEEK TEN: BAD NEWS/GOOD NEWS

Before leaving for Boise, the bike went for reconditioning at the Reedley Bike Trax Shop because the front two gears weren't shifting. Upon my return, the manager, Paula, informed me they had great difficulty trying to fix the gear shift. The broken part cost $88.00 to replace. However, the obsolete parts were unavailable. To convert the bike to a modern set of derailleurs would require a new set of all the parts, because the gears must synchromesh, and the cost would be near $600. In essence, Old Faithful had died the death of "no parts, no repair". I had 20 days to buy a bike, or cancel the trip.

After consulting Paula, and several bike shops, a pall of dejection loomed. On a whim, I checked the Fresno Bee want-ads on the off chance that someone might sell a suitable replacement. Of the nine items for sale, one listed a 21 speed bike. The family was selling because the daughter, who wanted a cycle to go really fast, had lost interest. Dad, a six foot six-incher, was its present rider. With the basic info, I began researching the internet, asked my daughter's advice, and checked several different sites for comparison values and body sizing tips. The cycle, a specialized light weight (19 pounds) Allez, had Shimano gears, three front sprockets, seven rear, (21 speeds altogether), finger tip shifters up and down on ram horn handle bars, two water bottle holders, new brakes and tires, rear rack, a mileage meter/speedometer, and a listed value of about $1,500, but sold for $200. Both the Reedley Bike Trax Shop manager and top mechanic declared it a good deal. It tested to 17 mph.

On shakedown cruises, four flats occurred in less than twelve miles each day. Paula replaced the tubes free of charge saying that the Slime Inner Tubes must have been defective. She wanted a safe and enjoyable trip. I replaced the outer tires with thicker thirty dollar thorn resistant Michelins, and lo and behold the tire problems ceased. After a hundred miles of testing the bike rolled two miles an hour slower (15 mph), but had no more flats. For the trip, I'll carry two spare tires and three extra Slime Inner Tubes. Maybe this old fogey has realized the importance of getting the right gear. Getting the bike to fit my body height and desire for comfort was a matter of adjustments and tweaking. I won't be in a race, but four mph faster than the old Italvega would be appreciated.

PREPARATION WEEK ELEVEN: RIGHT EQUIPMENT

With two weeks to go, we drove to Pasadena, CA, to celebrate Sammy, our daughter-in-law's graduation from veterinarian school, which allowed her to add DVM, Doctor of Veterinary Medicine, after her name. Family, fun, and feasting, but no riding. On Saturday we visited Santa Barbara for last details and work on the Borgaro estate. My wife, as trustee, tied loose ends, keeping the financial situation straight for her four sisters. I replaced a bathroom light and washed walls in preparation for painting when we return. Santa Barbara hills provided two days of twenty mile climbing, however, there was no time to take on the challenging San Marcos Pass, a 1,400 foot climb, north of town. The Allez bike handled well, but required shifting to the second lowest gear to handle one particularly steep grade. No doubt more challenging hills await on the Lewis and Clark Trail.

A benefit of visiting S.B. was the introduction to the REI store (Recreation Equipment Incorporated), outdoor activity being the stock and trade of this business, but it was amazing how much space was devoted to bicycling: bikes, helmets, gloves, camping equipment, car carriers, clothing, camelback (water)packs, GPS and location devices, safety glow vests, shoes, sun glasses, skin protection, maps, food supplements, panniers, carrying bags, rain gear, rear view mirrors, reflectors, night lights, sweat reduction clothing, tools, tires, tubes, tents, water bottles, wheels, lubricants, and every kind of specialized gear imaginable. Let's just say that biking fanatics drool when they enter. I escaped with just a few items and $200 poorer, but bike trip richer.

Tuesday began as a disaster. I forgot for the second time my dental cleaning appointment (why we returned Monday). Although I'm retired, I continue as a driver instructor during the school year, and there was a class of three students for Driver Training. The teens are good students but it is cutting into time needed for training. And then came the fifth flat on the rear tire. The streets of Dinuba were littered with nuts, bolts, screws, nails and sharp items on the road bed. On the thirty-second mile, the tire caught something hidden from sight and instantly sounded the wub-wub-wub of a flat. After a half mile walk home, and some moaning and groaning, the tire came off the wheel to reveal green slime throughout the inner casing. Wiping off the wet residue revealed a large star shaped split near the air valve. I cleaned the interior of the tire, inserted a new tube, repacked the casing, and put in ninety pounds of pressure. Now the tire rubbed ever so slightly against a portion of the derailleur. The wheel had been trued, but the rubbing continued. The only remedy was to ride until wear took about a hundredth of an inch off the tire. A high pitched hum accompanied the four mile practice circuit around the city. My butt was a little more comfortable due to a lamb skin pad over the gel seat, but got sore after twelve miles. Twelve miles seemed to be the limit of strength and discomfort endurance, typically time for a ten minute nutrition break. A succeeding ride has not been as painful, so I may be developing numbing calluses. Nevertheless, hand numbness continued even with gel gloves and memory foam pads added inside. I repositioned my hands every eighth of a mile at the very least. Hopefully, good old strengthening would overcome the hand annoyances.

PREPARATION WEEK 12: GEAR

Susan and I are going through the check off list of things to do before we leave: cancel the paper, mow the lawn, water fruit trees, acquire a gardener to care for the property, houseclean, obtain a house sitter, check out our camping equipment, have mail collected, notify neighbors and others of our routes and whereabouts, pick up maps from AAA (American Automobile Association), set up email addresses for those wishing to follow the trek, pack all the essentials especially medicines, cell phone chargers, toiletries, and clothing. The following is our needed items list:

CAMPING GEAR

8' x 10' stand up tent

Fold up aluminum table

Inflatable mattress

Inflation device for mattress

Shovel, fold up

Rake, small

Broom, small

Canopy, tented plastic

Coleman stove, 2 burner

Coleman lantern

Axe/hammer

Extra tent pegs

2 sleeping bags

Cooking utensils box

Picnic basket

Thermos

Coleman white gas

Astro-turf carpet for tent entry

3 thin plastic sheets

Ice chest, medium

6 days of clothing x 2 persons

Toiletries

BIKE GEAR

Crash helmet

2 Slime inner tubes

2 700mm tires

Cateye mileage/speedometer

3 sized hex wrenches

2 ankle pant clips

Lime yellow vest

Lime yellow short sleeve shirt

Lime yellow long sleeve shirt

Tire repair kit

Tire pump for a bicycle

Gel padded gloves

Camelback water pack

Sunglasses

Weatherman multi tool, small

Hatch back bike rack

Chain lube

Water purification tablets

G2 Gatorade, 30 bottles

Chamois Glide (saddle sores)

Extra gel pad material

Sunscreen

Mosquito repellent	Poncho
First Aid Kit	Bike shoes, hard soles
2 folding chairs	Protein bars
	Guide Book to L. & C. trail

MISCELLANEOUS
Lap top computer
2 medium jackets, his & hers
2 heavy jackets, his & hers
Pen and paper
Books for reading

Monday I met with my Senior Center buddies called the ROMEOS (Retired Old Men Eating Out). They asked questions, like so many others, now that the word is out. Some thought I was crazy, stupid, or needlessly taking a risk; others bet I wouldn't make it. A large number believed I was too old for this undertaking. Still, there were people who thought the trek would be inspiring. Well, so far, inspiration was only a word, and talk was cheap if I didn't put my money where my mouth was.

Susan felt frazzled. She had a departure list of perfection longer than my arm: she didn't want anyone but our closest friends to know we were leaving-fear that burglars would invade while we're gone; don't put on the woodshop burglar alarm-if it went off it would annoy the neighbors; the house had to be spotless for our house sitter; prepay bills; clean out the fridge; wash clothes and bedding; replace our old mailbox with a locking one; set up the tent to see if it was usable; last doctor and hair appointments; buy a Kindle to read books while waiting on the road shoulder; buy a watch and hard soled shoes for riding.

On Wednesday our parish priest celebrated his fifteenth anniversary of ordination. We sat down to a dinner of posole. A friend asked whether I had had the bike blessed before going.

"Yes! Please, anything will help!" Susan responded.

The bike was now blessed. Last minute congrats (premature?) and wishes of luck and last good-byes.

At home we began the final countdown to the trip. We've decided to drive our Subaru Forester. All things were ready, final cleanings, last gardening touches, laying out and checking items, and packing. Today the temperature was 98*. I checked my feet and they were getting cold.

DAY 1: THE PREJOURNEY BEGINS

Friday, June 1, 2012   Dinuba, CA to Yreka, CA   Sunny/dry 98*

It was not an auspicious early start for a beginning. With all the last minute packing and house cleaning for the house sitter, we left at 10:15. The initial route led through fertile green fields of the Great San Joaquin Valley. In the bright sun, verdant row crops and orchards bearing late spring growth decorated the sides of the asphalt road. The farms displayed manicured geometric plots of the most fertile soil in the world. Golden grain fields and hills gave California its nickname "The Golden State". Maybe there is some gold in them thar hills.

Along the highway corridor were city businesses looking for auto traffic profits. Except when stopping for lunch or shopping, cars moved with windows rolled shut keeping the cool air conditioning inside. It was 90* by lunch time. We spelled each other at Sacramento so as to take naps. North of the capitol city lay the rice fields of Colusa, Willows, and Williams, and then began the change into poorer red soils and rolling hills of sparse yellow grass suitable only for cattle pasture.

Our Red Bluff visit was with Raul and Kate Grimes who, forty years ago on the first bike trip, had been my first stopover in the El Monte/L.A. area of California. Like forty years ago, they couldn't believe a retired teacher maniac would go on a long distance bike trek from Astoria, Oregon to St. Louis, Missouri.

The late afternoon drive took us past Redding into the deep green of jagged mountains, densely forested firs, pines and the treasures of California under brilliant puffy cumulus thunder clouds in a baby blue sky. Upon sunset, black silhouettes on the timbered ridges hung on the western horizon, while cattle dots punctuated the deepening shade on golden fields.

After 500 travel miles we rented a motel room in Yreka, then, for old time's sake, drove by the 1905 clapboard house in Montague, where we had lived six years, twenty miles from the Oregon border. After 28 years, everyone in the neighborhood had moved or died. Back at the motel, with the laptop computer set up, Susan fell asleep the moment her head hit the motel pillow. I finished the day's diary. We had arrived without incident. And it had been a gorgeous California eye feast. Not a bad day after all.

DAY 2: PREJOURNEY AND THE REAL START

Saturday,   Ft. Stephens State Park to Astoria, OR   Overcast 68*
June 2, 2012

A great night's sleep is the way to start a great day. Departing the sparse scraggly pine covered hills of Siskiyou County, we began the long ascent to Mt. Ashland, Oregon. Each mile north, the hillsides and mountains became more plush with a green forest velour. Scattered clouds playfully shadowed the mountain textures with blotches creating a brindled cow effect. Ashland, famous for Shakespearean plays, and Medford, the metropolis of Southern Oregon, hid homes and businesses among the tree canopy up the hillsides. They were modern in every respect, but they, like many of the towns along the I-5 corridor of central Oregon, ran at a different pace than the big cities, slower and less trendy/sophisticated. Perhaps called blue collar logging towns, the folks were salt of the earth hardworking Americans. While stopped at Subway in Roseburg we spied a second hand book store locating one of our missing Sue Grafton novels-<u>H is for Homicide</u>. Only <u>I is for Innocent</u> is missing. Across the street, about to exit the car to pump gas, the attendant stopped us in our tracks.

"If the right people see you, it is a thousand dollar fine. That's state law. Only Oregon and New Jersey have it. Only station attendants may pump gas," he warned.

Deeper into central Oregon, the hills undulated frequently.

I was tempted to say: "These aren't too bad. They're climbable. If a truck can make it over, then so can a bike".

Well, that theory was about to be tested. Floating clouds created off-and-on overcast. The scenery varied breath taking versions of tall and short forest, bare rock ledges and carpeted hillside, small ranches nestled in mountain creases and the broadening expanse of Willamette Valley farming paradise. Green, green, green. Pears, apples, oats, berries, cattle, sheep. Quiet, peaceful, pleasant four-lane travel.

There was no missing the entry to Portland. More and more homes and businesses crowded the highway. More buildings were under trees. I-5 changed to six lanes. More freeway entrances and exits. More signage. More directions to pay attention to. More interchanges.

Route 30 to Astoria paralleled the great Columbia River. How strange to see large ocean going vessels tied up at docks a hundred miles upriver.

Log decks lined river banks along with stacks of freshly milled lumber. Industrial plants manufactured commodities at small hamlets and shops.

After acquiring a motel, and ascertaining the Catholic church location in Astoria for Sunday mass, we ate at the Pig and Pancake Restaurant. Susan remarked that we still had enough time to go to land's end, Ft. Stevens State Park, watch the sunset, and maybe I could actually start the trip, which would save backtracking after 8:30 a.m. services. Sure enough, we ate quickly. I rushed to the motel room, put on riding clothes, secured the bike to the car rack and drove. From the various diverging park trails, I selected one that lead to the Columbia River. Offloading the bike and putting a wheel into the incoming tidal rush, I lost grip, dropping the bike into the sand (not a good idea for the gears). Fortunately, no harm. Using an eye dropper, I sucked up water into a bottle for pouring into the Mississippi. If arrested for transporting a horrible germ, or river snail, or virus across state lines, my criminal path started here.

A bonehead mistake. In the hurry to depart the motel, I forgot my reflective yellow vest in the suitcase, making Susan worry. The bike trip started in the evening gloom. Susan drove ahead for two miles at a time to assuage her fears, in spite of the fact that I had head and tail lights on. The trip was uneventful, except that I rode over a two mile long drawbridge causeway in the dark. I won't do that again. I didn't mean not biking. No-not riding in the dark on the busy highway without the florescent vest.
12.3 mi.   elevation: 25'

8:00 p.m. start of the bike trip 6/2/12 on the Columbia river shore near the Pacific Ocean. Baptism of the tires and collecting Pacific Ocean water in a bottle.

Bicycle and Subaru support vehicle with bike rack at the Columbia start.

DAY 3: LAST MOMENTS ON THE COAST

Sunday, June 3, 2012   Astoria to Clatskanie, OR   Overcast 70*

There were things to do. At 7:00 we put on our faces, washed down sweet rolls with coffee, pilfered apples for energy later, loaded the car, left for 8:30 Mass, returned to the motel to change into bike riding clothes and set the bike on the car rack. We drove for Fort Clatsop, the site where the Lewis and Clark Discovery Party wintered over in 1805. Historic movies and displays in the National Historical Park Visitor's Center exampled the life and times of both Indians and the L. & C. group during their four brutal months of a rain drenched winter. Outside was a replica fort where the thirty-three explorers stayed.

I wondered what the intrepid L. & C. team would say about the country they had explored. What changes would they note about the territory encountered on their 3,000 mile odyssey. Would the same sights and sounds inhabit the route? How would travel have changed? Would there be better trails and roads? Would Indians and wildlife they had encountered still be in abundance? How had the land and people changed? Would food sources be abundant? What had their groundbreaking journey unleashed? Had Americans used their resources well? Would pioneers be proud of America's developments? Certainly the nation had changed.

A park patch and hat were purchased to dispel Doubting Thomas's who thought I'd just hide in seclusion emailing fake stories about the trip. Plus Susan took photos for other evidence. At 12:30, we returned to last night's quit.

Donning a yellow safety vest, safety helmet with a small mirror, and black gloves, filling the water bottles, and kissing Susan, it was off to St. Louis. Susan planned to drive ahead in increasing distances experimenting with how much confidence she had in my safety and endurance. At first, she drove to the far side of town, then in increasing steps three, four, eight, then nine miles, checking progress at easy-to-spot pullovers. A quick drink and snack, then off again.

It seemed that the Columbia riverbanks wouldn't have challenging hills, because the river rose so gradually, yet there were steep road ascents of two and more hundred feet. When a rider must shift down to the lowest of twenty-one gears, it was probably a 6 or 7 percent grade, which was tough enough for 375 horsepower diesel trucks. On the steepest grades, my speed was normally between 4.5 to 5.3 mph. As the crest began to round over, pedaling readily changed, which quickly merited a shift up in gear. Normally, I switched small rear sprockets first to a higher speed, then the front larger sprockets, but experimentation was ongoing to find the optimum gearing for the type of hill being tackled. The best thrill was coming over the hill crest with a long descent. At first, the speedometer seemed wrong, telling me the bike was racing at 25 mph to the trough. As time progressed, there were hills where I exceeded the 35 mph speed limit-no car passed me. Once, I encountered a nearly perfect flat section. Speed was never below 15 mph, although there were stretches of 19-20, so that I covered nine miles in 31 minutes. That's not fast by automobile standards, or Tour-de-France professional riders, but for yours truly that was hot roddin'.

At Clatskanie, Susan was telling me that I should quit for the day since it was 5:30. There might not be a good motel at my goal, Ranier, fifteen miles away. Being such a contrarian, and still feeling strong, I disagreed, wanting to make the first day a fifty miler. I could make it by 7:00. Okay, I made a deal. If Susan would pick me up at the top of the extended grade exiting Clatskanie, 3.4 miles, I would agree to a local motel. She could arrange the room and meet me at the top. The climb was seriously steep. We had traveled it yesterday by car-an unrelenting 4.5 to 4.1 mph grind. Vehicles, many pulling boat trailers, having finished weekend jaunts to the coast, were blasting past me. I gave Oregonians credit though. They were bike friendly, moving over to give clearance. And there was something to be said for the Oregon Highway Department. They built hill roads with consistent grades allowing steady riding. It was a thirty-five minute tussle to the top, where Susan was waiting. Aww! I wanted the reward of a fast coast downward, but a deal was a deal. I put my sweat soaked clothes into the front seat (me in them) and accepted a reverse ride to Clatskanie.

Susan already had bags in the room. I just needed to bring in the bike for the night, then shower. The laptop computer, set on the table, was slow warming up. This, our third motel on the trip, had working WI-FI. We dined at a pizza parlor which served the most tantalizing meat balls and spaghetti. I wanted carbs for riding tomorrow. Returning to the motel, I sensed how much my body was stiffening up, got a towel, and changed into a bathing suit to soak luxuriantly in the spa. Muscles gave up aches and pains. It felt so good, I returned to the room and dragged Susan down to enjoy the wonderful benefits of a hot soak. Now wasn't it a good thing that I thought of stopping here for the night?

41.6 mi.   53.9 mi. to date   elevation: 40'

Fort Clatsop National Park near Astoria, Oregon, where the Lewis & Clark Discovery party wintered over 1n 1803.

Parking lot of the motel, first full day of bicycling

Highway 30 east of Clatskanie, OR, under drizzling skies.

DAY 4: ON TO PORTLAND

Monday, June 4, 2012   Clatskanie to Portland, OR   Misting 62*

It's Oregon, so what did I think? Rain. At the motel breakfast nook, I asked the manager about the wet pavement.

"Is this what the weather is usually like?" I inquired.

"Yeeesss," she answered with a puckering face.

I was wondering if the rain came in sheets or squalls. Instead, it usually misted, maybe drizzled, and not all the time in all places. When Susan dropped me off at yesterday's stop, the sky was overcast with heavy segregated gray clouds. The ground was damp without any drops, the temperature expected to be 62*. Within 200 feet, wearing a short sleeve yellow jersey proved insufficient protection from the dank chill. Returned to the car, I added a forest green nylon windbreaker under the shirt. Ten minutes later my body warmed, adapting to the cool air. Off and on, heavy mist collected on jacket and helmet to the point that they were sodden with drips rolling side to side across my vision under the helmet visor. But it wasn't pouring.

Where yesterday the highway was lined with three foot tall grasses, heavy ferns, and brush before thick forest or rock outcroppings, today the edges of the road exhibited hidden homes and manufacturing sites behind lines of trees. The shoulder was cluttered with gravel and bark debris from passing logging trucks. Of course there was the typical trash cast aside by careless motorists, but the odd item thoughtless passengers tossed was banana peels. The closer to "civilized" townships, the more trash, and now and then chunks of metal to be avoided. Exits on the right needed special care because drivers sped past, then signaled at the last moment they were turning in front of me.

With the mostly gentle rolling hills providing a steady 15-16 mph, we reached St. Helens for a Subway sandwich lunch. After a 40 minute nap, I prepared the bike when a passing vehicle stopped and a burly fellow spoke through the open window.

"Nice bike. Where'd you come from?" the driver asked.

Chitchat revealed he had taken two long rides himself, one from Vancouver, British Columbia, to Cabo San Lucas, Mexico. But with honking horns in the parking lot, we broke the bike gab and he pulled away. I looked to hop the bike over a small round yellow curb, cross the sidewalk, and rejoin Highway 30 before the stoplight changed. That was when the rain slickened curb slid my tire sideways. Down I fell straddling the bike with my legs trapped in an awkward standing spread. Unable to get a purchase to raise up, and exposed to all the highway traffic watching my clumsiness, I burst into laughter. The joke was on me. It just cost me "face" and a nasty gash across my right ankle. The whole time Susan was oblivious because she was reading her Sue Grafton mystery in the car thinking I'd pedaled off. She didn't find out until hours later, but she did realize that I'd taken off without a helmet. Three miles down road she caught up to switch my baseball cap for head protection.

I want to be as discreet as possible as I say this. I wore padded biking shorts to alleviate soreness from riding. The effectiveness lasted maybe thirty miles. But the padding is stiff. Thus, when pulled up across the privates, the stiff material encountered certain manly hairs. After riding for a couple of leg pumping hours, no amount of shifting, sliding, finger pushing or poking lessened the torment of wiry hairs stabbing into private areas. Lotion or Vaseline was not the answer. So, while in the restaurant restroom, I removed said shorts. And what a relief! Also the lamb's wool padded seat cover was taken off. Only the gel seat protected my rear end from saddle sores. Damage done, calluses in place, this sufficed the next twenty miles.

For the rest of the day, the goal was northern Portland. Miles slid by. The St. John's Bridge loomed 250 feet over the Columbia River. Using the roundabout approach, the bike climbed to the bridge entrance and wheeled across the pedestrian walk, above the spectacle of hundreds of boats, machinery, houses, and docking areas below. A series of errors after 4:00 made the rest of the day agonizing: physically tired; not having a nutrition snack since 2:30; mentally weary; uncertain of the direction to go after crossing the bridge; missing Susan's directions to take a particular route; keeping pace with the traffic along busy Lombard Street; dodging junk on narrow streets; becoming lost on a difficult bridge crossing over the rail lines; finding Susan but making the mistake of saying: "Let's get this over," then pedaling off to 122nd Street northeast of the Portland Airport on Marine Drive's bike friendly but narrow lane; aching the while from sores, poking hairs, and a sore butt; utterly spent, I pulled into a parking lot, twenty-seven miles without a break. Susan drove us to Aunt Betty and Uncle Larry Warmack's home in Battle Ground, Washington. Beginning at dinner, rain deluged throughout the night.

74.4 mi.   128.3 mi. to date   elevation: 100'

DAY 5: UPRIVER

Tuesday,   Portland to Cascade Locks, OR   Overcast/misting 68*
June 5, 2012

Although the weather report predicted rain would cease in the afternoon, the start off was anything but dry. Marine Drive dedicated alternating bike path to the left off and just below the river road. However, the left side had slapping damp grass standing two to three feet tall while across the road prickly blackberry vines and stretching tree branches scratched, requiring constant dodging. When the path stayed north on Marine Drive, it gave an unobstructed view of the river twenty feet away with only three joggers braving the rain. The half mile wide river eased among low rounded hills of a 10 mile wide basin. Clouds shrouded the silver-gray river, empty of boats.

With sunshine breaking through in late morning, I crossed under I-84, turned left and aimed for the historic Columbia Gorge Trail in expectation of safe travel due to lighter traffic. It was a trade of one problem for another. At first, the trail was populated with lovely overarching tree lined estates gazing at the deep gorge. As the climb ascended a 6 percent grade, homes became more modest, but the shaded road never seemed to level off during the four mile roller coaster upward climb to Corbett. Lunch in a market was not enough to sustain the ups and downs of the crest drive. An overlook of the Columbia, held a marker declaring the scenic hardwood forest was 600 feet above I-84. Enough roller coaster. Less than a mile later a cutoff drop traversed the right escarpment into the trees. With rain stinging my face I squeezed the brakes dry to maintain a safe speed all the way down, expecting to reach flat I-84. Instead, Highway 30 continued east at the bottom along the cliffs. And still the road rose and fell. A photo stop at Multnomah Falls provided a needed break. All I could think of was food. At the information booth, a guide informed that it was legal to ride on the Oregon interstate. I was tempted to hop the fence, cross the railroad tracks, and put the bike over the cement barrier wall to start smoother riding, just 300 feet away. Susan convinced me to stay on Highway 30 for the safety, since the map indicated a short distance until it junctioned with I-84. Bad decision. The succeeding four miles were filled with steep roller coaster inclines. My legs ached all the way to Bonneville Dam.

I-84 turned out to be wide, safe nearly level, and pro-biker. For the most part, the Columbia had been hidden from sight among the curving bends of the river, so I expected a grand Bonneville tour spectacle. Not so, not so. The uniformed guard (Department of Homeland Security protection of all dams) stepped out of his white guard shack to halt my menacing tired biker walk. It was 5:10, visiting hours were over.

"Come back tomorrow," he said.

At Cascade Locks, we stopped. Before dinner, I shed muddy clothing, lounged in a warm spa bath, and changed into clean clothes. The Char Burger sounded like any ordinary burger joint until entered. The walls were decorated with Indian arrowhead collections, deerskin clothing, Indian blankets, old farm implements, and historic rifles and guns. We ordered supreme burgers, which they proved to be. But the real enjoyment was looking out the picture window at the steep sun-draped forested blue canyon mountains. Indian salmon fishing stands jutted out from the banks of the riverbed. Lewis and Clark had to be in awe at such grandeur. The baby blue river glided under a hundred foot high silver bridge connecting Oregon and Washington. Railroad beds lined both sides of the river, paralleling the highways on each side.

42.4 mi.   170.7 mi. to date   elevation: 135'

Columbia Gorge bridge, near Troutdale, OR

Ascending the first serious climb around Corbett, OR. 6/5/12

DAY 6: BONNEVILLE AND THE DALLES

Wednesday,   Cascade Locks to The Dalles, OR   Sunny 58*
June 6, 2012

Breakfast at the Char Burger was a tourist treat both because of plentiful working-man food and the eye feast of river majesty. Scenic pleasure continued to the overflowing white, pink, red, lavender, purple and deep purple rhododendron hedges lining the entrance to the Bonneville Dam. The lady guard warned to stay on the road, no stopping, and no going anywhere but to the visitor center. A loaded yellow school bus emptied its class as we entered the main doors. Their first objective was the restrooms. Displays of Lewis and Clark exploits and historic events of the dam were on the left. Elevators dropped folks two floors to the fish ladder observation windows, where the students oohed and aahed as salmon, shad, and lampreys passed through the murky yellow green water. Outside two electric generation plants hummed as they produced power for half a million homes. A new water lock system allowed barges and ships to ply both up and down the river. At the fish hatchery two 450 pound gray sturgeons lazed in a pond, as well as millions of fingerlings in other cement containment basins, being raised as future river fish.

While Susan bought groceries, I put on gear in the cloudy air. It was supposed to be dry, with a 100 percent chance of rain for tomorrow. At 12:20 I slid onto I-84. Travel flowed well except for the long rises. If I were complaining now at a 200 foot climb, what would I do when it was 2,000 feet? The forest diminished, trees becoming deciduous. Black outcroppings of basalt rock tilted on both sides of the river. Traffic hurtled along the Interstate as I pedaled at 14-20 mph with the wind sometimes pushing from behind. Road debris now was mostly tire tread, mixed with bungee cords and assorted plastic car parts. The blue Columbia, on the left, flowed west toward the sea.

At Cascade Locks, I took an hour's nap. It wasn't fair to Susan having to while away her time as I snoozed. Yet my body craved sleep. I entreated her to start taking little exploratory trips to enjoy some of the sights that I won't stop for. She should be able to let me go to the next significant stop without feeling the need to plug along a few miles ahead of me. I have enough military savvy and personal discipline to know what I can do, how much I can push, and when to call a halt. I suggested she go 22 miles to The Dalles, get a motel room, and explore as she saw fit. Although she wasn't tethered to me, this wasn't an easy request for her. It seemed two hours would be sufficient before I could roll into town. I was wrong. Tail wind aided a burst of speed to crest a mount. Susan was behind at a rest stop I had visited but, unfortunately, I had never spotted her. She was surprised that I had so easily slipped by.

WI-FI service was troublesome. Some people got a signal, but not us, or the signal was poor. Two motels failed to supply a good signal, so we refused their services. Figuring it was the eight year old age of the laptop, I wanted to buy a new machine. We shopped a couple of stores, and even got advice to try a Verizon solution. In spite of my insistence to buy an immediate replacement, even if we had to retrace our steps to Portland, tiredness won out. Susan got a room at a less expensive motel, Cousins, which had all the amenities, a great laptop signal, and a dinner special: burger, beer, and bottomless fries for $6. The spa felt wonderful, too. And, in a few minutes we'd succeeded with email.

42 mi.   170.7 mi. to date   elevation: 200'

DAY 7: MIXED BAG

Thursday, June 7, 2012   The Dalles to Arlington, OR   Sunny 70*

Please, Please, Please, all my good friends and readers: Do not forward the emails. If there were to be any publicity, we would prefer to be back home. I know it's tempting, but there is a reason. The midnight crooks may come to visit while we're gone.

DIET. For those who have wondered, food is what the cycling body craves and needs. Breakfast, in a diner, means protein, usually a big omelet or eggs and sausage with coffee; in a bed-and-breakfast motel it means a bowl of Cheerios, Raisin Bran, or oatmeal, at least three eggs, sausages, three cups of coffee, two cups of orange juice, two small breakfast rolls, but never pancakes. Lunch is typically sandwiches, either turkey or ham on wheat bread, fruit (apple, nectarine, orange), carrots, pickles, greens, lots of water, juice. Snacks, usually every hour, are a can of V-8, water, or Gatorade (to replenish salt loss), a piece of fruit, or protein bar. Dinner is generally the biggest meal I can find. Twice I ordered the biggest burger made. Otherwise it's been pasta carb packing for the morrow.

Clothing. I put on sunscreen to prevent burning. If cloudy, I wear a long sleeve green windbreaker, under a florescent yellow vest (like the highway workers), long pants with ankle clips (to hold cuffs away from the bike chain and gears), white athletic socks, and hard soled Reebok white net mesh tennis shoes (quick drying and prevents loss of compression on down strokes), black gel gloves (which prevent sunburned backs of the hands, but do not prevent sore or tingling hands), and a white safety helmet with an attached adjustable mirror to see traffic behind. If sunny, I wear either a long or short yellow florescent shirts that wick away sweat. Because drivers saw the long green sleeves protruding from the yellow shirts, they honked since I have the appearance of a University of Oregon booster.

Rain. Because it rained through the night, I delayed in the restaurant hoping it would quit. No such luck. Finally, at 10:30, I ambled to the car, put on bike gear, and rolled down I-84 for three miles, then stopped for irritation relief using Vaseline. Back on the highway, trucks sloshed by soaking my clothes. And then, joy of joys, the rain let up all the way to road marker 109 exit. Partly cloudy skies watched our park lunch, west of the John Day Dam near Rufus, OR.

Fish. At the park sat a man in a white van with a sign: *Sport Fishing Rewards/Register Here*. He worked for the Bonneville Power Authority

(BPA) in an astounding way. The program was to catch the Pike Minnow, a native predatory fish that had an amazing appetite for smolt, small salmon. Once this fish reached nine inches, its appetite changed from insects to salmon fingerlings, posing significant danger to salmon. The goal was to reduce, but not eradicate the species. What was the program? A registered angler earned $4.00 for every fish brought in over nine inches in length up to the first one hundred fish. Then the award climbed to $5.00 for every fish up to 400. Afterwards the award rose to $8.00 per fish. Some anglers fished every day from May through October, earning up to $50,000-$60,000. It was the price BPA pays as part of its contract to protect the salmon and provide inexpensive power. Although some persons threw away the fish, most were rendered-turned into cat food. Orientals steamed the Pike Minnow, but it was not a prize fish like salmon or trout. The program was unique to the Columbia River.

Road. I-84 rose slowly eastward with the river. Occasionally talus and rock scrabble had fallen down the cliffs. Sometimes ponds or created gullies prevented rock falls from bounding onto the highway, and there were plenty of falls in evidence. In fact, it seemed that the road edge was marked with a numbering system to allow work crews to locate exactly where a rock mishap had occurred. The mileage from Portland was listed in silver paint, but the mile was divided into hundredths. So a number reading 87.14 located where a rock fell. Anyone may phone in the exact position to the highway department. Surely there were other reasons for the system.

Once, while a noisy freight train lumbered by on the right, a startled doe jumped from its resting place in a gully not ten feet away. The train was no surprise; it was the unexpected sight of an approaching bike. More and more sagebrush and dry sparse grass appeared amid protruding rock chunks. Across the river, the Washington side became more rounded, brown, and dry. Trains rumbled along the edge of the banks on both sides of the river.

Geology. Trees no longer filled the dry yellowing slopes of the Washington bluffs side. The Oregon side contained mostly shear black tiers of stark volcanic rock bluffs up to 600 feet penetrating the sky. Winds delayed until the bike neared massive Gibraltar-like cliffs near the highway and then spat forth their invisible tornadic wrath at unsuspecting vehicles. White three-bladed wind turbines above collected power from the gusts.

The barrenness of the steep sided gorge was due a cataclysmic event fifteen thousand years ago. In the Missoula area, a glacial dam held back an enormous lake behind a thousand foot tall glacier. When the ice lake decayed the ice plug at the bottom, setting the waters free, the dam gave way to an 800 foot high wall of water tumult moving at perhaps a hundred mph. It smashed everything in its path. Huge boulders were moved hundreds of miles from their origin. Earthen bowls (depressions) were created from some of the swirling rock and debris. Coulees of Washington were such creations. The gigantic flood raged downwards gouging the Snake and Columbia Rivers on its way to the ocean, and in part entered the Willamette, Oregon area. Geologists averred that this calamity occurred several times.

Day's end. Susan agreed to advance to Arlington in search of a motel, with me thinking to extend an extra nine miles, then backtrack. She noticed clouds in the west behind were thick and menacing. Two miles ahead there was clear sky and sunshine. Certainly, I could race well enough to stay in the lead. That was true for six miles. On the seventh mile, a long incline slowed the bike to gear two, about 5.5 mph. Then splats began. Little white hail stones stung my skin. Soon water sprayed upward from the rear wheel drenching my backside, and splatters dribbled off my helmet. Exposed in an oxbow of the cliffs, winds buffeted while thunder boomed, and lightning leapt from cloud to cloud. With half a mile to go on a metal bike to the protection of the next rock canyon, a race against electrical death began. Once inside the rock formation, I moved farther inwards until the end of the crease, pulling off the road, passing a tall metal sign which could act as a lightening rod. Then I called Susan, assuring her of my safety. When the storm burst moved on, I regained the bike and pedaled, spinning rain slosh off the pavement onto my clothes and face. The last miles I sped downwards at 27 mph, squeezing the brakes several times to wipe them free of water slippage, and entered Arlington, aiming towards the motel. Susan reported that after my call, a 10-15 minute cloudburst hit town. I won't need a shower tonight since truckers were so generous giving me a spray bath as they drove by.

My body. Five out of seven days, the day started with a nose bleed. Cold wind caused a drippy nose. Eyes itched especially at the outsides. Hands lost numbness as soon as riding stopped. The rear end aches eased after a half hour, even though I used a product called Chamois Glide on the skin. Upper and lower muscles needed a good hot bath or spa sit to loosen up. My right knee ached. The gash across the right ankle still hurt. Feet were sometimes numb during riding, but recovered quickly. A muscle rub usually helped. A nap always sounded like a priority idea. Whose idea was it to do this? I want my mommy!

58 mi.   270.7 total miles to date   elevation: 300'

Cycling into the hills NE of Walla Walla, WA.

DAY 8: INTO WASHINGTON

Friday, June 8, 2012   Arlington to Lowden, OR   Windy 70*

Pizza is the secret. As a town, Arlington closed up at 6:00 p.m. This also meant the bank, medical clinic, hardware store, social services, grocery, liquor store. Dinner choices were a burger joint, a restaurant with no cars around, and the pizza place. We ordered a loaded large pizza pie looking to save one third for later. Sure enough, we enjoyed pizza for breakfast before I put a leg over the bike seat and started off. The secret ingredients gave me great energy, averaging 24 mph for the first twenty miles. The tires were blazing down the road. It wouldn't have had anything to do with the ten mile an hour tailwind, could it? How do I know it was ten mph? As I gained speed the gusts pushing against my back lessened until there was no wind at ten bike mph. After that, speed just magically picked up.

The river canyon became drier and less tall. Sand and rock talus fallen from bluff heights created yellow-brown slants dotted with sage brush and small clump grass. At the Highway 730 turn off north, the land reduced to rounded hills, dotted with farms. Huge mechanical irrigation pipes on wheels crawled across green fields. After forty-five miles, we lunched at the Umatilla (you-ma-till-ah) Marina Park, hiding behind a walled picnic table, due to severe wind gusts. White caps filled the river where it had been only slightly choppy minutes before. A large storm cloud was working its way up the river canyon.

It seemed, if the storm cell passed, we might have a big cycling day, since the wind was at my back. I rolled under a junction underpass, and started up a steep incline when six black jacketed motorcyclists passed, then pulled over in front of me, blocking the shoulder. To avoid them, but still pedal, I turned right into the soft red-black gravel off the pavement. Just as I was about to pass, the lead motorcycle pulled forward about 250 feet, and the others followed blocking. A second time I edged to the right, again the leader not seeing what had occurred.

The last rider called out: "Sorry, man".

More farms and ranches appeared right and left as the road twisted with the rising river bed, then entered a canyon dressed in 500 foot golden decaying bluffs. Trains roared below the cliffs on both sides of the river. Once I outraced an engine hauling a hundred cars for two miles, but was slowed by a large curve, where it passed at the Washington border sign. Susan and I snapped photos, before making a decision: proceed six more miles and call it a day at 4:00?, or increase mileage for sightseeing near Walla Walla? I chose mileage, leaving the river.

That was a hardship decision. Highway 12 started with a flat stretch which later threw in steep rises with a cross wind. Speed slowed to ten mph. Just before Touchet (too-shay), a particularly nasty climb began with a warning: "TRUCK LANE 1000 FEET". It was a foretaste of the mountains to come. Trucks moved to the right lane and growled at the downshifting needed to scale the two mile ascent. The bicycle joined the grunting, grinding ascent. There was nothing else for it. Keep the pedals churning in the lowest gear. Look down, not up. Crank one pedal at a time. Atop the rise, nearly spent, I pushed toward the town. Paying attention to my body, at a convenience store, I gave the reward it craved, milk. But my expectation of a motel was dashed. Fortunately, Susan had already scouted ahead. There was no inn here or in Lowden, not even a place to camp. Walla Walla was the next boarding opportunity. Not wishing to regress all the way back here in the morning, I chose to do six miles to Lowden before quitting at 6:20. Tomorrow, Susan will return me the eleven miles from Walla Walla to this stop. The motel's last available room was outlandishly expensive due to tourist season and local college graduation. Three wonderful things happened afterwards. A hot shower, baby back ribs that melted-in-the-mouth-and-fell-off-the-bone at Smith's Restaurant, and a long spa soak with the two of us exchanging tired achy leg massages.

88 mi.   358.7 total to date   elevation: 400'

Oregon/Washington border 6/8/12. Notice the padded white seat cover

Susan posed with the Subaru with the bike rack on the hatchback.

DAY 9: WIND AND RAIN

Saturday, June 9, 2012   Lowden to Dayton, WA   Windy/Stormy 68*

Wind-is it a friend or foe, a blessing or curse? We backtracked to Lowden (loud-en) under two tiers of clouds indicating coming rain. The day's first segment was short as we spent an hour touring the Whitman Mission National Historic Site a few miles west of Walla Walla. Then it was back on the road. Outside the car, the wind was blowing more forcefully than yesterday. Because of the chill air, I dressed in a heavy cotton shirt, green windbreaker, and the yellow vest. A steady crosswind, at 14 mph sounded good, but as a cross, the force acted like an invisible pillow fight retarding progress. In addition, the gentle incline prevented speed faster than ten. If the wind were strictly behind, the bike could make good time; if the wind cross cut, speed was reduced by 3-4 mph; at a 90* angle a five mph decrease; but, directly into the wind, the bike reduced speed by 7-8 mph.

The Port City of Walla Walla for years had been the onion capital of Washington. But in twenty years the region had converted to grape vineyards and wineries, making big changes to the city. The outer rolling hills sprouted large wheat farms whose grain rippled in the wind like shivering green worms. Ranches sported pastoral horse pastures and hay fields. Manufacturing smoke stacks have been coming into the area.

Leaving town on Highway 12, the road rose and fell on an inevitable increase of elevation. There were many ranchettes and colorful homesites that I ignored with the coming rain. At first it was drizzle, then steady rain, and occasional splatters. Speed slowed to eight mph on the climb, in the squish of water under the tires, slosh of water soaking both shoes, a cross wind, and dodging gravel along the shoulder. Normal width of the bike path is 24-30 inches, but on major highways it is between 4-8 feet wide. The Washington Highway Department did a decent job cleaning the road bed, but gravel was a constant problem for bike tires. As an auto safety technique, rumble strips (gouged out asphalt that causes a Brrrrrp! Brrrrrp! as vehicles glide across) were not on the road edge, but in the center, where the double solid yellow line divided the traffic. When possible, vehicles rumbled across and back as they give me extra safety room, but there was always rain slosh as they passed.

The owner of the Dixie Market welcomed a bedraggled bike rider. He mentioned the area produced wheat, peas, and garbanzo beans. We lunched at a small table in the rear with his wife and dog, Sonny, looking on. The road would have a serious climb, then drop, rise, and level off. True to his word, I cranked for 1 1/2 miles with sheets of water sliding down the road shoulder as vehicles shushed past. Cross winds ended as the road descended on the other side, coasting at 22.

At Waitsburg the highway turned right. Susan didn't like me riding in the rain. I responded that it wasn't really any more dangerous, if I stayed careful. Although still uncomfortable, she agreed to let me continue on the basically flat route to Dayton. By the time I splashed into town at 4:25, she had a room, and I was cold and soaked. After my hot shower, the rain stopped.

43 mi. 401.7 mi. to date elevation: 1600'

DAY 10: MASS AND THE PASS

Sunday, June 10, 2012   Dayton to Clarkston, WA   Sunny/clearing 51*

At sixteen hundred feet elevation, Dayton, WA, possessing the oldest working county courthouse (1887) in the state, had a population of 2,600 serving the surrounding farms. It contained thirteen churches (200 persons per if all are church attendees). Two interesting businesses. First, the Book and Brew, a bookstore pub/family restaurant where one may eat, greet, and read at leisure. A peruse of the Dayton High Summer Reading List had books I didn't read until college or after. Second, the Country Cupboard Bakery and Deli, supplying delicious fresh baked goods, breakfast and home décor and gifts. I bought two packages of red Republican and blue Democrat fertilizer (actually chocolate) to send back to my ROMEO senior kibitzers in Dinuba because of all the political wrangling we do. Dayton had no public laundromats or motel washing machines. We delayed leaving town because mass did not start until 11:00 a.m. I hoped to go as far as possible after 12:00, at least thirty-seven miles to the 2,785 foot Alpowa Pass.

How did the conquering bike hero suit up now? First, liberally applied Goldbond Medicated Powder, followed by Vaseline, a swipe of Chamois Glide to ease saddle soreness, then padded shorts without underwear, since stitching created uncomfortable wrinkles between skin and bike seat throughout the day. (Who's to say whether lotion was helping or if my calluses were toughening? By thirty miles or so my rear was numb/annoyed, so it's shifting from cheek to cheek until I can take a 10-15 minute break.) Long pants were put on when the sun was bright, or if it would rain. Always, always the yellow shirt/vest, helmet, gloves, and now sunscreen. I tried wearing wraparound sunglasses until my sweat smeared the glass. The sunglass style fogged up and prevented wind from cooling the eyes. Because the tennis shoes were soaked from yesterday's rain, I wore hard soled hiking shoes, which have long slick laces. Racing down a slope, the lace loop snagged the left crank nub in such a way that it was difficult to unhook the loop without losing balance and crashing. From now on the laces will be triple tied.

Due to the gentle rolling hills, farmers seemed in love with rugby, well at least rugby style jerseys. To prevent soil erosion, tractors plowed horizontally across the hills leaving wide strips of tilled brown dirt, green wheat, and harvested yellow stubble. This made the contoured hillsides look like an artist had taken broad swipes with a paint brush. There was no visible irrigation, which made this dry land farming. It is astounding how much John Deere machinery a farmer acquired to make a go of his acres. I can't begrudge a farmer his boat or camper for all the long hours and hard work put in.

Leaving Dayton, the road rose steeply. Susan promised to meet at the top of the incline. Two miles later, the road continued to rise, level, and rise again. But the road never revealed more than a quarter mile of forward visibility before it twisted into the hidden side of the next incline, then kept climbing. Susan was waiting, but not at the top. At 4.8 miles, it didn't matter, break time. The ridge changed to a 6 percent downgrade, which became a five mile careen at a hair raising speed of 39 mph, with the crosswinds buffeting the bike sideways. It was necessary to apply the brakes to prevent a disaster. Next followed a series of climbing segments at nine or ten mph, declines of 10-15 feet, a stiff climb at 4.5 mph, and then started all over. Frustrating, because there was a 12 mph tailwind that couldn't be taken advantage of, the reason being that all the riding was uphill—no level areas. I had to regain all the elevation lost in the five mile downhill. Today may have been my lucky day. In the brown canyon's twists and turns, I came to a warning sign reading: *Severe Crosswinds Ahead*. Yet, in the next five miles, no cross or headwinds occurred. By Pomeroy we were back to 1,700 feet. As is typical in the rural towns, everything was closed on Sunday, save for a gas/convenience store. Out of Pomeroy, the route meandered steadily up to the 2,785 foot Alpowa Pass, where the final section presented a brutal truck lane climb.

A rest stop sat at the wind tossed summit featured a nearly level Irish-green panorama of vibrant mesa cropland. I was surprised but uninterested. The agony of the biker shorts, used as underwear, had caused enough grief. Removed, and riding commando style, I whisked down the last twenty miles of dry rugged canyon walls to Clarkston on the reverse of the ascent. Thirteen miles of coasting were pleasant at 27 mph in the face of a 10 mph headwind. At the end of the brown gorge descent, a headwind resisted fast travel on the flat into Clarkston, taking an hour to conclude the last seven miles at 8:20 p.m. The road made a grand S-curve, right, then left, around a wide forebay of the Snake river. In the late evening, families occupied the bay and side lakes with fishing poles in hand, picnicking parties, and lovers kissing everywhere.

67 mi.   468.7 mi. to date   elevation: 740'

DAY 11: HELL'S CANYON

Monday, June 11, 2012   Hell's Canyon   Sunny to cloudy 72*

Friends, this may be your one and only chance to comment. Not that it will change what or how I write, but what are your thoughts? Too much information? Not enough? Different info? Too much "that's not an appropriate thing to email"? Be straightforward; you know that the truth hurts only me.

Day of rest. On the Hell's Canyon water route leaving Clarkston, middle class homes lay twenty feet above the highway. Sixteen passengers on our aluminum hull jet boat watched gently rolling dry hills pass south from Lower Granite Lake into the Snake River. Within two miles the hills became decayed 300-500 foot bluffs as we entered canyon. A highway ran along the Washington (right) side linking homes thirty-seven miles upstream to the cities. (People here wanted a share of privacy, independence, peace and quiet, but not too far from the lure of civilization, phone, and electricity, satellite dishes, boating, RVs. Why value rural independence but move next door to another house?)

Meanwhile the elevated precipices increased along with the ruggedness of the gorge. Light yellow grass frosting coated chocolate cake cliff tiers rising up the twisting and turning V shaped valley. Rock formations changed with every bend in the river: smooth hills; crags; 500 foot bluffs; crumbled stones lining the waterway; angular steep grassy slopes; four, five, six-sided columnar formations; gnarled jumbled blocks; prominences jutting into the water; teetering boulders ready to slip from precipices three to four thousand feet above. True isolationist farms and homes appeared on short stretches of river soil. Closed mines, a stamp mill, and hotel hinted a forgotten history of rough, tough pioneer fortune hunters. Some ranches persisted. Many folks came, poured out their blood, sweat, tears and lives, then departed, and the stories have gone with them. At one time power companies wanted to dam the narrows, but President Ford ended the plan when he assigned the gorge to the National Recreation Area list. At Johnson Point, the canyon rose 7,000 feet, the deepest canyon of the country, but it is only for the hardy soul. Its length and immensity deserve preservation for future generations to enjoy in awe.

Tidbits. Lubricant was applied after spotting the beginning of rust on the bike chain. Pharmacy and light shopping. Right ankle gash seemed to be getting better but remained sore, inflamed and red. Light eating day.

Laundry. It usually takes two hours to write this email. After dinner and a hot bath or spa, I would rather close my eyes, but then I'd forget to write the next day. Now that I've ridden 468+ miles, haven't I proven I can do it? So I'm quitting and coming home! (Just kidding.) Not funny, says Susan.

0 mi. biking   200 mi. boat ride 468.7 biking mi. to date   elevation: 740'

Taking a lunch break at Heller Bar Lodge on a jet boat cruise up Hell's Canyon 6/11/12.

Rafters on the Snake river headed for Hells Canyon.

DAY 12: INDIANS, ROADS, AND MOMMA

This is the second writing. With two paragraphs to go, our old laptop malfunctioned. It kicked itself off the internet and word processing at the same time. It's 11:30. Time to start rewriting. GRRRRRRR!

Tuesday,   Clarkston, WA to Orofino, ID Sunny to stormy 67*
June 12, 2012

The prediction of thundershowers, or the threat of a lynching, was the best way to get me up and out of town. I stuffed my pockets with bed-and-breakfast bananas (potassium) and apple cider packet mix (fluid intake) on my way to packing the silver mini SUV. Susan headed to the post office (to send off my political "fertilizer" packages) and Wal-Mart. On the bridge linking Clarkston with Lewiston, an urgent pit stop warning sent me down the bank to a fortunately located restroom just below. (Ever notice how often urgent pit stops occur at a least convenient moment?) Crossing to Lewiston I circled under the bridge taking the Highway 12 bypass along the river shore where joggers, cyclists, and morning risers were using the park exercise challenge course. Clarkston and Lewiston were attractive, neat, clean and well maintained cities enjoying late spring. For two days, families have been out on the river banks fishing. I crossed the bridge and turned into a five mph headwind onto the Highway 95 junction heading east on the north side of Clearwater River.

"Should I ask permission to ride the highway?" I pondered, passing the Idaho State Police Office. "No. It is better to ask for forgiveness ten miles upriver".

Water diverted left skirting stony river islands thick with tree stands. The U-shaped canyon slowly squeezed inward as bluffs gradually rose. Slopes appeared to have been covered with an enormous pool table cloth. Between road and river thirty feet away were deciduous trees, grasses and purple camas flowers. Each ascending mile, the gorge became taller, greener, more narrow.

Eleven miles later we visited the Nez Perce National Historic Park at Spalding, where the visitor's center held an exquisite collection of Indian jewelry, clothing, tools, weapons, photos, and artifacts. A video and ranger presentation gave details about Indian life. The Nez Perce were instrumental in preserving the Lewis and Clark expedition, but their lives were dramatically changed afterwards. With the intrusion of white settlers, at first, the Nez Perce were confined to a reservation area of 13,000,000 acres, but due to greed for gold, a subsequent treaty reduced the area to 7,000,000, and later to just over 1,000,000. Finally, the land was divided into individual parcels, thus reducing ownership even more, while "absorbing the natives into White man's life".

In the old days, 20,000 Indians appeared at The Dalles Falls. Obeying the Salmon Chief's instructions, they celebrated thanks to the Great Spirit for the fish. Everyone returned to their camp homes for four days, thus insuring that salmon would return the following year. (Ecologically wise!) Then fishing began. Tribes were assigned their places, even non-local tribes were assigned to Hobo Island for a share of the bounty. Men, tethered with ropes tied to their waists, stood on fish ladders and platforms jutting out from the rocks into the rapids. In their hands were twenty foot long poles holding loop nets with slipknots. When a fish entered the net, the knot slipped, the net closed, and the fisherman would lift a sixty pound salmon from the raging water. In addition there were long gaff poles, gill nets, wiers, and other fish traps. Everyone participated in the bounty, catching, drying, storing the year's supply of food. If it was a poor fish year, then it was accepted that the Great Spirit had determined it to be so. This was true with plants and animals. Greed was unacceptable. And no one could eat of the new year's food supply until all of last year's was consumed.

In the 1900s the government forbade the river fishing, in part because white men could not get the hang of it. After a generation passed, the skills were lost to the natives. Agricultural water claims reduced and eliminated the flows that salmon needed to spawn. Later, the government established that the Indians would always receive 50 percent of the annual fish take. The Indians have not taken 10 percent, more likely 2-3 percent. The Indians maintained their attitude that if they take care of the earth, Mother earth will take care of them. (Ecologically sound? Advanced?)

If the President of the United States were going to apologize to other nations for past wrongs, then he should consider apologizing to each Indian nation individually for the government wrongs committed. Better yet, issue a Presidential Order mandating the government to keep the words it promised in its treaties.

More than you ever wanted to know about shifting: My bicycle is a 21 gear Allez, with three sprockets in front (low, medium, and high gears) connected by a chain drive to seven sprockets of differing sizes on the rear wheel hub. On the front, the smaller the sprocket the lower the speed. At the rear, the reverse is true; the bigger the gear, the slower the speed. If the gears are set at L-1, it is in the lowest gear/slowest speed (super granny) for climbing the highest slopes, and L-2 would be slightly higher speed (granny). If the gears are set at H-7, they are set for the fastest speed possible depending on the right conditions (straight, level ground, proper tire pressure, tailwind, downhill, or any combination).

So what? Old timers understand the shifting concept well. If too much strain is put on an engine, then damage/destruction can occur. Going up a long steep hill makes the engine work harder. There is a point when the engine starts to lug. If a driver pays attention and shifts to a lower, easier gear, strain is reduced on the engine, the car continues to climb, but at a lower rate. This protects the engine. Applied to bicycling, when a rider comes to a rise, if he shifts before the lug begins, he saves his legs from forcing out too much energy. If so, the legs cramp, begin to tire, and lose their endurance on a protracted climb. When paying attention, the rider shifts as soon as he senses an added power demand. The ideal is to keep the legs churning at a rate that moves comfortably with only a slight demand. On level ground, with no wind or negative factors, the bicycle rides at fourteen mph in H-5. With a headwind of five mph eleven to twelve, and a ten mph headwind maybe nine to ten. Coasting downhill is, in my estimation, a waste. For once, a cyclist can open it full throttle, in H-6 or H-7, gaining valuable time lost in the ascent, denying hazardous factors, of course.

More than you ever wanted to know about asphalt: My observations of the pavement leave me with five categories of quality:

A = extra smooth quiet glide-perfect for fast riding; a little bit more dangerous in the rain since there are no places for water to trickle away from imbedded asphalt-gravel points.

B = slightly rough, would cause an abrasion if fallen upon; good for moving rain off asphalt; easy comfortable; slightly slower riding.

C = jagged rough; causes friction whirr; noisy; moves rain nicely; good car tire friction; rougher on bike tires; may have scattered gravel or snow-sand at road's edge; slows speed; sometimes has a sticky feel for speed.

D = broken, chipped, pock marked, paint chipped sections; many layered (older layers below); uneven flow to the edge of the shoulder; frequently suffering from loose gravel and asphalt debris.

F = pot holes; broken edge of the white stripe; missing asphalt at the edge; rumble strips caused by farm equipment or rotten asphalt; rain cracks that are broken, raised, split apart at least one inch, or are about to break loose; terrible traction; dangerous sidewise throw of asphalt litter; sharp dropping angle edges; causes "rolling" of tire sideways off sharply angled asphalt edge; harsh bangs and bumps between flat stretches causing tire damage.

After leaving the Nez Perce National Historic Park, on the south side of the Clearwater River, I mused about the crumbling 18 inch shoulder of Highway 12. That may be a kind, generous description. For the next twenty miles the road bed was, at best, a D level of pavement, and in too many places the white line was the actual road edge with 6 inch drop offs. Around curves, vehicles approaching from the rear forced me over to the point of running off into the slanted gutter of grass and rocks. The shoulder usually had a thick layer of loose gravel. When possible, if no cars were visible in my small helmet mirror, I would drift onto the road bed, keeping a constant traffic sight-and-sound check.

After our 2:30 nutrition break, I told Susan I'd see her in Myrtle. There were off and on rain showers through the rest of the day. She missed the sign, because it was small and covered by overgrown vegetation. About three miles after Myrtle, it happened. Thump! Thump! Thump! On a wide arching bend in the river I had my first flat. Well, simple! Pull out the handy dandy cell phone, punch in the number, press send, and wait for-no reception! Oh! Oh! It was the height of the towering mountain and fir forest above me, blocking satellite connection! I walked a half mile to the actual bend in the river. No reception. Pushing the bicycle along the right gutter section was too tricky to walk safely, so, when safe, I crossed the road to walk against the cement barricade three feet away from oncoming traffic. That lasted 300 feet. Too dangerous. For safety's sake, I hopped over the cement barrier and began walking the river embankment along the 6 foot wide berm holding up the roadbed. Twenty feet below, the fast moving river was cutting into the riprap. Okay for a few hundred feet until the berm narrowed, in spots, to slants dropping precipitously downward immediately into the river. In one area the barricades had actually been undermined by erosion. Back onto the shoulder. An oncoming driver, hurrying in his red pickup, decided to pass between a truck going upriver and me. A narrow miss.

Leaving the cement barricade wall, I crossed back to the cliff side and called Susan four times with no contact. Decision: move to a safer area. After a mile-and-a-half hiking, I came to a flat area for truck pullout on the north side. Knowing Susan would eventually realize that I was later than our agreed time, I waited. But after a half hour I crossed the highway again to flag down a motorist who would notify my wife. An Idaho State Patrol van passed me waving. (Justice for not asking permission to ride the highway?) Three cars later a man realized my predicament, and U-turned back, just as Susan drove up. I profusely thanked him for being a good American. Susan had been only a mile away around the next mountain curve. No cell phone reception in the steep canyon.

It took over an hour to change the tire. The green slime filled tire seemed okay, but for some reason it would not take air. New inner tube. Furthermore, let's just say I was ignorant about why the rear tire would not go back on the holding notch of the frame. I was trying to force the wheel through the two brake pads with a pressurized tire. When I wised up and let out the air, the wheel went on so much easier. Orofino was ten miles away. I told Susan to go ahead, since it was already past 5 p.m., and we'd call it a day. Great! Eight miles later, the second flat occurred. I called immediately. Reception! Susan came immediately around the bend, being a mile away, but this time in phone range.

We got the last room in the second hotel. A hot shower later, we ate in a most authentic Mexican restaurant! Interior walls in bright yellow with blue scribing accents on the wainscoting lower wall. Detailed Mexican scenes painted above. Decorative pottery, sombreros, bottles and paraphernalia surrounding the walled booths. A visual treat. And the food was wonderful. Wanting to get at least a jump on the night's email, I started writing at 9:30 p.m. When the computer threw the email program off at 11:25, I sat in moaning disbelief. I had violated the first rule of religious computing. *Save! Save! Save!* Momma said there would be days like this. 2:47 a.m.

40 mi.   508.7 mi. to date   elevation: 1,027'

Wednesday morning

P.S. Susan tried talking me into shortening this treatise before sending. She thought it was way too much. I guess the teacher in me will never die. For those of you who read it all, my condolences. For those of you who just skimmed, my understanding.

DAY 13: YESTERDAY WAS THE UNLUCKY 13

Wednesday,   Orofino to Syringa, ID   Sunny, partly cloudy 67*
June 13, 2012

It took 20 minutes on the kitchen floor of the hotel suite to change the tire without leaving slime smeared all over the place. I took a chance with the last spare inner tube; it was inserted without benefit of a tube liner. Maybe a mistake, but two flats in ten miles? Because of a kink in the liner, a section was wadded up, a possible friction point. The first flat had been a pin hole which didn't slime-seal. The second was a blow out opposite the intake valve where the liner was located. Any other succeeding flats meant either back to Lewiston, or on to Missoula (and skip going over the Lolo Pass?) Neither a sporting goods store nor the department store had the correct inner tubes. Four boys on bicycles told us Olive's had bike supplies in Orofino. For an auto parts store, Olive's had car parts and lumberjack needs, tools, chain saws, logger supplies, hardware, and guns, guns, guns. Just about every type of rifle, sniper weapon, and semi automatic sold, save for a cannon. The owner said diversification was the rule for success in the rural towns. Several people remarked that the road for years was just as I had described it. The state claimed it didn't have the money for repairs. And, Oh, Yes! There were two perfect inner tubes!

Retracing back to the green and white mile 38 marker, I harnessed up and pedaled, this time looking at the ground and in my circular rear view helmet mirror. Again, if no vehicles were coming, the bike veered onto the roadbed until traffic appeared. It took 6.8 miles to return to central Orofino. Thereafter the road became cleaner, but the shoulder remained dangerous. So, the next 46.2 miles, was spent in the right lane, if no cars were approaching from the rear.

At a nutrition stop eight miles from Orofino, a cell phone reception check. I couldn't locate my phone. We searched high and low, even calling on Susan's cell. No signal. We drove back to the hotel. No luck. We tried calling my number again. No answer. Could I have put it down back at marker 38? Susan tried again.

"I think I can hear it," Susan exclaimed.

Anew, I tore apart all my boxes, bags, and suitcase. Nowhere.

Then Susan said, "Here it is".

She had put it in her overnight bag in the rush of leaving and had forgotten about doing it. She pleaded "stress". So, back to the last forward location, Greer, where we had lunch.

After repacking the car, Susan, sitting in the driver's seat, asked, "Where's my phone?" She jumped out of the car and franticly began searching for her cell.

I said, "There it is in your seat. You were sitting on it. You're such a Hard A--". We both burst out laughing.

The rest of the day was spent gradually rising upstream with the river. Every turn revealed heavy dense forest pines on the right, and across the river, picture perfect scattered stands of trees. The mountains did not appear taller because the river rose up to greet them. Road crews in lime yellow vests were weed whacking tall grass. In the late afternoon, a pickup driver didn't want to grant any room at the edge of the road. Without even honking, he roared by, causing me to dodge into the soft gravel. Then his red boat trailer, wider than the pickup, sliced within inches of my left arm. A hundred feet ahead, his right wheels dug into the shoulder along with his boat trailer, kicking up dirt and gravel. He was either sleeping at the wheel, or in a hurry to try out his new fishing boat. He corrected and roared on.

A group of five compactly outfitted cyclists, two women and three men, passed by in Kamiah (cam--ee--aye). I caught up with them at Kooskia (koo-skee). Starting from Astoria, June 2, they were heading to Bangor, Maine, camping all the way, averaging sixty miles a day. I'm such a piker! I could barely keep up with them on a stripped bike. Everybody stopped at Syringa. We signed for a rustic log cabin at River Dance Lodge, appropriately named "Lewis & Clark" with its own hot tub sitting on the front deck admiring the Clearwater River across the way. There was no TV or WIFI in the cabin. The manager told us that there would be no cell phone reception until we reached Missoula, MT. Nobody could bother us soaking in the hot tub, watching deer wander across the lawn, and listening to the quieting forest. An hour later, I joined the campfire to trade stories/lies with the lodge crew. Life is rough for us pioneers.

53 mi.   561.7 to date   elevation: 1,440'

Cabin at River Dance Lodge on Clearwater River
6/14/12, near Syringa, ID. Spa on the porch.

Finishing the email journal in the cabin.

DAY 14: THE WILD AND SCENIC LOCHSA

Thursday, June 14, 2012   Syringa to Powell, ID   Sunny 67*

While I rode on, Susan tried, with difficulty, to make a call by land phone. MCI had changed our card number without telling us. Fortunately, they "allowed" one call. (Apparently by former police officers now working for MCI)

Before Syringa, the Clearwater River had slowly shrunk in size to about 200 feet in width. Cottonwoods had been dropping their white fluff for miles along the narrowing and twisting stream. Swift moving water was cutting the banks on both sides. Secret water courses, hidden in the trees, burbled on the left. A steep rocky face was broken up by ferns, low thick growth, under copses of trees, with boulder faces wet from seeping spring water. Occasionally a boulder joyfully tumbled from its perch, skittered across the road leaving chunks, and skipped into the river for an early bath. For the next sixty miles, the road was 90 percent class A asphalt, the perfect smooth ride off the main highway. The shoulder, to the right of my happy 18 inches of riding space was perhaps two feet of grass, before it darted downwards at a 70-80 degree slant to the river ten feet below. No guard rails, except at curves. Occasional trees or foliage broke the severity of the embankment. No roads or buildings were in evidence on the south side of the Clearwater, and no more fishing guide boats, as there had been before mile marker 90. Hundreds of brightly colored butterfly bodies littered the road bed, collateral damage from speeding vehicles on the highway cutting through the forest.

At 10:00 a.m., we stopped for breakfast at Lowell, "Where a little bit of heaven and a piece of paradise meet at the Lochsa River and the Selway". The town sign read: *Population 24*, crossed out to *23*. A mystery: the elevation read 1,280, which made Lowell, eight miles upstream, lower than Syringa. In the restaurant were the five intrepid bikers from yesterday, just finishing their meal. We chatted. A sixth rider, from New Zealand and a day-and-a-half behind, was looking to catch them in Missoula, having started two days later.

A couple, dressed in matching royal blue square dance shirts invited us to the Country Music Campout at mile marker 122. Other breakfasters praised the weeklong event for dancing from 1-4 p.m. and evening music too, no rock and roll. Surely, the way I had been cruising, I would be far past by the time things got going. But Mother Nature had a way of changing one's plans. Highway 12 followed the Lochsa River beginning at Lowell. A five mph headwind coupled with more frequent inclines slowed my gears to H 3/4. Curves became more numerous and there were fewer chances to pick up speed on straight-aways. By marker 112, the river had narrowed to about 125 feet, checking its speed with bends every quarter mile. The shush! shush! of the water spilling over boulders reduced to whispers as bands of pine and fir separated road and river. Occasional islands appeared splitting the waters. It was possible to look at an angle into the river to glimpse submerged yellow mossy logs and rocks. By 2:00, sated with the scenery, we went to the Country Music Campout at mile 122. Folks for thirty-two years had been coming every first full week of June and August to this outdoor event. People sat listening to county music, conversed, danced, and even jammed with other musicians, open to the public. What a treat! And the five cyclists were there too.

From marker 122, the road constantly rose, in H 2/3. The river slowed itself every 1/8 of a mile due to the bends. There were boulders and rapids which would have destroyed Lewis and Clark canoes descending the river. Dense forest. Turbulent water with dead snags jammed into the rocks. Every few hundred feet another spring, rivulet, creek, or river merging with the Lochsa. Since the direction was upriver, however, the river width shrank mile by mile. By day's end it had slimmed to thirty feet.

Tuckered out, we called it a day at Jeffrey Johnson Campground, or so we thought. The locked gate said: *Not Yet Open To The Public*, though we knew the bikers had entered to camp. A half mile hike distant, one might enjoy the hot springs. No luck for us. Susan carted the bike and me ten miles to the next heavily timbered campground, Wendover. We selected a site by the river near a family, and set up camp in the forest. Susan left to find water. None was to be had. The park was open without water, except for untreated river water, which was what the campers next to us were using. It was 7:30. I was weary to the point of being unhelpful/grouchy, and Susan was frustrated, being unable to cook. Trying to obtain a camp payment envelope and information on the water situation, she discovered, on the entrance billboard, a notice that the Lochsa Lodge and Restaurant at Powell, 3.5 miles east, was open. Had we realized its closeness, we would have gone there first off. Our maps were not helpful in this case. Leaving everything "as is", we drove. The lodge had rooms left so we took one, and then sat down to dinner. With dimming sky, we raced back to stuff camping gear into the car and bolt for the lodge just as night fell.

61 climbing miles   622.7 mi. to date   elevation: 2,900'

Cycling Hwy 12, east of Lowell, ID. The tiny
white spot before the truck is a bicycler.

DAY 15: LOLO PASS

Friday, June 15, 2012   Powell, ID to Missoula, MT   Sunny 67* or ?

During breakfast we discovered working WIFI in the lodge restaurant, allowing us to send two day old email. And who entered the restaurant? The five bikers. Natasha (Auburn, CA, 5th grade teacher), Robert (Arkansas), Louie (New York education administrator), Molly (Wisconsin, 5th grade CA teacher, cycling back home as a surprise without telling her parents), and Phil (Grand Rapids, MI, retired). They linked because of "Uncle" Phil's internet ad, calling themselves "Uncle Phil's Possum Posse Day Tour 'merica". After a big breakfast, they were tackling Lolo Pass, thirteen miles beyond. Again, we swapped stories and posed for mug shots. However, a backtrack to Jeffery Johnson Campground was necessary for me to make up the 11 1/2 miles skipped last night. A 15 minute head start was given at 10:45.

Usually Susan sat, read, or walked for exercise in the stop areas, until I passed, then caught up three or four miles later. Her intent, especially in an area of no cell phone reception, was to make certain all was well. If so, as she passed with three honks of the horn, I nodded my head several times, meaning go to the next stop a few miles ahead; if things were great, five left hand fingers indicated go ahead five miles; if getting tired, two spread fingers meant two miles more; a right hand finger pointing sideways meant pull over at the next wide pullout. This system worked well, except today required frequent stops.

In the last three stages of ascending Lolo Pass, the increased unrelenting incline sapped energy rapidly. Stage 1: The national forest beauty and the splashing river did not reduce the 11 1/2 mile upward strain to the lodge. It had become onerous to concentrate on anything but the climb. Stage 2: The road increased to L-2/3, about six mph with headwind. Susan provided fluid intake after three miles twice, although I did carry Gatorade/water all the time in case I needed to hydrate more often. Stage 3: At 1:00 at the pull out area for snow chains, a grueling L-1 climb began up the 8 percent grade. Pedal. Breathe. Pedal. Breathe. 3.1 mph. The Little Train That Could (nursery story): "I think I can. I think I can." Pedal. Sweat trickle. Sweat in the eyes, clothes soaked. Sweat dripped on the nose. Susan offered respite after 1 1/2 miles. Only 5 1/2 miles to go. Pedal again. Grind. There were no leveling-off shelves, only continuous climb. Traffic was light, maybe three cars every 5 minutes. Tireless sun burned sunscreen slathered legs. The seat hurt. Another break at mile marker 172. Just four miles left. Chewing the last apple for energy, I pushed off. It was too difficult to think or compose ideas. Snow sat across the bare clear-cut peaks landscaped with slash and tree stumps. Liquid break at marker 174. Pedal. I had been reading mileage markers all day: 150...152...162...169...before the big seven mile climb. Ahead was the best reading all day: *Lolo Pass 1 Mile.* No more breaks needed. Grunt. Puff. Puff. Puff. And then the road crested into the visitor center's level parking lot. Free coffee. Ranger information. 2:30 lunch. Picture taking time: arrival proof standing against the Lolo Pass sign: *Elevation 5,235'.* Yahoo!!!

Forty-seven Miles to Missoula. Entry into Montana caused three things happen: 1) lose one hour (Mountain Standard Time), 2) no sales tax, and 3) the roads supposedly got better. One might surmise that going downhill would be a relief. It was, in that I didn't have to pedal; it wasn't, as soon as the asphalt cup holes and gouges surfaced. These treacherous divots, caused by snow removal equipment, began jamming my tires. Bang! Bang! Thump! Thud! Ka-thunk! A yellow and black warning sign at the road's edge: *Steep Descent 25 mph Recommended Next 4 Miles.* At thirty-two mph the holes, camouflaged by tree shadows crossing the roadbed, punched the forward tire left or right. A fall would spill me head-over-heels in a lacerating skid along the asphalt. Slowing was the only option. Not wanting a flip over, I squeezed the brakes with gradually increasing force, which took a half mile to stop. Readjusting my descent speed, I stayed around 24 mph for a mile. After the second mile, when the jarring divots disappeared, I unleashed the rolling tires to a 44 mph speed. On the fourth mile the slope eased, as did the conditions on the pavement, for the better. To add injury to speed, a Montana mosquito bit through my Lycra bike pants on the way down, leaving a welt on the right rump. That was one rocket propelled mosquito.

Then began sweet 22-24 mph cycling on good shoulder, wide road, with downhill beauty, but not like thick timbered Idaho. A trickling brown brook steadily grew alongside the road, watering the declining number of trees. Woods descended into a widening grassy but sparsely treed canyon. At marker 16 the first ranches with red barns appeared tucked among stands of Douglas Fir. Soon the canyon was two miles wide. Quickly the tree life diminished in density to scattered copses of trees, on the eastern side of the mountain rain shadow. A collection of ranchettes imitated ranch life with a horse on two acres. Highway 12 shifted north in late afternoon sun at Lolo, providing the gift of a twelve foot wide shoulder, well paved, and clean. Missoula, population 50,000, home to the University of Montana, and, according to the free tourist guidebook Susan picked up, Montana's cultural hub, was a place for rest.

65.3 mi.   688 mi. to date   elevation: 5,235'/3,223'

Lochsa Lodge Restaurant Near Powell, ID, where we met the group of 5 cyclers headed to Maine.

Bragging and exhausted at the crest of Lolo Pass 5,235 ft. in the Bitterroot Mountains, ID.

DAY 16: MISSOULA

Leisurely wake up. Finished laptop composing. Coffee. Slow gathering of wits. Put bike on carrier. McDonald's for egg McMuffin and more coffee.

"I already got one," a 7 year old towheaded boy said to his mom, on the walk to McDonald's play place.

It started me thinking about how children tell their parents: "Mommy, mommy, watch me. Daddy, look at me". In a few years, the words become: "Let me do it by myself". Soon kids stop communicating, comfortable in themselves or their friends, and then the eye rolling and embarrassment at their parents' foibles begins. And sometimes outright disdain. It is difficult for children to see their parents as imperfect persons. They want perfect mothers and fathers who never tell the same bad jokes, or make mistakes, or cheer too loudly, or blunder publicly, or pass gas, or are socially inept, or aren't cool enough. It was hard on me to realize my parents weren't perfect. They did the best they could for seven children. They sacrificed in so many ways for my brothers and sisters.

I was the first to college. I stood on the shoulders of my parents and college teachers to see beyond my limited horizon. Learning came at a social cost while keeping my nose to the study grindstone, wanting every penny's worth of tuition to pay off. I was tightly wound religiously, trying to be perfect, and disappointed when I wasn't. I won't lie, cheat or steal, and I know how to persevere when others give up, considering myself a workhorse for God.

Not until after the army, and at 26 years of age, did I begin to like myself, to accept that I am not perfect, but I did get a lot of things right. At 32, the right woman accepted my oddball sense of humor and character faults and we produced two bright sensible top-of-their-class kids. They got the best traits from Mom and Dad, and also some of our weaknesses. On this, the eve of Father's Day, I hope and pray that they can accept themselves, and perhaps forgive their father for not being perfect. They are my perfection for the future.

Nestled in a five mile wide bowl of low mountains partially forested on one side and heavily on the other, Missoula is a modern city without traffic congestion, graffiti, or visible decaying sections. In the spring it holds both a farmer's and Saturday market for crafts. Main streets are business lined for miles. The motels and visitor's center have colorful picture maps showing all the desirable locations on easily referenced streets. Red brick buildings dominate the main older city. Homes on the hillsides or in quiet neighborhoods are sequestered from the commercial streets. Big franchise box stores have found this to be an excellent location. A few stores and shops keep up the illusion of an old wooden western facade, but around the corner reveals aluminum siding. A youth oriented town, because of the University of Montana Grizzlies, there are open air events, restaurants and music festivals. Bicycles are universal for both young and old. Wide streets have bike paths and designated street marker lanes.

Wise Susan had joined me up with Adventure Cycling Association, a non-profit cycling club headquartered in Missoula, our day's primary destination. And guess who was there? The five bikers buying supplies. All of us had our pictures taken to be posted on the Wall of Fame. At the recommendation of Robert, I bought a Brooks leather needle nose seat because he said that would relieve the rear end pain. It needed to be broken-in experimenting with seat adjustment for the next several days. I'd continue being sore until then. Much good advice and information came from the five and store personnel. Best of all, my bike now has a lock. How silly I was to think the weight of a lock and cable was too much to carry.

Having napped, the rest of the afternoon was spent gathering supplies from stores, fruit for nutrition breaks, (Cherries are now in!), books for reading, and sunscreen. At 5:00 we attended mass at St. Francis Xavier Church, a national designated historical site. The exterior was a three story tall flying buttress brick edifice for a congregation of 600. The interior was decorated with handsome stained glass windows, a choir loft, a large pipe organ, and above, on the rounded ceiling, religious scenes that would rival Italian houses of worship.

For dinner, at Hohut Mongolian Grill, diners selected from a wide variety of meats, fish, noodles, vegetables, placed all in a bowl, poured a sauce of choice, then gave to a chef. In front of him was a six foot in diameter round stove with a hole in the center for scraps and waste. He took the bowls, dumped the contents on the griddle, flipped two cutting tools/knives and proceeded to chop, scoop, and mix one's dinner, moving around the circle tending to all the other mixtures as well. When the meal was cooked, he scraped the concoction onto a plate and handed it to the customer standing on the periphery. Talk about immediate service! The food was delicious and reasonably priced. Returning for seconds wasn't just permitted, it was recommended.

Susan went to do laundry while I typed, soaked in a hot tub, and put on the new bike seat.

0 mi.   688 mi. to date   One more pass to climb.

DAY 17: ON TO GREAT FALLS

Sunday,   Missoula to Lincoln, MT   Showers/partly clearing 70*
June 17, 2012

Do you think an almost 68, year old is a hero for bicycling the Lewis and Clark Trail? Better clue you in. Last year, at the Adventure Cycling Shop, a 78 year old woman came in with her group. She was excited about her accomplishment, vivacious and exhilarated. An 18 year old fellow biker crept through the door looking like the world was about to eat him. But that's not all. Several years back, an 89 year old man came through on a coast-to-coast trip. Wall-of-Famers.

Tidbits. Eat your hearts out Californians. Gas here is $3.64 at Costco. No sales tax. There is so much country five miles outside of town, with kayaking, tubing, hunting, and fishing, that no one bothers going to the National Parks. A casino is the name for a bar. With the purchase of a liquor license, a gaming license is thrown in. You don't have to be an Indian.

Behind the low wooded hills circumscribing Missoula were the heavily timbered blue mountains. Because it was raining when we woke, I dragged my heals getting started, eating another McD's breakfast. With sun breaking through the clouds, I cut through the corner of Montana University, crossed a bridge over muddy Clark Fork River, and joined Highway 12 until it linked with I-90, and then Route 200 heading east. The first twelve miles coursed through stratified layers of dusty magenta rock, skree, and pines surrounded by talus fallen from mountain heights. Looking ahead was like peeking at cleavage, a hint of what's there but not seeing what's behind because the road twisted and turned with the Blackfoot River. Road marker 12 broke with the canyon into a wide green velvety pasture valley. Ranches spread out to the low hills cloaked in woods, which then rose toward the taller blue peaks. The idyllic scene had entranced many a city slicker who bought a piece of heavenly ranch, and then discovered months of winter, six feet of snow, long commutes to town for doctor appointments or supplies, fence mending, irrigation, hay baling, veterinarian bills, wind damage, repair, etc. Many of these picture perfect ranches were for sale.

A restaurant stop at Potomac, marker 16, provided us a visit with teacher Bill Stockton, who was the only high school science teacher in a 110 student high school on the Flathead Indian Reservation north of Missoula, from where he commuted. He taught AP Biology and six other science subjects in alternating years. Their four day week started at 7:55 a.m. and ended at 4:00 with a thirty minute lunch. After school he coached football and basketball. To make ends meet he worked in the restaurant, and just had a daughter born. (I thought I was busy.)

By 3:00, only thirty-seven miles had been covered. My rump was sore from breaking in the new saddle seat, and energy was waning (actually will power). Snacks changed to bananas, nectarines, and trail mix bars, with hope an energy burst would last to the fifty mile junction, where camping might be the night's rest. The road had been pretty steady in gentle climbs with lots of wide open pasture, occasional rolling ascents, and sweeping curves up through wood cuts or past scraped rock walls.

I'd been stopping nearly every six or seven miles because of saddle soreness, so it didn't faze me to turn in to the Mandatory Watercraft Check Point rest stop at mile thirty-seven. Two veteran Fish and Game wardens, Darrell and Curt, explained the reason for a stop-Kansas boaters.

"Are you kidding?" I asked.

Darrell pulled out before and after photo sheets showing items, a six inch long PVC pipe, and a fishing rod and reel which had been in a Kansas lake for one week. A type of fresh water infesting snail had completely covered both items. Originally spilled by a European cargo ship's bilge water into the Great Lakes, the snails were migrating into the rivers and lakes of the Midwest. The snails ate everything, including algae. Water, which had once been murky, soon became clear to depths of five, ten, twenty feet. Nothing else lived. The only way to eradicate the snails was to drain the lake, let it completely dry out, causing the snails to die. Even a little water, like in the boat bottom or the damp carpet of a fishing boat allowed them to live, and then spread to the next body of water the boat entered. States already affected include the Midwestern States, Arizona, Nevada, and California. The job of these two men from the Montana Wildlife and Fish Department was to prevent the spread of this harmful snail species into their state.

Looking at the map, my stopping place was just seven more miles, but then, looking farther ahead, it was another twenty-six miles to Lincoln. It was getting cold in the shadows. If we took an early camp stop, it meant crossing Rogers Pass would add an extra thirty-three miles to the eighty-eight after Lincoln to reach Great Falls, a total of 121 miles for tomorrow, and there would be nothing in between. I ate another nectarine, and pressed on through golf course perfect canyons and fly fishing river bends that a diehard angler would give a month's salary to fish.

Now numb, it didn't make much difference to the bony interior of the gluteus maximus. Ride on! For safety's sake, Susan let me charge ahead four miles, then pass if I were okay, to the next seven mile rest point, especially since we were again in a dead spot for cell reception. At 8:15, I rolled into Lincoln, MT, where Susan located a motel. I ate a Father's Day steak, and concluded with phone calls and email.

81 mi.   769 mi. to date   elevation: 4,700'

DAY 18: THE WIND GIVETH AND THE WIND TAKETH AWAY

Monday,   Lincoln to Simms MT   Partly cloudy, mountain 56*
June 18, 2012

Yesterday, the real reason I pushed on when tiring, was the twelve mph tailwind I did not want to lose. On the nearly level straight-aways, it was easier to maintain speeds of 15-17, even though it was obvious the road still rose with the river. Today, cranky, sore, and anxious to begin, I started off in the chill mountain air, late at 11:00 from Lincoln, MT, along Highway 200. While adjusting a rubbing rear tire, a gentle five mph tailwind arose. On to Roger's Pass. Off the roadside, dilapidated lodge pole barns and pioneer out buildings lay together with rotting gray tree stumps and surrounding rotting slash. At the snow chain turn out, the wind died out, making the final climb an L-2 without terrible strain until the crest. Here was the cruelty of the Montana Highway engineers. The road inclined at a consistent slope, yet with a perverse sense of torture, the last 300-500 feet of a climb were increased in angle, kind of like adding two inches to the top step of stairs. I believe it was deliberately done to irk cyclists. A blue and white sign said: *Point of Interest 1/4 Mile.*. At the top, the only noticeable item was the sign: Roger's Pass Continental Divide 5,610', a natural photo op.

Now the truth about the quality of Montana roads stood out. Rumble strips are gouged to the right of the road edge's solid white line, leaving about 18 inches of space to the guard rails. The pavement is class A, smooth and swift, without snow removal cupping and divots. The guard rails are too close for a biker on the shoulder. An errant twist of the handlebars, gusting truck, or a jutting cliff rock might put a hand or bike parts into the guard metal. Without visible traffic behind, I floated across the rumble strips, centered in the lane, and rolled down the 6 percent grade speeding up to forty-four mph at times. Two cars drew up behind and, when there was an opening, passed. Three miles zipped by. Meanwhile, the forest rapidly changed from dense to scattered to sparse, and then to dry yellow sere hillsides. Black Angus and Hereford cattle dotted the land. The road, however, continued downward in a series of steep undulating waves. Down 400 feet, up 350, down 400, up 600, down 800, up 600.

Stopped at the Dearborn River for lunch, sitting on red folding chairs while eating lunch, we enjoyed fruit watching the aspens flitting their leaves in a small protected river gully, perfect for an Indian camp. The fluttering leaves suddenly flapped ferociously as the afternoon heating stirred the air. In moments the wind was blowing 20-25 mph. Oh boy! A tail wind! The truth was a different matter. It was a crosswind from the north, on my left. Progress was aided by a slight angle of air to the back, but the force of the crosscut reduced forward momentum. Actually, it was necessary to lean left into the wind to stay balanced against the force. Add to this the roller coaster prairie hills, and speed was sorely affected, besides making it impossible to stay inside the 18 inch shoulder along with the rumble strips. Cars, passing by, momentarily blocked the wind so that the reduced gusting caused the bike to unbalance, leaning more to the left. Even more so with trucks coming from the rear. At times the bike fell towards the truck when its passage blocked the wind. Gusts from opposite side's approaching trucks added wind forcing the front wheel to twist right towards the soft shoulder of sand and grit. The biggest danger was falling into a truck passing from behind. Whenever there was no rear traffic in my helmet mirror, I would dart into the lane for better control.

Going uphill, demanded L-1 speed, three mph, fighting against the gusts, until the windless blocking of a roadcut through the hill. Exiting the hill cut, the wind resurged with a fury. But there was the downhill stretch, right? Not so fast, literally. Heading down was treacherous. Once the speed reached twenty-four, the sideways blowing forced the bike to balance-lean left. But, since the wind came in gusts, suddenly the bike would be falling left in the cut. Corrected to upright, it would then be hit with another blow to start a right fall. It was necessary to slow down to stay alive, especially considering traffic coming down the same hill. Then the wind blew even more fiercely, to the point I had to pedal down hills. This was spirit breaking riding. Storm clouds looming just south and my sore, sore, sore, sore butt finally ended the struggle. Was the saddle being broken-in or was my rump being broken? I gave up at Simms, thirty miles short of Great Falls.

We drove into the big city because there were no motels along the drive from Simms to Great Falls. It was not enticing to camp in threatening weather. I noted on the map that since we were close to Glacier National Park, we could take in some sightseeing.

Susan said: "I'm not going 200 miles off the trip and back for just a day in the National Park.

Calculating, I replied: "It's only 141. We could easily do it in a day".

Susan responded: "I'm not going unless we'll be there several days. I'll go if you say that you're done on this trip".

This is where I opened my smart-ass mouth and said: "Okay, I'm done".

At this, Susan wheeled over to the right and stopped the car. She actually called my bluff!

Sheepishly I had to eat my words: "Okay, I'll keep going". Nothing like a judge, jury, and executioner in the car with you. I'd rather deal with the wind.

57 mi.   826 mi. to date   elevation: Who cares?

Rogers Pass at the Continental Divide, Highway 200, between Belt and Lewistown, MT, a 90 mile day 6/21/12.

DAY 19: TIMING IS EVERYTHING

Tuesday,   Simms to Great Falls, MT   Showers/clearing 59*
June 19, 2012

The Weather Channel wasn't kidding: 60 percent chance of showers, tapering in the afternoon, rain at night, winds fifteen to twenty-five, temperature 59*. Looking out the motel window, the sky was darkly overcast, the ground wet, and wind blew strongly. We packed quickly, left our room by 9:00, but slowed at breakfast with map planning, weighing the options of going back to yesterday's dismal stop, and linking with tomorrow's route. Sodden clouds all about us, we decided to retrace to yesterday's stop, then return to Great Falls. Hoping that the rain would diminish by the afternoon, we crossed the street to Roger's Jewelry to repair my broken expandable watch band. The shop sold Yogo sapphires, found only in Montana. Beautiful but expensive. No charge for the repair. What a deal!

On to visit Great Falls and Lewis and Clark exhibits. Unfortunately the upper bluffs of the Missouri are populated by numerous industrial sights and businesses. The five falls sat in a gorge a hundred feet below the prairie. A dam, was built sufficiently distant to harness hydroelectric power without hindering view of the four visible falls, with one submerged, cascading over the rock plateau falls. Under threat of rain, we explored the Lewis & Clark National Historic Trail Interpretative Center, overlooking the Missouri River a hundred feet below. Of all the L. & C. presentations seen so far, this was, by far, the finest set of dioramas, artifacts, information displays, pictures, film, and interpretations of the Discovery Party.

At 1:00, we exited into spitting wind. No food so far provided energy or desire to tackle the menacing weather, until a Subway tuna sandwich. Rain showers had missed our location stops. The return to Simms was punctuated with occasional rain squalls. At 3:00, in a mild drizzle, the yellow vest over long sleeves of the green windbreaker began the make up distance back to Great Falls. For three miles, in crosscut winds like yesterday, the bike struggled down the damp highway dividing isolated ranches one to two miles away. The U-shaped valley, spreading across two miles of irrigated fields, widened with passage of each highway marker. Rounding an ancient brown promontory, the wind ceased, the drizzle-mist ended, the sore butt stopped complaining, and the cramping left thigh eased. A run with H-6/7 speed recovered thirty lost miles.

Flat down-sloping pavement passed more and more horse ranches, farm equipment, and machinists' shops. The frontage road at Vaughn, provided relative safety on an eight inch shoulder.

The approach to Great Falls looked like a lived-in forlorn city, populated with tired looking trailers, industrial yards both neat and derelict, overly spread out land parcels with buildings of modest and middle class means, weathered and paint peeling. No motels appeared on the long Highway 200 approach until inside the city. Although there were a few lanes for bikes, this city was not bike friendly like Missoula. Susan and I had played leap frog effectively to reach Grand Falls by 6:10. Behind, thunder chased us toward the motel. As we unloaded the car, raindrops spattered, letting up momentarily. Later, we ventured to a restaurant for dinner, just before a gully washer pummeled the streets. We walked dry to our room at 7:55. Each outdoor excursion missed the wet deluges by moments.

Susan discovered that I miscalculated day seventeen, missing twenty miles. And that wasn't all. She detected consistently when low blood sugar and weariness clouded my thinking and judgment. Navigator supreme, she has kept me on route, been master procurer of supplies, completer of odd chores, agent of motel accommodations, lunch buddy, laundress, soother of cramped muscles, slatherer of sunscreen, editor of writing mistakes, best birddog, collector of things I left behind, and support captain behind and before my riding. This may not have been the right time for her to give up her summer, but in no way could I have reached this point without her. Perfect timing, *For Me.*

34 mi.   860 mi. to date   elevation: 3,312'

DAY 20: THE LONG AND THE SHORT OF IT

Wednesday,   Great Falls to Belt, MT   Showers to sunny 71*
June 20, 2012

The Charles M. Russell Museum is a five star attraction worthy of any historian's interest. An estimate of time needed to explore: a rifle buff (an outstanding collection of the guns that won the West) two hours; cowboy and western bronzes (two); miniature wagons (two); buffalo (two); Indian artifacts, clothing, bead work, headdresses, peace pipes, arrows, par fleche (six); history (six); art (one day); the life and Western art of Charles M. Russell (two days). This is a museum that keeps on giving. Words cannot bring to life the extensive Native American exhibits and the Russell art of the vanished West. This Must See Attraction leaves the spectator in awe. We spent but 3 1/2 hours (not enough time) before exiting into a cloudburst-washed parking lot. Perfect timing again.

Leaving Great Falls at 2:30 revealed cyclists, staying in the local neighborhoods, enjoying relatively safe smooth riding, but not on the main streets. Only two people were on bikes, and I was one of them.

Highway 200 lead east on wonderful class A pavement, wide shoulder, and gentle rising into the vast undulating prairie. The green swells, similar to eastern Washington State, stretched outward to distant broken yellow bluffs. Giant fields of wheat, alfalfa, and grass stood in the sun. Aluminum wheat silos lined up four abreast in the fields. Up and down the pavement ran, climbing and dropping fifty feet. Some steeper sections took half a mile to reach zenith, then plummeted. Little Belt Mountains stood to the south. Blue Highwood Mountains rose on the left, but no flat land. After twenty miles, the road dropped precipitously into a narrow wooded canyon cut by a small river. At a truck weigh station, a highway patrolman discussed travel to Stanford, no lodging or amenities in the next thirty-six miles, with three major climbs. We set camp at Ft. Ponderosa, a grassy glade beneath skinny mature cottonwoods near the town of Belt. The longest day of the year, the second shortest distance covered.

24 mi.   884 mi. to date   elevation: up and down

DAY 21: I WON'T DO THAT AGAIN

Thursday,   Belt to Lewistown. MT   Overcast to sunny 79*
June 21, 2012

It wasn't the horn blasts from three separate freight trains moving on the other side of the trees, nor the tent occupants next door waking up, nor the revving engine, nor the birds singing that woke me. It was the high pitched cheerful echoes of children playing in a woodland park. Immediate repacking of our camp took an hour-and-a-half. Caught unprepared for a campout, we didn't have better breakfast fare than peanut butter and jelly (Simply Fruit) and nectarines. At 10:30, bathed in sunscreen, I climbed a gentle long ascent out of the narrow canyon. Small ranches dotted meandering Otter Creek as it gouged the brown earth and grass. Thirteen miles of 7 mph toil at M- 1/2 up the gradual slope. When the road topped the treeless butte, land rolled ahead under high plains grass and wheat farms as far as the eye could see. Lewistown, the next large city with supplies, amenities, and WIFI, would be a demanding eighty-two mile day. That was before we learned about the detour.

All around, a checkerboard of dried fields and leprechaun green was dotted with hardy self-sufficient ranches four or five miles apart. For miles the road rose and fell with a five mph wind. Snow fences intermittently lined the highway. And then two enormous climbs, the last a thousand foot rise over the shoulder of a mesa. Stanford, population one thousand, offered essential services, a pool, grocery, and a proud school. Lunch in the park. The local ranger station, identifying that the road would be very straight with small dips, but a detour of an extra seven miles, due to a washed out bridge, counted fifty remaining miles to Lewistown.

Tired and saddle sore, I may have finally figured out the right combination of seat adjustment, clothing, and padding. The crosswinds were mild enough to be a blessing, but the constant elevation rise resulted in nine to ten mile speed per hour. At Windham the road detoured for twenty-two miles around a pale green table mesa.

A curious sight began. Ranchers packed their hay, not in rectangular bales, but in one ton coils. Here and there piles of ten or so lined up, then fifty or sixty stacked in pyramids, and one stack, doubled coils on end with a triangular roof above resembled a Parthenon of hay. Another set of haystack rolls looked like a jet plane. The closer to Utica and beyond, the more hay stack art. Ranchers competed in an annual contest, vying for honors of the most ingenious way to arrange the stacks. People drove from miles around just to see the year's hay artistry.

Horses and Hereford cows were my observers. Cawing birds flitted and dove to chase trespassers from getting too close to their nests. In the setting sun, mountain shadows revealed hidden field creases and textures. The town of Hobson cornered the highway junction at marker 59. At 6:45, with Lewiston in range, there could be no dawdling. Eat, drink, pedal. The first black tree silhouettes appeared on the evening horizon.

When 8:15 came, Susan commented, "This is too long of a day".

I told her to forge ahead to get a room in Lewistown, thinking I could finish in about an hour. She followed me until 8:45 then took off for town.

It wasn't the way I figured. Cross winds became headwinds, more higher/lower hills, the deepening dusk, and fatigue factored into slow riding. We had agreed to stop at the first part of Lewistown. Because the sun was set, evening gloom all around, and my body spent, I stopped at the first motel, a Super 8, and called on the cell. No answer, just a message machine because her phone was silenced. I would remain in place until Susan came to get me. My cell phone registered only one bar of power remaining. After five minutes, and no response, I rolled farther downhill to the next motel, again leaving message. When Susan finally called, the reception was so broken, that she had to call back three times. I didn't want to ride anymore; it was too dark; my body had called it quits; no more gas in the tank. More broken reception. She had a room at the Yogo Inn on the other side of town. With twitching rubbery legs, I coasted downward two more miles, and found her on the corner of the inn at 9:50 p.m. She had rented the last room. All the other motels were filled. Big events in town-celebrity golf and baseball tournaments. Restaurants were closed. The only eatery open was McDonald's; never did two quarter pounders taste so good. We came back to the room, got our swim suits on and soaked in the spa after closing time at 11:00. While Susan set up the computer, I lay back on the bed, too exhausted to type. After an hour, restless leg syndrome kicked in. Susan massaged my legs so I could fall asleep again. Too much cycling ambition in one day. Too weary. I won't do that again, at least until next time. No WIFI for the next few days.

90 mi.   974 mi. to date   elevation: 3,963'

DAY 22: IT WASN'T A GOOD DAY

Friday,   Lewistown to Winnett, MT   Overcast to sunny 73*
June 22, 2012

I sat alone typing in a bar in Winnett, MT. Susan was unhappy. Men bellied up to the bar. Ladies gathered around a microphone singing Karaoke. This was the social center of town. It ain't what you think. Let's back up.

The morning wind was blustering the trees outside. Still so exhausted it took a while to wolf down a rancher's breakfast, pack, and finish what didn't get written last night. We overlapped the 11:00 departure time to send the latest email bulletin. Then we drove to the Montana Department of Transportation and the Charles M. Russell National Wildlife Refuge Office at noon to get road information. Chatting with Jackie, Donna, and Mike gave plenty to mull over including camp sites, parks, available services, worthy places to visit, and a whole lot about Williston, ND (more info later). But conversation did not lessen the winds. Weather predictions warned possible thundershowers and gusting east winds up to twenty-four mph. I bicycled at 1:30 while Susan bought groceries. There would be four days before the next large town, no cell phone, and probably no WIFI.

Overcast wind played havoc all day. The exit from town gradually rose for four miles, before turning into an L-2 grind for three more. Nothing spectacular in the climb, except the twelve to fifteen mph headwind that steadily increased. Twisting road directions made no difference; the wind was always in my face. By the wooded pine crest of the pass, after seven miles, 53 minutes had elapsed. A wonderful downhill lasted approximately two miles with constant wind buffets, until the true demon winds took over. If I dared to get the speed above ten mph, the gusts would put me in my place. Grasses bent over. Hills offered no protection, nor did road curves. No trees provided a windbreak after the pass. As the valley spread out to wider pastures, there were only treeless open fields.

The blustering was relentless. Each nutrition stop, the wind seemed to abate, yet as soon as the bike moved, the ferocity picked up again. For sure, after 3 p.m. the wind would let up! Oh, how deluded humans were in the face of Mother Nature! From mile post 113 the gales increased to full throttle, making forward progress eight mph, then four. It was like swimming in howling maple syrup. Now, I don't have to exaggerate about Montana wind. Houses had sandblasted paint on one side. Montanans have no need of fans. Laundry, put on clothes lines, dried in three minutes. Parents have been forbidden to name their daughters Gale. Children were sent to school with ten pounds of rocks in their pockets to prevent being blown away. Carpenters don't need paper to sand their wood. Cattle all leaned to the west. Fish had scales only on one side. Birds don't flap their wings. Persons wearing dresses or kilts were arrested for indecent exposure. Politicians were not allowed to debate-there's already enough hot air. Tornadoes avoided Montana like the plague. There was no air pollution-it was all blown to another state! Nine miles short of Winnett, marker 136, I gave up.

Racking the bike on the carrier, at 7:15 p.m. I let Susan chauffer to Winnett. First, she searched for the campground, but there were no signs, and few people on the street. A family group chatting at a fence asked if I were the cyclist riding in from Lewistown. Reputation had preceded me. They said that the camping choices were the dry grass baseball field across the street, or the park, by the highway, neither with restrooms. With the cafe closed at 6:00, the only chance for eats was the Winnett Bar. Two burgers later we surveyed the camping options, Susan still wanted to find the campground promised in Lewis and Clark Cycling literature. She was tearfully upset enough to ask me to drive because this was not what she expected. A rickety weather beaten decrepit abandoned building near a sign proclaiming HOTEL was all that was visible. We ended up in the park, the size of a small house parcel, set up the tent, and if we needed the facilities, well, "just go to the bar". It would be open until 2 a.m. Susan hated the dirty ramshackle bar restroom for washing up and brushing teeth.

The bar "fee" for my WIFI typing (as Internet Man), was to sing "Sixteen Tons" and tell a joke. And now you know the rest of the story.

45 mi.   1,019 mi. to date   elevation: too windy to tell

DAY 23: PORTAGE

Saturday,   Winnett to Mosby, MT   Sunny low 80s
June 23, 2012

Okay, so I cheated. Susan said after a thousand miles, and a day like yesterday, it was okay to "portage" the bicycle. I always obey my wife. (She rolled her eyes.) So there!

Winnett, population 150, was the county seat of Petroleum County. Its entrance road was a graveyard for rusting machinery, old cars, lumber piles, scrap, and rusting metal piles. It was decorated with wide streets, ice shattered curbs and sidewalks, and widely spaced old buildings with flaking paint. Homes were modest/poor in the derelict town. Even so, folks had strong pride in its school, down home friendliness, and welcome for strangers.

After last night's camping debacle, dogs barking, birds tweeting at 3 a.m., no middle of the night restroom, no shower, highway traffic motoring by, and drunks hooting from the bar down the street, we were cranky. The park sign declared that sprinklers came on daily at 8:00. We hurriedly broke camp and drove to the Kozy Korner Cafe, featured in Gourmet Magazine in 2004. We waited until the café opened at 7:00. Owner Buck's dry sense of humor greeted us at the door: "Open sign's been on for five minutes".

I replied: "We're slow readers".

He chatted as three old timers came in, while wife Ellen busied herself making eggs.

"No cinnamon rolls today. She's making pies," said Buck.

Two more men, dressed in orange biker shirts entered, Dave, a 4th grade teacher from Boulder, CO, and Anders from Norway. They had arrived last night from Jordan, MT, seventy-six miles east, but with the tailwind I faced. The lucky guys left St. Louis May 27 and had reached two-thirds of their goal of Portland. We exchanged road info before I retraced back to mile post 128.

With a mild breeze blowing at 8:30, I exited the car, removed the bike from the rack, kissed Susan and got two mosquito bites on the shoulders. In four miles I met the bikers again and swapped more stories. At 9:15, glided into Winnett for the second time. Already the wind had picked up to ten, the predicted air speed. Within the half hour it was up to at least yesterday's 25-30 mph level.

Since leaving Lewiston's forested eastern hills, the land had dropped into a wide butte-sided canyon. A curious observation. The tops of the 400 foot cliffs ran for over thirty miles with no trees above, and none at the base, just dry dirt. However, on the sides of the buttes, half way up, pines lined the walls horizontally the entire distance. From time to time they switched from the north side of the valley to the south, yet the tree phenomenon continued. Apparently water seeped out the layers of rock strata in sufficient amounts to keep the trees on the hillsides alive, but there was no moisture above and below. Ranches occupied the valley floor scattered with black Hereford cows. Each mile down the valley the cliffs dropped lower and lower, and the opposing side appeared to melt into soft rounded mounds more eastward. Gusts tilted the yellow, lavender, purple flowers and waved grass on the road shoulder 90* toward the highway's fence. Weeds? Hardly. The ranchers mowed the shoulders and reaped a harvest of alfalfa, their one ton hay rolls left in the rain ditch for later collection. Further east, sage brush cropped up on hillsides as more brown and yellow dried grass became visible to the horizon. The land, bit by bit, became more arid, yet had ranch oases and vegetation as green as ever.

According to the Colorado and Norwegian bikers, Dave and Anders, supposedly the land would become flatter with fewer climbs. Not so. Like giant elongated waves, the rises demanded extended three to five mile elongated four percent climbs. Sometimes the watershed rippled due to frequent creeks, otherwise the declines were ancient washes devoid of green. Trees were evident only when a creek or stream permitted enough water to sustain life, and this sparsely.

Heavy thirty-five mph winds continued hampering forward progress. The next and only respite was Mosby, a rest area at Marker 159, at the top of a serious climb. Pines sat one hundred feet below in an arroyo. All in, I stumbled to a sunny wind-tunnel picnic bench as Susan gathered the food basket and cooler for lunch. It was dragon mouth toasty and blowing. Montana's rest area restrooms provided a constant radio weather report through a speaker system. The forecaster predicted low 80s and gusts to thirty-one. Bushed, I slept for an hour.

Waking, I gave Susan a proposal: "Let's drive to Jordan, get a motel, shower, rest, and not come back".

A second invitation was not needed. Off we went. For fifty-five miles the land became desiccated. All trees vanished in the first six miles. Buttes changed into dirt mounds, the yellowed outcroppings of shale resembled huge dinosaur bones being unearthed from underground tombs. In the distance were volcanic cinder cones. Interspersed ranches irrigated with circular crawling mechanical watering systems.

Sand Springs (church, store, and tot playground) was the last spot on the map before the barren thirty miles to Jordan. Five miles beyond, a man and woman struggled, cycling into the gusts. Their pedal speed could not have exceeded four mph. They seemed provisioned as there was nothing until they reached Jordan; I didn't want any more wind struggle. If Lewis and Clark could portage, so could I. (Portage means to take boats/canoes out of the water and carry them around a waterfall or other hazardous obstacle.) And I had Susan's permission.

Actually, she leaned over and said: "Thanks for portaging. I dreaded having to go through country like this". I don't feel one bit guilty for cheating.

Simply put, Jordan was an oasis in the Montana desert land.

33 mi.   1,052 mi. to date   elevation: 2,598'

DAY 24: PORTAGE TO FT. PECK

Sunday, June 24, 2012   Portage to Ft. Peck   Overcast/late sunny 90*

Jordan (population 340 in town), county seat of Garfield County, sported two motels, two gas stations, auto repair, a hospital, a Wildlife Refuge office, a Department of Transportation yard, three restaurants, and eight churches. The congregations must come from miles around, averaging forty-three townspeople for each church. Most streets were gravel/rock. Small maintained yards told how much pride folks had in their homes. The restaurant cooked plenty of hardy food at a fair price.

St. John the Baptist Church had about 120 attendees, on the feast of the Baptist. John lived according to truth, not to the political leader of his time. He argued against Herod's immorality; it cost him his head. Who resists moral wrong in our society? Have we gone in step with our political leaders, neighbors, friends? Popularity does not determine the right course.

The wind blew fiercely from the time we woke, so we portaged toward Ft. Peck. The Jordan oasis was more than a green relief in the desert, flowing thirty-seven miles. Opposed to what Anders and Dave told us, the eastern exit from Jordan was not flat. Probably those massive fjords of Norway and the boulders in Colorado have confused their thinking of what flat means. Steep climbs of 200-600 feet were common until a highway rest stop, when the road turned north. Here the earth crusts were broken and scarped by erosion that transformed plains into arroyos and gullies.

From Mosby east, the land was once part of a shallow inland sea 65,000,000 years ago, probably not deeper than 600 feet. Dinosaurs and ancient denizens of prehistoric seas prowled the hot marshy subtropical coastline. The fossil record told of crocodiles, turtles, toads, lizards and small creatures inhabiting wetlands. Many of the best examples of dinosaurs on displays around the world were collected from Garfield and McCone counties. The finest Tyrannosaurus Rex skeleton, as well as thirty other partials, were found in the Hell Creek Formation which extends over eastern Montana and the Dakotas. If one knew where to look or had an educated guess, luck may discover a dino. Gravel layers in brown, tan, orange, black, yellow, and white strata rock lay bared by wind and river erosion. Table mesas with hard capstones resisted the rains better, so they appeared as thousands of "Twinkie" cake mounds or elongated horizontally striped hills. The scene was beautiful, but, without services, a lonely ninety-six mile distance from Jordan.

We scooted north passing the eroded mounds toward Ft. Peck. Perhaps there were a dozen isolated ranches on the fifty-nine mile section. The car was whipped left and right by buffets up to 45 mph. The overlook on Ft. Peck Dam spillway proved the ferocity of the winds. One's voice was ripped away from the lips, so conversation was difficult. Howling gusts pushed spectators sideways, requiring leaning into the wind to stand.

Ft. Peck Dam is the longest hydraulic fill dam in the world. Blocking the Missouri River, it provides sixteen hundred miles of shoreline, double California's coast. Benefits included flood control, hydroelectric power, irrigation, social and cultural transformation, fishing and recreation. As a project, Montanans claim FDR saved the state with this dam in the Depression by employing over 10,000 New Deal workers. The visitor center exhibited an excellent assemblage of dinosaur fossils and ancient inland sea creatures, all locally disinterred. Paleontologists literally have field days locally, on the hunt for bones. This was a first class dinosaur exposition.

The town of Fort Peck resembled homes set in a park of wide grassy lawns unfenced between neighbors, tree lined drives, and vistas overlooking the Missouri. According to the store clerk, most residents worked for the Army Corps of Engineers at the dam. Town offered few services for remote NE Montana: a theater offering a live performance of "All Shook Up", a hotel (hunting lodge), post office, a closed restaurant, no school, but a cafe and a gas station down the road. Ft. Peck Hotel is a rustic sportsman's paradise with taxidermy trophies on the walls, photos of hunting successes, pictures of fish catches that didn't get away, and a bragging parlor next to the fireplace near the bar.

0 mi. biking   1,052 mi. to date   elevation: 2,090'

DAY 25: CIRCLE 'EM UP BOYS

Monday,	24/200 rest stop to	Overcast to sunny 97*
June 25, 2012	Circle, MT	

Dr. Shannon, I have sinned. The breakfast spread at the Fort Peck Hotel had the biggest most scrumptious, yellow and brown cinnamon rolls just sitting on a plate chest high as we entered the dining room. I weakened. I let temptation win. I had the most savory sugar coated smile after biting into one soft creamy puffed confection. And there were no regrets. I licked my fingers all day. It tasted soooooooooooo good!

Returning fifty-nine miles by car from Fort Peck on Highway 24 to U.S. 200, we revisited the stark landscape, steep rises and dips, and the rare appearance of visible ranches, save for the bank of a dozen postal boxes on two side roads. Coming at us, an ambulance, a fire-rescue vehicle, and a white pickup passed with flashing lights as we pulled over. Several miles later a dark gray State Highway Patrol truck was turning about on the narrow road. To our right was a passenger vehicle with its roof crushed and possessions strewn all about the shoulder. I told the officer we hadn't seen this the day before.

He answered, "It just happened".

The speeding emergency vehicles were on the way to Glasgow Hospital sixty miles away. How were the authorities notified? There was no cell reception. The prognosis was iffy.

At the rest stop, I dressed, applied sunscreen, checked water, then killed a precious hour talking to a carload of travelers about the bike trip. It was disadvantageous when interested or curious strangers delayed departure. Significant because today's temps headed to the upper nineties. Thankfully, the headwind died down. I climbed the first of two distant ascents, with three tall interrupting loop de loop hills hiding other shorter roller coaster hills, all substantial climbs. But true to his word, a farmer I spoke to last night at the hotel was right. In twenty miles the land would cease with the hill climbing. For the first time, I was cruising easy rises, flat grassland, with real speed, even in the heat. Our 2:00 lunch stop at the B.S. Café (Brockway Supper) cooled us off while gazing at the gas propelled model airplanes suspended from the ceiling. At 3:00 the bicycle did a speedy thirteen miles to Circle.

In the motel, a group of men known as the "grasshopper guys" spoke with us. Their work for the federal government was to count the nymph grasshopper population within a specific area and estimate the threat of serious infestation/potential for reduction using a new pesticide. The basic rule was: If you notice the hoppers, you already have a serious problem. As nymphs, they ate the alfalfa or crop as fast as it grew. The survey and experiment was to determine how little of an application would provide the maximum effect. Eradication was not the goal, but reduction. Application would be done in checkerboard fashion so that beneficial insects could survive to do their jobs. The motel manager warned them not to go to the other side of town which was named mosquito heaven.

Critters. Talking with the grasshopper guys reminded of all the different critters seen on this trip-raccoons, marmots, coyotes, squirrels, rats, beaver, rodents, rattle snakes, skunks, and numerous other wildlife. White tailed deer have scampered across the asphalt. (One buck was licking the double yellow line on the Roger's Pass-not long for this world.) Sometimes the animals were bloated road kill, or desiccated skin and bone off the shoulder in the grass. The powerful odor of death could be detected far away if the air was still. The first forty miles of Idaho Highway 12 was littered with the bodies of dead birds. The time I had a flat tire and walked 1 1/2 miles, there were fifty or so feathered fliers of all sizes and colors. After Orofino, ID, thousands of butterflies, swallowtails, monarchs, whites, blues, yellows, brown and whites lay on the pavement, continuing into early western Montana.

At first I wasn't sure, until it became clear, insects were deliberately flying into me. Bees, grasshoppers, gnats, flies, and unknown bug splat were colliding with unusual frequency into the bright yellow bike shirt I wore for safety. The flyers must think I'm some kind of giant sunflower. Today we both were bitten by deer flies. The winner for annoyance? Mosquitoes. Susan can work morning or evening in light short sleeved clothing without a lump. Yet, with DEET wiped on all exposed skin, long sleeves and pants on, my body is a mosquito magnet. If Lewis & Clark complained about the skeeters 208 years ago, I'm in for trouble.

The original plan was to follow the Missouri River from Fort Peck, MT to Williston, ND. In talking to locals, it has consistently been described as an area to avoid. The locale was wild and unruly. Traffic ran heavily on narrow roads; trucks didn't stop; there was a lack of law and order. A gold rush was going on, Black Gold. People were streaming to the area where fracking the oil-bearing shale was occurring at a furious pace. Common salaries ranged $40, $60, $80 an hour for jobs. Montana locals claimed it virtually impossible to obtain any services. All motels were full up for fifty miles around with no available apartments. Rentals charged

$1,700 per month. Groups of men rented a house together for $2,400 a month. Those trying to outwit the system brought campers, paying $700 per month to park on a farmer, rancher or home owner's yard, without water, hookup, or any amenities. The job market cut into business life. Wal-Mart no longer bothered putting merchandise on shelves; customers came in grabbing everything off pallets. Employees did not stay around. High pay pulled them away to the oil fields. McDonald's opened just for lunch, closed; opened for dinner, closed; couldn't keep workers. It was the same everywhere. Because the fracking had been so successful and lucrative, many political heads had blinders on. Local law enforcement was overwhelmed. The crime rate soared, even filtering down to Sidney. A teacher out jogging was murdered there in January. The owner of the B.S. Café in Brockway, sixty miles away, wore a pistol on his hip when we walked in for lunch today. He claimed the criminal activity was reaching out even to his area. Montanans said it was the Wild West. Supposedly, North Dakota's governor urged citizens to arm themselves.

The daytime DUI rate skyrocketed. Since men worked round the clock, having finished the graveyard shift, they started partying and got caught. The highways had little white crosses along their routes-not the custom used by Hispanics in California, yet it meant about the same. Each cross indicated a traffic fatality posted by the State. But here, the difference meant the accident was a DUI. When the road from Ft. Peck to Williston was redone, 120 crosses were removed. It wasn't that way a few years back.

Even though we made a side trip to Fort Peck to see the dam and exhibits, the bicycling route was revised well south of the oil boom area.

31 mi.   1,083 mi. to date   elevation: 2,437'

Vista of Montana miles, one of the few level stretches.

DAY 26: GLAD WE LEFT EARLY

Tuesday,   Circle to Glendive, MT   Sunny, predicted 101*
June 26, 2012

Knowing that the Weather Channel had predicted 101* for today, it was imperative to leave as soon as possible. At 8:20 the bike headed out on road 200 S. A mild breeze kept my face comfortable as the sun made itself felt. Thick haze on the horizon obscured the last long ridges of climb. Sand colored fields alternated left and right, with the opposed side emerald green. Mother Nature seemed fickle. Where fifty miles ago rugged scoured stretches appeared to be desert, within a few miles the dry land farms reappeared, green belts resumed, and fertile earth yielded beauty in the folds of shallow valleys. Irrigation by thunderstorm governed and eroded the flatland over millennia. A drop of rain falling on a rise, slid to a lower level dragging a grain of silt, met another drop, and another, picked up more grains while descending in the watershed. Enough grains over time grated against softer silt material, removing, then gouging soil in ever increasing amounts. Water meandered, choosing the path of least resistance, cutting into layers of sediment and rock, creating myriad reshaped formations in the earth. Every gully, wash, arroyo, canyon differed from all others. Each watershed formed unique fingers which wandered in crooked projections, without repeat. Montana's features have been blessed by Mother Nature's carving. Hay, wheat, and bean fields filled the undulating landscape.

Can someone tell me? When does a beer can or water bottle become trash? Banana peels? Food wrappers? In the store were such things already trash? Were they trash while driving down the road? Apparently travelers have an inborn sense of when things were no longer of value and so tossed them out speeding vehicle windows (perhaps hoping to slam dunk their garbage into a "fortunately placed" dumpster or trash barrel? *Not.*) Americans are depositing waste into the very beauty they admire. What would happen if containers had, not a five cent deposit return, but a $25.00 charge on each container? Would Americans take pride or entrepreneurship in keeping the landscape unspoiled?

With the temperature in the nineties, ten miles from Glendive, radiant heat added hot stiff breeze. On a three mile long rail siding, gray and maroon grain cars sat waiting for the wheat harvest to begin. Heat waves shimmered on rock piles of a gravel company. Ahead rail yards were jam packed with pipes destined for oil fields. I secured the bike on the car rack at 1:30 and rode into town. Our motel room was not ready. Workers were installing a new door. So we set out for Taco John's Tuesday special half price deal. The electronic bank marquee announced 108*. Because we had to-dos on our list, we prowled town, took photos to send for my 50th high school reunion, a haircut, laundry, washed the car, new gloves (lost my pair), and bought an internet cord for places that might have wall access requiring a cord. After my haircut, because rain started falling, I covered the black bike seat with plastic to protect the leather. While in the hardware store, rain and lightening cut loose.

A floor clerk talking on his cell phone said: "If you don't like Montana weather, just wait fifteen minutes".

Later at dinner, the Weather Channel ran a thunderstorm warning for the local area until 8:00 p.m. Then the TV ticker tape caption ribbon revealed storms had hit Brockway with 60 mph winds and hail, and Circle had 70 mph winds and quarter size hail. Everyone was warned to stay inside and away from windows, etc., etc. Tomorrow? 82* and a 25 mph tail wind. Our fortune continues. Glad we left early.

46 mi.   1,129 mi. to date   elevation: 2,078'

DAY 27: GOODBYE MONTANA, HELLO NORTH DAKOTA

Wednesday,   Glendive, MT to Medora, ND   Sunny 82*
June 27, 2012

I told you, it was the pizza! After gorging on a large loaded pizza last night, today's riding was the cat's meow. With breakfast completed at Subway, Susan mailed photos for my 50th high school reunion, while I headed east on I-94 racing over the last of Montana's diminishing hills. At 10:44 the first puffs began, then there were ten mph tail breezes. Man! That pizza was working magic! The bike zoomed on the highway and climbed as never before, miles zipping by. Fifteen, sixteen, some stretches seventeen mph. Half way to our day's goal we stopped at Wibaux (wee-bow), the last Montana town on I-94, taking advantage of its rest area. The visitor center's western style furniture was the goodbye scene with the Montana hostess.

And then fun began. Twenty mph winds blew me across the border. North Dakota rippled its landscape. Flat stretches with few trees, except around dry land farms, and gentle rises into the eroded hills of the badlands. Speed, matching the wind, eliminated any cooling breeze until I crested hills where faster winds wicked sweat away. Consistent speed.

Medora, gateway to Theodore Roosevelt National Park, held the Dakota Bike Shop. Neither the owner nor the mechanic could repair my Cateye Speedometer (which had stopped giving info). They ordered a helmet mirror for my broken one, then tried unsuccessfully to end the mild rubbing of my rear tire. Their opinion was that the flatness of the tire tread indicated excessive tire wear, yet a new heavy duty tire produced worse rubbing. I used my original thin racing tire after all the mechanic's ministrations. The old tire, which the mechanic declared worn out, was thicker than their replacement, so it would be kept as a replacement in case the thin one was destroyed by road junk. When the two mechanics wanted to replace my Shimano gears with new ones to stop the slight rubbing, at that point I realized I had become a walking dollar sign in their eyes. I left $41.67 lighter in the pocketbook with only a helmet mirror on order and a switched tire.

Our motel keys didn't open the door, requiring a room change. Heat worn, we devoured every food item choice in the buffet restaurant. In the slanting sun's glare and deepening shadows of the eroded Badlands, we drove into Theodore Roosevelt National Park. On the mesa we eased past prairie dog town, then lowered into the river flats where a herd of buffalo grazed, deer crossed the road, and a black wild horse nosing over a rancher's pole fence tried to lure a penned mare to escape with him. Later, at an evening program, Ranger Laura spoke of the ecosystem of grasses and animals disrupted by the invasive grasses and domesticated animals not native to the prairie. The modern ranger program was reintroduction of native grass species and learning how to use animals in harmony with the inborn habitat.

We've been having memory loss mishaps. Lost so far: a pillow, bike gloves, a bathing suit, and sun screen, which gave more storage room in the Subaru, but that didn't make us happy. I had misplaced keys and clothing, saddle cream, forgotten to put on lotions, left helmet and gloves, and exited stores without items we paid for. Putting things back in the same location every time seemed simple, but weariness made one absent-minded. Or was it the water?

66 mi.   1,195 mi. to date   elevation: 2,248'

Beside the car on vista point of the North Dakota Badlands.

Descent into the North Dakota Badlands, Medora,
and Theodore Roosevelt National Park.

DAY 28: TRNP, HAROLD, MEDORA MUSICAL

Thursday, June 28, 2012   Medora, ND   Sunny 85*

Theodore Roosevelt National Park is a celebration of T.R.'s love for nature. As a young man who had lost both his mother and wife the same day, the North Dakota badlands were the healing potion for a distraught man. Involving himself in every aspect of western ranching and hunting, he came to value quiet beauty and respite given in the West. He himself claimed that had it not been for living in the North Dakota badlands, he would not have become president. The park is a center for rejuvenation of native grasses and bison. Other uninhibited creatures roaming the park are prairie dogs, elk, and wild horses. A thirty-six mile loop allows visitors a leisurely drive around eroded giant moundscape.

Geology lesson. Striated layers of the steep mesas are multiple shades of yellow, orange, black, and grays. Sandstone caps at mound tops are strong and impermeable enough to resist erosion. Underneath are various soft muds of the ancient inland sea. A layer of black lignite coal is too thin and weak to burn with intense heat, but it can be ignited by lightening or human cause. In some cases the fire has burned into the layer creating enough heat to change the rock above into orange scoria. Bentonite is ancient gray volcanic ash from activity hundreds of miles away, which swells when wet with rain, soaking up to fifteen times its own weight. When dry, it shrivels to look like popcorn, which makes it impossible for plants to take hold in the soil, and its softness gives the cliff sides a slick melted appearance, hence the uncovered bare look of layer cake lines in the mesas. Trapped in the bentonite are petrified trees and rounded brown concretions that look like cannon balls in mud. Rain, washing down the creeks and arroyos cut into the soft lower mud removing the underlayment to the point that the sandstone cap was undermined and collapsed as the soft mud disappeared beneath. Mesas were cut by the meandering river, separated from the prairie above and reduced to a lowered mound.

Medora, named for the wife of a French marquis who came to make his fortune in cattle raising, is a restored town dedicated to family vacationing. Though only about one hundred souls live there year round, not counting the ranchers, the town comes alive catering to summer tourists. Buildings renovated and restored in the western façade tradition attract visitors with a love of all things western, good restaurants, the Cowboy Hall of Fame, a museum, and three unique playgrounds. Many college students provide the workforce to run all the TRMF (Theodore Roosevelt Medora Foundation) businesses.

The rejuvenation of Medora was due to Harold Schaefer, a generous businessman and enthusiastic promoter extraordinaire. In 1944 he sold Glass Wax under the brand Gold Seal, followed by Snowy Bleach and Mr. Bubbles (bubble bath for kids). His generosity was legend and his treatment of employees was first class. He was political and influential, but the heart of his devotion was to restore the decaying town, little by little. He and wife Sheila began in 1962 by restoring the historic Rough Riders Hotel. One thing lead to another and he ended up owning 75 percent of the town. In 1965 he asked a university professor to create a show, the beginning of the Medora Musical. His requirements: high energy song and dance, the history of Theodore Roosevelt and the badlands, humor, patriotism, cowboys and horses, western music and a little bit of religion. Where some shows may last a year, and be considered successful, the nightly Medora Musical has continued for forty-eight summers, each year being rewritten and updated. An evening's entertainment in the Burning Hills Amphitheater, under the summer evening stars is a five star must.

0 mi.   1,195 mi. to date   elevation: 2,248'

DAY 29: TODAY SUSAN AND I SPLIT UP

Friday, June 29, 2012   Medora to Richardton, ND   Sunny 89*

I know you don't want to hear it, but it's true, Susan and I split up. This morning after breakfast in the Elkhorn Café, Susan stayed in Medora, and I went east on I-94. The bike shop had promised that the helmet mirror would arrive at noon. The problem was that waiting until delivery time meant starting late, then pedal fifty-eight miles in the Midwest heat wave. Instead, Susan poked around town while I headed east towards Dickinson. However, every five miles I phoned to let her know how the new thin tire was doing. There was a 20-25 mph headwind without severe interference in progress.

North Dakota land featured a gentle series of hillocks and swales; dry land canola, beans, barley, peas, sunflowers, wheat and hay, with easy climbs along the cement gray corridor. The calls did not receive happy news of a mirror acquired, so I kept pushing on, consuming the bottles of water in the heat. A 2:10 arrival at Dickinson, was reason for a Subway lunch and another call. No delivery yet. Giving Susan the option to wait until 2:30 or get a refund, I sat down to a tuna sandwich outdoors and conversed with Dakotans. Susan drove up at 3: 10 with the mirror. It had arrived at the bike shop right at cut-off time. Not only did Susan let me out of her sight, but she had the confidence that I could cycle without immediate support nearby. Maybe separation is a good thing.

A final bit of information from the National Park. There is an invasive insect named the Emerald Ash Borer, not native to the Americas. Discovered in Michigan probably in crate wood, this Asian insect has no natural enemies. Escaping into the forests of Michigan, it is responsible for the deaths of over fifty million ash trees in the U.S. and Canada since 2002. The larva burrow under the bark of a tree in S patterns. Once infested, the tree is doomed. This insect has the potential to wipe out all ash trees in the Americas. Oddly enough, the pest does not move once in an area. People taking infected firewood to a new location, like when on vacation, spread the creature. The TRNP is 50 percent ash trees, hence the concern to prevent further spread into the West.

Early in the day two fully equipped heavy duty bikes leaned on the side of the Bunkhouse Motel. Dave and Ann, dressed in fluorescent yellow jerseys had taken a year off work to see the United States. Starting in Minneapolis, MN, they traveled the East Coast to Florida, west to

California, up the Pacific Coast to Portland and then they were heading home, a trip taking them over 10,000 miles. They had suffered over one hundred flats. These were the two bikers we had seen fighting the headwind between Mosby and Jordan where I portaged. They were made of sterner stuff. I'm a piker.

What's on the highway besides trash and the usual car debris? The most common items are tire recap shreds and wires, followed closely with nuts, bolts, and metal pieces. Someone with a mobile electromagnet patrolling the road edge could end up with a load of scrap metal. Other discovered items include clothing, shoes, fishing equipment, cowboy boots, ice chests, CD's, tools, rope, water coolers, red flags, sunscreen, sunglasses, and bungee cords, mostly broken. Today I salvaged five black cords.

Two kinds of passenger vehicles pass by. The majority honk 300-500 feet away, acknowledging a long distance biker on the highway. Some go further, hand pumping out the window, waving, or saluting, whether in the first or second lane. Then there is the practical joker, who waits until ten feet away, always in the closest lane, blasting an earful as he passes by. Usually I haven't been startled, but every once in a while....

In the late afternoon, where the highway reduced to one lane each way for summer asphalt repair, a squad car with lights flashing zoomed by. Moments later three more patrol cars shot past. Four miles ahead, they caught up with a couple in a car at exit 78, our planned break spot. Susan carefully went around the crowd of cars, followed by me squirming through the bottleneck. Near their car's cracked front windshield, a man and woman were separated for questioning. We moved on to finish our snack. Susan motored ahead six miles to Richardton for a motel. On arrival, I was annoyed the car wasn't at the exit, likely forcing me to cycle over the bridge an extra mile to town. But, just over the arc of the overpass was the car patiently waiting with relief for tired muscles. Perhaps it was true, absence did make the heart grow fonder. And it was good to know Susan would give a ride to the motel.

58 mi.   1,253 mi. to date   elevation: 2,464'

DAY 30: NORTH DAKOTA

Saturday, June 30, 2012   Richardton to Mandan, ND   Sunny 90*+

After a hearty breakfast at Clara's Diner, Susan stayed behind to visit the Cathedral of the Prairie in Richardton, an early 1900s twin-towered church and Benedictine monastery, while I started. Last night before dark, we had passed the four story brick structure that stood above the little town of 300.

A pronghorn antelope jumped from its tall grass cover to race along the interstate shoulder ahead of me. He outpaced me for a quarter mile, until encountering his secret fence hole, clambered through, and disappeared in a few quick leaps.

North Dakota's I-94 was a class A surface with an eight foot wide shoulder for rain runoff. The shoulder was further separated by two rumble strips into a five foot wide strip and a second set of twin 18 inch strips, a left and right side next to a grassy drop. If I paid attention to my far right zone, I could cycle smoothly and safely, protected from the traffic. However, gravel and tire debris, which were constants, required side to side weaving. Timed incorrectly, or when distracted by the landscape and moving to the middle of the shoulder, the rumble strip jarred the handle bars, reminding the biker to move back to the correct 18 inch space.

Since entry into North Dakota, isolated oil donkeys dipped their heads up and down pumping oil from wells below ground. Nearer Dickinson, more donkeys were in evidence. On one hill, topped with a storage tank, a flame-out of excess natural gas seemed like a tank ready to explode. The back side of the hill revealed men operating heavy equipment, aware of what was occurring. Their job was establishing an 500 foot x 500 foot oil rig pad for a new well. In the distance were other pads being developed.

Two miles below the surface of western North Dakota is a rich oil deposit called the Bakken. In some places there is sufficient oil to be extracted with the normal oil well process. The new technique of fracking produces four times the daily liquid production. Thousands of jobs have come to an area desperate for money.

From the Visitor Guide of the National Parks of North Dakota: "Each new well means another drill, rig, well pad, pump jack, debris pit, flare pit, storage tanks, and access road on the landscape. Each new well requires 2000 'trucking events' to complete its setup and to begin pumping oil. Noise and dust from heavy truck traffic and pumping equipment is constant. Numerous flares can be seen in the formerly dark night sky as excess natural gas is burned off." The controversy has raged over a year whether to extract or leave the resource. Meanwhile the land and communities have been deeply affected.

This is the land of gnats and no-see-ums. Pesky gnats may fly around or onto you, land on eyeglasses, blocking vision, and they bite. They are tasteless but may have protein if consumed. My breathing habit climbing a hill had been to purse the lips sucking in air while inhaling. That proved hazardous today. Having sucked a gnat into the right lung, I began coughing and harrumphing for the next seven miles. It took much time for the body to create enough mucus to dislodge the vermin with a big "pitui". Now, no-see-ums are different. You can't chase what you can't see. These insects land on clothing, slip through the weave, and sample flesh underneath giving a sharp hot sting. Slapping at them does no good. The correct technique is to rub forward and back with pressure to crush the pest. Anything less than total annihilation allows continued biting.

Farther east I-94 proceeded on longer lower hills, though the slopes may run for two miles at a gentle slant. Travel was faster on the flats, usually more than 20 mph, climbs of 8/9 mph, and long down hills, frequently 25 mph and higher. Heights rarely exceeded a hundred feet from trough to crest. The countryside resembled a gently rolling green sea with graceful swells and dips. No herds of elk or antelope have yet been visible. Trees existed only at farms or habitations, indicating that rain is insufficient for woodland unless human hands assist nature. Intersecting roads occurred every five or six miles, often with off ramps to brown-orange dirt farm access roads. One road, the "Enchanted Highway", exhibited gigantic scrap metal sculptures toward the south.

Thunderstorms were predicted for Bismark, but by the end of the afternoon, none had occurred. Early morning had five to ten mph eastern head winds, virtually windless in the mid afternoon, and upped to ten mph in the late afternoon. Hill climbing became suffocating if the bike speed matched the wind, eliminating cooling off. My new friends were the Cloud Brothers, cumulus clouds, cruising across the interstate. If I kept my speed in concert with the clouds, the bike could stay in the shadow for a couple miles, a clever way to stay cool while the temps were in the 90s.

68 mi.   1,321 mi. to date   elevation: 1,644'

DAY 31: NORTH DAKOTA 2

Sunday, July 1, 2012   Day of Rest/Touring the Missouri   Sunny 90*+

Appearances can be deceiving. Looking west, down to the Missouri, and across the other side, it may seem that the land is flat. No siree! The gentle dips in the topography continue right up to bluffs along the river. Thousands of erosive years have not reduced the scenery to tabletop smoothness. Today's car tour north of Mandan, Bismark on the east side of the Missouri took us up and down rolling farmland and river bottom. Corn, beans, and giant hay rolls dominated the land views cut by baby blue water winding upstream. Cottonwood sentinels stood on the river banks. Many homes and farms were positioned to take maximum view of the river and sunset.

But there is a curious difference here. Homes have at least two heavy duty vegetation lines, and farms four sides, a square, of wind/snow breaks. These are not the windbreaks of California, a line of eucalyptus. Typically the front line is 100-200 feet of low growing closely planted bushes. Next is a taller different variety of dense bushes, with a third row of pines or another species of tree. Experienced farmers usually have a fourth row of lower permanent vegetation forming a virtual living stockade against blowing wind and blizzard snow drifts. Newbees (new homeowners) have maybe two or three years of surrounding growth. The unlearned have no protection.

Many farms had huge stockpiles of hay rolls; some appeared to be rotting. Last year, North Dakota realized an excellent hay crop, while the rest of the Midwest endured drought. Ranchers became desperate to the point that Texans came north seeking hay. In spite of a glut of last year's plenty, new hay was being harvested.

The weather, according to locals, has gone crazy. The winter of 2011 had so much rain and snow runoff that Ft. Peck operated its spillway wide open to prevent overtopping the dam. This created disaster downstream. Smaller dams were forced to open their spillways wide. Minot, ND was flooded as well as other towns downriver. The winter of 2012 was unusually mild. The temperature never got below 0*, though it usually dropped to -40* below. Several people have said 2012 was like spring. This year the winds were the reverse of normal, blowing from east to west, with hotter than normal temperatures. The entire Midwest has suffered in heat and drought. It's important to be aware of the weather here, since thunderstorms are practically a daily prediction, even if they don't come true. But this year storms have not materialized.

As a river, the Missouri seems to be a sleeping cat, lazily curling from bank to bank leaving elongated sandbars at bends and mid channel. It does not appear deeper than twenty feet and is perhaps 250 feet wide, recognizing that it does change its bed over the years. The lack of water may be due to the drought locals are talking about. Cottonwoods do not have the ability to stop erosion, as 10-15 foot high bluffs have caved into the water at various spots, leaving a tangle of snags clinging by their roots on the shore. Outdoors lovers play on fishing or houseboats, kayaks, canoes, or just splash in the sandbar water. This image doesn't match the films of rampaging waters flooding bottom lands, destroying homes and farms. The dam system has greatly controlled flooding but mother nature gave warning in 2011 that humans are not in full control of the river.

Tidbits. Unlike Californians, all North Dakotans had an accent except when talking to other North Dakotans. Stop signs had no companion white limit lines on the street, although white rectangles indicated where pedestrians may cross the street. On Sundays, one could expect towns to roll up the streets and not work: church, fishing, or stay home. Patriotism was alive and well in the Midwest. Buildings were draped in bunting well in advance of the coming 4th of July parades and fireworks. Parking areas were decorated in red, white, and blue painted poles, and flags were found everywhere. Already bangs and pops of fireworks sounded off from anxious kids. Gas sold $3.47 a gallon. Family and local restaurants served fine meals. Most homes had cellars. To water the lawn, it was necessary to have a well (water table is about twenty feet down). Homes commonly were built of either brown or red brick, or aluminum siding. There were no fences dividing neighboring yards. People were honest and trusting.

When the Subaru had traveled twenty miles this morning, en route to Washburn, I told Susan that I was tired of climbing hills, that riding along the bottomland suited me just fine.

She said: "Well, you could end it all by just riding to the east side of North Dakota, and you'll be at the Mississippi. You could pour in your little bottle of Columbia River water and be done".

I asked: "How far is that?"

She: "We're about half way, so about 150 more miles".

Me: "Let's see, fifty miles a day, we could do it in three days".

She: "How about it?"

Me: "You want me to skip thirteen hundred miles just so we could quit and go home? You don't want me to suffer any more?"

She: "Sounds pretty good to me".

Me: "Nah! I'm going all the way".

One of us is crazy. (Besides, we later realized the east side of North Dakota is the Red River.)

A private foundation administered the Lewis and Clark Interpretive Center and a mock up of Ft. Mandan (winter stay of 1804 for Lewis and Clark) near Washburn. There were similarities to Ft. Clatsop in Oregon: triangular shape, pointed defense poles, eight low slung rooms, fire places, blacksmith forge, storage areas, gate. The difference was that vertical housing logs at Ft. Mandan are well suited to deal with snow at Mandan, while horizontal poles resist the constant drip Oregon rain. At the visitor's center, many authentic items were on display from the L. & C. Discovery party, as well as local history. We crossed the river to the west side, stopping at Knife River Villages National Historic Site north of Stanton, where a replica of an Hidatsa earth lodge gave a glimpse of tribal life 200 years ago. The reality of the numerous hills yet to be encountered was driven home on our return. This may be a river basin, but the Missouri has not leveled the watershed emptying into it. It will be rock and roll landscape to St. Louis.

0 mi.   1,321 mi. to date   elevation: 2,144'

A mock up Mandan village, where the Lewis
and Clark party wintered over 1804.

Replica of the Lewis & Clark accommodations at Mandan.

Interior of earthen lodge at Knife River Indian
Villages National Historical Site, Stanton, ND.

DAY 32: HOW TO CELEBRATE YOUR ANNIVERSARY

Monday,   Mandan to Linton, ND   chance of T-storms 90*+
July 2, 2012

That's right! Our 35th anniversary. Now what should we do??? I've "tortured" Susan for thirty-two days. Switching places so she can cycle, and I become the car support isn't going to happen. Making a fur coat from all the road kill??? I don't think so. Being the he-man that I am, I asked Susan what she wanted for the anniversary.

She said, "You don't want to know! I'll give you one guess."

"Let me think. It has four letters and starts with Q.... Ain't gonna happen".

We did go to the Medora Musical. (She reminded me that we took a Hawaiian cruise last December as an early celebration.) We've been moteling it, eating out, seeing the great American landscape at a pace that gives enjoyment. And at least Susan doesn't have to put up with my zaniness or humor until I start writing these emails. What else can I do? Now, the hairy frontiersman knows how to romance his own true love. Popsicles! Her favorite treat. Problem is, they're hard to transport in a baking ice chest even with ice. Guess I'll just have to owe her. *Big Time!!*

Gloom hung overhead all day, but it wasn't because I failed to find a suitable present. The boom of distant thunder echoed across the parking lot, coming from a boiling cloud to the southwest, the rest of the sky overcast. Maybe it would pass after breakfast. Nope. The cloud played delaying tactics. At 9:10, I prepared as drops fell around me. Starting from Saturday's stop, I wheeled down to Mandan's Main Street and turned left. After a long passage through a busy business district, Susan, in the car, pointed out the safer Memorial Highway to cross the Missouri into Bismark. With thunder in the distance, I rode toward the airport. On the three foot wide asphalt bike path paralleling the highway, I met Jim and Diane who were cycling from Michigan to Seattle. They had already covered forty-five miles by 9:30, heading west towards the heavy clouds. Ten miles south appeared to be escape from the threatening dark billows. Hah! The cloud hung near me like a buzzing gnat, occasionally splatting me with a few windblown drops but never wetting my clothes. It never advanced directly over me, staying just far enough off to the southwest all afternoon. No lightening occurred.

Three miles south of the airport began the day's rigorous climbing. These were not the fearsome roller coaster hills of Montana and western North Dakota. Rarely did the mounds rise more than 200 feet high, but they did have the aggravation frequency and slope equal to earlier ascents. My knees complained. A light east crosswind kept sweat in check but, by noon it disappeared as the humidity rose. Cooling could be had by pedaling faster.

The scenery delighted with a series of picturesque farms and pastures. If a man wanted to tire his wife with beauty, he needs only to drive Highway 1804 on the east side of the Missouri. Each new valley revealed a garden spot of pines and firs with homes-a feast for the eyes. Bottom land was identifiable with windbreaks on the right. On the left side of the road were windrows, but mostly hay fields and pasture. The first corn fields grew in the bottom land, along with wheat, sunflowers, beans, and the omnipresent hay rolls. Beyond mile marker 40, trees ended as the asphalt drifted nearer to, then farther from the Missouri. Still, the overcast hovered, keeping the air cool.

A strategy for scaling the hills. When encountering a series of running mounds in quick order, speed downward as fast as possible. *Do Not Coast!* Coasting gives away valuable momentum. A faster momentum at the bottom pushes the rider farther uphill and requires less cranking away in the lowest gears. Shifting is important. The moment gravity takes its toll, making the legs feel heavy, change to the next lower gear to keep the churning as fast as possible. Done properly, the rider is propelled farther up the slope reducing the amount of "grind it out" time, helping a cycler's legs last longer.

By 3:00 the sun was poking through the clouds, and the humidity at 70 percent was oppressive. Because we secured lodging in Linton, our course veered east off the river road. The last thirteen miles felt as if there were no air to be had. Breathing was a chore. A headwind popped up giving just enough relief to join the 83 Highway before retiring for the day.

A bath later, we looked for our anniversary dinner. Bars had pizza, but we wanted something else. The only game in town was Webo's Restaurant. Now, I really know how to treat a lady! We started with a margarita and pina colada. The evening's special was burgers with a salad bar thrown in. We both ordered the German burger with Swiss and sauerkraut and loaded up at the salad bar. Everything from scratch: broccoli, cucumber, potato, mixed fruit, macaroni, greens, and all the great toppings. The burgers were fantastic. I know how to treat a lady! (Am I off the hook for my anniversary present?)

70 mi.   1,391 mi. to date   elevation: 1,719'

DAY 33: HUMIDITY IS MY COMPANION

Tuesday, July 3, 2012   Linton, ND to Selby, SD   Hazy to sunny 90*+

The old timer farmers in the Webo Restaurant gave a sidelong once-over look that said real men don't wear skin tight black bike shorts. It wasn't worth responding. We sat quietly, ate and left. I told the waitress she could inform the guys that real men can wear skin tight shorts if they have biked 1,391 miles from Oregon. That would raise a few eyebrows.

North Dakota still had a few surprises left. First, yesterday's final stretch defeated my strategy for scaling hills. The last twenty-five miles had such elongated rises that racing up them was not in the cards. In addition, the winds played friend and foe games switching from southerly headwinds to easterly crosswinds, cooling in the 70 percent humidity, but reducing forward speed. Strasburg, the birthplace of Lawrence Welk, got a nod in passing. Two road crews, conducting land moving operations at Baumgartner and Rice Lakes, were raising the causeway four feet and building two bridges on each side, by October, for waters to pass from upper watersheds to lower, and then meander to the Missouri. Engineers proclaimed it cheaper to build bridges than culverts. Work had to be done before freeze began in October. Farther on, a hill side was scalped and boulders set aside. Scoop buckets filled empty trucks with dirt as fast as they circled the loading loop. A half mile away the dirt was dumped into water beside the present causeway. A huge yellow Caterpillar 6 pushed the material into proper location. Back and forth the trucks raced while slow/stop signs regulated traffic. The highway traffic guard, holding his red sign, said the rocks would be used to provide embankment erosion protection. Scalping the top two feet of soil removed boulders. Because the State Highway Department needed rock fill, ranchers happily sold excavated rock piles as fill, and returned the dirt piles to rich clean farm soil. Everyone benefitted. Crews have kept the ND roads well maintained and clean.

Twenty-five miles later it was photo time at the South Dakota border. SD had the flattest landscape so far, with long gentle elevations. Permanently tilted tree limbs faced west from constant easterly winds. The Missouri River had been dammed to create four massive reservoirs called the Great Lakes of South Dakota, Oahe, Sharp, Francis Case, and Lewis and Clark. Other lesser inland bodies of water, were not great in size, but numerous. Call them ponds, watering holes, swamps, marshes, ditches, temporary lakes, etc., but they were everywhere, ubiquitous as mosquito havens.

Today I ate gnats, felt too many no-see-ums before learning how to smash them, and fed bloodsucking vampire flies. During a rest break, while sitting in the car with legs extended out to the grass fields, flies were attracted to my sweat. They bit through the white athletic socks drawing blood. Susan at first didn't believe in vampire flies until her ankles were attacked. Now when I biked off, she methodically shooed all flying demons out of the car.

The routine settled into a nutrition, water, butt rest break every five miles. An apple, nectarine, banana, or granola bar. More than a gallon of water consumed before lunch due to sweating. Even with the padded bike pants, my rear end hurt. Saddle cream, applied daily to the new seat, didn't seem to soften it. Bag Balm, which milk farmers use to ward off chapped skin, and the padded lamb's wool seat cover helped to some degree, but, after thirty miles, made little difference. Shifting around relieved soreness for a few minutes, but eventually both rump sides hurt. Even my arms, from prolonged riding in the same leaning position for extended periods, were sore. Hands still numbed. Relief became the five mile break, just enough time to recover and press on.

In the town of Herreid (Herry-id) I stopped in the market wearily bringing a container of grapefruit juice to the counter peopled by two cashiers.

One woman said, "You'll have to take that to the other counter". I stared dumbfounded, until she added, "Unless you have a question".

I replied, "No, I'm too tired to ask a question".

Then she asked, "Are you just passing through?"

"No. I just came from California to enjoy all this South Dakota humidity".

The other woman responded, "If you like it so much, why don't you take it back with you".

Another excellent road crew was resurfacing a thirteen mile stretch. With traffic stopped at each end, in the blistering heat, truck after truck of asphalt was dumped before the spreader machine, followed by the rollers. Not only was the fresh pavement hot, but the black absorbed the sun's radiant heat glaring it upward. Every worker had that "beat by the heat" look when I arrived at 3:30. A signal woman pointed out they should already have quit at 2:00. The boss wanted them to work Thursday, after the 4th, but the crew said no. Regulations indicated that they were to get the rest of the week off Wednesday through Sunday. So the boss was pushing them work extra long to finish the section before the Fourth of July. The signal lady waved me to start before the waiting cars, allowing a biker, to christen new asphalt. Upon reaching the opposite end of the paving, one sweat drenched, grime encrusted, orange shirted crewman was scraping up loose matter with a shovel.

I shouted in passing: "I'll bet you can't wait for quitting time".

He shouted back: "You got that right".

Selby's entry posted a *Speed Limit 45* warning. Within 500 feet a second sign said: *Speed Limit 25*. At the burger stand, the only café open on July the 4th eve, we watched a lone sheriff deputy nab two criminals for exceeding the speed limit in the speed trap. His holiday overtime was making money for the town. A trucker pulled over across the street with a long white and blue steel rectangular sand mixer device, on his flatbed truck, destined for oil wells being drilled in Dickinson. He explained that eight trucks, using vacuums, collected different sands, combining sand and water to pour down a drilled well to stabilize the well casing. The valuable oversized cargo, 11 feet wide and 74 feet long, worth a million dollars, couldn't legally be driven in North Dakota on holidays. Escort cars weren't needed, but the law required flags front and behind (a clue to all the red flag debris lying along the shoulders of the highway). He was nervously waiting until the 5th to move again. Five other truckers, delivering the same type of machine, pulled over.

Due to fires in Colorado, and the heat wave in the Midwest, the TV said most city fireworks shows in the state were cancelled. Firefighters had been sent to the forty-one wildfires burning in the West. Even the fireworks booths had been asked to stop selling. Humidity does not stop things from drying out.

57 mi.   1,448 mi. to date   elevation: 1,904'

Entering a stretch of flat ground in South Dakota 7/3/12.

Biker's 68th birthday Highway 34, along the
Missouri River, east of Pierre, SD.

DAY 34: CELEBRATE!

Wednesday,   Selby to Pierre, SD   Hazy, 25 mph winds 80*+
July 4, 2012

It's NOT the pizza! Looking through the picture window, at breakfast, the southerly winds were whipping the flags straight out, side to side, while tree limbs bent in the 25-30 mph gusts. Everything pointed to a miserable headwind day. Breakfast, of raisin bread and honey or peanut butter, was spent with an older couple regaling their travels and local info. By 9:10, winds had subsided to ten mph. It was time to face the music. Sunscreen and gear on, I dove into a surprising tailwind. Over the bridge south of town and into farmland, the blows switched to the east which helped against the already humid morning. Several miles later, a section of hilly road had been completely scraped off on both sides in preparation for paving, but lay with scattered gravel and hardened bumps permitting motorists half use of the highway. In a few hundred feet the danger was evident with no center divider, a deep drop off to the right, and lots of potholes to negotiate. The west side, however, was devoid of automobiles with nearly smooth easy riding, even with gravel. It didn't take genius to switch over to the unoccupied side. Although there was fear that stones might puncture a tire, safety was worth it, and it was faster than the travel lane populated with vehicles. It provided three miles of enjoyable riding.

After the last white and orange construction barrier, wind turned again from the north. The next miles were easier, until the tailwind reached 25 mph. That's when I hit my stride. Music came off the tires as they hummed over the grooved cement highway. Whirr! Whirr! Whirr! Hummmmm! Flat roadbed permitted the fastest flat sustained riding to date, 25-27 mph, in H-7, covering nine miles rapidly. For a second time, a longer than usual distance time was finished before a nutrition break, making our day's thirty-six mile goal to Gettysburg, SD, seem too little. We had been thinking to quit early, respecting humidity and heat. As an old farmer might say, "Never look a gift horse in the mouth", I won't look a gift wind in the mouth. A 25 mph tailwind can't be bought when you want it, nor can one get overcast skies to suit. The morning haze and clouds had kept heat from bearing down. So the plan was revised: How close would the wind get us to Pierre, eighty-eight miles from Selby? Miles slipped by, yet no water/nutrition break was ever skipped, knowing that heat stroke could sneak up quickly.

From the beginning of the trip, old rickety barns and abandoned farmhouses have stood desolate at the highway and SD was no different. Lives, dreams, and fortunes of so many people lay in unoccupied buildings.

What does it take to make a farmer or rancher? An agricultural specialist who knows and understands the soil, what it can and can't provide; a believer who has faith in mother nature, even when she devils with wind, hail, snow, freezes, scorching heat, drought, insect plagues, floods, and crop diseases; a stout-hearted individual who works from dawn to dusk, even later; a gambler who takes calculated risks on what and how to raise; a believer who hopes for fair banking, and good laborers; an entrepreneur who buys a $100,000 tractor and all the equipment needed to run a farm; a chemist who knows insecticides and the legal application regulations; a contractor who builds barns, silos, bins, sheds and outbuildings to house and protect; a bean counter who deals with a narrow profit margin and is subject to the whims of the market and middlemen; a plagued martyr who suffers the prickly pear "cactus" of government red tape. A farmer/rancher is probably one of the most disciplined careful individuals to walk the earth. To succeed, she/he must be.

By mid afternoon, at Agar, a lunch stop, numerous trucks wheeled up to the town's many huge gray cement grain silos, deposited their loads, and returned south. Trucks had been few all day. Why so many now? A company was on the job, harvesting golden wheat during the fourth of July. Though the road was packed with haulers, never did they seem in a hurry shifting into gear, running down the highway, or passing me, in the sweltering heat. Still, the tailwind blew favorably, cooling every sweaty climb into Pierre. (pronunciation: pee-er)

Pierre sat on a bluff overlooking the Missouri. Two bridges crossed to the west, and upriver was the dam forming Lake Oahe. A shower and Italian dinner later, we strolled to the free fireworks show along the river. Actually there were thousands of shows, the official city sponsored one, and then everybody else. This was not a popgun style of small town explosions and pretty flares. Fireworks were legal here. A few citizens shot off puny roman candles. Many bought their own mortars and fired off every sort of starburst device that professionals do, exactly what happened along both sides of river front, on and in boats. Thousands of bangs, booms, cracks, blasts, and starry colors splattered into the night air. Some private parties even out did the city's spectacle. A lot of money went up in smoke. Everyone celebrated. Including the vampire flies and mosquitoes because I had walked to the river dressed in shorts.

89 mi.   1,480 mi. to date   elevation: 1,490'

DAY 35: IT'S MY BIRTHDAY!

Thursday, July 5, 2012   Pierre to Ft. Thompson, SD   Overcast 80*+

So what if I got up late! I have a right to be tired and grouchy. Besides it's my 68th birthday! No cake or pie or soda, just a little extra shut eye. Plus extra carbs and coffee for breakfast. Shopping: fruit, bread, pickles, sunscreen, glyburide, gasoline. So what if I left at 11:50. It's my birthday!

The decision to leave was based upon cooler predicted temperatures brought on by the overcast with a 30 percent chance of rain and a 15 mph eastern headwind. (On Tuesday, Pierre had 101*, but with the humidity and heat index, the Weather Channel claimed it was like 112*) Mother Nature doesn't often give two gift horses in a row. Under clouded shade along the bluffs was an eye treat for an artist. Silvery blue water sliced the Missouri shore's soft yellow curves coursing around islands of tall grass.

Riding today was punishment contending with withering headwinds making progress slower, sucking more energy out of yesterday's wearied legs. It was hell when rises and dips spilled all the altitude gained in the last half mile just to repeat the process. In concert with the wind, it was a torment pedal by pedal.

Steady but slow advance along Highway 34 eastward continued until the nearly vacant De Grey boat launch. Then began the first killer half mile climb, not as long as the Lolo or Roger's passes, but every bit as demanding. Cracks across the pavement every twenty-five feet made the ride go ka-thunk, ka-thunk, because the broken section edge joints no longer fit smoothly. For a car, that might be a slappity slap. For a bike rider, it's boom, boom on an already sore fanny. The second killer L-2/1 climb began at mile marker 239 in Hughes County and lasted until marker 245, a deceptive twisting set of curves which disappeared into the dry prairie height. A quick decline lost most of the upward progress, only to reveal two more succeeding steep climbs as the prairie rose just beyond one's view. Mounting a third height were three more strenuous tilts, with no relieving flats, followed by two more, again out of sight until upon them. When I stopped for my break Susan declared a five mile climb. And there was still a climb ahead. Hah! When I finished that one there were two more to the county line. Rain had spit on me the entire route, enough to dampen but not soak. All the time, ka-thunk, ka-thunk. Throbbing knees begged for no more. At last, straight, nearly level ground into the face of the wind. (I have officially renamed this stretch Heartbreak Hill.) Then at mile 248 was the coup de gras, three quarters of a mile "I Give Up Hill." To professional cyclists in the Tour de France these are pimples. But to all wannabees, I challenge you to beat these three killers with a twenty mph headwind.

By comparison, Hyde County had such smooth pavement! I cheered when the ka-thunking stopped. Legs felt like overstretched rubber.

The next ordeal was no-see-ums which toll-taxed any warm creature (me) entering their territory. They had very small territories, of maybe ten square feet, which meant thousands of toll taxes to pay. Biting flies did not allow rest even in a gale.

At Mac's Corner, I gave up, no motel or services except a gas/convenience store. Dispirited by ferocious winds, I cheated by asking Susan to portage me the twelve miles to Fort Thompson, a small Indian reservation town of 1,300, home of Big Bend Dam forming Lake Sharp. Four businesses operated in a sad dilapidated community: Dakota Market, Shelby's Mini Mart and Gas, Lode Star Casino, and Lode Star Motel. We also saw a post office, health center, and a Boys/Girls Club. The casino offered a daily special of a huge prime rib steak, hash browns, and all you-can-eat salad for $10.95. Admittedly, casinos provided enticing meal deals to lure in the gamblers. Need I say more? I pigged out. Am I ashamed of portaging twelve miles? No! It was my birthday!

46 mi.   1,526 mi. to date   elevation: 1,440'

DAY 36: WELFARE

Friday, July 6, 2012   Ft. Thompson to Platte, SD   Partly cloudy 90*+

Fort Thompson, a small place with few amenities, appeared careworn. Failed deserted businesses sat idly on the highway. IHS (Indian Health Services) and PHS (Public Health Services) medical centers stood next to each other. Government built modest aluminum siding homes were spread throughout the area along with ramshackle trailer homes. A casino poker tournament on Thursday was the only activity in evidence.

Riding the bluffs out on Highway 4, then Route 50 southeast of Fort Thompson, was similar to yesterday but without wind. There were two severe uphills. It finally happened. I met a hill I couldn't climb! The asphalt resurfacing crews had dug up both sides of the road, leaving hard packed underlayment covered by plenty of sand/gravel. The bike wheels sank into the sand. I had to walk the bike 200 feet until there was enough hardpack. Humidity was stifling by 11:00. Entering Chamberlain we looked for a fast food place that served bottomless soda. Nothing else would quench my thirst cravings. McDonald's satisfied the bill. The bank across the street gave the temperature as 89*. We sat cooling off until 1:45. Susan found a thrift store to acquire more reading books while I sweated off soda on a long ascent heading to I-90.

Supposedly I'd only ride east seven miles on I-90. But with its superior surface and only ten mph crosswind, leaving the interstate was out of the question. Many map lines, squiggled ahead on Highway 50, warned of hills. However, Highway 45 showed twenty-five straight and true miles earning a change of course at exit marker 289. Fast travel was rewarded by the cloud brothers who kept shade overhead for miles. Mother Nature continued her beneficence raising the wind speed to twenty when I turned south. It was necessary to be either faster or slower than the breeze to acquire a cooling affect from the wind. Nearly level ground gave the highest speed possible, H-7, for twenty miles.

The high prairie was populated by lonesome farms of corn, wheat, and hay. As homesteads slid by, my thoughts prompted that these fiercely independent folk couldn't be welfare recipients. Somebody likely would prove me wrong with a single example, but the evidence was there: well kept buildings and homes, equipment, stored crops, healthy fields.

So what? How does welfare benefit the taxpayer? The welfare recipient? Is there a payoff for the money taken from farmers or other wage earners?

Is it then given to the poor, those out of work or luck, the dysfunctional, the malingerers, the indolent, or the manipulators? The Robin Hood Effect? Shouldn't recipients repay, in some form, the generous financial boon they have been given by taxpayers? What is expected of those who receive welfare? It seems requiring repayment of long term welfare recipients (more than a year's dole out) would accomplish two purposes: payback and reshaping one's life. What would happen if long term welfare recipients were given a relocation option, maybe with a few more dollars, to immigrate to farming communities, working for their checks, perhaps as a form of indentured servant? They could live under contract in a healthy environment, provide assistance to a farm, get in touch with their deeper selves, develop independence, learn a farm related trade, absorb skills that Agriculture people exude, help populate the Midwest, and be productive. If given such an option, how could that be termed degrading? Of course, it could never work, farmers are too fiercely independent. And no welfare recipient would ever want a fresh start. Oh! If a farmer ever abused a person-it would be the death of the program (which never happens under our present system, right?). Most of all, it would have to be administered by highly paid bureaucrats who know nothing about the needs, ins, and outs of farming. The retired Montana, North and South Dakota farmers surely couldn't develop a program, set reasonable requirements, and run it better than the government. No, let's keep welfare running the way it has always "succeeded".

Platte, at 6 p.m., was a good time to finish.

74 mi.   1,600 mi. to date   elevation: 1,601'

DAY 37: TIDBITS

Saturday, July 7, 2012   Platte to Tyndall, SD   Partly cloudy 82*

Today started with the city fire alarm going off. Shorty's Bar and Grill in Platte burned down. Smoke was still in the air as we left. With the advice of the innkeeper, it seemed that avoiding Highway 50 would also avoid river bluff hills. Well, kick me in the pants and start last week. Highway 44 is nearly flat, if you are in a car. It is a road that constantly inclines to the next gentle slope that isn't visible yet. My bumble brain also chose to face the 5-15 mph north wind that grew to a strong east headwind. Since there were few places to change course until Parkston, I paid the foolish price of exhausting my legs for forty-two gusting miles. Turning south on Route 37, a wonderful fast cement straight road with few rises provided cruising amid thousands of acres of corn half grown. I roasted in the late afternoon, finally turning east for the last wind grueling miles.

6:30. Tyndall (tindel), pop. 1,200, owned the longest approach we've encountered in the state. It was the end of my rope (for today). Windworn, overheated, hands and legs cramping, wiped out, I brought suitcases into our tiny motel room and for the first time lay down on the bed for an hour. Customarily, I took a shower right away to revive. Susan massaged both cramping, itching hands back to life. It took inordinate time to clean up and motivate the body for dinner. Susan discovered that when I'm weary, I don't think or calculate as well, hence, the corrected distance below. I had shorted myself fifty-seven miles on Day 34.

At the Sedona Pub and Grill, typical restaurant of small towns, was the daily special: broasted chicken, potato, and salad bar, $7.99. I ordered the special. Nicky, the waitress, came back apologizing that it was such a hit, that there were only two chicken pieces left. We bantered a bit. A price break could be given.

"Okay with me," I thanked.

Susan had returned to the table with her salad, so I looked for a plate, filled it and sat back down.

Nicky returned. "We're sorry to tell you, but the cook thought we were done for the day and threw out the last two pieces of chicken. What else would you like? And we'll throw in a load of hash brown potatoes."

I ordered the local fish, walleye. Then I asked, "That was all-you-can-eat salad?"

"Yes," she confirmed.

"Well, this just isn't my day. You were out of tomatoes and broccoli".

"Oh! You should have told me," she apologized.

"Your saving grace is the most wonderful potato salad. May I have more?"

"Yes". In a few minutes she came back. "The meal is on us. You had enough trouble".

Carla, the owner, came to the table, assuring that they didn't mean for us to have such a problem. Then she discussed how she had come from Texas for an engineer's job that didn't materialize. Noticing that the pub business was for sale, she asked herself,

"I haven't ever had anything to do with a bar. How hard could it be?" So she bought the business. Her two biggest problems were having too many employees, and how much inventory to have on hand for a town of twelve hundred.

The bar had originally been a bank built in 1909, burned down and rebuilt. But it failed during the Depression. She indicated the picture behind us. All three bank employees died due to the failure. One of the young men had been embezzling, the other knew about it. The Depression revealed the shortages, so both men shot themselves in the bank. The president, an older man, believed the failure would badly reflect on him, entered the big vault down stairs, and shot himself, too. We insisted on paying the full bill for our great meals and interesting conversation.

Tidbits. It appears that 90 percent of SD towns are under fifteen hundred population. Counties are arranged in checker board squares on maps without special designated map coloring. Patriotism is healthy in SD. Many towns have a memorial hall, American legion, or some tribute for those who served in the military. Not only does every town have multiple churches, but at remote crossroads, there are churches and graveyards. For days thousands of motorcyclists blatted past on every roadway. Must be the Sturgis motorcycle rally. Hunting licenses are $40 for two deer tags, three pheasants per day. Fishing Licenses run $25 for all fish, lakes and streams.

The Platte newspaper warned about rabid skunks, forty identified last year. Skunks are the most common road kill, followed by raccoons. Partridges are stupid; they fly right into cars. Deer hit by cars do massive damage to vehicles. Tortoises and frogs are new road kill items. In spite of Lewis and Clark's descriptions of enormous herds of antelope, elk, deer, bison and other wildlife, there have been no such sightings. How did they come to disappear?

Every farm used dry land irrigation, but looks are deceiving. This year's drought limited corn to half normal height, with seed heads already

313

sprouting. It bodes badly for winter cattle feed. Ranchers may have to sell off their herds. Few mechanical water wheel systems exist. Many ponds, mini lakes, and golf course water hazards are fetid. No rain fell in two weeks, and the last was a 15 minute squall.

Enormous hundred foot silos and granaries poke out from the countryside. A large number concentrated together usually means a settlement. Trucks ran up and down the roads bringing grain supplies to the insatiable silos. Hundreds of rust red railroad cars lie on sidings waiting to be filled and carried to the cities.

There is a sadness at seeing the ugly side of some Americans. This hasn't been limited to one state, race, city, or locale. When looking at the vast beauty and variety of America, it is shameful to see the callous disregard for public lands or the property of others, when Americans thoughtlessly dispose of trash out the automobile window.

"It's not my property. It gives jobs to road crews picking up the trash. It's no big deal," may be the thinking of only 5 or 10 percent of citizens.

Yet the moral authority of the rest of the country is not forceful enough to deter such behavior. These are Americans sacrilegiously destroying the bounty of America's land, one piece of rubbish at a time. Call it a pet peeve. Say I'm starting some bleeding heart green movement. Tell me I'm making a mountain out of a mole hill. It is one thing to accidentally have something fall off a truck, or get blown off by a gust of wind, it's another to make the roadside a dumping ground. It doesn't matter? Then there should be no complaint if an Adopt-a-Highway clean up truck empties the waste in a perpetrator's front yard. Call it a sickness of some American souls. Now, don't get me started about graffiti.

76 mi. 1,733 miles to date elevation: 1,418'

DAY 38: DAY OF R & R

Sunday,   Tyndall to Yankton,   Cloudy a.m./sunny p.m. 84*
July 8, 2012   SD by car

    Rest and recuperation. For the last several days the fortunes of cooler weather accompanied us. Today, overcast kept morning temps down, so there were no winds to speak of. After mass, we drove twenty-nine miles to Yankton realizing the reality of hilly flat land. No decision yet of whether this was portaging. We visited Eunice Reis, our daughter-in-law's grandmother. Together we brunched at JoDean's Restaurant, a memorabilia collector's paradise. Besides offering a gigantic buffet spread, the interior sported a bigger-than-a-barn western setting, housing antique bar counters, organs, farm tools, signs, vehicles, butter churns, washing tubs, rolling pins, ice boxes, armoires, license plates, fishing equipment, etc. located on the walls above heads. In other words, the owners collected everything old and found history in cast offs.

    I wasn't good company taking a two hour Sunday nap in a recliner, so Susan and Eunice toured her senior apartment facility without me and had coffee in the dining room with other residents. Many of the owners decorated recessed hallway doors with humorous notes, patriotic Americana (in honor of July 4th), and signs creating a happy place for retired people.

    In mid afternoon, Eunice gave the local tour at Calumet Bluff, where Lewis and Clark gathered Indian chiefs for presents and a peace council in 1804. It overlooked Gavin Point Dam from the Nebraska side. The center displayed engineering feats, fish and wildlife, historical clothing, and films. The dam itself created Lewis & Clark Lake, fifty feet above the lower river, providing hydroelectric power, flood protection, and recreation benefits, in addition to clear river travel all the way to St. Louis.

    Tornadoes are a fact of life here, so we paid attention to daily weather predictions. For protection, most Dakotans build insulated and waterproofed basements. Although some are woodshops or storage rooms, many are like Eunice's grandson's home: furnished family room, two bedrooms, hobby room, bathroom, the whole under-the-house living area being a getaway from the summer heat. Windows atop basement walls at ground level let in sunlight. What looks like a modest one thousand square foot home is doubled with the basement.

This computer is slowing down, dying. It can't keep up with typing speed, so it drops off typed letters-typos. Occasionally it challenges known spellings or changes a word to some other. It has thrown me out of the word processor program numerous times, before I have made a backup save. Sometimes it can't acquire the WIFI signal available to others. We should have replaced it in Portland. I'm thinking of re-encouraging it with a .357 Magnum.

0 mi.   1,733 miles to date   elevation: 1,205'

DAY 39: UNTITLED

Monday,   Tyndall to Vermillion, SD   Partly cloudy 84*
July 9, 2012

It was tempting. No one would ever have known, unless I told them. We drove back twenty-nine miles to Tyndall where we stopped on Saturday, deep in the corn crop. Sluggish may be too kind for how the start began with every part of me begging for cutting down the miles. The trip is finally taking its toll. Massages temporarily relieve muscle aches but don't last; groggy breakfasts; mental mistakes; worn out by lunch; continued saddle soreness; taking shorter rest periods so we can get to a motel to cool off/shower; joking about quitting; temptation to portage. However, today was a bright sunny start and fast wheeling.

At Tabor, I desperately needed a restroom when the "pancake effect" kicked in. Two garage mechanics wanted to see the bike. The town of 400 was populated by Polish and Czechs, who have a Polka mass at 5:30 Saturdays. There was even a street with my grandmother's maiden name, Szymanski. Back on the highway, I found quarters lying in the gravel for our laundry needs. All along the route I've prospected money dropped in the street.

With one notable long climb, cycling was fast on the flats, speed creating a breeze. To my right, on the south, rose the blue distant bluffs carved by the Missouri, at times blocked from view by the foreground lines of trees. Hay rolls lay parked in the ditches. Corn sat in the fields waiting for rain. Cows, blank-faced, stared at my passage. Heat shimmered up from the pavement. Vehicles lazily drove past. Barnyards appeared lifeless and untended, regardless of how neatly kept. A road crew burying pipes stood around at near standstill. There was no hurry in the summer sun and oppressive humidity.

At 1:30, not expecting to gain much speed, the bike rolled down a precipitous ramp decline into Wal-Mart's parking lot back in Yankton, suddenly shooting downwards. I desperately grasped the hand brakes, barely turning the handle bars to avoid smacking into the truck delivery wall. In the baking heat, I located Susan's parking space, locked the bike to the rack, and walked into the air conditioned shopping mecca. With supplies replaced we enjoyed a Subway tuna sandwich inside, deliberately delaying, avoiding the soaring outside temperature.

From 2:15 on, Highway 50 passed from Yankton into the everlastingly beautiful countryside. Although an orange construction sign announced road work for the next ten miles, it was closer to fifteen, with the entire north highway being ripped up to be reconstituted and repaved. The south side two lane was split by orange pylons with traffic moving slowly and me on a wide shoulder. There were no really good spots to pull over for breaks. At 5:15 we terminated in Vermillion, population 10,000. Humidity had won. I wasn't human until a shower, leg massage, and an hour's nap revived me.

Vermillion is the home of the University of South Dakota Coyotes and the Dakota Dome, a completely enclosed football stadium. High school teams on playing fields scrimmaged in late evening. Fast food joints catered to college clientele, while dorms, apartments and frats sided the main road. Except for some businesses, lawns dried up without sprinkler systems. Dakotans don't waste water on grass, figuring when it rains the grass will come back

54 mi.   1,787 mi. to date   elevation: 1,150'

DAY 40: OUT OF SORTS

Tuesday, July 10, 2012   Vermillion, SD to Sioux City, IA   Sunny 89*

I woke cranky and out of sorts. Susan couldn't do anything right by me. I moaned and groaned about getting going early, but wouldn't get in gear. Yesterday's email needed adjustments before posting, and I balked at everything Susan suggested. On the way out of town we got mixed up on the directions. Fred, an administrator from USD, straightened us out. The university enrolled around 9,000 students majoring to be doctors, lawyers or MBAs. (Agriculture and Engineering are in the northern university in Brookings.) Vermillion revolved around the college.

In his words, "If you took away the college, there'd be only a few bars and closed businesses".

Back on the ka-thunk, ka-thunk pavement I kept grumbling to myself. At the correct turnoff, Susan sat patiently waiting. The bean fields and corn were already hot. A short hill climb approached a farm house partially hidden by cornstalks. In the car, just on the other side, Susan poised with camera in hand to snap my descent down a majestic slope into green lush glory. A left turn at Whimpy's Bar, in Burbank, shot a straight arrow roadway past green Missouri forest bluffs four miles south.

Although the plan was to break every five miles or so for muscle relief, I disregarded that when Susan pulled over in a sunny spot. Already hot, I deliberately passed her.

"Go to the shade," I yelled out meaning I wanted rest under the bunch of trees a mile distant. Susan passed the first farm inlet with trees, pulled over, then drove off to another place in the sun. I passed by her to the next farm, crunched up the shaded gravel driveway, plunked down and took a solo shaded break, my stomach grumbling. No one was home, though everything spoke of a small, well maintained yellow house and farm buildings. Rested, I stopped next to the driver's door.

I said, "Go ahead, but stop in a farmer's driveway. No farmer will refuse you shade. And if he does, tell him your big ugly husband is coming".

Susan has been reluctant to stop in farm driveways.

My attitude is: "What's the worst that can happen? Ask you to move? Besides, the answer is always no, unless you ask".

The book Bicycling the Lewis and Clark Trail said a safer frontage road paralleled I-29, but a mile into Elk Horn, the road did not appear. A local woman reported that others had been confused too. She recommended going back to I-29 to reach Sioux City. The bank marquee read 87* at noon. Under the bridge before the entrance ramp, taking a water break, I discovered that the right pedal was broken and cracked along the spindle.

A saga of breezeless sticky biking over the freshly tarred stones began on the shoulder. I will not need new tires for the remainder of the trip because now they have acquired two extra inches of asphalt tread; the bike is so much taller, that now I fall off when coming to a stop. (Not!)

The next detail is not very nice. All morning, into the afternoon my stomach was not friendly. Now it turned enemy! Without getting graphic, I created enough methane to heat a hundred homes for a month in South Dakota's worst snowstorm. Even when we stopped for a Subway lunch at marker 2, the flatulence did not cease with a pit stop.

We cooled down in a corner until 3:15, until I rode on Military Road entering Sioux City, Iowa, to locate a bike shop replacement of the broken pedal. Snaking around miles of middle class houses set in the hills, a steep climb, I crested a small hill. On the way down, picking up speed on the sidewalk, the bike approached a cement wall with no room for bicycling. Thinking to slide sideways to the road, I encountered a concrete driveway jutting a slab two inches too high. The jarring front wheel smack rotated the handle bar forward and down. This position made grasping the brake levers nearly impossible.

After a half mile of dangerous cycling with the rotated handlebars, I stopped at a corner Wonder Bread bakery seeking the nearest bike shop. The cashier wasn't certain, but a bald-shaven burly man in a bright yellow shirt knew exactly. He gave the instructions right, left, right, left. The cashier, in her eagerness to help a poor lost soul, enthusiastically wrote out the directions. In the car I realized that her eagerness proved too exciting- every turn was a right turn! For once I had paid close attention and we arrived exactly as yellow shirt said, at Albrecht's Cyclery. The blue shirted owner had a mechanic on the bike in moments. I went outside to invite Susan in to cool off, but she was gone. Thinking this could last a while, I stood around watching my bike jiggle behind a wall partition.

In five minutes the mechanic said: "All done," as he adjusted and tightened the handle bars. "Let's settle up," I replied.

"Okay, that'll be $10.65". (Pedals are sold in pairs.) This was fast service without gouging desperate customers.

Susan picked me up, returning to the AAA office where she renewed membership and acquired driving info. I needed their restroom. At 4:50, it was time to call it a day. Accidentally missing the directions to the nearby motel, we ended up on the south side of Sioux City. While cooling down and typing this email I needed the restroom again. (It couldn't have been that delicious Italian meatballs and spaghetti from last night, could it?) Well, after a shower and dinner everything was copasetic. Now don't mess with me until I'm done digesting my Texas Road House full rack of melt-off-the-bones ribs.

40 mi.   1,827 mi. to date   elevation: 1,135'

Dropping into the gorgeous green farm belt
SE of Vermillion, SD. 7/10/12.

Unique motorcycle sculpture envied by most tourists, Whiting, IA.

DAY 41: CORN

Wednesday,   Sioux City to Missouri Valley, IA   Sunny 89*
July 11, 2012

Old town Sioux City sidewalks suffered from ice broken cement. Narrow streets have caused traffic engineers to change them to *One Way* to improve circulation. Abandoned buildings stared sooty and weather worn, and yet a construction renaissance was renewing downtown vitality. The city spread five miles. In the south, a collection of malls, centrally located, perched on hills next to one another, instead of being sprinkled among residential areas. Clientele must drive far distances to take advantage of sales. In essence the 83,000 population serves the industrial needs of agribusiness and cattle with granaries, rail yards, machinery, farm equipment, butchery, welding, and repair services.

Our AAA tour book identified Sioux City as having thirty-eight Lewis and Clark bicentennial murals in the Southern Hills Mall. Finding them was a chore, for several people had no idea of their whereabouts. When located on a wall above our heads, only two murals remained. The mall had begun removing them this very Monday. Two workers in dark blue jump suits gave directions to the mall office. The woman manager explained that they were being removed for remodeling, and would be given to a good home. However, if interested, she would give leftover souvenirs. Down a maze of corridors and a locked store, she led to a storeroom stacked with boxes of posters, tote bags, coffee cups and note cards, offering selected souvenirs for my ROMEO friends (Retired Old Men Eating Out) in Dinuba.

Yesterday's intestinal distress continued, causing purchase of anti-Montezuma's revenge medicine, which took all day to calm my stomach.

The day's ride banked down the recommended path of K 45 toward Sloan. The bicycle book thought this safer than the I-29 freeway. I beg to differ. There was no shoulder. The right white line was the exact edge of the roadbed with a 2-4 inch drop-off into gravel. Heavy traffic, in both directions, slowed in the narrow lane before passing me at 35 mph. Many industrial businesses had short dangerous entrance and exit openings. Three hazardous miles later, Susan transported me to the freeway entrance, although being on the interstate did not make her comfortable in the least. Agreeing on our next meeting point, I rejoined the busy interstate pedaling on wide black asphalt. Iowa weeds stuck up from the grassy road shoulder.

Fields sprouted soybeans and corn. Corn stalks stood like army soldiers at attention, shoulder to shoulder, flapping their green lapel leaves in the gentle breeze. Birds dive bombed my passage, protecting their nests.

At Sloan, we stopped for a Subway tuna sandwich again, and cooled off. Travel resumed at 2:00 but we switched to K 45 to see if the route had improved in seventeen miles. Yes and no. The traffic was considerably diminished, but the paved lane was as narrow as before. In addition, Iowa heat and humidity had caused certain pavement sections to swell patches higher than originally steamrolled. Lots of bumps to watch for. For the most part, miles and miles of corn passed boringly by. At Onawa (AH-nah-wah), a fellow sitting in shade said the town held claim to the widest main street in the U.S.-four central lanes, with a side cement divider left and right providing a business frontage road with diagonal parking, eight lanes in all! At Whiting I stood next to a welder's artistic fourteen foot tall orange motorcycle for a photo op. Blencoe, River Sioux, Mondamin, or Modale were without services. Susan located accommodations in Missouri Valley to cap off the day.

What grows in Iowa? Corn, corn, corn, soybeans, corn, corn, corn. Now you knew this was coming:

What does an Iowa farmer get when his wife scolds him? An earful

When do Iowa farmers wake up? Ear-ly

What do children call their hot corn farmer father? Pop

What is an Iowa corn farmer's favorite frozen dessert? A Popsicle

How does an Iowa corn farmer play piano? By ear.

What kind of voice does an Iowa opera star have? Husky

How do Iowans describe the worst part of town? Seedy

What does an Iowa stripper wear? Tassels

What foot problem do all Iowa farmers have? Corns

What do Iowans eat with their steak and potatoes? Cobb salad

What is the only rank Iowa soldiers can achieve? Kernels

What are the three crops grown by Iowa farmers? Seed corn, half-grown corn, harvest corn

Describe an Iowa horror movie. Earie

Name the favorite style of humor for Iowans. Corny

How do you know an Iowan woman is getting a phone call? Ear-rings

What kind of crime do Iowans commit when chasing others? Stalking

What do bald Iowa farmers wear? Ear-wigs

What is the source of propulsion for the Iowa navy? Row, Row, Row

What kind of chickens does an Iowa farmer raise? Cornish hens

How do we know Iowans are good farmers? Because they are outstanding in their fields

How do Iowa doctors treat hearing maladies? Irrigate the ears

What do deaf Iowa farmers have when they can't hear their scolding wives? Peace

Where do Iowans bury lawyers? In Nebraska

How do Iowans grin when reading these jokes? From ear to ear

Now you know what goes through the mind of a hot, tired bicyclist in the middle of a sea of corn.

49 mi.   1,876 mi. to date   elevation: 1,007'

DAY 42: SIZZLIN'

Thursday,   Missouri Valley to Glenwood, IA   Sunny 93*
July 12, 2012

East of the I-29 Interstate lie the Loess (lowsss) Hills, a 200 mile stretch of fine silt brought down by the Missouri in mild flood plains thousands of years before the river cut a deeper gouge west. Loess means loose in German. When the land dried, wind blew the fine soil eastward into lengthy dunes. The loam is very rich as attested by the dense forest and vegetation filling every inch of ground. Below the hills is some of the finest farmland in the world. This gigantic phenomenon occurs in only one other place in the world, the Yellow River Valley in China.

Today's trail launched from the center of Missouri Valley by crossing over the rail yard lines. Narrow highway L-20/183 crept through weed choked ditches, then skirted in a crescent arc east and south along the Loess Hills. Steamy heat oppressed the twisting climbs along the foothills, but morning shade balanced with shadows playing over the road. If no traffic was coming in either direction on the hills, it was easy to glide to the east side of the road, under the tree canopy to stay cooler, then correct back to the right when an approaching southern car was audible in the distance.

Paralleling the road, the north/south rail line has had no traffic for several days. Several rail crews and yellow heavy duty maintenance engines were busy replacing ties, rails, crossings, and other Union Pacific needs. Many homeowners preferred country living along the tracks, gazing at the lush bottomland rolling before them. The road wound up to Honey Creek in the hills. Without any air moving, it was difficult to breathe in the forest thickness. Short breaks in open air on the other side allowed breathable gasps. Over and back the road twisted on the Loess.

Council Bluffs posed a maze of difficult driving through town until the chamber of commerce secretary handed maps and typed out directions. Skipping lunch, we followed the directions, even though there were hazardous areas. We nearly exited the city without eating. At a distance, major shopping glinted in a shimmering industrial center. Subway became our cool down until 2:30.

I'm no expert, but let me describe humidity's affects on the human body. It's like putting blankets over your face. After three minutes, carbon dioxide is sufficient to make your lungs want to escape from under the covers. There is no place to get a deep cool gasp of air. If there is a breeze, move the body towards it, raise your arms and let the mild cooling begin. No breeze? Witness the perspiration ooze from every pore in the body. Clothing is instantly soaked and sticks. Relief comes in the form of either moving to create a breeze, or use a fan. (Air conditioning has changed the Midwest, making it bearable, but requires one to remain indoors.) Sweat trickles from under the hat. (What? No hat? It's humid and you have no hat?) Perspiration soaks the mop called hair, slides down the ears, over the eye brows. Wiping it away is temporary, and nearly useless. Eyes sweat. A salty forehead trickle reaches the eyes and stings. Unless the eyes are wiped, the stinging continues. Length of time in the out-of-doors saps strength and desire to do things. Speed of achievement slows. Languor takes over. The mind gets fuzzy, tires quickly, loses focus. Lacking enough liquids to replace the sweat, a dizziness hints that more serious effects-heat stress or heat stroke-are on the way. The body's biggest enthusiasms are to sit down, get something tall and cold to drink, and wait for ambition to go away.

South of Council Bluffs, the L-35 trail over the Loess Hills was another beautiful excursion up and down and over the crest of the formation, all in miserable climate. Desire to cover at least fifty miles was defeated by the wear of atmosphere.

Still in Iowa? Did I forget to tell about traveling through one hundred thousand miles of corn?

You knew this was coming:

What do Iowans call comedian hippies? Corn flakes

What is the only day of the week Iowans don't bake in the summer sun? Fry-day

By what adage do all Iowa farmers live? Ear no weevil

Why has the Iowa Goodyear blimp followed me for the last three days? For a refill

Do Iowans bury dead skunks, opossum, and lawyers? No, only skunks and opossum

Where do Iowans bury skunk and opossum road kill? Where they find them

Why do Iowans only bury skunks and opossum? They have redeeming qualities.

What redeeming qualities do Iowa skunks and opossum have? They have hearts and guts.

Why don't Iowans bury lawyers in Iowa? They have no hearts, no guts and you can't tell one end from the other.

Why won't Iowans bury lawyers in Iowa? They stink up the place.

42 mi.   1,918 mi. to date   elevation: 1,017'

DAY 43: TRACKS

Friday,
July 13, 2012

Glenwood, IA to
Rock Port, MO

Overcast to sunny 98*

Out of fear from yesterday's heat exhaustion, we left the motel just after 7:00. Rain drops on the car increased our concern after the Weather Channel predicted thunder storms. The trek began along 34 West.

I ceased being a fan of the rolling Loess Hills. Unsure of the correct direction, I called Susan who back tracked to make certain I was pointed correctly. Another delay, but the clouds were heavy, brooding and cooler. Junctioned with I-29, frontage road L-31 provided superior paving and little traffic coursing through ever present corn fields. At a fifteen foot embankment running for several miles, a man with his boy and girl bent over catching catfish bait at a side creek on the right. They identified soybeans growing up to the dirt levee of the Missouri. Gravel road ahead lead to a boat ramp. The seemingly harmless brown roiling river was about a football field wide, fenced by tall cottonwoods. Two fellows, launching a 14 foot aluminum craft, pooh-poohed the T-storm threat.

"Twenty percent chance means no rain, even though we need it," they mocked.

At marker 124, when the road cut back east over the interstate, an opportunity occurred to watch a BNSF (Burlington Northern and Santa Fe) rail crew hard at work. Have you ever really looked at railroad tracks? Have you ever wondered how they are repaired? Leonard and foreman Ben supervised the safety and progress of the rail crossing repair. It is a sight of extreme precision and efficiency. Each rail machine device has a single dedicated purpose. Device 1 (D1) slowly rolls while mechanical arms pull and drop rail spikes only from the left side. D2 only removes right spikes. D3 Lifts the rails three inches to slide the cleat plates off the tie. D4 grasps and pulls out the old tie from the outer side, dropping it. D5 with an electro-magnet picks up spikes and cleats. D6 places new ties perpendicular to the track. D7 scrapes out rock. D8 lifts the rail three inches to slide a new tie under the rail. D9, loaded with rock, spreads it between the ties. D10 is a rock sweeper throwing chunks forward and down. Two individuals walking behind, check the progress and accuracy of the fill. D11 raises the rail three inches and slides two new cleats in place. D12 and D13 drive left and right spikes into the ties. The last two walking crewmen check quality. The forty-eight man gang has the goal of 1,650 ties per day in twenty days to complete the section from Hamburg to Pacific Junction, about twenty-eight miles. While the rail bed is being redone, all freight trains are shifted to the west until completion. However, this spur normally carries great amounts of coal. An empty car is worth more than a loaded one. When the empty returns to the coal yard, a check is paid.

Susan wasn't happy that I had stayed observing and talking 45 minutes with the railroad gang. Having driven ahead to find a good break spot, not knowing that I had stopped to talk and observe, she became worried when I hadn't shown up on road L-31 and came back looking for me. It was my fault, not phoning her, but all the worse, the early start was foiled by my curiosity.

Quiet road moved along the Loess Hills bottomland and crossed bridges over I-29 repeatedly until pavement changed to gravel. Clouds continued to keep sun rays at bay. I pedaled onto the interstate entrance ramp because no reasonable side roads were available. Nine miles down the interstate I left corn fields and the Loess Hills toward Hamburg just as the sun broke out. Instead of a vibrant town, the 2006 economic downturn was everywhere in the vacant stores and homes. Our furnace lunch in the park was interrupted once by a passing car. So many Midwest towns have likewise become desolate, populated by empty, dust ridden stores whose clients moved to where jobs might be.

Back to the trail, Road 275 on the map seemed a straight easy route. That was true for two miles until the Missouri border crossing. Instantly the pavement became as wrinkled as a raisin. Cracked cement and macadam chip chunks fell off the edge. Usually roads at the end of state lines are poorly maintained. Missouri state's portion of Loess Hills instigated roller coaster torment. Heat relief came from light breezes at hilltops, or by pedaling fast in the stifling forested troughs. Any stop was breathless.

Contour farming created artistic corn row patterns, rounded and twined around hillsides as if a giant rake had carved a Japanese stone garden.

At Rock Point, I swore off hill climbing. Wishful thinking. Susan rented a room, where we cooled down at 3:30. Out of clean clothes with the nearest laundromat eight miles east, we chanced a two mile ride west to the interstate, discovering a truck stop with a lone coin washer and dryer. The BIG (Black Iron Grill) offered a rustic decor rude dude scraps-and-peanut-shells-thrown-on-the-floor restaurant. An early evening sunset graced planning for tomorrow's destination of St. Joseph.

55 mi.   1,973 mi. to date   elevation: 972'

DAY 44: IT'S NOT A PERFECT WORLD

Saturday, July 14, 2012   Rock Port to St. Joseph, MO   Sunny 99*

Packed at dawn, the car headed to Egg McMuffinville. A whining undisciplined girl came in with mom. It was obvious that the girl was going to have it her way regardless of what mom told her. After directions by the mother, she sat in the wrong area, then waltzed around while mom was in the bathroom with the younger child, and began whining again as mom exited the restroom. We walked outside to eat.

Our 7:10 goal was St. Joseph for lunch. The bike entered I-29 at marker 110, but left at 107 for the safer west side Road 111. Freshly paved straight smooth black asphalt ran through the corn blocks! No cars in five miles until Susan moved by. No wind. Fast rolling. In eleven miles two vehicles came by. When an empty coal train passed, I waved. The engineer blared a Whooh! Whooh! The route ended when it crossed east over the highway. Unfortunately, again the road roamed up and down the Loess Hills causing cussing of both hills and transportation department engineers for aggravating my knees. These weren't terrible hills, but sore knees don't let you forget who's doing the work. Mound City's bank thermometer registered 84* at 10:02. The landscape was pristine scenic touring, a mixture of field swerves among the geometrical patterns, yellowed with tassels fertilizing corn silk. It was hard to believe the crop was in danger due to the drought. So much green and yellow, without rain for three weeks and 90* temps.

Scenic touring did not mean safe touring. Quiet roads connecting towns posed the deception that fewer vehicles meant safety. Too often the road lacked a shoulder or, if there was shoulder, it was cracked/broken/chipped away, and dropped off onto gravel which may twist the wheel or puncture a tire. Most drivers of trucks and farm trailers or heavy equipment gave wide berth when possible, or patiently waited for oncoming traffic to get by before they passed. It was common for small passenger cars to hog the lane, refusing to move over. Once in a while drivers seemed to deliberately drive the lane center so as to teach the bike rider a lesson.

"The road is for cars, not bikes," they seemed to say.

On rare occasions a driver's approaching wind roar indicated he was bearing down, the only safe maneuver being to dive into gravel. Bridges, always narrower than the road, created tricky crossovers before traffic coincided with a biker. On town cross streets, drivers frequently were not always looking for a cyclist. Every side street entrance presented gravel piles, 200 feet before and after, threatening to bog the front wheel, twisting it sideways out of control. And then there were the guys in a hurry, who couldn't delay ten seconds for an approaching car on the opposite side to pass by me so they, in turn, could safely pass the bike. No, they must pass full throttle between the two of us. In a way, bike riders need nerves of steel.

On the other hand, almost none of the foregoing pertained to the Interstate system. The shoulder ranged from four to eight feet wide, separated from the road edge by a rumble strip warning. For the most part it was clean, free of tire shreds, trash, and loose gravel. Never had a truck or automobile driver come too close. Occasionally, right side shoulder debris forced me to dodge left for a moment or two.

Okay, the question: Isn't it illegal to be on the Interstate? No entrance has ever posted a sign prohibiting bicycles. Police, sheriff and state trooper cars have passed without halting me. The California freeway rule declares if there is no parallel road within one mile left or right of the freeway, one may ride on the right edge. So far the Interstate felt safe, except when traffic increased near cities.

When the Loess Hills road subwayed under I-29 after twenty miles, I chose to walk up the grassy flank of its bridge to enjoy good road prior to marker 79. Susan, circling a hill to the actual 79 entrance, noted I had skipped a significant ascent. Well, almost. I still had to climb to the entrance ramp. But then, for fourteen miles, there were Loess Hills that even the Interstate could not avoid. I kept hydration stops until quitting at 11:45. With the bike stowed on the car rack, we drove to St. Joseph for our earliest cool down lunch. I wasn't overheated. [Lesson learned?] I didn't portage; the city was west, far off the Interstate. I was safe in 99* and 82 percent humidity.

Since cycling concluded before noon it seemed we had time to see the sights. Not so fast. The Interstate highway signs which indicated food, motels, and services left out the fact that a car had to travel six miles to reach St. Joseph. Searching for a diner and motel gobbled up time on heavily trafficked modern Frederick Avenue and 29 Business loop, where most commercial ventures were located.

The ancient downtown, a decayed inner city, was nearly deserted. City fathers had neglected far too long the city core which stores and shops fled. Old buildings were boarded, bricked up, patched and peeling, windows broken, roofs rotting, surrounded by old mansions and grand hillside homes which had seen better days. Poor people living in the shabby homes didn't have the money or know-how to restore. The hillside community suffered city abandonment.

Crossing the river on the pale green cement and steel intertwining overpasses, expecting St. Joseph development across the river, we ended, surprised, in empty Kansas fields amid a few industrial sites. At least we spent ten minutes in Kansas. Back downtown we hunted for a park indicated on the map, turned past deserted businesses, and eased under a bridge toward the Remington Nature Center. It was closed, so we ambled to the boat launch dock and splashed river water. The real reason we came to the river? To dine at Terrible's St. Jo Frontier Casino. Actually, it was just hunger. We like buffets, but endured second hand smoke. This trip has been enough of a gamble, so we didn't throw away money at the slot machines or gaming tables.

There were times today and many days in the past when I would be irritated. Perhaps Susan selected a stop point a bit farther than I wanted, or delayed, stopping in a shadeless area. Petty things get on one's nerves while struggling. Today's realization arrived that the world is not perfect because I want things just so. What good would it do to get angry, yell, or criticize? We were both hot and tired. Susan has to be bored with start, stop, wait, where is he? She waits in a hot car often parked in the sun, although she claims she's okay as long as the windows are open. She reads in fits and starts. And then sooths my poor ego. This is not the path to glory and acclaim. As if I have been the perfect companion, griping about every new ache and pain and detailing what I've observed. Maybe I'm learning that the world is not built to my specifications, that there is more than my perception of the world. Rather than curse circumstances, it's better to make the world a nicer place with kind words and a touch of humor. Or treat one's wife to a good meal.

49 mi.   2,022 mi. to date   elevation: 823'

7/15/12 Checking to see if the Missouri had real water.

DAY 45: A TOUR AND COMEUPPANCE

Sunday, July 15, 2012   Kansas City, MO and into Kansas   Sunny 100*

Sometimes the best part of resting is that you don't get much done. Though my ideal would have been to luxuriate in bed until noon, I had promised to chauffeur Susan to Kansas City. With a carbohydrate motel breakfast, we drove I-29 south, with knees grateful for not pedaling fifty-three miles of rolling hills toward K.C. Each mile revealed more drying grass and wilting corn. Tree leaves languished yellow and brown from the drought.

During a tour of the Harry Truman National Historic Site in Independence, MO, we watched an introductory film about Harry Truman before a guided tour of his home. A modest and unassuming man, Truman made tough important decisions. As ex-president, he walked about town, met folk, and autograph hounds, but kept his home private, and shunned publicity.

Lunch at Hardees, another name for Carls; both restaurants sport the same corporate famous star. Then onward to K.C. Although the Kansas City Royals were playing a day game in the stadium, we were unwilling to join the fans in the 100* stands.

Susan owns a doll house and, consequently, an interest in miniatures. She wanted to tour the AAA gem attraction Toy & Miniature Museum near the University of Missouri, Kansas City. The map gave the exit as 66A, which didn't exist. Taking the 67 exit through a forest of park trees did not link us up with the correct street, no matter how we turned to intersect. The more we drove the twisting hills, using the general map, the less we found streets listed. At last we connected with a major street and felt we had our bearings, when we encountered a small blue sign with white letters titled ATTRACTIONS, pointing the way to multiple sites. However, no mileage was given. On we drove nearly missing a second blue sign indicating a right turn. A distant drive until a stoplight with five intersecting streets each with a crooked angled street name. Which way? We guessed wrong, turned and corrected twice more. Again a long drive until we knew we were close to the University. No sign. However, if we had come from the opposite direction there was a sign! Oh! A marquee on the lawn.

We ascended a steep entrance to park in the shade, noticing a family returning to the only other car in the parking lot.

"The museum is closed one day for maintenance," said the family.

"What????? On a Sunday? On a family outing day? During tourist season?" I griped.

The local family gave us alternate attractions to explore. At the town center plaza we enjoyed cruising past unique architecture, but avoided shopping or hiking in the heat. Instead we chose to leave the city and immediately got lost again on the winding hills. Having wasted nearly two hours fruitlessly driving in K.C. we asked a man gassing his car to point us to a freeway.

At 3:00, thirsty, tired and missing a Sunday nap, we escaped across a bridge to Leavenworth, Kansas. Immediately Susan pointed to a Subway shop where we could get a drink. I passed it. Then there was a 7-11. I passed that, too, thinking town was just ahead, driving on, completely missing the city a mile on the south.

I asked Susan, "Did you really want to see Leavenworth?"

Her reply was: "I don't <u>have</u> to see it".

In a tiff, tired and thirsty, I reacted with hostility that she did not answer the question, then doubled back to Subway. The humid atmosphere had converted our emotions into testiness.

Thirst quenched, clearing the emotional air, and wiping away thinking cobwebs, we approached the entrance of Fort Leavenworth, the oldest operating military base west of the Mississippi (1827). Next to it is Leavenworth Federal Prison, ringed with concertina barbed wire. With the hope an ex-G.I. might tour the Army base, I asked the guard, who said yes, but he must inspect the car and contents. With all the camping gear and travel paraphernalia, it would be a long process, and that ended the request. But the soldier asked for my driver license, escorting the car around the guard post to the off base exit before returning the license. The tragedy of 9/11 has disrupted American faith, trust, and confidence once enjoyed before terrorists changed the social fabric of society. Sunday-deserted streets but charming 1890s brick façades graced downtown Leavenworth (35,000), still a going city but with notable empty buildings and stores.

In Atchison, KS, we parked at 4:54 (closing time 5:00) at the Railroad and Amelia Earhardt Museum fronting the rail yard. The docent encouraged us to take our time exploring, for she had many tasks to do, accepting more visitors to a proud museum full of hometown memorabilia. Our touring appetite sated, we returned to St. Joseph via the tentacled freeway system. I got my nap, barbecue for dinner, and comeuppance when the laptop again kicked me off before saving with only this last paragraph to finish.

0 mi.   2,022 mi. to date   elevation: 823'

DAY 46: HIDDEN TREASURE

Monday,	St. Joseph to	Sunny/part cloudy 95*
July 16, 2012	Chillicothe, MO	

Since this trip began, we've had to compromise where to explore the Lewis and Clark Trail. First, in 1804, they rowed on water for the most part until the river depth forced them to hike overland. No modern routes exactly follow their footsteps. At best, some roads parallel the river for a distance. Second, it seemed that every road within twenty-five miles of the Missouri River claimed to be the Lewis and Clark Trail with posted official brown and white signs. Third, in certain instances, trails in the guide book were dangerous or took long out of the way circuitous routes. Fourth, scenic does not identify the actual route of L. & C. Fifth, a bicycle trip does not equal an 1804-1806 boat, perogue (wooden canoe), horse, and overland trek. Finally, anyone may choose his/her own interpretation of which way to honor the epic journey of the Discovery party. Today, we chose to head east on Highway 36 directly towards Hannibal, MO, staying about one hundred miles north of the Missouri, later changing southeast to St. Louis.

Rising 7 a.m. morning sun created a new danger-drivers behind were blinded by golden orb's glare. Tilting my helmet didn't help. Fortunately, after exiting town, fewer vehicles occupied the connecting eleven mile Route 6 link. Farms and ranches of east Missouri exhibited a slightly different climate. Rain, and consequently vegetation, seemed more plentiful. Fields, defined by tree lines, gave a park-like scenario. Crops sang the same tune, corn, corn, corn, soy, corn, corn, corn. But now hay rolls and pastures crept into nooks and crannies. Untrimmed ditches were colonized by tall weeds, wild flowers, and thick volunteer vegetation. But the drought had begun its affect here too. TV news said 80 percent of the nation was experiencing some form of drought.

Highway 36 ran four straight lanes east-west, divided by a center grass strip. Hills continued yet rarely rose more than fifty feet on gentle slopes. A lack of mile markers prevented judging distance covered. No morning breeze. At 9:10 the rear tire went flat. Fortunately, Susan was still behind me, having just completed a water break. Needing a tire and tube, I used the old Michelin, reassembled the wheel, and had a perfectly functioning tire that had been given the kiss of death in the Medora bike shop.

Raccoons have become the common road kill. At last the mystery of Idaho's dead birds in June has been solved. In the spring, fledgling birds, learning to fly, had no awareness of the speed of passing traffic. Consequently, they became victims of their own innocence.

We purchased gas for $3.24 a gallon in K.C., but on Highway 36 it was pricier at $3.28. What are a few pennies when Californians spend $3.89? At 11:00 small cloud brothers traveled in a northeasterly direction leaving cooling shadows on the roadway. Frequently I was able to cycle under one for a mile.

We reached Hamilton, our minimum forty-four mile goal, for the day at 12:06. Subway has become our lunch spot. Why not? Ubiquitous franchises with fresh healthy sandwiches fairly priced, and a place to cool off.

Susan, gazing out the picture window across the street, glimpsed the Library and J.C. Penney Memorial Museum, a pure discovery, since it wasn't listed in the AAA tour book. James Cash Penney started out as a clerk, then became a partner in the Golden Rule stores. Later he bought out his partners and changed the name to J. C. Penney. Not a devotee of charging customers what the traffic will bear, he espoused good value for money spent, trained staff and helped shopper decisions. By inventing product testing, his methods revolutionized department store business, selling nothing which hadn't been certified as value. Items from the start of his business until death were on display. His humble birth home was proudly enshrined and a wall mural adorned the town's entrance building. Eastwards the road turned flat and fast to Chillicothe (chilly-caw-thee). Huge cumulus clouds scampered overhead reducing radiant heat with a fifteen mph southern breeze. At 3:30 travel ended assuring two days travel to Hannibal within our grasp. Chillicothe was not the first town we've seen with murals, but theirs were many and big.

69 mi.   2,091 mi. to date   elevation: 797'

DAY 47: THE FIRST IMAGINEER

Tuesday, July 17, 2012   Chillicothe to Macon, MO   Sunny 101*

Coming down to the end, it's time to take stock. The heat and humidity are bearable as long as there is frequent hydration and air movement. The right body half tanned darker than the left due to southern exposure. Sun-bleached clothing wears stains and snags. Tar and road grit discolor the riding shoes. A putrid odor from hand sweat emanates from the gloves. Washing them every few days is necessary. Glasses, having fallen off the nose with bumping incidents, sit crooked with roughened metal edges scratching skin under the eye. The right ankle gash from Day 3 has mostly healed, the scab having come off, but there is a sensitive reddened area around the scar. Complaining never solved the butt soreness, cramping hands, or aching knees, so it became a matter of toughening it out. Each morning most physical ills disappear after a warm up ride, only to return after ten miles. The bike is grimy, but oiled and in good running order. Tires have held up in spite of three flats. The gear shift has a persistent jump-down of two sprockets, and one catch on the up-shift. Susan and I have our moments of disagreement, but the partnership is still strong and well coordinated, and we can laugh at ourselves. We started to think about the end. But *no!* The trip will not go to the East Coast. Pedaling out before 7:30 remains a challenge, even though it would solve the heat problem. Breakfast is necessary but not always prompt. It always takes more time to pack up than we want. Bike clothing cannot be put on until saddle soreness lotion has been applied. Then check the bike and load gear. Also, it takes forever to give Susan a good-bye kiss.

Early morning sun forces eye squinting and head dropping to avoid staring into glare. From the highway, hardwood trees line the fields, now more yellow/brown scorched. Corn is no longer king. Hay and soybeans rule. Large tree stands have begun to fill in where fields dominated. Still there are vast plots of green. Terraced hills rise to different terraced fields, then drop down a level or two, for a mile of farm flats. Without mechanical irrigation, all scenes are ravaged by drought, except for weeds poking up. It is certain farmers are about to lose their crops, which in turn means no cattle feed, which means food and beef prices will skyrocket next year. On TV, governors are already asking for emergency relief. What kind? It's not as if the President has an ocean of water to dole out. A withered crop is still a loss even if the government throws a trillion dollars at the problem.

Stopping only for water and fruit breaks, I finished forty-one miles by 11:00 a.m. Humidity incited wringing wet ascents, cooled when coasting down the other side. More long flats and long gentle climbs. At Macon, overheated, I hung the bike on the car rack. Cycling another mile was out of the question. Susan rented a room while I barely could function. Inside, I needed an hour's cool down before summoning the energy for a shower. While eating turkey burgers, Susan produced a motel brochure about Marceline, a town we had passed twenty-six miles earlier, the boyhood home of Walt Disney.

Having the liberty of a free afternoon we backtracked to Marceline. The city hadn't displayed a billboard sign advertising Disney's boyhood home, but it proudly savored his legacy taking a portion of the central street "Kansas" and renaming it *Main Street U.S.A.* Disney's memories of his Midwest boyhood inspired the façade of his theme park's Main Street. Though he lived here only from ages five through ten, the impact stirred his imagination and observations of animals, nature, trains, and farm life. The Walt Disney Hometown Museum occupied the former railroad depot holding letters, photos and family history, as well as theme park models, train paraphernalia, and cartoon samples. On the outskirts of town, were his Dream Tree and The Happy Place (barn) so endeared to him. A sign claimed that this was the birthplace of Imagineering. The actual red and white house where he lived was privately owned but viewable from the road. The sights would have been missed if Susan hadn't perchance spotted the leaflet.

59 mi.   2,150 mi. to date   elevation: 869'

DAY 48: SCOURGE!

Wednesday, July 17, 2012   Macon to Hannibal, MO   Sunny 105*

It's so ubiquitous we don't even recognize it for what it is. Every town and city and state suffers from it. As a living witness on a cross country trip, I can say no community is safe from it. Right in our faces, we see it neat and clean and professionally produced. It's taken for granted. That's the way it is. It's the American way. When cleaned up it reoccurs. No politician has ever fought to get rid of it and, in our present culture, would never ever dream of outlawing it. It is the most pervasive form of pollution affecting our country--political advertising.

1. How many times must we read the name Jones or Smith or Gonzalez or Johnson in Red, White, and Blue (or some other color combination)? How many entrances and exits from town, the shopping district, or our neighborhoods need to be billboarded, plastered, ground signed, picketed, staked, flagged? Are Americans so dumb, so unaware, so politically non-involved that the name must be thrust under our noses everywhere? And if we flee to another locality the pollution is there with some of the same names and perhaps a few new ones in another campaign.

2. Is this "getting out the message?" What message is on a name banner?

3. We can't turn on a computer, tweet, listen to the radio or watch TV without some form of political advertising foisting a candidate's name into our awareness.

4. What's the quality of the message being hawked? Invariably it is a negative "spot" belittling the opponent, dragging the opponent in the mud, pointing out all the terrible reasons why So-and-So is such a bad individual unworthy of office. What does the candidate really stand for? Rarely mentioned.

5. Political pundits are no better than hucksters offering all their "wisdom" in the attempt to prove the opponents are a pack of liars, ne'er do wells, out of touch buffoons, slipshod performers, contemptuous clods, unlike their "sterling" choice, the honorable So-and-So. In the end both candidates end up So-and-Sos, or SOBs.

6. This all will end. We'll take down the political signs, forgive and forget, and get on with our lives, right? Won't everyone make

nicey-nice? Negative campaigning is so strong it leaves a bitter after taste lasting long after the final sign is removed. The losing party prepares vitriol to subdue opponents in the next election. And the public returns home with a sick feeling that the wrong person got elected. Who wants to follow a bad leader? What is the cumulative effect of years of bad mouthing one's spouse? Then what is the cumulative effect of political badmouthing? Why support the political winner whose negatives were so flamboyantly exposed? Do we not end up saying, "They're all a bunch of bums. Throw the bums out!"?

7. Party loyalty has become more important than the good of Americans. "My party or nothing". Vote only for the party line. "Vote only for Republicans". "Vote only for Democrats". Think for yourself. Re-election has become more important than service to America. Why have our elected representatives not dealt with the national debt? Our Federal budget disaster? Foreign trade deficit? Pork barrel spending? Welfare reform? Manufacturing out sourcing? Tax reform? Political funding reform? Jobs? Government waste? Immigration? Our borders? How do politicians continue to spend money we do not have on new pet projects or niceties we simply cannot afford? Any citizen who spends money like the politicians would be hauled into court. The political atmosphere is toxic. Political intransigence is the order of the day.

8. Is the negative campaigning lost on our high school students learning about the democratic process? Will teens use the similar scathing attacks on fellow students to win a student body office? Let's not be naïve. What kind of example have we been given?

9. Expenses have exploded. Commercials, TV spots, advisers, researchers, sound bite producers, advance men, cosmeticians, clothiers, posters, badges, news ads, hype, hype, hype, all to glamorize the candidate. It costs money. Donations, please. What used to be a soap box debate, maybe throw in transportation costs of perhaps a few hundred dollars, has escalated into a frenzied money guzzling campaign. The candidate with the largest fundraising war chest typically becomes the winner. What could be accomplished with the same finances used to cure diseases, build infrastructure, repair aging and decaying inner cities, reduce welfare, rehabilitate criminals, solve problems? Has the nation gotten its money's worth?

10. Campaigning lasts too long. Why do the candidates determine how long they are allowed to annoy us? Campaign posters have been on display since the start of this trek beginning June 1. Every state is a continuing battleground of advertising innuendos, exaggerations, half truths, outright lies. Who and What to believe? Some campaigns start two and four years before election day. Americans are bored and turned off by a prolonged unrelenting process. What's wrong with a six week, forty-two day period, that seeks the real philosophies, skills, and proven abilities of the candidates with televised debates?
11. The present system does not inform. It denigrates. Politics, as currently practiced, is a scourge on the American public.

The foregoing was a result of observing ad signs on a lone farmhouse lawn as I rolled past, with memories of the superabundant political campaigns waged in every state. Susan termed this email a too long and overblown rant. The Bill of Rights guarantees freedom of speech. As an American I'm asserting my opinion no matter how right or wrong, no matter who agrees or disagrees, no matter whether I have crackerjack or crackpot ideas. But I'll be darned to let politicians believe they are the only real thinkers. So, my fellow Americans, what do you think of our political process?

This morning's 7:00 departure made all the difference for the predicted high temp of 105*. Heading into the blinding sun glare was a concern, but so was the danger of heat exposure like yesterday. The day's fortunes began with level ground cutting again through green but distressed King Corn country. Vegetation rattled withering orange leaves, even the mature trees. A breezeless thirty mile jaunt on baking pavement concluded at 9:00. Taking three minute water breaks and standing kept the race pace up. Once, Susan leapfrogged ahead to a shaded farm intersection. As I approached the silver Subaru, a woman in a brown car pulled alongside her, looked hurriedly, and pulled out. I gave my shrillest piercing whistle barely in time for her to recheck, and stop short, just as I shot by at 19 mph. The rest of the morning whizzed by uneventfully. At 11:25 I quit at the entrance to Hannibal whose marquee announced 94*. The remainder of the day was blistering.

At a barn playhouse, Mark Twain impersonator, Richard Garey performed a hilarious show "Mark Twain for President". Using actual lines from the humorist, he created a program as relevant today as a hundred fifty years ago. A dinner cruise aboard the Mark Twain paddle wheeler proved to be a quiet romantic sunset along tree silhouetted banks of the Mississippi. A banjo, guitar, and ukulele playing musician serenaded with lots of sing-a-long old time favorites. Forty years ago it had been my fantasy to ride a steamboat or barge down the Mississippi on my first cross-country bike trip. Fantasy fulfilled.

60 mi.   2,210 mi. to date   elevation: 470'

DAY 49: HANNIBAL

Thursday, July 19, 2012   Hannibal, MO   Thunderstorms

Clattering sounds woke me. Susan usually rises before I do, but she was still in bed. The A/C was off because it was too chilly last night. Had I turned on the heater by mistake during the night? No. Then peeking out the curtain, I spotted puddles on the cars and the parking lot. Rain. Rumbling clouds heralded a passing thunderstorm. Streets were just wet, a welcome relief from yesterday's 105*. The day was a cooler, 96*, yet still uncomfortable.

Hannibal (population 17,900), is not like the flat land sloping down to the Mississippi I had imagined. The city sits on a group of hills fronted by a narrow waterfront. Railroad tracks and a flood levee run along the river shore. Frequently, coal trains and auto container cars shake the ground with mini earthquake vibrations. Cliffs on the west river itself are painted in varying layers of colored shale. Lazy brown Mississippi water inexorably courses southward past thick wooded islands and moored barges. To the north are two bridges, one for trains, and the taller for vehicles crossing into Illinois. The eastern banks are heavily forested, undeveloped low bottom land. A majority of Hannibal's buildings are two story red brick, some older than the 1900s, needing paint to cover blemishes. Wooden buildings are mostly white, partitioned by narrow two lane streets with broken asphalt, smeared cement patches, and chipped concrete sidewalks. No parking meters. Mark Twain's influence dominates the historical downtown.

The Mark Twain Museum displayed interactive exhibits from the author's books and life, surrounded by many of his quotes. Fifteen original Norman Rockwell illustrations for Twain's books were hung upstairs above the steamboat and whistle platform. Tickets also gained admission to the original boyhood home, and interpretive center.

By 1:00 the sun had sapped us once again. After lunch and liquid, we scouted Highway 79 to determine its safety and worthiness for the journey to St. Louis. Being too poor a trail for cycling, I selected Highway 61, busier but wider. Susan had opportunity to use Lover's Leap, but declined to jump off the cliff of an Indian Legend. Guess I'll keep her. After a cooling nap, we listened to a free evening jazz concert of the Frank Trompeter Band in front of the Twain house, then went to a buffet. Tomorrow starts the last days of bicycling.

0 mi.   2,210 mi. to date   elevation: 470'

Mark Twain Riverboat dinner cruise on the
Mississippi River, Hannibal, MO, 7/18/12.

Lover's Leap near Hannibal, MO. View of Mississippi.

DAY 50: LUCK, AND THEN SOME!

Friday, July 20, 2012   Hannibal to O'Fallon, MO   Overcast 82*

Rising early was an act of self preservation from weather. Everything packed, open the door, and surprise, surprise! Full overcast. The weathercast predicted 92* with possible morning clouds. Well, halleluiah! We took advantage by leaving early 6:30. Highway 61 began looking like a poor choice because it was narrow, small shouldered, already filling with vehicles, and contained hills. The first water break at seven miles seemed neither a thirst nor humidity problem, and 12 mph was satisfactory speed. Susan kidded me once for giving her a dime found on the road.

"You'll stop for a nickel or a dime but you won't pick up a $5.00 bungee cord?"

So when she opened her window I handed her a black bungee and said: "Here's $5.00".

In spite of being vigilant of road trash, some piece of junk lifted off the ground and smacked the bike frame creating fear of a flat. However, no damage. The traffic volume thinned out, half of which were trucks.

Thirty miles by 9:20 gave thought to surpass Troy, sixty miles south of Hannibal. No sun or humidity trouble yet. The road flattened in gentle ascents and descents, affording prolonged bike speed. The popular crop is corn, with soy beans still in second. And then it hit me. For hundreds of miles these two crops, along with hay, were the major items seen growing. Where were the tomatoes, lettuce, squash, cucumbers, radishes, beets, turnips, berries, or melons? They were found at salad bars, so where were they raised? Was it cheaper to truck them in than to grow them? It's clear why stone fruits are not planted here-harsh winters. But not even a humble roadside fruit/veggie stand existed. It appeared only corn on the cob for humans or corn for cows and pigs was being raised since North Dakota.

Troy's 11:30 lunch, under blessed overcast, invited an additional twenty-five mile reduction of the journey's final distance. Cycling down the on-ramp, the bike encountered a high lip drop-off with a shoulder of crushed yellow gravel. Speeding vehicles from the rear gave no leeway, forcing the bike tires to dodge into the shoulder's crunchy stones, jarring steering control left and right. Two hundred feet later the tires hopped onto solid cement and the afternoon trek commenced. Each mile thereafter, traffic volume increased. Susan became agitated about safety. I promised to stop two miles farther. It turned out to be Road P, the one needed.

Crossing the high volume highway was a challenge, but once across, it was back to pedaling, encountering three of the steepest short hills of the entire trip. The day ended at 2:00 in the suburb of O'Fallon on the perimeter of St. Louis. Without cloud cover, today's distance could never have occurred. This circumstance afforded the opportunity to scout trail's end, whether maps added unnecessary distance, or streets prohibited cyclers. It turned out that the bike was on the perfect route. Saturday would be the last fifty miles.

How to celebrate?

85 mi.   2,295 mi. to date   election: 541'

DAY 51: MISSION ACCOMPLISHED

Saturday, July 21, 2012   O'Fallon, MO to Hartford, IL   Sunny 98*

We prepared Friday for the last haul with Pantera's loaded pizza-no leftovers. The 7 a.m. start on Salt River Road directly faced the golden morning sun. Morning joggers trotted under tree shade trying to get cool exercise. A club of thirty bicyclers, with their backs to the sun, crowded the opposite roadside. Few cars were moving, it being the weekend. Suddenly, out in the grass edge, a ball of gray rabbit fur bounded forward, darted toward a chain link fence gate, and squeezed through. The street lead out of town to brushy undeveloped grassland before linking with Highway 370, which resembled a freeway. The entrance ramp lead to an eight foot wide shoulder plagued with trash. City cycling was like playing dodge ball weaving between the chunks of retread tires, car parts, rocks, and junk galore. Except for the golf clubs which had fallen out of a vehicle. (Susan forbade salvaging the clubs.) Six miles of on or off-ramp crossing later, the bike exited to Highway 94, the Lewis and Clark Trail, marked by brown and white signs. The traffic motion device left turn light didn't detect a bike rider, so I had to wait two light cycles for a car to trip the signal.

A mile north the road slimmed from four to two lanes. In a grassy ditch was a U.S. flag apparently fallen off a car. Picking it up, I affixed it to my camelback water pack, giving me a caped crusader look, as I cruised rustic back road farms. Susan removed the flag at a the next stop. Highway 94 was a bit circuitous, but less trafficked without the danger of trying to cross the Mississippi River using I-70, a major artery, into Illinois. Why go to Illinois? Didn't L. & C. start from St. Louis? Yes and no. That's the town everybody knows. But Lewis declared that the start of the journey began officially from the mouth of the Dubois River, now called the Wood River, in Illinois.

Pedaling the sticky pavement through twisting miles of corn was laborious. Absent wind hindrance, it should have been speedy travel, but the sticky tar surface approximated an ascending road. Generally flat means 16-17 mph, but it was a task to get 12. Thickets and masses of trees on the right meant the Missouri was beside me. Then the road carved to the left out into the sun away from cool Missouri tree shade. Slow travel made the final ride interminable through the vacant farmland. At last a narrow arched 1920s auto underpass for the railroad allowed me through, twisting left, perpendicular to Highway 67, three miles from the suspension bridge crossing the Mississippi. Susan snapped a photo as I scaled the pedestrian walk of the cable crossing.

Midway on the bridge, I halted to watch a square faced river tug push fifteen barges toward the Melvin Price Dam and Locks two miles distant, as the captain deftly maneuvered between the cement bridge supports, or his river days would be finished. In the visitor center of the dam a timed computer training device challenged tourists to pit their skills against a barge training simulator with currents and sand bars. Maneuvering a thousand foot long set of barges is a tricky feat, requiring powers of sharp focus, prediction of currents, wind, early positioning of the flotilla, knowledge of hidden sandbars, and seamanship.

Descending the bridge slope, the path turned right. Susan honked. I didn't want to stop. With nine miles to go, the heat affecting me, thirst making itself felt, and honking irritating my weary head, all I wanted to do was get the trek over with. I halted, leaned the cycle on the grass, and sauntered back hearing her voice.

"There's a bike path up on the levee. Why don't you take it?"

Now I'm hard headed. I don't like to change in the middle of something. When I'm hot, don't bother my stubbornness. But with my resistance at an all time low, I listened to my wife and climbed the yellow grassy embankment into the most wonderful cool breeze. And the sight of the mighty Mississippi was quietly impressive. Because of the drought, water level was at its lowest in recorded history. The Corps of Engineers had kept the main channel dredged and open to 14 feet, but this required river pilots to push less heavy smaller cargo loads so the barges did not ground on the mud/sand bars.

The bike path atop the levee runs eight feet wide, divided by a broken yellow stripe for traffic control. Generally flat with bumps, the path gives riders a great cycle ride. Some caveats however. The path dips down from time to time, with a stop sign, and warning: *Bike Riders Must Dismount and Walk Their Bikes Across the Road.* Conoco Oil Refinery runs service roads under the levee path to their boat docks, making dangerous intersections, thus the stops. If a rider isn't alert or ignores the warning, two fifteen foot bright yellow guard arms in blocking positions will cause a painful accident. Paying attention permits bikers a narrow two foot wide space to pass perpendicularly to the route. Ignore at one's own peril.

At 11:20 I stopped at the new 200 foot tall monument of the Lewis and Clark Confluence Tower (actually two towers). Susan took pictures, but when I spotted a blond headed 6 year old boy splashing in the water fountain geyser shooting twelve feet in the air, it was too hard to resist. I ran through the icy water twice, clothes and all. It broke the overbearing pall of the heat spell. Refreshed, I cycled to Lewis and Clark State Park a half mile away, site of the first Corps of Discovery winter camp in 1804. More pictures. Inside the visitor center, I met George, the guide, who began his introduction to the center and displays.

Instead, I saluted him and said: "Reporting sir. Mission accomplished".

"Where did you ride from?" He had seen me put the bike on the car rack next to his car. "From Oregon, sir. 2,344 miles".

It was then his jaw dropped. Many bikers had started from Camp Dubois, but I was the first one he'd met who had finished there.

We toured the facility's excellent start-of-the-trail exhibits, including a full scale mock up of the original boat but it was difficult to read in depth. We had seen so many L. & C. exhibits. Two little old ladies had overheard about the cycling exploit, quizzed about the trip, and secured a photo. Next, we took a gravel road to the river's edge, where I pulled out the vial of Columbia River water carried since June 1, and spilled contents from half a continent away into the Mississippi. To complete the symbolism, I put the wheels of the bike into the river. After lunch we returned to the two towers for a 150 foot elevator ride up to see the actual confluence of the two rivers. Back at the bottom, I once again walked into the cold geyser shower, then changed clothes, and went to celebrate.

This may not be your style of celebrating. I wanted a bottle of orange juice and Popsicles for Susan. Alton, IL, had an expensive glass bottle of juice, but not acceptable Popsicles. Realizing I had not bought a souvenir hat to mark the occasion, we rushed back to the visitor's center, where the cashier had closed at 4:30. I pleaded with her, using my worst phony sad puppy dog face, to sell a hat, without opening the store. She agreed. I now possessed tan baseball style hats from both ends of the Lewis & Clark Trail.

Acquiring a motel on Saturday proved challenging. After a shower, a rack of baby back ribs, and Susan's flat iron steak, I wanted to treat her to a York Patty Mint. At the grocery, I left with sweet treats but also a mysterious box in a plastic bag.

"I notice the irony of 'No Sugar Added' Popsicles and the candy you bought," exclaimed Susan.

Sunset was beginning, so we found a park to watch the flamingo pinks, iridescent oranges, and magenta clouds color the evening sky while enjoying the Popsicles. The end of a perfect saga.

49 mi.   2,344 mi. final distance   elevation: 470'

Crossing the Clark Bridge over the Mississippi
with 12 miles to go, 7/21/12

Trip completed in front of the visitor center at Lewis
and Clark State Park, Hartford Illinois, the actual
start of the Lewis and Clark exposition.

Replica of the keel boat L. & C. used at the expedition's start.

On the bank of the Mississippi spilling the
Pacific Ocean water into the Mississippi.

Cooling off under the geyser water fountain at the Lewis and Clark Confluence Tower, Hartford MO.

DAY 52: THE ARCH

Sunday, July 22, 2012   St. Louis, MO   Sunny 101*

Whoa! We're not used to all this celebrating! A whole bottle of orange juice and seven Popsicles and BBQ. (Because the WIFI was not connecting, we switched motels to send the journal conclusion and this installment.)

Locating a local Catholic Church with WIFI, was another problem, so we drove eight miles to one seen in O'Fallon. Already the weather news had declared a heat advisory for the next five days-over 100* and humidity at 45 percent and rising. Today would only be 101*. Too late for the 8:00 mass, we went to the Waffle House for breakfast. Cacophony reigned: waitresses yelling out orders, cooks calling back, banging and clinking plates, talking over the diners. Yet it was a happy place. Customers were packed at the door waiting for a table, for a good cheap breakfast. We made the 10:00 mass, where, afterward, a homeless mother and daughter stood outside begging for money. A parish mother explained to her child that she didn't donate because the begging woman should use the proper channels the church already had established. It's always a dilemma. Do I help with money now or send them to the office for organized help?

The day was free!!! What to do? Visit the Gateway Arch. I-70 passed a series of red brick buildings, most taller than two stories, into the heart of St. Louis. Closer to the industrial center, more of the burned out, gutted, graffitied derelicts appeared. Road construction for a new interchange and bridge were in full swing. The exit to the Arch and Busch Stadium was well marked leading into rough paved streets lining the waterfront. A parking structure charged $5.00. Slanted red brick pavers secured the sloping banks of the waterfront, while chain mooring davits lay silently waiting to tie up paddle wheelers or other water craft. If it were the ocean, an observer would declare that the tide had gone out, the river being so low. Tugs slid by, pushing barges. Railroad cars lined both sides of the Missouri going to the rail yards or to their new destinations. Helicopter and boat excursions were sold from floating docks at the water's edge. A twenty foot tall brown cement wall hinted of flood protection needed along the river. Above was a park and perimeter walk

Wide tan stone steps climbed upwards between the triangular shaped stainless steel legs of gleaming St. Louis Gateway Arch. Craning one's neck to see the upward sweep is sufficient to make a person lose his balance. A long line of day tourists already stood perspiring in the noon swelter waiting to enter the underground national park entrance to the arch. There were no drinking facilities outside for the thirsty. A 40 minute delay for security to check bags hindered crowd processing, then downwards into a cavernous room where air conditioning and drinking fountains refreshed the tourists; ticket booths sold entry passes; crowds wandered; shops sold souvenirs; and movie theaters showed documentaries. Children approached the Westward Expansion Museum gawking at historic, animal, Indian, and Lewis and Clark displays.

A film depicting the construction of the Arch detailed a mind boggling story of the precision, design, construction, weight, and machinery of the monument. No worker lost his life during construction. Suffice it to say that when the final section was to be fitted in place, the engineers needed seventy tons of pressure to separate the two legs four feet wide to accommodate the final piece. The legs were only one-quarter inch off dead-on, 630 feet above the earth. Simple in concept, most complicated in execution.

To get to the top of the arch, we clambered into a round tin can car that held five people crouched over, sitting. When the doors shut, it was possible to see though a small window to the interior structure of the Arch's electric boxes, cables, angled switchbacks and circular staircases, as it glided up. At the top, excited tourists hurried to climb the last steps into the upper curve. A series of narrow slit windows permitted viewers to peer out. Visitors oohed and aahed, gazing below at miniature trains, cars, and buildings with nearby ant people. The magnificent scene gave view to the East from whence the pioneers came, and opposite to the West where they went. It is a perfect shrine of the Westward Expansion. Many photos were taken next to signs indicating the 630 foot elevation.

At 4:30 we turned attention to the stately green domed Old Courthouse, also part of the park. We felt our skin crinkle in the sun and sensed humidity's thirst. Susan bought a disposable camera after hers lost battery power during the arch tour. She wanted to finish taking pictures while I groused about thirst and hunger, and my starchy innards craved a nap. By the time we left the park, taking two long wrong turns to reach the car, conversation dropped to zero.

"Let's just get out of here".

I-70 brought us back to the outskirts motel in St. Charles, stopping to have an early dinner. In the safety of our room we tried to read, but ended up with the long delayed naps. Email for Day 51 could not be sent though, as the motel's internet was down. I considered ending further blog entries, but Susan posed a question.

"Why have a log written before and during peddling but not afterwards as we return home?"

So it seems the writing shall continue.

0 mi.   2,344 mi. to date   elevation: 470'

Louis and Clark statue by Eads Bridge, St. Louis.

A neck bending look up at the Gateway Arch over ST. Louis, MO.

DAY 53: THE UPPER DECK

Monday, July 23, 2012   St. Louis   Sunny 102*

It truly felt awkward to rack the bicycle and not be cycling. With clothes washed, Egg McMuffins eaten, coffee downed, civilian clothing donned, and a semi-lazy morning underway, we searched for a motel with a better WIFI source. The Weather Channel warned of a 104* heat spell.

First stop, Busch Stadium to buy tickets for tonight's baseball game, this being a once-in-a-lifetime visit to the St. Louis ball park, with the added bonus of the L.A. Dodgers as the opponents. Finding the ballpark wasn't as much trouble as buying tickets. Parking signs listed a $5 charge. I stopped in the shade of a tall building but left the motor on for the air conditioner to cool Susan. It was also an attempt to tell a policeman that we weren't parked. I ran across the street to right field's nonexistent ticket office. Three red Cardinal automated ticket computer machines sat out from the brick wall. Being in the sun, the LCD screens were burned black from the midpoint down-unreadable, except by awkward crouching, covering the screen with hand, head, and hat. In time the screen became visible, but protecting it, while selecting and buying seats, was another matter. Without a stadium seating chart on the computer, purchasing was a pig-in-the-poke enterprise. Being a penny pincher, cheap upper deck $15 tickets were fine, so I chose first base side figuring the sun would set and we would be in the shade. Back at the car we drove around the decayed downtown area of broken pavement, gutted windows, and graffitied brick buildings posting $10 parking fees for doubtfully safe empty lots.

Rethinking the purchase, we turned back to the ball park to change seating. The second time through allowed view of Center Field ticket windows, but when I exited the car, none were open. Inside the iron gates a worker pointed me to a window. It was closed. Another guard, inside an office, suggested the left field side ticket vendors. A woman cashier identified my tickets as being in the sun until one hour after the game started.

"Could I switch the tickets?" I asked.

"No," she replied.

"Why not?"

"The game is nearly sold out," responded the ticket lady.

"Oh, I get it. It's because of the Dah-jahs!"

"No. It's because of the Cardinals," retorted the baseball rival. Dejected, I walked back to the silver car waiting in the heat.

The Cathedral Basilica of St. Louis was visible above the trees with its forest green domes. The cavernous echoing interior was decorated heavily in gold and colorful mosaic tiles, including walls and ceiling. The three church domes symbolized the Trinity, with the central being the largest. Prominent scenes depicted acts of Jesus, apostles and various saints, Latin and English bible quotes, the eight beatitudes, and historic groups who came to establish the faith. Side chapels contained plaques recognizing former bishops. Impressive religious art.

Lunch was a merry-go-round. Jack-in-the-Box wouldn't accept bills larger than a twenty. We couldn't find enough change to pay. The cashier was going to let us "pass" when we found a few more coins. She gave back change although we had provided the exact amount.

Meal done, we headed for Anheuser Busch Brewery, to see the Clydesdale horses. We couldn't help that a free tour of the facility was forced on us. (Wink! Wink!) A 45 minute guided walk through the towering red brick buildings showed the process, grains used, giant vats, bottling, and packaging processes. Busch produced 36,000 barrels of Budweiser a day. Midwesterners needed just eighteen hours to consume it, according to the guide. Of course, we were also forced to consume two samples of the beers produced. I tried a lemon wheat and a raspberry wheat, while Susan tried a Bud Lite Lime. Throughout the brewery we had noticed Cardinal mania. Everywhere, men and women, girls and boys, wore red shirts, or jerseys with player names on the back, and it was no different in the beer tasting room. I inquired of the six fellows at the next table if they were going to the game.

"Yes," they replied.

Pointing to a guy at the same table in a blue tee shirt, I asked if he were going to root for the Dodgers. They laughed.

"I came from California just to see this game," I revealed.

A fellow said: "Then you won't mind them losing". The Cards had just swept a four game series with the Cubs.

With just over two hours till game time, when parking would become a traffic jam, we searched, frustrated, hunting our selected motel, its distant location off the freeway, hidden in a maze of conflicting streets. Having wasted time prowling down wrong paths, we rented an available motel right off the interstate, stashed our belongings, hustled to our favorite fast food, Subway, for another tuna sandwich, and zoomed along the expressway to the stadium exit. Uh oh! Cars tightly jammed in the left lane waiting for poorly synchronized traffic lights, which created interminable delayed turns toward the ball park. Cutting right, I found drivers were unaware of the double left giving us ready access to the city. On a street paralleling the stadium, a parking garage posted a $5 charge. Easy park, but an eight block walk in the shadows of radiant city buildings. The parking lot next to the stadium had upped its price to $15.00.

Inside the right field entrance, directions led to an elevator up four floors to the loge. An elderly black lady conductor sat in her elevator chair with a battery-operated fan cooling her as she brought people up to their sweltering correct levels. Upon exit, vendors were selling water for $5.25 a 16 ounce bottle and beer for $8.00. Unwilling to part with bucks to buy a half interest in the Cardinal franchise, I told Susan I'd just go to the restroom to drink from the sink. Climbing stairs, we located our seats one row from the top of the stadium, facing the sun, and greeted the other nose-bleed seat fans. A half hour before game time, I sought to buy a drinking cup for water. Downstairs, a woman cleaned up the bench where her children sat.

She said, "Oh you can just ask at the refreshment stand. They give cups free."

Sure enough the concessionaire lady gave two cups with ice, then filled them with water. I thanked the franchise for not taking advantage of folks in the heat. A moment later I discovered there were drinking fountains. Susan was pleased with the cold cup, and talked me into transferring to a vacant seating section in the shade.

"If the people come, we can move," she defended.

The temperature board read 102* at the game's start. Humidity had to be over 80 percent. Shade protected us for 40 minutes as people slowly drifted in to the stadium.

With the Cards in the lead after the first inning, we returned near our original seats. The fortunate part was a warm breeze blowing between the fans' legs behind us. Lower down, fans had no breeze in stifling air. How could the players survive in such breathless conditions on the ball field? Maybe 65-70 percent of the seats were occupied-so much for the game being sold out. Later the announcer gave paid attendance at 42,000+. Capacity was 46,861, so it seemed many ticket holders were no-shows. Cruz smashed a three run homer for the Dodgers in the second inning. In the fourth, fans began leaving the park, it being so miserably hot. This gave us the chance to move to the top row where the blowing warm air evaporated our sweat. But at 9:30, with the Dodgers ahead at the end of seven innings and the temperature 92*, we chose to leave, having had the

Busch Stadium experience. In our car, the radio announcer declared the game was five to three in the bottom of the ninth. Three outs, Dodgers won! Such a heroic survival in the upper deck meant Susan and I deserved a soft serve ice cream, but we ended up with ice cream sandwiches.

0 mi.   2,344 to date   elevation: 585'

DAY 54: THE POST JOURNEY BEGINS

Tuesday, July 25, 2012   St. Louis, MO to Little Rock, AR   Sunny 107*

The heat warning would last until Thursday. Everywhere grass had turned brown, except for those sprinkling their lawns. Distressed trees wilted. TV news told stories of uncommon fires, which usually occur on the west coast-sparks igniting dried grass. Highway electronic signs warned: *Fire Danger.*

The Ulysses S. Grant National Historic Site, southwest of the city, once titled White Haven, a thousand acres now reduced to nine, was the childhood home of his wife, Julia Dent. The great Civil War general married a southern belle, whose parents were staunch slave holders. Grant opposed slavery on moral grounds. He resigned his military position after 1848 and farmed next to his in-laws. Side by side with the slaves, he performed all the manual labor needed, at the great disapproval of the in-laws, but earning the respect of the slaves. At the Dent house there were heated discussions and arguments about slavery. When the Civil War broke out Ulysses returned to the army as a colonel to fight with such conspicuous skill and care for his men that he was advanced to general for the Union. His manner was not to brag or defend. He believed actions spoke louder than any verbal defense. This skill continued when later politically attacked as President. He would listen, but not be caught up in useless debate. His trust of all men, became his weakness, and led to his financial ruin. However, his memoirs, written while he was dying of throat cancer, were a success, saving his family.

After buying White Haven in the 1860s, Grant intended to turn it into a horse ranch. In the historical park, slave life and jobs were exhibited including an exceptional interactive set up. Anheuser Busch owned the property, termed Grant's Farm, for the raising of Clydesdale horses.

Highway 67 headed south through hills of trees, scorched corn, and sere fields. Few farmers had water pump irrigation. Strata of lavender rock shale poked out from bulldozer cuts. At the southern end of Missouri, and the northern beginning of Arkansas, land flatted out, with rivers coursing lazily under road bridges. In places kudzu was visible. Kudzu was introduced in Mississippi to prevent flood damage. The plant sent down a root every foot or so, thus anchoring the leafy fast growing plant which soaks up water. It quickly covered bare spots of earth, but it did have a drawback. The vines climbed any plant or tree encountered, overwhelmed them, and greedily absorbed all sunshine. When a plant was fully encased, it died from lack of sunlight. The remnant was a ghostly green form in the woods. Abandoned shacks and out buildings suffered the same fate. Given time this plant will leave the South in a drapery of green.

Fewer businesses lined south Highway 67, and sites were less well kept or cleaned, possibly explained by humidity depriving persons of any desire to be outdoors. Crossing into Arkansas revealed abject poverty and hard times. At first, farms appeared to have weeds just along the highway edge like all other states. Closer inspection revealed weeds deep into poorly maintained fields. Trees perched in corners and mid field required plows to dodge around them. Volunteer plants, sprouting willy-nilly, infested the land. Hodgepodge growth indicated unabated takeover by Mother Nature. Modest houses mixed with collapsed barns and ramshackle mobile homes. Some residential and business lots had the look of hoarders who collected toilets, house appliances, lawn mowers, and the castoffs of others. However, the first signs of diverse crops were visible: tomatoes, watermelon, onions, peas, string beans, and cotton. Highway 67 had an unfinished twenty mile gap, but, after it resumed, farms became manicured, organized, and orderly. Three University of Arkansas campuses were located on the highway, Newport, mile eighty-four, Searcy, mile forty-four, and Beebe, mile thirty. Otherwise there were few traffic destinations. Little Rock supplied Mexican dinners. My knees have stopped hurting.

0 mi.   2,344 mi. to date   elevation: 300'

DAY 55: PUBLIC SERVICE

Wednesday,   Little Rock to Hot Springs, AR   Sunny 107*
July 25, 2012

The development of the William Jefferson Clinton Presidential Library memorializes what he did for Arkansas and the nation. A presidential library is not built using federal money. Private donations were needed. Thirty dilapidated acres of river front, rail station, and a furniture finishing plant in the seamiest industrial section of Little Rock were donated. Construction began in 2001 on a white cantilevered building reaching over the Arkansas River. The train station had been abandoned for years, with its rusty rail bridge still crossing the river. Revitalizing the train station began with clean up and painting before internal remodeling. The building was converted into the Arkansas State University Clinton School of Public Service which grants Masters Degrees in Public Service. Due to chemical waste dumped by the furniture company before current ecological concerns, seventeen feet of toxic soil pollution had to be removed.

The Presidential Library, mainly constructed of recycled materials, contained 20,000 square feet of exhibition space, 2,000 square feet of penthouse living quarters atop the ecological green roof, and 152,000 feet of total archival space. When the building was dedicated in 2004, the keys had to be handed over to the Federal Government. Official presidential documents must be stored in federal buildings. Thus, all 80,000,000 documents over his eight years in the Oval Office were contained here. Remember, his presidency began as the computer age was beginning, so most documents were on paper. The library contained the only full sized replica of the Oval Office in any presidential library, with Clinton's personal memorabilia and books on display in it. Bill has been known from time to time to sneak from the rooftop penthouse down to spend moments revisiting His Office.

Bill Clinton became Attorney General of Arkansas three years after college, and governor two years later, the youngest one ever elected. He was turned out of office after four years, the youngest governor ever removed. In his own words, he was good at what he wanted to do, but bad at doing what others wanted to do. Lesson learned, he was reelected four years later, and for four successive terms, a total of twenty years. A champion of the mixture of races and equal opportunity, and a master of thinking of the grand picture, he was elected to the presidency for two terms. The sheer number of positive outcomes of his administration were overshadowed by his lapse of good behavior and his cover up. Academics will be researching the impact of his public service for years to come. Arkansas steadfastly heralded its home state hero.

Several blocks away was the famous/infamous Little Rock Central High School. In 1957, nine Black teens, attempting to integrate the segregated school, were repulsed when Governor Faubus ordered the National Guard to stop them. Because of the state's disregard of the Supreme Court's order to proceed with integration with all due speed, President Eisenhower ordered the 101st Airborne to ensure that integration did occur under force. Prejudice and violent behavior of white teens and adults rocked the school and community, let alone the nation. In 1958, the first black student graduated from the school. The next year, 1958-59, the school board decided that there would be no classes at any high school, being labeled The Lost School Year. All nine 1957 students received the Gold Medal of Freedom, the highest civilian award, presented in 1999 by President Clinton.

Our final southeast visit was Hot Springs, Clinton's boyhood home, and home of Hot Springs National Park, at 107*. TV news reported a fire had been started by a crew cutting roadside weeds when a blade ignited grass about an hour north. Flames jumped Highway 10, causing the town of Ola to evacuate all twelve hundred citizens. By the 10:00 News, a thousand acres had burned. This kind of fire was not supposed to happen here. No rain was in the forecast.

After a catfish dinner, we toured Hot Springs Mountain Tower in the national park taking the elevator up 650 feet for the panoramic view. Smoke from the fire to the north rose on the horizon. When the hot springs were discovered, entrepreneurs sought to make money by promoting their healthful bath properties. Through the years, the region became a famous health spa destination but degraded into a befouled creek sided by shabby firetrap bath houses. When a series of fires destroyed the ramshackle early dwellings, the Federal Government stepped in, establishing requirements for building plans, safety, and health ordinances. Better facilities were developed attracting more visitors including presidents, Babe Ruth, baseball teams, actors, gangsters such as Al Capone, and thousands who came searching for the elixir waters of the Hot Springs. Water, heated by liquid descending into deep pores and earthen cracks, grew 4* hotter for every 300 feet of descent, caused by naturally occurring decaying radioactive elements. Eventually the water resurfaced through faults leading up to the lower west slope of Hot Springs Mountain, and voila! Hot bath water!
60 mi. driving   elevation: 632'

DAY 56: HAIL! OKLAHOMA HAIL!

Thursday,	Hot Springs, AR to	Partly cloudy 104*
July 26, 2012	Weatherford, OK	

Monotonous stifling weather and bright sunshine removed any desire to rearrange items in the Subaru giving Susan more leg room. Off to Hot Springs National Park. Susan and I collect national parks, Nature's treasures in America. Since no one walked the streets, easy parking. The former Fordyce bath house served as the park's visitor center until October during revamping and remodeling of the original Ozark center.

Bath houses received superheated water from forty-seven deep underground fault outlets on Hot Springs Mountain, explained the ranger guide. Once the Federal Government set regulations for developing the heated waters, very ornate hotels and bath houses were built for rich white people to spend their wealth on the curative powers of the springs. They flocked to spend a week or weeks taking the baths, men and women in separate large quarters. After guests disrobed to wear a toga-like sheet, they were escorted to a marble tub, where they submerged in 98-100* water for 20 minutes. An attendant scrubbed them with a loofah, one time use, then given as a souvenir to the bather. Next, a steam cabinet for 20 minutes, followed by a sitz bath for ten minutes, a needle spray booth, a sauna, and, finally, a 20 minute cool down on a white lounge chair, ended by a massage if desired. Dressed, at the end of the process, clients entered a salon with classical piano music surrounded by wicker chairs, billiard tables, and writing desks with stationery to write letters to friends about their pleasant experience.

Word of mouth spread enthusiasm to come to the baths, and come they did by the thousands. Bath houses paid men to lure vacationers away from the competition and to attend Dr. So-and-So's bath house, because he was an expert in these matters. Although there was some flim-flamery going on-no minerals have been discovered to cure any specific diseases or maladies-people did feel good after the physical attention. Modern devices used for physical therapy were developed for broken legs, arthritis, and muscle recovery. However, the African-Americans who attended the bathers were prevented from using the baths. Eventually there was a bath house developed for people of color in the early 1900s. With the advent of modern medicine and antibiotics many of the maladies could be treated elsewhere. Steadily the bath houses declined in number until only two operate now.

In Missouri and Arkansas, Baptist churches populated the countryside, entries and exits to cities and, of course, all traffic routes in town. Not including other faiths, the telephone book listed sixty-seven Baptist churches alone in the area around Hot Springs. By comparison there were a mere eight Catholic churches in the area. Seems like this is Baptist country.

Yesterday, we bought gas for $3.11 a gallon, then drove a block to see $3.09 on the sign. We was robbed! A warning posted on a gas pump declared: *Drive Off Without Paying, Go to Jail for a Year, or Pay a $1,000 Fine, or Both.* Apparently enough thieves have stolen gas, that the state passed a severe law.

By 11:30 the 102* atmosphere was searing. We drove for an hour just to be on our way to I-40 and homeward bound. Masses of cumulus clouds filled the sky but did not cool. As the miles grew, so did the weather. Route 270, then Route 71, was not supposed to be scenic, but the woodlands were flush and dense and rolling along Lake Ouachita. Unlike the order in towns, rural roadside businesses operated on one's home property in the grass or beside older buildings. Country subsistence work. Highway shoulder grass had not been cut down, maybe due to the wildfire cautions. In the distance an enormous cloud roof fomented a northwest thunderstorm. My prediction of being under clouds in ten minutes was delayed to thirty until joining the I-40 at Ft. Smith. Electric signs everywhere warned: *Extreme Fire Danger.* A turn west pointed toward Oklahoma.

The radio disc jockey announced a severe storm warning had been issued by the National Weather Service for northwest Arkansas.

"Heavy rains, lightning and thunder, quarter inch hail, 60 mph wind gusts. If you're outside, head in to a strong building. Stay away from windows and electrical and pipes".

The announcer tried to play music but every few moments he interrupted with more severe warnings, his uppermost concern, until he ceased all music.

"Half inch hail in Washington County. One-and-a-half inch hail. Two-and-a-half inch hail at Mt. Berg". On and on he reported.

Susan asked whether to pull over at the next rest area. I concurred. A mile from the stop, rain began, then deluged as she entered the rest area. Down came a maelstrom. It was difficult to look out the windows. Visibility was cut to ten feet. Streams raced along the gutters. Raindrops hitting parked trucks were whirled upward in a curling arch over the trailers. Small hail bounced off cars, sidewalks, park benches, and roofs. Our car thermometer plunged from 104* to 74*. The torrent continued for ten minutes, slackened, and then stopped. Outside, I checked the leather bike seat and tied a plastic bag over it to prevent water damage. The sheepskin cover and pad had kept it pretty dry. We drove out at 3:30 toward Oklahoma City, the entire time with the radio revealing the thunderstorm's activity which had not yet hit Fort Smith.

The D.J. reported the temperature at 105*, saying: "We really need this rain, but not the hail". Just as we were leaving the radio reception area, the radio static announced the deluge hitting Fort Smith.

The West was a mass of brewing clouds lit up with intermittent lightning flashes. Although all was overcast, our path cut between two massive cloudbursts. For the bone dry grass and corn, it was too late for water. Sporadic showers of no significance occurred. The storm, sliding sidewise to the northeast, had not dropped much rain. Many trees had already given up their leaves. The natural topography was gently waving, and the dirt, a deep orange meaning a presence of iron, was poor farm soil. Trees became fewer, smaller, sparse. Heat crept back to 100*. The motel manager said that T-storms last year were so severe that the insurance companies lost heavily, paying off car dealerships for hail damage to new cars. In the spring two hail storms had occurred but the companies weren't insuring, or were only partly covering the hail damage. She said that the Oklahoma City TV ads begged customers.

"Come down and make a deal," they advertised. "Thousands of cars available, only a little hail damage. Thousands on hand. Come on in".

Hail! Oklahoma, Hail!

375 mi. driven   elevation: 1647'

DAY 57: THREE STATES

Friday,	Weatherford, OK to	Clouds 98*
July 27, 2012	Albuquerque, NM	

During breakfast, a local man, Tony, engaged us in conversation. He had arrived in Weatherford at the end of the 1976-84 oil boom. Money and jobs were to be had, but housing was impossible, as well as rentals and trailer camping. Everything was at a premium for prices, just like Williston, ND. Tony purchased land for a house and built the restaurant he ran for sixteen years. He was bought out by a man from Los Angeles, who thought $300,000 was cheap for a successful diner, gift shop and full bar. But city people do not think about small towns. The new owner eliminated all the veteran help and started new, angering the locals. The tourist trade was not sufficient to keep the concern going. It changed hands two more times before it burned down. Tony had carefully carried on his business, made friends, and helped others. In turn they supported his restaurant. He traveled to Mexico to purchase items for his souvenir shop. Owning houses and lots in Mexico, he said he would never return. Under the present lack of law-and-order, four of his brothers and a sister were murdered five years ago. Known by people across the border, he had no intention to check on his land or buildings. Now retired, even with his losses, he had visited Hawaii and Japan. Because he liked the area and the people, he helped around the motel.

"Between money and people, it is better to have people who like you," was his mantra.

On the eighty mile drive to the border, yellow/brown crop land rolled to the west, with a few juniper trees set in red/orange soil. Corn stands were dry and dead, hay rolls in small groupings, horses and cows scattered. The soil seemed incapable of raising truck farm vegetables. A few white wind turbines were visible in groups of 10-20 on hill crests. In Elk City we toured the National Route 66 Museum, a collection of cars, route signs, gas station emblems, license plates, hubcaps, and memorabilia of the famous highway now replaced by Interstate 40, nostalgic memories of the ancient Chicago to Santa Monica interstate route.

Crossing the Texas border brought a sudden increase of green scrub brush in gullies and washes, but the orange soil continued. A blue and white sign announced a visitor center a hundred miles west. Apparently Texas felt there was nothing worth seeing until Amarillo. Lunch in Shamrock lead to their claim-to-fame Tower Conoco gas station and U Drop Inn Café, the one immortalized in the Disney cartoon <u>Cars</u>. As once described, Texas is miles and miles of miles and miles. The sere prairie flattened. Ranches dotted the lonely horizon. Numerous horse trailers shuttled horses on the highway. In the morning perhaps one out of five vehicles was a truck, by late afternoon it was half.

At the Visitor Information Center in Amarillo, Susan collected brochures, while I wasted 23 minutes trying to gain access to their WIFI. Texas tan grass and scrub was clean and neat to its state border, although some Texans piled debris, broken cement, asphalt, and other rubbish in rural dead ends. A set of buttes on the horizon revealed age old erosion, but it was difficult to see evidence of a river or wearing down of rock. Was it possible that a gigantic geologic rift occurred millions of years ago, thrusting up a long line of meandering rock cliff from the plain?

At New Mexico's border, bluffs continued, but the rolling terrain had more exposed jagged rocks collapsing down from their perches. Slowly vegetation acquired a slight green hue. Above, white puffy clouds were growing larger and scudding west! Winds created a counter flow pushing the cumulus 25 mph ahead of us. Twice rain pelted with heavy drops in a rain shadow effect up the hillsides. New Mexico was actually greener than Texas. A few farmers had mechanical circle irrigation systems producing the only green vegetation around. Certain road business signs proclaimed themselves to be trading posts or world famous, but after a hundred miles of advertising, they turned out to be isolated tourist traps. Small New Mexico towns had businesses visible from the Interstate, but they were cluttered, messy, and unflattering for their communities.

The time zone change gave an extra hour to the day. Albuquerque shared a golden late afternoon. During the long drive we had not noticed the steady gentle rise in elevation.

465 mi. driving   elevation: 5,312'

On the return, home, a look at the Boca Negra area petroglyphs near
Albuquerque with a view of the desert I had crossed 40 years earlier.

DAY 58: ROCKS

Saturday,   Albuquerque, NM to   Sunny 82-92*
July 28, 2012   Kingman, AZ

What better way to celebrate New Mexico than with rock carvings at Petroglyph National Monument in Albuquerque. It looked like a pile of black rocks tumbled down the serpentine buttes. But what a pile of broken basalt chunks! A jagged trail climbed through ebony blocks containing million year old air bubbles. Hikers clambered up, rock by rock, to read the ancient designs, spirals, rectangles, handprints, animals, birds, symbols and spiritual messages of rock carvers from 8,000 B.C. until the 1800s. No one knew the significance except the original carver, not even present day Indians. Over 24,000 designs have been discovered. At the edge of Boca Negra Canyon, a housing development prevented the feeling of park remoteness and magic, but there were many areas to visit. Warnings of rattlesnakes in the area were posted. But exploring amid the rapidly heating black rock meant a rapid tour.

Westward the pink-orange dirt rock on the ground led away from habitation into the desert. Scattered clouds on the horizon promised afternoon T-storms, scarce vegetation, no farms, and bare land. After thirty miles, scrub plants appeared with occasional green groundcover. Gallup, a long town, was sequestered in chunky orange brown rock hills. The area was principally a rail switching yard that catered to Route 66 history and tourist trade. Above stood the Magallon Plateau featured and famed in Zane Gray and Louis Lamour western novels, and populated by Navajo and Hopi Indians. Vertical orange bluff precipices meandered in weaving box canyons, perfect for movie making background.

For eighty miles yellow billboard signs advertised Indian City. Amid the cliffs of the Arizona border was a shabby collection of business stalls, where jewelry, knives, trinkets, and pottery were for sale. This scene repeated on three other occasions with miles of advertising disgracing the landscape.

Heavy gray clouds massed into stormy overcast. Canyons vanished becoming rolling desert. A pale green fuzz coated the ground. Soon a squall splashed. Puddles lay beside the highway and in trenches. Then miles passed without rain. The hit-and-miss squalls continued while a gigantic deluge to the south was letting loose. Desert vegetation proved the monsoon rains were having a favorable effect on the land.

As the road approached the mountains ahead, evergreen trees grew in profusion. The ascent to Flagstaff delivered us into a forest of fir and pine, but as we slowly descended in altitude, the trees again diminished in number and thickness. Down the road, the gas needle neared empty. We ducked into Williams, gateway to the south rim of the Grand Canyon. Gas prices approached those of California: $3.79, $3.89, $3.69. A station off the beaten track demanded $3.59, cash only. A twenty dollar bill fueled to Kingman. Further descent brought us out on the desert, side by side with train tracks supporting lines of 100+ double-decker container cars. Kingman ended our travel day with cheap gas ($3.23) and a heavenly Arizona sunset.

485 mi. driving   elevation: 3,333'

DAY 59: HOME AT LAST

Sunday,	Kingman, AZ to	High clouds/sunny 100*
July 29, 2012	Dinuba, CA	

A busload of Japanese tourists had left the motel before we woke at 6:30. Last night they were abuzz taking pictures of the sunset, Joshua trees, desertscape, and their kids enjoyed the swimming pool. This morning they were as quiet as church mice. Local mass was 10:00, too late for a good start. Google located a 10:30 mass in Needles, sixty-two miles ahead. Thus we could have breakfast, make distance and still attend church. The car sped down the dry sandy desert with light traffic, small scrub plants, cholla, sage, snakeroot, yucca, on either side but no trees. Huge power plants, mining refineries or manufacturing sites were plunked in the middle of nowhere. Across the Colorado River no *Welcome* sign to California greeted as had all other states. Farms flourished near the flats beside the river, but up the slopes were hard scrabble rock and sand. It is dumbfounding how flash floods have pushed heavy rocks and boulders from the mountains three, four, five miles down the alluvial fans. It looked like a giant had played marbles with the rocks tumbling them in scattered piles of creamed coffee sand.

Our arrival was an hour and twenty minutes too early in Needles, so we drove around town. Many poor homes were in disrepair, yet some folks had begun remodeling. Several businesses had plywood sealing up their showcase windows and doors. Others were abandoned in sandy lots devoid of curbs and gutters. New businesses were trying to live off old Route 66, or serving the boaters and weekenders at the Colorado River. With still an hour before church, we drank coffee at McDonald's, where four packed bicycles leaned against the wall. After half an hour I struck up a conversation with the oldest of four Japanese cyclists. Kim, 42 years old, the interpreter, was the only English speaker, who struggled, but made himself understood. He was accompanied by a girl, Sunny, 15, a 12 year old boy, and a 20 year old man. All were biking from Los Angeles to New York City. He asked about a bicycle shop, but none existed in Needles. Bullhead City or Kingman (thirty mile trips) were their best bets. They wanted maps, so I gave advice to ask at visitor centers at the entrance of states where they could get free maps and info.

Kim asked if there would be guns.

"Not unless you cause trouble," I responded. "No. Most Americans are very friendly and helpful if you ask".

Foreigners have a negative image of wild gun toting Americans which we have brought on ourselves. American movies have created a fear in foreigners that there are so many trigger happy evildoers that we need guns for our protection. What has happened in England or Japan or China that they do not need guns? The price of our right to bear arms has been the highest murder rate in the civilized world. I know, I know. It isn't the gun that did the killing, it's the person. Then what about American persons? Why do we have so many killers in our midst? Where have we gone wrong? What has happened in our American society? Don't disagree/complain to me-talk to the parent or spouse of a murder victim. Explain away how gun ownership protected their loved one.

Then I asked Kim what they needed at a bike shop.

"Grue and pitches," he pronounced.

"What?" I asked.

"Glue and patches," he corrected.

"Oh, for flat tires," I realized.

My bike supply box contained unused patches and glue, small metric cycle wrenches, and the tin of Bag Balm for sore butt riding. He was very appreciative, took pictures of us with Sunny, and asked for our email address. We just made mass. The sermon was about the five loaves and two fishes. Giving from what you have, and today it was patches.

After Needles began a series of long ascents up to 5,000 feet and down, repeated several times, through black basalt broken from cracks in the desert surface and deposited along the pink and light tan sands far out into the desert. Rocks, washed down from the mountains, gave the jumbled look of someone who put boulders in a blender, and then poured the grindings upon the earth.

Trucks, by law, moved to the right lane, while lighter vehicles passed them on the left. Of course, there were zoomers who believed that seventy mph was just too slow to drive in the desert. The speed limit was never meant for them. Thus, at every slight gap between vehicles, at every opportunity, any time a car didn't hit the accelerator to pass a slower vehicle, they would swoop around with their beefy engines growling away.

How can a desert get any more arid? Enter the Mojave Desert to find out. Bleak with white wind turbines on treeless horizon mountains, scant grass lay between the cracked stones of the arid sand strewn desert floor. A planned lunch stop at Ludlow found an overflowing parking lot at 12:30, long lines to the bathroom, and longer lines to order at the Dairy Queen

Restaurant. We left without eating. The onramp DQ sign read: *Thank You.* Barstow, fifty miles beyond, a protracted drive, would be a better chance of less crowding.

Ever since Oklahoma City I have been studying scenery with awe, trying to remember my coast-to-coast bike trip completed forty years ago. Route 66/Interstate 40 had been my path. I had covered this route, but couldn't remember long segments with no cities, stops, or relief in the demanding desertscape, amazed that I completed that trip on a ten speed with only crude equipment, a sleeping bag, and $250.

Daggett and Barstow loomed out of the rail yards with fast food places which I skipped, looking for my favorite burger joint. To tell the truth, I blew the chance to stop for lunch. Having passed fast food row, the Subaru joined Highway 58 towards Mojave City. Turn back ten miles or on to Four Corners? On I drove up and down sandy hills until 2:30. Subway, (Guess what we ate?), pit stop, and gas at $3.79. Does California dispense better gas because of the high prices?

The freeway passed the lone entrance to Edwards Air Force base, curved northwest to Mojave in the barren desert, finally climbing the Tehachapi Pass. Strangely, the terrain and ground cover changed almost immediately. Golden brown grass, a few trees, some houses at first, more in time, and little communities dotted the canyon with refineries tucked on the hillsides. Train tracks paralleled the road after Tehachapi Summit at 4,089 feet, before the six miles of steep downgrade. Doug Fir and Digger Pine trees blanketed the hills. Closer to the 2,000 foot level, trees gave way to the gold of California. No other state has exhibited such brilliant colored dry grass. Descending farther still began the eye treat of farm greenery. In the ninety miles from Bakersfield back to our Dinuba home was the cornucopia of plants not seen in the other monoculture crop states-grapes (table and raisin), tomatoes, melons, alfalfa, beans, squash, broccoli, lettuce, peppers, melons, almonds, oranges, lemons, peaches, persimmons, nectarines, plums, walnuts, pecans, strawberries, and more. Road side stands sold farm produce.

We made three stops in Visalia: first, for the cheapest gas, second, a bank refill of dwindling cash, and third, the most important, a stop at In-N-Out Burger. Mmm-Mmm-Mmm good! I savored every burger morsel. At the entrance, a young man left his car blocking the driveway and walked to a hedge bordering the burger joint. It seemed he was making a pit stop, when it turned out he was checking out a girl in the drive-up car line across a hedge. Phone number in hand, he sauntered back to the car, as if nothing were blocking the driveway, and cruised off, the casual rude social disregard of macho youth.

For fifty-one days I pedaled across the country. Body sore, yes, but adventure strong. I didn't regret it. The enormity of mountains, hills, plains, flora and fauna, skylines and vistas, people and places, buildings and stories, have been a joy to collect. They are not possessions other than in my memory. I don't have to dust them off, just close my eyes and dream. I'm home in Dinuba. I get to sleep in my own bed. Dorothy, in the <u>Wizard of Oz,</u> said it best: "There's no place like home".

435 mi.   elevation: 900'

AFTERWORD

What Did I Learn?

People
1. Folks like to talk about their lives, jobs, kids, and opinions if you ask.
2. There are good and bad people, but mostly good in every place. Society cannot function if the bad dominate.
3. People love to show what they can do.
4. People love to talk even more about what they have done.

Cities
1. Blight kills the city.
2. Ignore or frustrate business and industry and the city dies.
3. Healthy parks, regardless of size, mean a healthy community.
4. Every town is proud of its school(s).
5. Fences do not guarantee good neighborhoods.
6. Safe bike paths accommodate community life.
7. Clean roadbeds indicate healthy communities.
8. Cities are not the choicest places to live. There are many conveniences. But so many Americans, having earned a higher standard of living, have moved away from the city to enjoy ranchettes or country style living.
9. Every TV news community publicized its bad citizens.

Land
1. The wealth of the United States is in its vast diverse lands.
2. Food grows where water flows. (California farm motto) The drought this summer proved farmer Jensen at Fort Peck, MT, right. The next war will be fought over water.
3. Most of the U.S. is still being developed.
4. Farmers are self disciplined masters of the soil, and by necessity, good businessmen dependent on 10,000 things that could and do go wrong.
5. Specialized farming is both a blessing and a curse. Efficiency, but witness drought and beehive collapse, and super bugs' affects on agriculture.

6. In the Midwest, everyone pays attention to the weather.

Religion
1. Every town has a church. Some towns seem to have more churches than they can support.
2. At least by number of churches, Americans have religious faith.
3. Churches do not determine how or whether people practice their faith.

Signs
1. The Lewis and Clark trail is so popular, that places where the Discovery Party never ventured have laid claim that the group was there, at least by the use of the brown and white L. & C. signs.
2. Some signs are funny to catch your attention. O'Fallon church: *Come In. We're Prayer Conditioned.*
3. Some signs are serious reminders. St. Louis interstate: *Hit a Road Worker $10,000 Fine. Lose Your License.*
4. Some communities have never bothered to check whether their signage directions are easy enough for a stranger to find the destination.

Lewis and Clark
1. Their two year odyssey is awe inspiring, considering the advances of transportation and modern equipment.
2. They would be stunned at the riches of land and minerals later discovered.
3. Both would be dismayed at the disappearance of buffalo, elk, deer, antelope, and other wildlife herds, the destruction of native habitat and forests, and animal and parasite infestations.
4. They would be ashamed at the treaties made with the Indians, and the later disregard and violations of faith and promises made by pioneers and the American Government to the American natives.
5. They would be insulted at the mistreatment and destruction of the Indian nations which they had so carefully united to the nation with promises of the great white father, the president.
6. The advances in science, technology and agriculture would amaze and impart pride of their learning and explorations.
7. Pollution, waste, trashing of the environment, and careless mining and ecological practices, would reduce the two preeminent explorers to tears.

Myself

1. Unless I continue to challenge myself, I will rust away as a "used to be".
2. My life is not over. The Good Lord is not done with me yet. So I'd better keep on.
3. When should I quit? Three minutes after my heart stops beating.
4. I'm funny if you get past my crusty exterior.
5. I like people when I make the effort to get past their crusty exteriors.
6. Teaching is so ingrained in me that I can't subdue myself. Witness all the stories and details I've sent along with this travelogue.
7. It's quite likely that my enthusiasm to teach has been too much at times. Fathers sometimes do that to their kids.
8. Sometimes in teaching you will never know who you touched or how you touched. But you teach anyway. You must have faith in your students.
9. Perhaps the most difficult discipline for me was not cycling, but sitting nightly before the laptop and composing the day's events.

My Wife

1. Considering the demands of this arduous undertaking, and how Susan had not wanted to give up a summer to support me, I haven't discovered a more devoted, self sacrificing, helpful partner.
2. The only things my wife complained about were the heat and humidity, my bad jokes, some of my writing, bicycling on the freeway, vampire flies when they bit, and that the trip wasn't over yet.
3. She is my soul mate, support, caregiver, corrector, anticipator, manager, investigator, trusted advisor (although at times I disagree mightily), financial backer, religious partner, and staunch ally.
4. She is my best friend and I could not have done this trip without her.

Life

1. Life is meant to be lived. Witness Stephen Hawking.
2. I have been blessed with a good life, by the grace of God and because I chose to follow the New Testament dictum: "Ask and you shall receive. Seek and you shall find. Knock and it shall be opened unto you".
3. Life has been the greatest gift given me, with all its pains, sufferings, wrong roads, delays, mistakes, dangers, threats real and imagined,

accidents and injuries, worries, illnesses, scars, losses, negative emotions, and all misfortunes I had to deal with. I can say with a straight face: "I did all that, and I'm still here". Or in the words of Julius Caesar: "Veni, Vidi, Vinci". (I came, I saw, I conquered.)

FREEDOM

This trip has been a testament to the greatest American right: Freedom. What is freedom? It is the opportunity to choose. We do not have to follow in our parents' footsteps. In this country we choose, not our parentage, but the path to follow when we leave home. We may elect to educate ourselves or ignore learning. A life of physical toil, or mental challenge is up to us. There is no one way to live. Our choices, each in their own manner, determine how our lives live out. Sloppiness or order, care or neglect, slipshod or obsessive, penny wise or pound foolish, thoughtless or thoughtful, wasteful or economical, detailed or generalized, city or country, legal or illegal, hasty or patient, moral or immoral. The choices are there for us.

Our environments are just places. If the present location is not the place to make our way or our fortune, it is up to us to take charge and choose a new land of opportunity just as our pioneer forefathers did. Careers often define who we are and what we have accomplished, but not always. Lewis and Clark did not make a career out of exploring the Louisiana Purchase. Some amateur tinkerers invented solutions technocrats have missed. Backyard stargazers have discovered comets and meteors. Bicycling across the country was one kind of choice, just as sports, or technology, or business are choices. It is the industry of a person that produces accomplishment and success.

What is worthy of our ambition? Americans do not applaud those who sit on their pants and holler. Regardless of one's enthusiasm, it is in the "Give it your all" choice that makes the difference. In the United States we are all equal, irrespective of race, sex, religion, background, or orientation. How is that? We have the greatest gift a citizen can have: Freedom. The opportunity to choose.

Printed in the United States
By Bookmasters